THE MEDIEVAL CHURCH SCREENS OF THE SOUTHERN MARCHES

THE MEDIEVAL CHURCH SCREENS OF THE SOUTHERN MARCHES

by

Richard Wheeler

Logaston Press

LOGASTON PRESS
Little Logaston Woonton Almeley
Herefordshire HR3 6QH
logastonpress.co.uk

First published by Logaston Press 2006

ISBN 1 904396 51 8

Set in Times New Roman by Logaston Press
and printed in Great Britain by
Biddles Ltd., King's Lynn

Front cover illustration: St. Margarets, Herefordshire

Contents

The Gazetteer

Location Map of Screens included in the Gazetteer

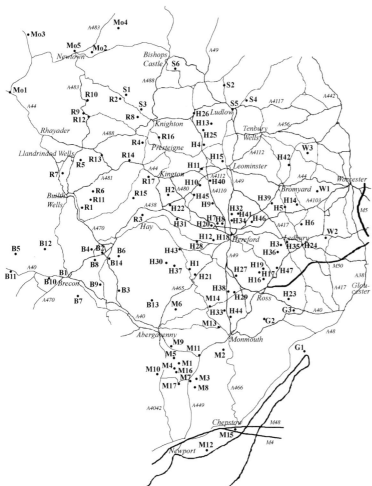

Montgomeryshire
Mo1 Llangurig
Mo2 Llanmerewig
Mo3 Llanwnnog
Mo4 Montgomery
Mo5 Newtown

Shropshire
S1 Bettws-y-Crwyn
S2 Culmington
S3 Llanvair Waterdine
S4 Middleton
S5 Ludlow
S6 Lydbury North

Radnorshire
R1 Aberedw
R2 Beguildy
R3 Bettws Clyro
R4 Cascob
R5 Cefnllys
R6 Cregrina
R7 Disserth
R8 Heyop
R9 Llananno
R10 Llanbadarn Fynydd
R11 Llanbadarn-y-Garreg
R12 Llanbister
R13 Llandegley
R14 Michaelchurch-on-Arrow
R15 New Radnor
R16 Norton
R17 Old Radnor

Breconshire
B1 Brecon Cathedral
B2 Bronllys
B3 Cwmdu
B4 Llandefalle
B5 Llandeilo'r Fan
B6 Llanelieu
B7 Llanfigan
B8 Llanfilo
B9 Llangasty Tal-y-Llyn
B10 Llanspyddid
B11 Llywel
B12 Merthyr Cynog
B13 Partrishow
B14 Talgarth

Herefordshire
H1 Abbey Dore
H2 Almeley
H3 Aylton
H4 Aymestrey
H5 Bishop's Frome
H6 Bosbury
H7 Brinsop
H8 Burghill
H9 Canon Pyon
H10 Dilwyn
H11 Eardisland
H12 Eaton Bishop
H13 Elton
H14 Evesbatch
H15 Eyton
H16 Fawley
H17 Foy
H18 Hereford Cathedral
H19 How Caple
H20 Kenchester
H21 Kenderchurch
H22 Kinnersley
H23 Lea
H24 Ledbury
H25 Leinthall Starkes
H26 Leintwardine
H27 Llandinabo
H28 Madley
H29 Michaelchurch
H30 Michaelchurch Escley
H31 Monnington-on-Wye
H32 Moreton-on-Lugg
H33 Pembridge Castle Chapel
H34 Pipe and Lyde
H35 Pixley

H36 Putley
H37 St. Margarets
H38 St. Weonards
H39 Stoke Lacy
H40 Stretford
H41 Sutton St. Nicholas
H42 Tedstone Delamere
H43 Vowchurch
H44 Welsh Newton
H45 Weobley
H46 Withington
H47 Yatton

Worcestershire
W1 Alfrick
W2 Little Malvern
W3 Shelsley Walsh

Gloucestershire
G1 Awre
G2 English Bicknor
G3 Mitcheldean

Monmouthshire
M1 Bettws Newydd
M2 Cwmcarvan
M3 Gwernesney
M4 Kemeys Commander
M5 Llanfair Kilgeddin
M6 Llangattock Lingoed
M7 Llangeview
M8 Llangwm Uchaf
M9 Llansantffraed
M10 Mamhilad
M11 Raglan
M12 Redwick
M13 Rockfield
M14 Skenfrith
M15 St. Pierre
M16 Trostre
M17 Usk

Acknowledgements

But for the patient and good-humoured assistance of a number of people this book might have taken even longer to write. In particular I thank Elizabeth Walker, Collections Manager at the National Museum of Wales in Cardiff, for arranging a private viewing of the spectacularly beautiful Christ figure from Mochdre church; Jennifer Evans, Library Assistant at the National Museum, for her unstinting help, including the endless photocopying of papers from *Archaeologia Cambrensis*; Kay Kays, Image Licensing Officer at the National Museum, for permission to use the photographs of the Christ and Mary figures from Mochdre; and to Olwen Stubbs of the National Library of Wales, for her assistance with the Parker drawings. On the subject of images, I am very grateful to Sara Long, for her work scanning and configuring many of the drawings and diagrams. All the photographs in the book are my own, with the following exceptions with whom copyright remains: all the Parker drawings are reproduced by permission of Llyfrgell Genedlaethol Cymru / The National Library of Wales; the Christ and Mary figures from Mochdre by permission of the National Library of Wales; and the screen designed by Gilbert Scott for Hereford Cathedral now in the V&A by permission of the V&A.

I also want to thank Gerralt Nash, Curator of Historic Buildings, and Ray Smith, Chief Conservation Officer, both of whom work at the Museum of Welsh Life at St. Fagan's, for their help, advice and encouragement over the course of this project; and for giving so generously of their time in 2005. My sincere thanks also to two medievalists: Hannah Wheeler, for carefully reading through the Welsh Marches chapter; and Dr. David Griffith of the University of Birmingham, for a wealth of valuable information and observations via email. I am indebted to Andy Johnson at Logaston for his support, forbearance, light but astute editorial touch and for allowing the image of the stone screen at Welsh Newton to occupy a full page (against his better judgement). Finally, I thank my parents – my love of old churches springs from their love of old churches – and I thank my wonderful wife Su, for the meticulous editing of the manuscript, for the tireless help and support, and most of all for being the person you are and for always being there for me. I dedicate this book to you.

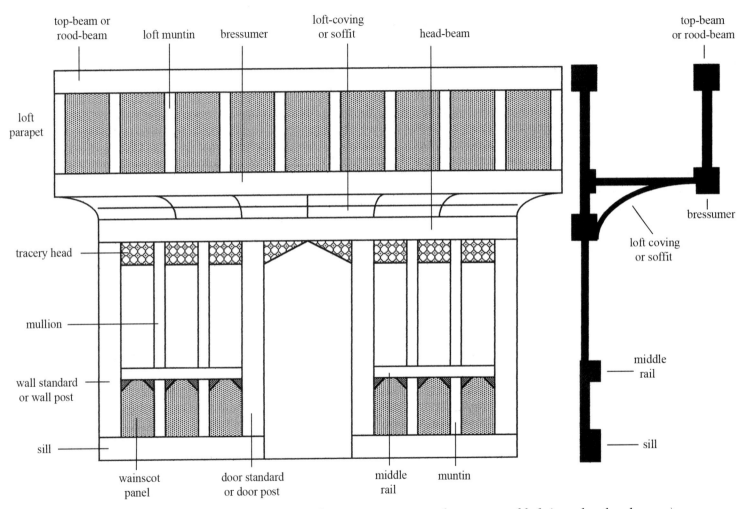

top-beam or rood-beam

loft muntin

bressumer

loft-coving or soffit

head-beam

top-beam or rood-beam

loft parapet

tracery head

mullion

wall standard or wall post

sill

wainscot panel

door standard or door post

middle rail

muntin

bressumer

loft coving or soffit

middle rail

sill

Front and side view diagram showing the component parts of a screen and loft (see also the glossary)

INTRODUCTION

The Middle Ages, and above all the fifteenth century, produced in vast quantities the most wonderful woodwork the world has ever seen.
F.E. Howard & F.H. Crossley

During the later Middle Ages (*c*.1300–*c*.1500) almost every church in England and Wales was furnished with a rood-screen. The rood-screen was erected at the east end of the nave in order to divide the chancel, which belonged to the clergy, from the nave, which belonged to the parishioners.[1] Church screens are found in Continental churches too, but the singular course of development taken by church plans in England and Wales ensured the fitting's near-universal adoption here. Uniquely, this course of development saw rood-screens evolve in relation to the treatment of the internal dividing wall between the chancel and the nave. In Continental churches this dividing wall never existed, and accordingly their church screens follow a very different evolutionary path

In churches with a chancel arch the rood-screen usually stood beneath, or immediately before, the arch. However, in churches whose side aisles extended east of the nave to flank the chancel, the rood-screen often extended north and south of the nave in order to span the side aisles as well. The rood-loft was a later development. Its assimilation into the fabric of churches did not become widespread until the second half of the 15th century. It formed a gallery directly over the rood-screen, and was used both to gain access to the Rood and as a raised platform for singers and musicians. As church layouts became increasingly elaborate, so other types of screen were deployed to further subdivide church interiors.

The rood-screen and rood-loft are so named because of their location immediately beneath the Rood: the carved figure of Christ on the Cross. The word 'Rood' is a corruption of the Saxon word for a cross, but later came to encompass both the Cross and the attached figure of Christ upon it. Flanking the Rood were usually the figures of the Blessed Virgin Mary and St. John the Evangelist; these three together forming what is often referred to as the 'rood-group'. The Great Rood was the pre-eminent image within every church, and was displayed high up at the east end of the nave in the fullest view of the congregation below. A number of methods were used to support the Rood and its attendant figures. Sometimes, it was suspended from chains attached to the roof of the nave or the crown of the chancel arch. More commonly, however, it was fixed to the top of the rood-screen or rood-loft parapet; or to the top of a rood-beam.

The physical and hierarchical prominence given to the Great Rood ensured its virtual annihilation during the Reformation. For the iconoclasts, concerned with what they saw as a growing cult of image-worship, nothing seemed more likely to trigger and sustain idolatrous behaviour than the figure of Christ at the head of the nave, painted and gilded, and even on occasion clothed.

The remedy was a simple one: everywhere, rood-figures were taken down and destroyed, often by burning. By association (and because of the carved or painted figures often displayed upon their west fronts) countless rood-screens and even greater numbers of rood-lofts were also destroyed; and this in spite of the fact that both were merely proximate to the Rood above, and had no specific iconographic or didactic relationship with it.

Today it is hard for us, in a land of scrubbed and whitewashed churches, to imagine the teeming splendour that was the late medieval church interior, alive with colour and gilding, imagery and carvings, awakened by the dance of candlelight. To beautify a church was itself seen as an act of worship, which gave to that place a voice to speak God's glory and mystery to others. All manner of fittings, which started out as functional additions to the church interior – pews, pulpits, desks, lecterns, font covers and roofs – were later to receive the decorative attentions of the carver, the painter and the gilder. Rood-screens were no different. Indeed, their unassailable prominence guaranteed them the most lavish treatment of all church fittings, and even in churches that displayed very little in the way of fine fittings what few resources were available were often channelled into the creation of surprisingly elaborate screens.

The glorification of God cannot alone account for the splendour of such fittings: inter-parish rivalry for the title of the finest church, or the prestige won by the patron through a lavish donation, are just two other factors that motivated the creation of ever-finer church fittings. There was also the instinctive motivation felt by the artist himself, to answer the nudge of his own creative reflex; to make something and to make it beautiful. Even the humble artist thrills to the thought of people both seeing his work and delighting in it, and the rood-screen and rood-loft provided the medieval church craftsman with a supreme opportunity to showcase his artistry.

Although the rood-loft came later and was initially distinct from the rood-screen it surmounted, a desire to create single unified fittings soon led to the careful integration of the two components. In the second half of the 15th century and the first quarter of the 16th century in particular, old screens were often pulled down entirely so that new and seamless pairings of screen and loft could be put up in their stead. For the late medieval churchgoer the integration of the two became so complete that the term 'rood-loft' came to refer to the whole ensemble of screen and loft. Like the rood-screen before it, the rood-loft was at first a purely functional addition to the church. However, it too caught the eye of the artist, and its even greater prominence eventually assured it even greater levels of enrichment.

Roughly 1,000 substantially complete late medieval rood-screens survive in England and Wales: a far greater number than in any other country. The relative abundance of surviving screens can be accounted for by a number of factors, of which the most obvious is that there were simply more to begin with (whereas the cancelli-type screens discussed on p.11 were generally erected only in the larger Continental basilican churches, rood-screens were employed in the very humblest English parish churches). Other factors that contributed to the survival of rood-screens include the fundamental utility of the fitting in churches without a dividing wall; the inconsistent interpretation of Orders during the Reformation (and the patchy nature of their enforcement); and, in a large number of cases, blind and unfathomable good fortune.

Of the screens surviving in the churches of England and Wales the vast majority – more than 90% – are of wood (and all but a handful of these are of oak[2]); the rest are of stone. In addition there are countless other churches which retain fragments of medieval screenwork, often reused in different fittings (such as pulpits), or simply displayed elsewhere in the church as a curio. Even in churches that have been entirely stripped of these fittings other associated features often survive, such as rood-stairs and rood-doors, testifying to the numbers of rood-screens and rood-lofts that once existed.

For every late medieval rood-screen that survives today, roughly nine others have been lost entirely, or exist only in a fragmentary state. Furthermore, as F.E. Howard and F.H. Crossley observe, 'there is no reason to suppose that those which have survived have escaped destruction because of their exceptional beauty. Indeed the reverse is far more likely'.[3] The tearing down of rood-lofts was even more widespread, and only a handful of complete examples now remain *in situ*. Of all the once-common fittings found in the medieval church, however, none is now as rare as the Rood itself. From literally thousands of original rood-groups, just five mutilated figures now survive. In accounting for such levels of destruction it is right that we identify the Reformation as pivotal, but to the vandalism wrought in the 16th century must be added that which took place in the 17th, 18th and 19th centuries.

Surviving examples of late medieval screenwork can be found in virtually every county in England and Wales (only Cumbria and Northumberland have almost nothing to show). However, in two areas in particular the concentrations are especially high: in the counties of Devon and Somerset in the South-west; and in those of Norfolk, Suffolk and Lincolnshire in East Anglia. In the South-west, Devon is pre-eminent, with almost 200 churches still containing late medieval screenwork. Somerset next door has at least 60. On the other side of the country, Norfolk has more than 200 churches containing late medieval screenwork, while Suffolk and Lincolnshire have roughly 100 apiece. More than half of all surviving late medieval screenwork is thus concentrated in just five counties.

Ecclesiologists with a particular regard for church screens have therefore tended to focus their attention on the South-west and East Anglia, often to the exclusion of other parts of the country. Devon has fared particularly well in this regard, and is perhaps the one county – ecclesiologically speaking – that could claim to be famed for its screenwork. Given the quality and quantity of the screenwork of the South-west and East Anglia, any favouritism is both understandable and reasonable. In these regions the higher concentrations of screens afford the best opportunity to analyse their construction, design and decoration, and to uncover patterns and chart influence. However, other parts of England and Wales that are rich in screenwork have been unjustly neglected. One might count among them the counties of Bedfordshire, Cambridgeshire, Derbyshire, Essex, Kent, Northamptonshire and Oxfordshire; together with those counties lying to either side of the Welsh border: Cheshire, Shropshire, Herefordshire, Montgomeryshire, Radnorshire, Breconshire and Monmouthshire.

Given the prominence of the rood-screen and rood-loft within churches up until the Reformation, and the obvious decorative appeal of these fittings, one might expect to find a great deal of readily accessible material on the subject. Unfortunately this is not the case. Although a significant amount has been written on the subject, much of the best work can only be found in little known periodicals or out-of-print books. This is particularly surprising given that the use of screens was more widespread in England and Wales than in any other country, and that nowhere in the world are the surviving examples more numerous or fine. Other ecclesiastical fittings for which we could never make such claims, such as stained glass, have fared infinitely better.

It was only in the 19th century, when many rood-screens and lofts were being pulled down in the name of restoration, did people begin to write about the subject with any degree of authority. Indeed, it was partly because of these losses that the fittings began to attract the attention of writers and ecclesiologists. For some, such as Sir Stephen Glynne[4] and the travel writer Richard Fenton[5], screens were simply one of a number of interesting church fittings that merited attention. For others, most notably perhaps David Walker and Archdeacon Thomas (both of whom contributed papers to the academic journals of the day[6]) church screens seem to have held a special and abiding fascination.

Two other figures from this era, both great lovers of the Gothic, should also be mentioned at this point: the Rev. John Parker and Augustus Welby Pugin. The Rev. Parker was the rector at Llanmerewig, Montgomeryshire, and was a gifted and meticulous draughtsman (Crossley and Ridgway describe his drawings as 'the acme of delicacy and truthfulness'[7]). During the first half of the 19th century he made numerous drawings of Welsh screens (and other fittings), supplementing his illustrations with detailed written descriptions. His commitment to accuracy saw him clambering over screenwork in order to take detailed measurements of the fitting in question. While doing precisely this at Newtown, he tells us, 'The clerk held the ladder which once nearly fell with me'.[8]

Parker's work on the screenwork at Newtown in Montgomeryshire is typical. Between 1829 and 1832 he visited the church on at least three occasions, carefully recording by way of words and more than a dozen images what he found there. At the time the screen and loft at Newtown were deteriorating fast, and soon after were dismantled (the parts being variously re-erected in nearby St. Davids, built in 1843–7). Without Parker's work, our knowledge of this important and beautiful rood-screen and loft would be very much the poorer (see plates 3–6).

Like the Rev. Parker, A.W. Pugin was a fine draughtsman and a fervent admirer of the Gothic. He was also a designer, architect and writer of considerable repute (and occasional notoriety). In 1851, a year before his death, his book *A Treatise on Rood Screens* was published. While the same disquiet about the fate of rood-screens informs the writings of both Parker and Pugin, the two men were essentially looking in opposite directions: Parker into the past, Pugin the future. Thus, while Parker sought to record with care and objectivity the minutiae of surviving church screens and lofts, Pugin was making a series of impassioned arguments for the relevance of such fittings today and tomorrow. His *A Treatise on Rood Screens* begins (somewhat portentously) with the following words:

> The subject on which I am about to treat is one of far more importance than the generality of men may be willing

to admit; it is not a mere question of architectural detail, respecting a few mullions and a transverse beam, but it involves great principles connected with discipline, and even faith.

Much of the best work on screens, however, was done in the first half of the 20th century, during a period of renewed interest in, and concern for, parish churches and their fittings. Driving the process was a recognition that many treasures were going unrecognised as such, and were not being afforded the protection they merited. Church screenwork, which had already endured its share of destruction and mutilation, was still faring badly well into the 20th century; a fact highlighted by Aymer Vallance[9] in the preface to his 1936 book, *English Church Screens*. In it Vallance lists many screens damaged or completely destroyed in the preceding 45 years through a combination of accidental fire and deliberate action: 'But worse and more insidious even than fire is the wilful damage by the responsible guardians themselves, sometimes ... with official sanction; but more often in defiance of all lawful authority'.

Vallance wrote a companion volume, entitled *Greater English Church Screens*, which covers the screenwork of cathedral, monastic and collegiate churches. Throughout his life he remained a champion of Kentish and Yorkshire screenwork in particular, contributing papers on the subject to a number of journals and periodicals. Part of Vallance's appeal as a writer is the force with which he counters what he perceives as myths concerning screenwork. In one unforgettable passage a person responsible for suggesting that rood-screen doors cannot be closed (in order to teach that the way from earth to heaven is always open) is dismissed as 'some witless dotard of a bucolic sextoness'.[10]

Two other notable books dedicated solely to the subject of church screens were also written in the first half of the 20th century. In 1908, Francis Bond's concise but wide-ranging book, *Screens and Galleries in English Churches* was published. A year later, the lavish two-volume work *Roodscreens and Roodlofts*, co-written by Frederick Bligh Bond and the Rev. Dom Bede Camm[11], appeared. This major study took the two men seven years to complete, and is still regarded as the standard general reference work on the subject.

Over the years many books dealing with the broader field of church fittings have included chapters or sections dedicated to screenwork. Of these, two in particular are worth highlighting: F.E. Howard[12] and F.H. Crossley's[13] book, *English Church Woodwork*, published in 1917, is justifiably still regarded as the benchmark volume on the wider subject of ecclesiastical woodwork. It covers the period 1250–1550 and analyses regional variation in construction and detail for the first time. In common with Vallance's *English Church Screens* and Bond and Camm's *Roodscreens and Roodlofts* it is richly illustrated with black and white photographs and line drawings. J. Charles Cox and Alfred Harvey's 1907 book, *English Church Furniture*, is concerned less with analysis, but represents instead the first attempt to draw up a comprehensive catalogue of surviving church fittings, including screens.

Of the work on church screens in periodical form, that carried out by F.H. Crossley and M.H. Ridgway is significant in its own right, but especially relevant here. During the 1940s and 1950s the two men carried out an exhaustive study of church screens and lofts in Wales. Concentrating on design, provenance and influence, they identified for the first time screens linked by common workshop centres. They also catalogued surviving

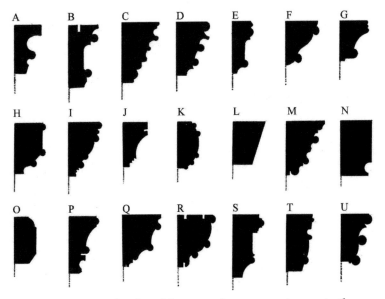

Southern Marches head-beams: eloquent testimony to the
richness and variety of the region's screenwork.
A Kenderchurch, B Lea, C Bosbury, D Eyton, E Elton,
F Leintwardine, G Yatton, H Leinthall Starkes, I Trostre,
J Kemeys Commander, K Llangeview, L Llanbister, M Heyop,
N Llandeilo'r Fan, O Merthyr Cynog, P Brecon,
Q Pipe and Lyde, R Shelsley Walsh, S Llandinabo,
T Madley, U Michaelchurch Escley

screens, and where possible gathered evidence of screenwork that was no more. The resulting papers appeared in *Archaeologia Cambrensis* (the periodical of the Cambrian Archaeological Society) and a more comprehensive or rigorous treatment of the subject would be hard to imagine. Unfortunately, quality does not guarantee dissemination, however, and this and other fine work remains, for the general reader at least, tantalisingly out of reach.

The reasons for this study of the screenwork of the southern Marches then are essentially twofold. Firstly, at the time of writing, there are no books in print dealing solely with the church screenwork of England or Wales. Chapters on screenwork have been included in recent books on parish churches and their fittings, but these tend to deal only fleetingly with the subject.

Secondly, the church screenwork of Wales and the border counties has never received the attention enjoyed by other areas, most notably the South-west and East Anglia. This relative lack of acknowledgement on the part of ecclesiologists is entirely undeserved. In terms of quality, Welsh and borderland church screenwork not only bears comparison with that found in the South-west and East Anglia, it often surpasses it, and nowhere in England can such variety be found, nor such a fiercely independent spirit of design. Furthermore, as well as a large number of fine late medieval screens, a disproportionately high number of rood-lofts survive in Wales.

Of these, a number – including those at Llananno in Radnorshire, Partrishow in Breconshire, and Llanwnnog in Montgomeryshire – are especially fine, and arguably rank among the finest achievements of the medieval woodworker. At little

Bettws Newydd, in Monmouthshire, there survives the most complete rood arrangement in existence. It consists of a rood-screen, rood-loft, and rood-tympanum (only the Rood itself is missing). Marooned in a handful of Welsh churches in the southern Marches are also a number of fine English screens, including most notably perhaps the one spanning nave and side aisles at Old Radnor in Radnorshire.

Conversely, on the English side of the border there are a number of churches containing fine Welsh screenwork. Of these, humble and hard-to-find St. Margarets in Herefordshire is justly famed for its crystalline rood-loft of silvery oak. At Aymestrey, also in Herefordshire, is a tall and elegant rood-screen reminiscent of those found in East Anglia. It is finely carved and closely related to the screens at Hughley in Shropshire, Astbury in Cheshire, and Gresford in Denbighshire. The primitive but characterful rood-screen at Pixley in Herefordshire is the oldest timber screen in the southern Marches, and one of the earliest in the country (it belongs in date to the 14th century). Meanwhile the screens at Llandinabo and Abbey Dore are of Renaissance character, but while the former is small and delicate, and was made just prior to the Reformation, the latter is big and bold, and was made after the Reformation (possibly by John Abel in the 1630s).

Herefordshire also boasts two important stone screens. At Welsh Newton is a rare rood-screen of the 13th century, whose pointed arches give it the appearance of a nave arcade. In Hereford Cathedral, meanwhile, a later stone parclose screen of a very different character partitions off the Audley Chapel from the Lady Chapel. Completed in c.1500, this elaborate screen has two tiers, each of nine bays and two half bays. It retains much of its original figure painting and colour decoration. Also made for Hereford Cathedral (but now housed in the Victoria and Albert Museum in London) was the once-famous metal screen designed by George Gilbert Scott, and made by Skidmore of Coventry in 1862. This showy and fantastical creation is constructed out of iron, copper and brass, and incorporates 300 cut and polished stones. It is, as Pevsner describes it, 'a High Victorian monument of the first order'.[14]

Together, Shropshire, Worcestershire and Gloucestershire contribute just 12 churches to this study, fringing as they do the eastern edge of the southern Marches. However, the screenwork of Bettws-y-Crwyn, Llanvair Waterdine, and Ludlow in Shropshire; and that found at Shelsley Walsh in Worcestershire, is of great interest.

For too long the significance of the church screens of Herefordshire in particular has gone entirely unrecognised. For Messrs Cox and Harvey[15], for example, it does not even merit a place in their second division of counties with notable church screenwork. There are probably two main reasons for this lack of recognition: firstly, the modest number of complete screens found here; and secondly, their lack of consistency in terms of design and construction. On the first point, it is true that Herefordshire cannot compete with the likes of Devon or even Northamptonshire when it comes to quantity. However, there are still close to 50 churches containing late medieval screenwork in Herefordshire (accepting that much of this is fragmentary). On the second point, it is precisely this lack of consistency that is so distinctive and precious. Put simply, Herefordshire was caught in a crossfire of influence that led to the appearance here of perhaps the most diverse collection of church screens of any English county. Characteristics deriving from the screenwork of Wales and the Western School to the west and south, the Midland School to the east, and numerous workshop centres, (including ones throughout Wales, and in Shropshire and Gloucestershire) can all be traced in Herefordshire.

In the context of church fittings, only a tiny handful of the screens and lofts described in the following pages have attained anything approaching renown, and only a tiny handful are much visited. The vast majority stand silently in small churches that speckle the secretive, folded landscape of the Welsh borderlands, little known and rarely seen. This forms the third reason for this book: to encourage exploration and discovery, and to provide a resource for the curious.

THE ORIGINS OF ECCLESIASTICAL SCREENWORK

And thou shalt make a veil of blue, and purple, and scarlet, and fine twined linen of cunning work: with cherubims shall it be made:
And thou shalt hang it upon four pillars of shittim wood overlaid with gold: their hooks shall be of gold, upon the four sockets of silver.
And thou shalt hang up the veil under the taches, that thou mayest bring in thither within the veil the ark of the testimony: and the veil shall divide
unto you between the holy place and the most holy.
Exodus, xxvi: 31 – 33.

For as long as there have been Christian churches there have been church screens. Indeed, the prototype for the Christian chancel screen lies in pre-Christian times. Of the precedents dating from this era the most striking is the veil partition found in the Jewish Tabernacle, or Synagogue. This was used to divide the Synagogue into three distinct spaces: the outer Court of the Tabernacle, where the laity would gather; the 'Holy Place', occupied by the priesthood; and the 'Holy of Holies', or innermost sanctuary, where the Tabernacle itself was housed. The veils that formed these partitions where richly coloured and embroidered, and were supported upon a framework of pillars and an architrave.

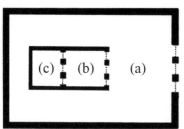

The plan of a Jewish Tabernacle or Synagogue: (a) Court, (b) Holy Place, (c) Most Holy

The hierarchical division of the Synagogue into three principal spaces, and the use of veil partitions, recurs in some of the very earliest buildings used for Christian worship.[1] Moreover, the veil is given a fundamental symbolic aspect for Christians (and its usage thus affirmed) by the tearing of the veil of the Temple at the precise moment of Christ's death upon the Cross:

> Jesus, when he had cried again with a loud voice, yielded up the ghost.
> And, behold, the veil of the temple was rent in twain from the top to the bottom.[2]

The Christian interpretation of this event – that through Christ's sacrifice a way was opened up between God and man – partly explains the curtain-like form of early Christian veil partitions, for such an arrangement could express two central themes of the Christian experience: mystery when the curtains were closed, and spiritual unity when they were open. The curtain veil had a further characteristic that made it suitable as an early screen: Christian worship was initially a covert activity that took place in existing buildings, such as private houses, and not in those built specifically for the practice of religion. Within such structures spaces had to be appropriated for the purposes of worship, and for the sake of flexibility, and with one eye on the authorities, a temporary partition was both a practical and sensible expedient.

Unsurprisingly, given their friability, no early Christian veil partitions survive today. The feature is known only from documentary sources and from its occasional depiction in wall paintings and mosaics. Sources dating from the 1st and 2nd centuries that refer to veil partitions are scant; but from the 3rd century onwards they become numerous and compelling. In the 4th century the Greek writer Athanasius talks of 'the veil of the church',[3] and in the early 5th century another Greek, Synesius, refers to 'the mystical veil'.[4] Also belonging to the 4th century is a wall painting uncovered in the Roman house of SS. John and Paul (the Chamberlains to Constantia, the daughter of Constantine). It shows the curtains of a veil being pulled aside, and a robed figure with arms spread wide in celebration stepping through into a sanctuary beyond.

This and other evidence suggests that the use of the veil partition by the primitive Church, be it for ritual or symbolic purposes, was once almost universal throughout the Middle East and southern Europe. The use of veils in the very earliest churches further west, and specifically in Britain, is less easily traced. However, such partitions were evidently a feature in Celtic and Saxon churches, and have their most conspicuous (and enduring) analogy in the Lenten Veil, or *Velum Quadragesimale*. This feature appeared as early as the 9th century, and was in widespread use throughout England from the 12th century up until the Reformation in the 16th century.

In a clear echo of the Synagogue's internal organisation, early Christian churches were often divided hierarchically into the Narthex, or outer nave; the Naos, or choir-nave; and the Bema, or sanctuary. In such churches, the Naos, or nave proper, was divided from the Narthex by railings or gates, commonly made from wood. By the 4th century, the nave and Narthex had become structurally integrated within a single shell, with communication between the two spaces commonly effected by triple openings in the dividing wall. This layout

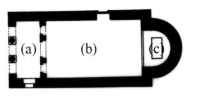

Church of Babouda, Aleppo, Syria: (a) Narthex, (b) Naos, (c) Bema

is well seen in the plan of the church of Babouda, built in the 4th century, close to Aleppo in Syria.

The wooden partitions that restricted access to the nave in the earliest Christian churches represent the very first constructional church screens. Their usage is evidence of the strictness with which the hierarchy of the Early Church was both observed and enforced, and also helps to explain why the solid screen gradually superseded the veil as the primary means of partition in churches.

In early Christian churches a screen was also used to divide the nave from the sanctuary beyond. Initially, this partition took the form of an architrave supported upon pillars (often four in number, like that found in the Jewish Synagogue). However, the supreme adaptability of this frame ensured its retention long after the veil had ceased to be deployed as a continuous partition. The architrave was found to be ideal for the display of sacred images, for example, and provided a prototype for the iconostasis of the Eastern Church, and the rood-beam or painted rood-loft parapet of the Western Church. Old St. Peters in Rome contained a partition of this type, probably erected in the 6th century or earlier. Besides the veil, the spaces between the pillars sometimes contained low, timber screens of lattice-work. These are known as cancelli (from which the word 'chancel' derives). With the veil partition all but outmoded, and with the security of the sanctuary now a higher priority (due in part to the increased numbers of worshippers), these cancelli took on a primary significance and were made both more substantial and more prominent accordingly. From at least as far back as the 4th century, they were sometimes erected without the columns and architrave that once accompanied them.

The earliest cancelli were of wood, and took the form of railings or balusters. To our eyes these would approximate more closely with altar rails than screens. Cancelli of this type stood in the Basilica of Paulinus at Tyre (in modern-day Lebanon) in the 4th century. Subsequently, other materials were employed in their construction, including metal[5] and marble. The church

Iconostasis of Torcello Cathedral (11th century)

of the Apostles in Constantinople, erected in the 4th century by Constantine, contained cancelli of gilded bronze. Torcello Cathedral in Italy, meanwhile, still houses a choir screen that consists of a colonnade which supports a blind arcaded iconostasis: between the columns to either side of the central doorway are cancelli that consist of finely carved marble tablets. Over time, cancelli became highly decorative, in a process that anticipated the similar shift in emphasis traceable in the parish churches of England and Wales between the 13th century and the 15th century. The rich openwork of some Continental cancelli also finds an echo in the elaborate tracery forms of the late medieval screenwork of England and Wales.

Early examples of both cancelli and colonnade screens can still be seen today, most numerously in the old basilican churches of Italy. Of all the early church types it is the Italian (and specifically the Roman) basilican church whose influence proved the most pervasive and enduring for the builders of later Christian churches. Basilican churches share many characteristics with those of the primitive Eastern Church, but draw heavily on sources distinctly their own. An obvious though misleading one is the secular Roman basilica, from which the basilican church derives its name.[6] This was a type of large meeting-hall used in public administration, and when Christianity began to emerge from the shadows it may have been into such spaces, appropriated rather than purpose-built, that it stepped. The plan-form of the purpose-built Christian basilica, on the other hand, owes more to that of certain pagan religious structures.

The small, subterranean 'Basilica' of Porta Maggiore in Rome is just such a structure. It belongs to the 1st century, and was probably the meeting place of a mystical sect. It has a number of characteristics found in later Christian basilicas, including an oblong plan-form (and thus a longitudinal emphasis), a nave separated from side aisles by arcades, and a rounded apse at one end. The slightly larger Temple of Mithras in London, built midway through the 3rd century, exhibits the same features. This

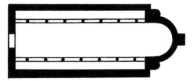

Temple of Mithras, London

later structure was used by adherents to the cult of Mithras, an early and significant rival to Christianity. Other sources, this time domestic and secular, may also have informed the planning of early Christian basilicas. These include the atrium and tablinum of the Roman house. The atrium, or inner courtyard, can be said to answer (albeit rather loosely) to the nave of the basilican church; while the tablinum, a small room opening on to the atrium, answers to the sanctuary. The Roman schola, or guild building, also features an oblong plan form terminating in an apse, and thus affords another possible source for the layout of the Christian basilica.

Initially, basilican churches displayed the familiar tripartite arrangement of narthex, nave and apsidal sanctuary. However, a rapid growth in the size and importance of the nave eventually made the narthex redundant as an internal space, and a two-unit plan-form evolved, (the narthex became in the process a purely external feature). In such churches the sanctuary was essentially extended to absorb the choir, by screening off and thus appropriating the westernmost bays of the enlarged nave with cancelli. Partitions of this type, both dating from the 6th century, survive in the Basilicas of San Clemente and Santa Maria in Rome. The change marked another step in the evolution of the hierarchy of church-users. It was now deemed inappropriate for the laity to set foot in the choir: a prohibition given lawful authority in 566 when the Council of Tours decreed that only for the purposes of taking Holy Communion would such an act be deemed acceptable. Subsequently, the basilican plan evolved side aisles and transepts, rather as the medieval parish churches of England and Wales were to centuries later.

By the 4th century then, the essential characteristics of the Christian basilica – an oblong plan form, a longitudinal axis, a nave flanked by side aisles, and a rounded apse beyond – were well established. In 313, Christianity received official patronage for the first time, from the Roman Emperor Constantine.[7] This triggered an explosion in church building, and the basilica, unsurprisingly, became the prototype for the majority of new churches that appeared thereafter.

The design of the Continental basilican church had a discernible but ultimately limited impact on English church planning. Neither the mission of Augustine at the end of the 6th century, nor the Normans in the middle of the 11th century (to name the two principal conduits of influence for the basilican model) could establish the basilica as the national church type in Britain. Augustine had been the prior of a Benedictine monastery in Rome, and was sent to England by Pope Gregory I in 596. He was made Bishop of the English a year later, and became the first Archbishop of Canterbury. The church of SS. Peter and Paul at Canterbury, founded by Augustine in 597 (but still unfinished at his death in 604) was basilican in form, and other churches of the type soon followed. Today, the remains of seven of these churches, all dating from the 7th century, can still be seen in the south-east of England.

Stylistically, these churches form a strikingly homogeneous group, and written evidence has made it possible to precisely date all but one. Although the churches vary in size and proportion, all are basilican in design. Each has an elongated plan form terminating in a rounded apse; six of the group have at least one porticus (or side chapel), and the church of SS. Peter and Paul has a narthex at its western end. From the remains that survive it is clear that at least five of the group possessed a triple arcade separating the apse from the nave.[8] The decision to erect three smaller arches should not be read as evidence that the early church builder was unable to span such voids with a single, larger arch, for such a feat lay well within his compass. Rather, as A.W. Clapham suggests, 'they seem to have fulfilled a double role, serving both as structural supports and as a form of iconostasis or screen'.[9]

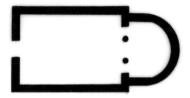

Plan of Rochester Church, of the 7th-century Kentish group, showing a triple arcade separating the apse from the nave

From his power base in south-east England, Augustine clearly intended to extend his reach (and that of Roman Christianity) into the heartlands of Celtic Christianity to the north and west. However, these efforts largely failed, and as his mission faltered so did the influence of his imported brand of church design. The churches of the Kentish group, although forming a remarkable cluster, represent exceptions to the unfolding pattern, and are striking for the highly contained nature of their geographical distribution, rather than for the reach of their influence. Likewise, the triple arcade separating the chancel from the nave did not, at least for the most part, establish itself in the mind of the English church builder.[10]

Excepting those of the Kentish group, the most significant early basilican church in Britain stands at Brixworth in Northamptonshire. For Clapham, 'Brixworth is perhaps the most imposing architectural memorial of the seventh century yet surviving north of the Alps'.[11] This mighty structure has been greatly altered down the centuries, but at its core lies a basilican church similar in character (if not in scale) to those of the Kentish group, and dating from *c.*675. It has a nave of four bays, a square choir and an apse beyond, but has lost its side aisles and the triple arcade that once divided the nave from the choir. The central arch of this triple arcade was loftier and wider than those to either side, and related in its proportions to the sanctuary arch beyond. Meanwhile, over the flanking arches were small windows, which echoed those still visible to either side of the sanctuary arch.

Four hundred years later, the Normans reintroduced the basilican model into Britain. This time, however, the influence was not restricted to a small geographical area, but was transmitted throughout England by the invaders, and is clearly discernible in a large number of churches erected in the 12th century in particular. In many smaller Norman churches – such as Kilpeck and Moccas in Herefordshire – the rounded apse is most clearly a basilican trait. The transepts of larger medieval churches

– such as Montgomery in Montgomeryshire, and Bromyard in Herefordshire – echo the porticus (or side chapel) of the basilican church. Transepts were in continuous use from at least as far back as the 13th century; the rounded apse, however, fell from favour during this period.

The 13th century, far from witnessing the universal adoption of the basilican format in England, instead saw the evolution of an entirely distinctive national church type; and with it the introduction of several strikingly un-basilican features. Two of these are especially noteworthy: the square east-end lit by an east window, which took the place of the rounded apse (and is entirely unknown in Rome); and the chancel arch, which became the principal structural division between the nave and the now unified sanctuary and choir. The chancel archway is essentially an opening cut through an internal dividing wall (itself, a feature not present in basilican churches); and, crucially, it was the treatment of this dividing wall over time that dictated the evolution of the rood-screen in England and Wales.

Of course, not all churches possess such a dividing wall. In Devon, for example, many churches were rebuilt in the Perpendicular era with no dividing wall between chancel and nave (and consequently no chancel arch), and were equipped instead with screens, often of prodigious length, which spanned the side aisles as well as the nave. Wales, too, is rich in architecturally undivided churches. In such churches, the rood-screen is no longer a fitting whose removal can occur with impunity, but an architectural component fundamental to the successful operation of the church. It comes as no surprise then that Wales, and most especially Devon, rank among the richest areas in the country for medieval screenwork.

For churches with a dividing wall, meanwhile, the primary course of development saw the chancel arch gradually enlarged. What had been no more than a small doorway in Saxon churches became an expansive archway in later churches, and as the archways widened so did the screens beneath. A secondary course of development, however, saw the chancel arch left untouched, but the wall to either side of it pierced. These openings took several forms, eventually becoming assimilated elements in a number of distinctive screen types. Here, the wall itself was adapted over time to form the principal means of demarcation. This is in contrast to the main course of development where progressively more (or, indeed, all) of the wall was essentially replaced with a screen.

THE GREAT ROOD

The cross to which the figure of our Lord was attached is gone, and the figure itself is somewhat mutilated and decayed. The height of the figure is 19 inches; the arms and feet are gone. The head, with its crown of thorns, is bent forward; the hair full, the brow deeply furrowed, and an expression of pain rests upon the face.

Archdeacon Thomas's description of the carved Christ from Mochdre in Montgomeryshire.[1]

The carved Christ from Mochdre

Today, the carved Christ from Mochdre lies entombed in a padded box in a basement storage room at the National Museum of Wales, in Cardiff. Despite its battered state it remains a thing of compelling beauty. The recent cleaning of the figure, which involved the painstaking removal of centuries-worth of grime and wax, has revealed precious traces of original pigment: a little brown remaining in the hair, some pink over the sternum and right eye, and fragments of red still clinging to the lips.

The carving itself is clearly the work of an immensely gifted sculptor, blessed with deep empathy for his subject. Sorrow and nobility, even resignation mixed with surprise, are still discernible in Christ's face. The articulation of the head and the fearless attenuation of the torso, tell of a body rebelling against a life that endures and a death that must be close. The effect is exquisite. The depredations of time and misuse have done little to lessen the force of the work, so we can only imagine its impact on the God-fearing parishioners of Mochdre more than 600 years ago, when it probably stood high up at the entrance to the chancel, brightly coloured and brought to life by the dancing light of its many candles.

The Christ figure from Mochdre dates from the 14th century and is one of only a tiny handful of medieval Rood figures to have survived in Britain. The word 'Rood' derives from the Saxon word *Rod* (sometimes *Rode* or *Roda*), and originally denoted the Cross alone. Only later did 'Rood' come to mean the Cross *and* the attached figure of Christ (in other words, the Crucifixion). As a type of religious sculpture, Roods were once common throughout England and Wales. Mark Redknap, the writer of a paper on the medieval rood figure found at Kemeys Inferior in Monmouthshire, notes that, 'Before the Reformation, such figures were standard in the large number of churches which dotted the landscape – for the 13th century, estimated at no fewer than 8,000 in England and about 950 parishes in Wales'.[2] Roods were placed in a number of locations throughout the church, but the Great Rood[3] (so-called to differentiate it from the lesser Roods found elsewhere in the church) was afforded unassailable prominence, high up at the head of the nave. This made it, for perhaps three centuries, the most prominent object in almost every nave in the country.

Depictions of the Crucifixion in early Christian Art are exceptionally rare. Indeed, Christ was very rarely depicted at all much before the late 3rd or early 4th century. The earliest surviving example may be the caricature image of a crucified figure with an ass's head, scratched hastily onto the wall of a house in Rome in the 2nd century. The initial reluctance to depict the Crucifixion has a number of sources. It evidently derived in part from a belief in the essential humiliation suffered by Christ – and thus vicariously by Christians – at His Crucifixion (this being a method of execution reserved for common criminals). There was also the problem of the infant Christianity being essentially an underground religion, the risky pursuit of which would be made only more hazardous by the creation of a visual language, which could prove its existence and identify its followers.

It took centuries, together with imperial sponsorship from the likes of Constantine, before Christianity was able to fully emerge from the shadows and become a public religion. This transition brought with it a pressing need both for new spaces in which to practice (and thus a new architecture) and a new art with which to communicate its beliefs. Thus, basilican churches began to appear in the 4th century, and the first faltering steps were taken toward the creation of a coherent and accessible visual language.

The need for such a visual language, however, brought with it a gigantic theological dilemma; one that simply could not be side-stepped and was to preoccupy Christians to a greater or lesser extent for the next 500 years. The central doctrine of the Incarnation states that God became Christ, in which case is it desirable – indeed, is it even possible – to *portray* Christ? A hatred of pagan idolatry initially led to often vociferous resistance to all forms of representational art (for example, an absolute ban on mosaics depicting God was strictly adhered to until the 12th century; a prohibition which sometimes encompassed depictions of Christ). However, the formulation of the Nicene Creed in 325[4] gave ammunition to those who took a contrary view. It declared that Christ was 'of one substance with the Father', and 'for us men and our salvation came down and was made flesh, and became man'. Such a belief, once established, not only meant that Christ's depiction was possible, it also meant that to avoid it could be read as adherence to the heretical belief that Christ's appearance on earth had been merely visionary. This crucial theological shift (coupled with Christianity's now pressing need for a didactic component) saw images of Christ beginning to appear, in what was now viewed as a necessary affirmation of the orthodoxy.

Having established that it was not only desirable but imperative to depict Christ, it became necessary to establish the essential characteristics – or signifiers – that would enable his identification in artworks. Thus we find artists beginning to wrestle with the problem of how to depict Christ. For example, now we readily accept the idea of a bearded Christ. However, whilst some early Christ figures did follow this archetype (e.g. on the sarcophagus of *c*.390 from S. Ambrogio in Milan) others prior to the 6th century appear as smooth-shaven (e.g. in The Miracle of the Loaves and Fishes mosaic of *c*.504 from S. Appolinare Nuovo, Ravenna).

With the establishment of certain conventions regarding the appearance of Christ, it was also necessary to identify which scenes from the life of Christ would constitute the most appropriate subject matter. For the reasons outlined above, a marked resistance to images of the Crucifixion endured, with notable exceptions, up until the 8th century. From this date onwards, though, the number of images of the Crucifixion suddenly and dramatically burgeoned, and the subject established itself as one of core importance in European art. The reason for this dramatic flourishing is not fully understood, but must derive in part from a recognition of the didactic importance of depicting the Crucified Christ, and of doing so in one of two ways. In the first, Christ is shown as victorious over death (thereby denouncing the notion that his Crucifixion was in some way humiliating). In the second, Christ is shown as suffering for the sins of mankind (thus reminding us that His sacrifice was a peerless expression of His universal love). Although the suffering Christ was to become pre-eminent in the later Middle Ages, both types essentially held simultaneous currency.

With the two forms established, their use spread throughout the Continent and found expression in a number of mediums, both two-dimensional (such as manuscript illuminations, painting and mosaic) and three-dimensional (such as sculpture in wood, ivory, metal and stone). The earliest surviving wooden Crucifix is the Cross of Gero in Cologne Cathedral, which dates from 969–76. It presents the onlooker with a life-sized figure of Christ in the northern European tradition: naturalistic, strained, exhausted, and at the point of death. The representation possesses certain traits seen in similar figures throughout Europe (including the four surviving Christ figures discovered in Britain). The head has fallen forward onto the chest and tuned to the right, the eyes are shut, and the figure exhibits the device of contrapposto, which expresses both more realistically the suppleness of the human body, and its weight. Precisely these features can also be seen in the monumental 12th-century Crucifixion from Le Puy in France (now housed in the Musée National du Moyen Age in Paris) and in the Welsh Christ figures of the 13th and 14th centuries from Kemeys Inferior and Mochdre respectively.[5] Other characteristics of this tradition are the elongation of Christ's body and the pronounced and often stylised modelling of His ribs.

Simultaneously, the other form of Crucifixion – showing Christ triumphant, or as the King of Heaven – began to appear throughout Europe. The earliest known example is a low relief carving on the wooden door of S. Sabina in Rome, dating from 432–40. The two mid-11th-century stone relief carvings of the Crucifixion from Daglingworth in Gloucestershire described below also exhibit these traits: a Christ figure very much alive, with head up and eyes open, often wearing a crown, and displaying none of the torment or strain of the other form. In place of the contrapposto is a rigid, straightened trunk, while the arms, rather than being stretched by the sagging weight of the body, are spread wide in a gesture of all-encompassing beneficence. These characteristics can be seen for example in the life-sized Crucifix from the Convent of Santa Clara de Astudillo in Palencia, Spain, dating from *c*.1150–1200 (and now housed in the Metropolitan Museum of Art's Cloisters

galleries in New York). They can also be discerned in the Monmouth Crucifix,[6] which dates from *c*.1170–80.

It must be acknowledged of course that the characteristics of each of the two types of depiction, far from being restricted to only one of the forms, clearly intermixed on occasion. So it is for example that we find a metal Crucifix figure belonging to the second quarter of the 12th century wearing a crown, but clearly of the 'suffering Christ' type. The 11th-century Lundo Crucifix is of the same type,[7] but here the Christ is not shown in a strained pose, but frontal and symmetrical, with arms outstretched in rather the same way as those of the Daglingworth Christ figures.

In England, the earliest surviving depictions of the Crucifixion date from Saxon times, and there is no doubt that the Crucifixion formed an important component of Saxon religious art. Saxon Roods tend to be made of stone rather than wood,[8] and were often placed above the south doorway of churches (i.e. the main entrance) and not over the chancel opening.[9] At Langford in Oxfordshire there is a re-set 'Christ in agony' type Crucifixion (complete with Mary and John) over the south porch, and a large headless 'Christ as King' type Crucifixion re-set into the side wall of the porch. Suggested dates for these figures have ranged from the 10th to the 12th century.

Holy Rood church at Daglingworth in Gloucestershire contains four notable pieces of late Saxon stone relief sculpture, all of which date from the middle of the 11th century. Two of these depict the Crucifixion. The smaller of the two panels was, until recently, mounted high up on the outside of the east wall of the chancel (a position it seems to have occupied for many years). It can now be found inside, attached to the north aisle wall close to the pulpit. Even allowing for the rigours of time and weather, this is neither a sophisticated depiction nor the product of a master mason. Christ is shown as if preaching from a rock, his arms outstretched. He does not appear to be attached to the overly-broad limbs of the Cross behind. There is no sense that

Langford: Two Christ figures; the larger one headless, the smaller flanked by Mary and John

his weight is being taken by the nails at his wrists and there is no agonised contrapposto.

West of this, but also mounted on the north wall of the nave, there is a second Crucifixion panel. Again, Christ appears to be standing and bearing his own weight. Here, the face is more clearly discernible and betrays none of the anguish found on that of the Mochdre Christ. The differences between the Daglingworth figures and later wooden rood-figures cannot be attributed solely to disparities of craftsmanship. Rather, a more impactful naturalism had established itself by the 14th century; one made possible by the emergence of the craft of woodworking, and the potential for expressiveness entailed in that craft.

As well as being in far better condition than the first Daglingworth panel, the second one is also of greater interest, for it shows Christ flanked by the Roman soldiers Longinus and Stephaton. Longinus stands to the left, holding the lance he will use to pierce Christ's side. Stephaton, meanwhile, holds aloft the sponge soaked in vinegar wine. Other depictions of the Crucifixion show the configuration that would come into general usage later; namely, Christ flanked by the figures of Mary and John. The outline of just such a rood-group, this one dating from the 10th century, can be found on the outside of the south wall of the church at Breamore in Hampshire. The same church contains a superb Anglo-Saxon inscription over the archway to its south transept, which in translation reads, 'Here the covenant is revealed to you'.

Although the transition from the 'Christ as King' type to the 'Christ in agony' type was probably a gradual one, a striking and influential prototype for the latter is recorded; one that may have had a dramatic and quite sudden influence on the adoption of such representations in England. Hugh of Leven was the head of a Cistercian community and the Abbot of Meaux in the East Riding of Yorkshire from 1339 to 1349. During his tenure there he oversaw the creation of a new Rood for the nave of the monastic church. Amazingly, rather than follow the stylised 'Christ as King' archetype, he chose instead to employ one of his own monks to sculpt a Christ figure from a living nude model (and this at a time when modelling from life was virtually unknown, let alone for the purposes of depicting Christ). Following the Rood's completion, permission from the mother house at Citeaux in Burgundy was sought (and granted) for lay people to be allowed access to the Rood, for the image was believed to have miraculous powers.

Prior to the 12th century it is clear that Roods were

Daglingworth: Two Christ figures of the mid-11th century; one flanked by the Roman soldiers Longinus and Stephaton

19

*The carved figure of Mary
from Mochdre*

occasionally erected without any accompanying figures (a fact evidenced by certain Saxon examples). From the 12th century onwards, however, it became standard practice for the Great Rood to be flanked by the figures of the Blessed Virgin Mary and St. John the Evangelist (thus forming what is often referred to as the 'rood-group'). Incredibly, as well as the Christ figure from Mochdre, the carved figure of Mary from the same rood-group also survives. Although battered and incomplete, like the Christ figure she retains much of the grace and stillness bestowed on her by her carver long ago.

The reason for the survival of the figures of Christ and Mary from Mochdre, but not that of St. John, remains a mystery. It is a striking fact that of the thousands of rood-figures that once graced the churches of England and Wales during the Middle Ages, not one survives intact or *in situ*. In fact, just four mutilated Christ figures survive from 400 years of wood-carving; one figure from each of the four centuries. Thus, from being among the most abundant of church fittings, rood-figures are now among the very rarest of ecclesiastical treasures.

In 1915, the head and right foot of a Christ figure belonging to the 12th century were discovered behind a wall in All Hallows church, South Cerney in Gloucestershire. These fragments are possibly the oldest pieces of figure carving in wood to survive anywhere in the country. The finesse and naturalism of the carving, given the virtual non-existence of the craft of woodworking at this early date, is startling. There is certainly nothing comparable in contemporary stonework (and precious little in stonework of a later date) to be found anywhere in Britain. Interestingly, the South Cerney pieces clearly belonged to a 'Christ in Agony' Rood, proving that Roods of this type were a feature of Romanesque religious art (Professor George Zarnecki has dated the South Cerney fragments to *c*.1130[10]).

*South Cerney: The head and foot
of a Christ figure of c.1130*

20

In about 1850, during repairs to the church of St. Michael (later All Saints) at Kemeys Inferior in Monmouthshire, workmen unblocked a long-sealed doorway that once gave access to the rood-stairs. Inside, together with a quantity of bones and skulls, they found the remains of a wooden Christ figure dating from the late 13th century. Aside from the head and torso, a foot of the same date together with two arms of a later date were also discovered. When complete, the figure would have been roughly one metre tall, making it almost twice the height of the Mochdre Christ. Like the Mochdre Christ, however, the Kemeys figure exhibits carving of great refinement. The face in particular is exquisitely caught.

A less refined wooden Christ figure, this time belonging to the 15th century, was discovered at Cartmel Fell in Lancashire (and exhibited at Carlisle in 1882, soon after its discovery). The figure retains its legs but has lost its arms. Although the basic characteristics of the depiction are similar to those shown by the other figures (it too is carved in three-quarters relief, for example), the modelling here is nothing like so deep or assured, and the piece is evidently the product of a less able wood carver.

These four mutilated Christ figures, together with the Mary figure from Mochdre, complete the list of surviving wooden rood-figures. Without these few scattered remains we would have only documentary evidence of the existence of this once-common form of religious sculpture, and almost no physical evidence whatsoever. Destruction on this scale, almost amounting to a kind of material genocide, is difficult to comprehend nowadays, and there is a temptation to believe that other wooden rood-figures remain hidden somewhere, awaiting discovery.

The precise date at which the custom arose of locating the Rood over the chancel arch – 'so as to rivet the attention of the congregation, or of the casual worshipper'[11] – is not known. Howard and Crossley argue that, 'it is certain that the practice was general before the date of the earliest Saxon churches',[12] and identify the suitability of the large expanses of blank wall that existed over chancel arches in churches of the Bradford-on-Avon type as backgrounds for rood-groups. Although evidence exists to support the contention that Roods did appear over chancel arches at such an early date, the practice does not seem to have become general until at least the 13th century.

With the custom of locating the Great Rood over the chancel arch established, the fixture evolved a wide variety of configurations and treatments. In terms of height, the figures varied from a few feet tall, right up to life-size or even taller. The outline of a Rood measuring eight feet in height survives on the screen tympanum at Wenhaston in Suffolk. The Rood that belonged at Cullompton in Devon, meanwhile, may have been taller still. Roods were also intermittently taken down and replaced with larger versions when churches were enlarged. This was particularly the case during the Perpendicular era, when walls were heightened and clerestories added. Evolving tastes and a desire to outshine a neighbouring parish also accounted for the upgrading of some Roods (just as such factors did with the adjoining rood-screens and rood-lofts).

Along with the generally-present figures of Mary and John, a number of other figures also appeared with varying frequency. These included saints, angels (in the form of cherubim and seraphim in the case of King's Chapel at Woodstock), the four Evangelists, all twelve Apostles (in the case of Braybrooke in

Northamptonshire) and even, very rarely, the two thieves (these once stood at Brecon, and still do at St. Fiacre-le-Fouet in Brittany). A later arrangement, and one that probably derived from Continental precedents, saw the grief-stricken Mary kneeling at the base of the cross (as opposed to standing apart from the Rood, as she clearly did at Mochdre).

Candles, lamps, tapers and torches (in a variety of configurations) were also fixed along the top of the loft parapet or rood-beam in order to light or honour the Rood. Records from the mid-16th century show that the rood-loft at Westwell in Kent originally supported 60 candlesticks (though this seems to have been an unusually high number). It was also common practice to illuminate the Rood by means of lights (typically in the form of candelabra) suspended before it on a cord or chain. These were generally raised or lowered using a pulley attached to the roof. Two pulley-wheels for this purpose still survive in the roof at East Hagbourne in Berkshire.

Of all the customs associated with the Great Rood, however, none would perhaps seem stranger to our eyes than that of clothing the figure of Christ. Whilst the practice was by no means universal, enough evidence exists to suggest that it was not uncommon either. Furthermore, the practice, far from being restricted to the later Middle Ages, pre-dates the Norman Conquest (at Canterbury, for example, there was a clothed Christ figure as far back as the early 11th century).

The Italian Crucifix known as the *Volto Santo* (or 'Holy Face') at Lucca in Tuscany provides one notable Continental precedent for the custom of clothing the Rood in England. This famous wooden Christ figure, dating from the 11th century or earlier, was clad in a long red robe both to honour and embellish it. During a visit to Lucca in 1050, Abbot Leofstan used the *Volto Santo* as the prototype for his own 'Ruby Rood'. This exact copy of the *Volto Santo* derived its name from the deep red of its robe. Leofstan had the Ruby Rood placed over the altar of the Holy Cross in the Abbey Church of Bury St. Edmunds: a high profile site for a sculpture whose characteristics were consequently adopted elsewhere.

Certain parochial inventories prove conclusively that the custom of clothing the Rood prevailed in parish churches too. The items most commonly used to dress the figure of Christ were cloaks, coats or robes (typically of velvet, but sometimes of satin or some other fabric), and shoes, which were commonly of silver. Thus, at Chilham in Kent, records show that until 1543 the figure of Christ from the Great Rood was clad in a green satin coat and a pair of silver shoes. As well as clothes, Christ figures were also festooned with jewels, gilt crosses, gold or silver rings, coins, pendants, and a multitude of other costly embellishments. At Canterbury, the Christ figure from the Great Rood wore a crown; an addition designed to emphasise the concept of 'Christ as King'.

'When I see on Rood'

When I see on Rood
Jesu, my *leman*,   lover
And beside him stonden
Mary and Johan,
And his rig *iswongen*,   scourged

And his side *istungen*,   pierced
For the love of Man,
Well ought I to wepen
And sins for to *leten*,   abandon
If I of love *can*,   know
If I of love *can*,   "
If I of love *can*.   "

An anonymous rood poem of the 14th century

It is clear that the Rood occasionally became in itself the object of the worshippers' devotion (as opposed to a mere conduit for the proper devotion of Christ as symbolised by the Rood). The giant Crucifix that once stood at Brecon – variously referred to as the *Golden Rood* or the *Crog Aberhonddu* ('Cross of Brecon') – was just such an object. During the 15th century its reputation for healing the sick brought pilgrims from all corners of the Principality, and inspired some of the best known Welsh bards to compose poems in its honour. Within the southern Marches, Ludlow, too, possessed a much-venerated Rood (the so-called 'Cross of Ludlow'). It was believed that it could save people from damnation, and became a much-visited object of pilgrimage that attracted believers from far beyond the boundaries of the parish.

Stories abound of the miracles that took place before Great Roods. A girl with spinal curvature, a woman with paralysis, a blind fisherman and a blind woman were all apparently cured after coming before the Rood at Malmesbury Abbey. Unsurprisingly perhaps, a desire to be buried before the Great Rood also evolved (though this was an honour extended to the privileged few only). Thus, two early Bishops of Worcester – Samson (d.1112) and Theulph (d.1123) – were both buried in the nave beneath the Great Rood. A number of wills survive from the 15th and 16th centuries in which the desire to be buried before the Great Rood is expressed.

During certain penitential phases of the religious calendar the Great Rood would be shrouded with a veil or white cloth as an emblem of mourning. This veil would cover the Rood from the first Sunday in Lent through until the Fourth Station of the Procession on Palm Sunday, at which point it would be drawn aside. At the conclusion of Evensong on Palm Sunday the Rood would be covered once more until Easter Eve. Unsurprisingly, numerous references to the rood-veil and its associated apparatus exist. During certain festivals it was also common practice to decorate the Rood and rood-loft with garlands and other vegetation. This custom is kept alive to this day at Charlton-on-Otmoor in Oxfordshire. On May Day each year a Cross of greenery is still set up on top of the church's rood-screen.

There can be no doubt that the increasing levels of observance directed at the Great Rood were the cause of violent antipathy during the Reformation (though it could be argued that, were such a custom as the clothing of the Rood to prevail, it might generate disquiet even today). Even if the Rood did not in itself become an object of worship, the clothing of Roods and the high level of maintenance enjoyed by the rood-group ensured that initial discomfort had developed into open hostility by the time of the Reformation. The increased realism of the later 'Christ in agony' type may also have been a contributing factor. With Christ figures becoming more and more lifelike, the attention directed at Roods could easily be read as something perilously close to self-worship. The antipathy to Roods during the Reformation did not result in the instantaneous destruction of all Roods. In fact some survived for more than a century. The life-sized Great Rood of Llanrwst church in Denbighshire, for example, was still lying hidden in the rood-loft there as late as 1684.

Although no medieval Roods remain *in situ* (in Britain at least) it is still possible to get some idea of the original appearance of this once-universal fixture, for a number of churches in England contain notable later arrangements. Of these, the rood-group

North Cerney: Modern Rood-group and loft, incorporating a superb Italian Christ figure of c.1600

doubt that medieval rood-figures were often lavishly painted and gilded. Mark Redknap, in his paper on the Christ figure from Kemeys Inferior, notes:

> It is clear that, in contrast to its present condition, the Kemey's Christ originally had a vivid and rich polychrome appearance, popular throughout the medieval period. Great care was taken in decorating the figure, so that at one stage it would have glowed and gleamed with gold leaf ... The secondary colour scheme appears to have included gilding on the hair, gold, red and blue on the loin-cloth, dark brown/ black beard, eyebrows and eyelashes, green crown of thorns, and flesh tones in pale pink, with red emphasising the wounds.[13]

at North Cerney church in Gloucestershire is particularly impressive. Above the chancel arch here is a rood-loft, erected in 1925 by F.C. Eden. Fixed to the top of its western parapet are the figures of Christ, Mary and John. The carved Christ is an especially fine example from Italy, and dates from *c.*1600. The accompanying figures of Mary and John are later. Although the colouring applied to the figures here is recent and may not accurately reflect a typical medieval scheme, there can be no

The desire to correlate the Great Rood's physical prominence with its mystical and didactic pre-eminence resulted in it being sited over the entrance to the chancel. This entailed the creation of a suitable platform for the fixture in this location. Prior to the introduction of rood-screens and lofts, the Rood was generally fixed upon a rood-beam (occasionally referred to as the *perk*, *candlebeam* or, in larger churches, the *trabes crucifixi*). This hefty timber beam was embedded into the side walls of the nave, just to the west of the chancel entrance. Besides the rood-figures, it had to support the various candles and lamps that accompanied the figures.

The height at which rood-beams were fixed varied greatly and was informed by such factors as the size and proportions of the church, and by the nature of the nave arcade. The massive rood-beam at Denston in Suffolk is set into the spandrels on

Cullompton: The massively carved 'Golgotha',
upon which the Rood-figures stood

either side of an extremely lofty arcade. It soars here just below the height of the clerestory. As well as being fixed to the top of the beam, the Great Rood was sometimes suspended beneath it. At Cullompton in Devon there is just such a beam, located even nearer to heaven than the one at Denston. It hovers just below the rafters, borne aloft by carved angels at either end. This beam forms a tie-beam on wall-posts, and is essentially a part of the roof structure. Amazingly, the foot of this giant Crucifix rested on the floor of the rood-loft far below. All that remains now of what must have been a massive and particularly arresting rood arrangement is the 'Golgotha' from the foot of the Cross. This huge and ruggedly-worked panel is carved with rocks, bones and skulls, and now lies in two pieces at the west end of the church.

The use of rood-beams in England dates back at least as far as the 12th century. The monk Gervase details one located over the rood-screen in Lanfranc's Cathedral at Canterbury before the fire of 1174.[14] This supported a great Cross, the figures of St. Mary and St. John the Apostle, and two cherubim. The rood-beam at Old Shoreham in Sussex is decorated with double billet mouldings, and may also date from the 12th century. Early in the 20th century, during repairs to the nave roof of Dodington church in Kent, a rood-beam of the 13th century, carved upon both faces with trefoil arcading, was discovered. However, by 1925 these precious fragments had been lost. The two sawn-off ends of another finely-moulded rood-beam, this one of *c*.1260, can still be seen at Binsted in Sussex. An early and complete rood-beam also survives (albeit no longer *in situ*) at Meopham in Kent.

Other churches with rood-beams still *in situ* include Bawburgh, Blakeney, Costessey, Potter Heigham, Scottow and Tunstead in Norfolk; High Ham in Somerset; Debenham, Denston and Worlington in Suffolk; and Hackford in Norfolk[15] (though again here the rood-beam is sawn off). In the southern Marches, a re-set rood-beam survives above the screen at Little Malvern in Worcestershire. Although relatively few rood-beams survive, numerous corbels that once supported rood-beams do (e.g. at Brecon Cathedral), thus helping to confirm the widespread use of this fixture. Occasionally, the bressumer of a rood-loft was left in place following the removal of the rood-loft. This beam is often mistakenly identified by later church writers as a 'rood-beam'. Pipe and Lyde in Herefordshire affords an example of just this. Pevsner[16] describes the beautifully carved timber beam here as a 'rood beam' when in fact it is the bressumer belonging to the church's missing rood-loft.

As rood-lofts came into general use, so Roods were fixed instead to loft parapets. Prior to this, Roods were rarely if ever attached directly to the tops of screens, for such a location was not generally thought to be elevated enough. For this reason (and even with screens well established) Roods tended to remain fixed to their rood-beams above the screens. Fixing the Rood to the top of the loft parapet, on the other hand, proved both effective and expedient. The parapet provided the perfect degree of elevation for the Rood, while the rood-loft itself (and its stairway) afforded a means of access for those charged with attending the Rood. Although the majority of Roods were fixed to the western parapet, some were fixed to the eastern one. The Great Rood at Llanelieu in Breconshire no longer exists, but the mortise hole into which its foot once slotted can still be seen in the eastern beam, adjacent to the rood-tympanum. The ghost of the Cross can also be seen, pale yet clearly discernible on the boarding of the tympanum.

An important consideration when setting up the Rood was the nature of the backdrop the figures would be seen against. The east window, whose glare tended to throw the figures into silhouette, was generally (though not always) considered undesirable. This was perhaps the principal reason why the custom of employing a solid background for the figures was established. In churches of the 13th century and before that had low chancel arches the expanse of wall over the arch provided the Rood with just such a background. This expanse of wall was often painted with a depiction of the Last Judgement and Resurrection (together referred to as *'The Doom'*).

A Doom painting of the late 12th century survives, albeit in a heavily re-worked and incomplete state, over the chancel arch at Patcham in Sussex. It was discovered in 1879 beneath 30 coats of whitewash. Another, this time belonging to the 13th century, survives over the chancel arch of the Guild Chapel in Stratford-on-Avon. It is described as, 'full of incident ... Many little figures climbing out of their graves, including a king, a bishop and an abbot'.[17] The recently uncovered 'Coventry Doom', in Holy Trinity church (next to Coventry Cathedral) is especially fine, and dates from the early 1430s. Perhaps the most spectacular surviving example though – and one that makes up for its lack of artistic finesse both by covering the whole expanse of the east wall of the nave and being largely true to its original scheme – is that found in the church of St. Thomas, in Canterbury.

As chancel arches grew and the wall spaces above diminished in area (particularly in the Perpendicular churches of the 15th century) a new solution had to be found if a solid background for the rood-group was to be maintained. Generally the space remaining between the top of the eastern parapet of the rood-loft and the top of the chancel arch was simply blocked up. Doing this created a feature known as a rood (or screen) tympanum. The same thing could also be done in open plan churches without chancel arches, essentially by extending the eastern loft parapet upwards. Here, the space between the rood-loft and the ceiling was boarded up with timber planking, plaster rendered laths or wattle, and sometimes even canvas.

At Bettws Newydd in Monmouthshire, the most comprehensive late medieval rood arrangement in existence survives (see photograph on p.272). It comprises a rood-screen, loft and tympanum, and serves to demonstrate how effective such an arrangement can be in a small church of single-unit plan form.

Llanelieu: squints cut through the tympanum

The tympanum in particular neatly divides the church into two 'rooms', as well as providing a solid background against which to view the Rood (which no longer survives). Two windows of three lights each pierce the tympanum. A rood-tympanum also survives intact and *in situ* at Llanelieu in Breconshire (see plate 9). This is decorated with small white flowers against a pinky-purple ground, and is also pierced by (albeit less formal) squints (see photograph above). Elsewhere in the southern Marches other mutilated rood-tympana survive. At both Aylton and Michaelchurch in Herefordshire, the sawn-off boarding of the rood-tympana can still be seen protruding from the ceiling.

Just as the wall spaces above chancel arches were once painted with 'Dooms', so it was with rood-tympana. Today, rood-tympana embellished with Doom paintings are extremely rare. Of those that have survived, the remarkable story of one in particular should be re-told here. In 1892, during the restoration of the church at Wenhaston in Suffolk, woodwork including the rood-tympanum was taken down and left outside in the churchyard (one can safely guess at the fate that awaited these pieces). During the night, however, whether by Divine providence or good luck, there was a torrential downpour. At first light the next day it was noticed that some of the whitewash covering the tympanum had been washed off, revealing the long-hidden figures of Mary and John, blinking in the sunlight. The vicar was immediately informed and the tympanum cleaned and re-assembled in a nearby schoolroom.

The 'Wenhaston Doom', as it came to be known, is by far the most spectacular remaining example on wood of this once-common form of religious art. Executed in the first quarter of the 16th century, the work is more than eight feet high and 17 feet

Michaelchurch: showing the cut-off tympanum over the screen

wide. It displays an array of figures and scenes in a composition every bit as wondrous and terrifying and visually complex as anything Hieronymus Bosch (who was painting at the same time in Holland) could have devised.[18]

With the onset of the Reformation, rood-tympana were not, as a rule, pulled down. Indeed, their very prominence ensured their survival, for it was recognised that once scraped clean or whitewashed the bare expanse that remained was an ideal hoarding upon which to display religious texts. The most common of these were the Ten Commandments – the '*Decalogue*' – together with the Lord's Prayer and the Creed. An especially fine set survives at Lydbury North in Shropshire (see photograph on p.156). These are written in an archaic 'black letter' text and, unusually, are signed and dated: Charles Bright, Churchwarden, 1615.[19]

Besides religious texts, such tympana often carried the Royal Arms; sometimes painted, sometimes carved, as affirmation of the sovereign's role as the new head of the Church. Lockington in Leicestershire and Kenninghall in Norfolk each possess a fine tympanum bearing the Royal Arms; the former belonging to Queen Anne and dated 1704 and the latter belonging to Elizabeth I. In the southern Marches, superb carved examples of Royal Arms survive at Elton in Herefordshire (Elizabeth I), at How Caple in the same county (William III) and at Ludlow in Shropshire (Charles I). A great many rood-tympana survived until the 19th century, at which point they were removed by Victorian restorers.

To further emphasise the status of the Great Rood, fittings known as 'celures' were often placed over the figures. A celure is

Elton: the carved Arms of Elizabeth I, now opposite the entrance

essentially an extra-decorated roof section (coved, vaulted or flat panelled), designed to act as a canopy of honour over the rood-group. Celures were generally supported in one of two ways. They could be entirely independent of the ceiling above; being supported instead upon timbers that projected out from the east wall, or north and south walls, of the nave. They could also result from the localised enrichment of the ceiling itself over the rood-group. In either case, the ornamentation of the fitting involved the use of the same elements found on the rood-screen and loft below (carved and moulded timbers, painting and gilding).

How Caple: the carved Arms of William III

A number of celures survive, including fine examples at Stowlangtoft in Suffolk and Almeley in Herefordshire (see photograph on p.201).[20] The latter is divided up by painted ribs (with flowers at their intersections) to give a chequerboard pattern of 40 squares, each of which has a Tudor rose at its centre. The Almeley celure dates from the early 16th century. At Glascwm in Radnorshire (also in the southern Marches) the wagon ceiling of the chancel extends to take in one bay of the nave, thus forming a celure. The fitting was only rarely used in larger churches; the only known example being the one in Manchester Collegiate (as was) which has since been removed.

With a rood-tympanum blocking any light previously available from the east window in the chancel, the problem of how to illuminate the Great Rood was a significant one. One solution (further to that of using artificial light) was to insert a window high up in the wall of the nave. Rood-windows (where they survive) are generally found in the south walls of naves, and vary greatly in size and style. At Culmington in Shropshire a tiny rood-window can still be seen, puncturing the wall fabric; and to the east of it a miniscule window to light the rood-stairs. Other small rood-windows of this type can be seen at Llanfilo (see photograph on p.190) and Partrishow in Breconshire, and at Kemeys Commander in Monmouthshire. At the other end of the spectrum is the arrangement found at Welsh Newton in Herefordshire (see photograph on p.256). Here, a large, gabled dormer window was added just west of the church's stone rood-screen. If this is not precisely coeval with the fabric of the church (i.e. *c.*1300) then it must

Trostre: the little cinquefoiled rood-window, which matches in its design the nave window to the west

have been put in soon after the church was built. At Grosmont in Monmouthshire is another fine gabled dormer designed for the same purpose and of a similar date (though this one is found on the north side of the church, and not the south).

THE DEVELOPMENT OF THE ROOD-SCREEN
IN ENGLAND AND WALES

'It must not be forgotten that it is the variety and development of the ground plan that has given us the wealth of variety and detail of the portion of the building we see above the ground.' Sidney Heath, *Our Homeland Churches.*

The Saxon Church

Although churches of the basilican type count among the earliest structures used for religious practice in Britain (e.g. the Temple of Mithras in London), an altogether different archetype informed the design of the majority of early Christian churches built in Wales and the west of England. The small sanctuary chapel imported by missioners from Ireland and the north was a humble, functional structure, relatively simple to erect, and designed to house an altar and occasionally a holy relic or image. Originally, such chapels were of single-chamber form, their entry being limited to the priesthood or the initiated. Members of the laity, who were not permitted inside and for whom the space was not designed to cater, were made to gather about the entrance for the purposes of worship. Such an arrangement would have been familiar to the pagan Saxons, for they were used to performing their rites outside, in sacred enclosures marked by wooden fences, earthworks or stone circles.

St. Piran's Oratory in Cornwall, long lost to the shifting dunes of Penhale Sands, is an example of this earliest type of Christian chapel. It was probably built by missioners from Ireland in the 6th or 7th century and, although later extended, was initially of single-chamber form. The Gallarus Oratory in southern Ireland, shaped like an upturned boat and probably dating from the 8th century, is also of single-chamber form. The survival of so few of these early chapels is only partly explained by the vagaries of time: their coastal setting, which made them vulnerable to successive invading forces, and their simple construction (they were often made of wood) were also factors militating against their longevity.

The anomaly of the priest sheltering inside the sanctuary while the congregation stood outside in all weathers, together with the influx of new worshippers triggered by Christianity's imperial recognition, was corrected through the addition of a second, larger chamber. With the chapel thus extended, the access doorway into the earlier structure effectively became a primitive chancel arch. In small Saxon churches of two-unit plan form this communicating doorway was generally extremely narrow,[1] and remained so until after the Conquest. Small archways of this type can be seen at Escomb in Durham and at

The plan of Escomb church, Durham

Bradford-on-Avon in Wiltshire. Despite the addition of a second chamber such chapels remained, for the most part, small structures. Uyea chapel on Shetland, for example, is just 27 feet long, with a nave measuring less than 17 feet.

With the addition of a second chamber, the archway between nave and sanctuary in the lesser churches remained little more than a small doorway until well after the Conquest.[2] During this period two factors in particular demanded the maintenance of this mural partition between nave and sanctuary. The lesser of these was the need for security, for the new worshippers formed, 'a rude crowd, often profane, and quite untried in loyalty'.[3] Far more important, however, were the symbolic and liturgical aspects of such a division, and specifically the importance of 'mystery'.

The mystic tradition in Christian worship ultimately derives from the beliefs and structures of the Eastern Church, while the policy of attempting to communicate mystery by screening off the high altar was a key feature both of Eastern and basilican churches. In the latter instance the colonnade-type screen (sometimes referred to as the 'mystery-type' screen) was both physically imposing and visually obstructive: two factors that made the altar beyond, literally (and metaphorically) less accessible to worshippers. During certain penitential seasons, the draping of a curtain or veil from the top of the screen communicated a further refinement of the mystery idea: namely that the holiness of the sanctuary did not remain constant, but rather that it fluctuated to the rhythm of the holy calendar. In the Saxon churches of Britain, veil partitions were used to close off the narrow doorway into the sanctuary. This completely masked the altar and heightened still further the already potent sense of mystery associated with this holiest part of the church.

Even when other forms of partition were developed in Britain, the related practice of erecting Lenten veils, to shroud the high altar and its associated fittings for the forty days of Lent, persisted. Although such a flimsy partition did not present a physical barrier to those wishing to gain access to the sanctuary, the crime of removing the veil was considered grievous indeed. In the late 9th century, King Alfred decreed that the tearing down of a Lenten veil would incur the then-vast fine of 120 shillings. Although the Lenten veil screened the sanctuary only during Lent, and was not the same as a permanent curtain screen, it seems reasonable to conjecture that the violation of one would be regarded as comparable with the violation of the other.

During this period, wooden partitions taking the form of a simple gate or grille began to appear in Saxon churches, replacing the earlier curtain or veil partitions. These were placed as would a door within a doorframe. Although it would be misleading to refer to such partitions as 'screens' it is certain that it was from such partitions that rood-screens were later to evolve. Today none survive, so we can only speculate as to their appearance. However, given the relative severity of Saxon church interiors, and the modest proportions of a fitting required to span so small a gap, they would surely have attracted very little, if anything, by way of ornamentation.

Norman Churches

The 12th century witnessed the further compartmentalisation of churches, and with it a need for partitions which could effect these changes internally. Along with two-unit plans, three- and four-unit plans also evolved. The new compartments were added longitudinally, and generally in a way that resulted in an incremental decrease in the scale of each chamber from west to east. Side aisles were rarely employed, even in the larger Norman churches.[4] Side aisles, the rounded apse common to small Norman churches, and the transepts used to extend the choir space in larger Norman churches, are all features that are essentially basilican in character. However, side aisles did not become established features until much later, and the rounded apse soon gave way to the square east end.

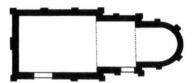

The three-unit plan of Kilpeck church, Herefordshire

Herefordshire boasts fine examples of both three- and four-unit plan Norman churches. Kilpeck and Moccas, both of which belong to the second quarter of the 12th century, have three-unit plans and show a pleasing west to east diminution in scale. At Peterchurch, which belongs to the mid-12th century, a square fourth chamber exists, over which the Norman tower originally rose. This space forms the choir, and communicates with the sanctuary to the east and the nave to the west via rounded arches. Here, the eastward vista, channelled as it is by the diminishing archways, is particularly memorable. The Peterchurch arrangement, of a tower over a square choir, is found in several churches of the 11th and 12th centuries: for example at Checkenden in Oxfordshire, Birkin in Yorkshire, and at Dalmeny in Scotland.

Although the main course of development during the 12th century saw chancel arches widened and rood-screens erected before or beneath them, the expansion of the chancel arch was not universal. One reason for this may relate to the location of subsidiary altars within churches lacking side aisles (i.e. most Norman churches). This factor is especially relevant as it directly impinges upon the development of the rood-screen. From an early date English parish churches had at least three altars. Besides the high altar at the east end there were usually two further altars, typically placed against the chancel wall to either side of the chancel arch. A narrow chancel arch afforded plenty of wall space against which to set these altars, and this may help to explain why the use of smaller chancel arches persisted through the 12th century, and into the 13th century. The problem with this arrangement (and the reason why it represents the exception and not the rule) is that it does nothing to make the high altar more visible to the congregation at a time when this was becoming more desirable.

The southern Marches is unusually rich in screen altars. Of the surviving examples, the two at Partrishow in Breconshire are the most notable (see illustration p. 196), for they stand adjacent to a late medieval rood-screen and loft. At Peterchurch in Herefordshire the screen no longer survives but two altar slabs do, flanking the entrance to the apse. In the same village, tiny Urishay Chapel also retains fragments of its screen altars. Documentary evidence records that two such altars also once stood at Llangwm Uchaf in Monmouthshire. In Norman churches with enlarged chancel arches the two subsidiary altars, instead of standing against the chancel wall, could now stand against the screen itself. Being of openwork this partition allowed views of the high altar beyond.

In decorative terms at least, the rood-screens of the 12th century were emphatically subordinate to the adjacent chancel arches.

At this time screens were seen as overwhelmingly functional: a status reflected in their plain construction and lack of ornament. Chancel arches, however, once they had shaken off any vestiges of doorway practicality, began to soar and grow rich with carved decoration (e.g. Rock in Worcestershire). As the space described by the chancel arch expanded, so did the rood-screen below; and as the screen grew, so its role as maintainer of the security and sanctity of the chancel became ever more manifest.

It is impossible to identify the point in history when a screen (as distinct from a partition such as a gate) first appeared beneath a chancel arch to fulfil this role, but we know that one stood in Canterbury Cathedral in the early 12th century. Sadly (but not surprisingly) no complete Norman rood-screens survive, so any conclusions regarding their appearance are necessarily conjectural. The only fragment with a viable claim to a Norman origin is the wooden railing now mounted over the chancel arch at Compton in Surrey. This piece is in the form of an arcade of round-headed arches on piers topped with Romanesque capitals. Kirkstead Chapel in Lincolnshire and Rochester Cathedral in Kent also retain screenwork for which a date in the late 12th century has been claimed.

The fact that almost no church screenwork has survived from the 12th century is not surprising, for it seems that little woodwork of merit (to say nothing of screenwork) was actually produced during this period. Indeed, for Howard and Crossley, 'England produced scarcely any woodwork of artistic importance until the latter part of the thirteenth century'.[5] The reason for this (and one eloquently expressed by the lavish chancel arches of the Norman period) is that this was overwhelmingly the era of the stonemason.

The early woodworker, charged with making a screen, had no precedent specific to his material to refer to. For this reason he had to turn to the stonemason for guidance. The results of the influence of the mason on the work of the carpenter are clearly visible in the screenwork of the 13th and 14th centuries, of which a great deal more survives.

The 13th and 14th Centuries

Church building in the 13th century was dominated by the alteration and extension of existing structures, rather than by the raising of entirely new ones. The most common changes were the lengthening of chancels, and the addition of side aisles to naves (and occasionally to chancels, particularly in south-east England). Entirely new

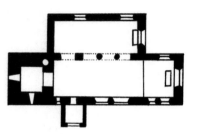

Llanfigan, Breconshire, a 13th-century church with an aisle of the 14th century

churches were generally of two-chamber form and, being that much larger from the outset, did not need the aisles that were added as extensions to existing smaller churches. The transepts of the 13th century tend to be larger than those of the 12th century, and a number of churches were given transeptal chapels. The influence of the layout of monastic and cathedral churches saw some larger churches given cruciform plans.

From c.1300 onwards churches were often completely rebuilt, (although the plans of many were still informed by what had previously existed on the site). During this period the popularity of the cruciform plan (and consequently, transepts) declined, and towers began to appear at the west ends of churches, as opposed to over their crossings. Side aisles continued to be widened and heightened; and with the insertion of larger windows and the addition of clerestories to naves, interiors began to flood with light. Crucially, this period also witnessed a shift in the balance of power between the two principal elements dividing chancel from nave – the chancel arch and the rood-screen. From the middle of the 13th century, although chancel arches continued to expand, the decorative treatment they received became gradually less elaborate. The treatment of the attendant rood-screens, on the other hand, became progressively more elaborate.

The 13th and 14th centuries together represent the formative phase in the evolution of the rood-screen; a phase which coincided with that of church woodwork generally. For most of the 13th century the craft of woodworking remained in its infancy, concerned with the functional to the virtual exclusion of the decorative, and operating very much in the shadow of the then-mature craft of stonemasonry. These factors – in particular the craft's immaturity and its reliance on the stonemason – led to the creation of rood-screens (and other fittings) that lacked what might be termed 'wood-sense': that consummate handling of wood that can only proceed from a deep understanding of the material and a measure of creative autonomy, and that is so gloriously a feature of church woodwork in the centuries that followed. Although the status of the woodworker himself would eventually match (or even exceed) that of the stonemason, in the 13th century he was an artisan of more modest abilities and pretensions.

The lowly standing of the woodworker prior to *c*.1250 is well illustrated by the example of the dug-out chests still found in many churches. Up until the middle of the 13th century these were constructed by hollowing out a solid tree trunk, exactly as a mason would a block of stone to form a coffin. The problems with such an approach are self-evident. While both stone and wood can be worked with a hammer and chisel, they remain fundamentally different in nature. Stone is granular and best worked in block form, while wood is fibrous and best worked in narrow lengths. When applied to wooden chests the mason's techniques are clearly wasteful of both time and timber. Subsequently, when chests began to employ the expedient of a plank construction the planks were usually left plain, yet were fastened together using elaborate metalwork. So, even when the chest was constructed in a way that respected the properties of the wood, the job of ornamenting the chest went to another.

It comes as no surprise, then, that the woodworker, when asked to make a rood-screen, was initially unable to comfortably address the challenges of such a commission. In the case of the rood-screen at Pixley in Herefordshire (see illustration p.242; which, although belonging to the 14th century, exhibits characteristics found in earlier screenwork) the carpenter's want of specialist knowledge is immediately apparent, for whilst the design of the screen here is entirely reasonable and structurally sound, it is also severely plain and hardly attractive. His handling of the wood has exacerbated the weaknesses of the design, for the timbers have been clumsily worked and are disproportionately massive (even accepting that the screen later supported a loft). Even those screens from the 13th century that display greater finesse – such as those at

Stanton Harcourt or even St. Mary's, Chichester – are marred to varying degrees by a fundamental lack of wood-sense.

Today, very few rood-screens dating from the 13th century survive. Even prior to the Reformation many were replaced or greatly altered as the taste for more elaborate screens evolved. Of those that have survived the earliest, by popular consent at least, is the rood-screen at Thurcaston in Leicestershire, for

Detail of the screen at St. Mary's Hospital, Chichester

which a date of *c.*1220 is often claimed (e.g. by Aymer Vallance in *English Church Screens*). A more plausible contender, however, is the screen at Kirkstead (St. Leonard) in Lincolnshire. This is probably coeval with the chancel fabric, and if so belongs to *c.*1230–40.[6] The screen at Sparsholt in Berkshire may not be quite so early, but it too dates from the first half of the 13th century. Slightly later, but unrivalled for its completeness, is the rood-screen at Stanton Harcourt in Oxfordshire, of *c.*1260.[7] The spectacular screen at St. Mary's Hospital, Chichester, belongs to *c.*1290, while those at Northfleet in Kent, Harwell in Berkshire, and Chinnor in Oxfordshire, are probably of *c.*1300.

Stanton Harcourt, Oxfordshire, showing the similarity between the east window and the screen above middle rail

In design terms these screens share a number of distinctive characteristics, of which the most fundamental is their post and beam construction. This technique is also apparent at Pixley. Although incomplete, the screen at Pixley retains its principal framing members, which comprise two wall standards (extending up to the wall-plate), two door standards, a sill, a middle rail and a head-beam. Throughout the 13th and 14th centuries most screens displayed the essential rectangularity that proceeds from a post and beam construction (though rarely is it as pronounced as it is at Pixley). The evolution of rood-screens during and after this period can be characterised as a gradual process of refinement and decorative elaboration, designed to improve upon and disguise this underlying framework. When rood-lofts began to appear in the 14th century the structural integrity of the post and beam method meant that screens were readily adapted to accept the accompanying lofts. Symbiotically, the addition of lofts informed aspects of the development of rood-screens, restricting for example their upward growth (at least in Wales and the west of England).

With most timber rood-screens of the 13th century the debt owed to the stonemason by the woodworker is at its most conspicuous in the upper portions of the screen, and specifically in the design of the mullions. These commonly take the form of turned and banded shafts, capped above and standing upon bases. In doing so, they draw heavily on window design of the period. This is especially noticeable at Kirkstead and Stanton Harcourt. In both, the chancel is lit by an east window whose design finds a clear echo in that of the rood-screen above middle rail height. The use of turned shafts as mullions, whilst mirroring forms common in stonework, was disproportionately time-consuming for the carpenter (and made only more so if the shafts were to have bases, caps and bands whose spacing was to correspond accurately from shaft to shaft). As a consequence the turned shaft gave way to the moulded mullion in the 14th century. Here, the cross-section was shaped by working along the grain (not across it) resulting in mullions that were quicker and easier to replicate.

As well as borrowing from the compositions and motifs of the stonemason, the carpenter also adopted certain of his construction techniques. He dowelled his timbers together, rather than using the expedient of mortise and tenon joints, and in doing so frequently arrived at compositions that lacked structural rigour. Whereas, in later screens the mullions would run from the middle rail into the head-beam (with the tracery heads slotted between), in screens of the 13th century the turned shafts often supported an arcade cut from continuous boarding that was itself slotted into the underside of the head-beam. This latter arrangement, seen at Kirkstead, Sparsholt and Stanton Harcourt (and again found in stonework) possesses only a fraction of the structural integrity of the former. In these cases the arcade supported by the turned shafts is unpierced and cut from thick board to give simple trefoil heads. At Thurcaston an unusual technique is employed, whereby the octagonal mullions are carried up to the head-beam, and the arcade of trefoil heads is made up of two thinner boards, which sandwich the upper portion of each shaft.

With the exception of the arcade of banded shafts, the rood-screens of the 13th century generally show little by way of decoration. Rather, there tends to be a subordination of the aesthetic role of the screen to the utilitarian. The various framing members – head-beam, middle rail, sill and standards – are either unmoulded or simply moulded, and the panelling of the wainscot is left entirely plain.[8] The screen at St. Mary's Hospital in Chichester[9] provides an exception to this rule, and shows the advances that had been made by the end of the 13th century. Here, the familiar turned and banded shafts are employed throughout; as are (albeit buried in the design) the trefoil heads characteristic of the period. However, narrower intermediate shafts subdivide the lights above the middle rail, giving a cage-like feel to the screen. These shafts reach only halfway to the head-beam. Meanwhile, the upper half of the design consists of a series of boldly carved triangular heads, each one crocketed and framing an encircled quatrefoil. The least satisfactory aspect of the composition sees the head-beam resting on shafts rising from the junctions between each triangular head and the finials topping each head. Both structurally and compositionally this is a little awkward. Despite these idiosyncrasies, however, the overall effect is inventive and enjoyable, (and clearly prefigures the expansive tracery of screens of the 15th century).

By the beginning of the 14th century the arcade was well established as the principal design feature underpinning the composition of screens; a status that was to remain unchallenged until the Reformation. In larger screens a multiplication in the number of lights also occurred (consistent with the general pattern of elaboration that evolved during the 14th century). In smaller screens, however, the triple division was generally maintained. Constructional and decorative refinements continued during the 14th century. New motifs and variations of form began to enrich the upper parts of screens; and new methods of construction more appropriate to wood began to evolve. The screen at Cropredy in Oxfordshire displays both advances. Dagger and mouchette forms bound across the top of the screen, and the arcade is subdivided by intermediate standards (again, pre-empting a feature that would become common in later screens).

Unsurprisingly, more rood-screens survive from the 14th century than from the 13th century. Those from the first half of the 14th century generally display features drawn from past models. The screens at Willingham in Cambridgeshire, Ewerby and Leake in Lincolnshire, and Kirk Ella in Yorkshire, for example,

all have the turned and banded shafts found in screens of the 13th century. At Geddington in Northamptonshire and West Thorney in Sussex the treatment of the traceried lintel supported upon the shafts is relatively simple; while at Rickling in Essex and King's Lynn in Norfolk the treatment is more elaborate. Crucially, in none do these shafts reach the head-beam. In character, many of the tracery forms of this period are recognisably Decorated, incorporating as they do trefoils and quatrefoils, mouchettes and daggers, ogees and cuspings.

In the second half of the 14th century and towards its close, however, screen builders began to look predominantly forwards, discarding past models in favour of new ideas. The screens at Lavenham in Suffolk and Merton in Norfolk both employ the framed construction with deep lights typical of the 15th century. Both screens have moulded (as opposed to turned) mullions, and highly elaborate tracery. The rood-screen at Barton in Cambridgeshire, of the late 14th century, has intermediate standards that extend to meet with the head-beam, with mouldings that are returned over each bay. The screen also has cusped and crocketed ogee heads with Perpendicular panel tracery filling the spandrels: in all, a design that has everything to do with the screenwork of the 15th century, and very little to do with that of the 13th century.

The rood-screens of the 14th century show the craft of screen-building undergoing a phase of transition, gradually but surely pulling itself clear of the influence of the stonemason, and moving ever nearer to the dazzling and self-assured craft it would become by the beginning of the 15th century. The problem of how best to reconcile the seemingly contradictory requirements for security on the one hand, and transparency on the other, had been elegantly resolved. The lower halves of screens respected the tradition of the ancient cancelli-type partitions, while the traceried lights above middle rail height respected the transparency demanded of contemporary religious custom. With the basic format of the rood-screen fully resolved, and freed from his habitual ties to the stonemason, the screen-builder could at last take flight.

The 15th and 16th Centuries

During the 15th and 16th centuries the development of churches was as much informed by factors social and political as it was by those purely architectural. Although the Wars of the Roses (1455–85) and the conflict in France had only a marginal effect on normal life in England, they contributed significantly to the impoverishment of the aristocracy, and to the undermining of its ability to build new churches. For the first time the role of church patron was taken up by the commoner, and many new churches were funded by parish subscription.[10] The shortage of labour in the aftermath of the Black Death had caused a steep rise in wages, and the burgeoning wool trade saw the emergence of a powerful and fantastically rich merchant class. With the country's wealth partially redistributed, the shift in patronage (and distribution) of new churches was often dramatic. The inversion is well illustrated by the example of Lavenham in Suffolk. The Perpendicular church here was begun by the noble de Vere family, but completed by the Spryngs, who were prosperous clothiers. The centres for the wool trade and the weaving industry, and consequently the areas with the finest Perpendicular churches, are Devon and Somerset, the Cotswolds, and East Anglia.

The wealth of the wool merchants led to the creation of some of the largest and most spectacular parish churches ever built. Lavenham and nearby Long Melford (both in Suffolk) could almost be cathedrals. Although chancels did not on the whole increase dramatically in size, naves were made longer, wider and taller, and became as auditoriums for preaching in. Side aisles were also widened to enable processions to pass along their length unhindered; and chantry and guild chapels sprang up, built with endowments from wealthy local families. Many completely new churches were built during this period. However, drastic rebuilds, which involved the sweeping away of large parts of the original structure, were predominant (especially in Devon). Elaborate and soaring towers, such as those at Boston in Lincolnshire and Chipping Campden in Gloucestershire are also characteristic; as are lavish porches, like those at Cirencester and Northleach in Gloucestershire. Numerous and expansive windows, at ground and clerestory level, made the huge interiors lighter than ever.

The change that had the greatest impact on the development of the rood-screen (and that inadvertently led to the survival of so many) was the abandonment of the wall dividing the chancel from the nave. In churches where this occurred the sole division between the two spaces was provided by the rood-screen, and the priesthood and congregation shared what was in effect a large open-plan space. As such churches usually had side aisles that extended for the length of the building, the rood-screen would typically extend to the north and south walls of the church, thereby dividing nave aisles from chancel or choir aisles. This development led to the creation of some of the most spectacular church screens ever devised, overwhelming to the onlooker as much for their sheer physical presence as for the richness of their carved and painted surfaces. The rood-screen at Uffculme in Devon is but one striking example. In its journey across the church it describes 17 separate bays, and is 67 feet long; while the timber used in its construction might best be measured in tons.

The adoption of the architecturally undivided church type was widespread by the second half of the 15th century,[11] and was especially popular in the South-west and Wales (though generally without side aisles in the case of Wales). There can be no doubt that the survival of so many late medieval screens in these regions is due in part to the lack of a dividing wall in such churches, and the resultant fundamental utility of the rood-screen. The choice for the Reformers (and others) was a simple one: either leave the screen intact, or replace it with some kind of dividing wall to maintain the demarcation between nave and chancel, nave aisles and chancel or choir aisles. With the latter proving unpalatable many screens were simply left *in situ* (though their paintings were usually defaced and their accompanying lofts pulled down).

Rood-screens that span the side aisles as well as the nave are not restricted to Devon, yet are rare in Wales and the southern Marches. One fine and notable exception is the screen at Old Radnor in Radnorshire. Here a diocesan anomaly resulted in an English type church and rood-screen becoming marooned in Wales.[12] The screen here is an arresting sight, and would have been more so prior to the removal of its original colour in the 19th century. Jonathan

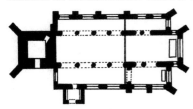

Plan of Old Radnor church

Williams, a visitor to the church in 1818, described seeing, 'The beautiful screen that divides the nave from the chancel, most richly carved in oak, painted and gilded, and bearing on it representations of saints and religious persons, placed in ranges, compartments or niches'.[13]

The rood-screen at Old Radnor displays a number of features characteristic of English screenwork in the 15th century, one of which is an arched form (see illustration on p.176). This form, the arcade, derived from stone precedents, but proved at least as suitable for timber screens. As well as being aesthetically satisfying, it also turned out to be an effective engineering solution to the problem of how best to support the weight of the rood-loft (which almost every screen of the 15th century was required to do). The evolution of the arcaded screen can be traced through a

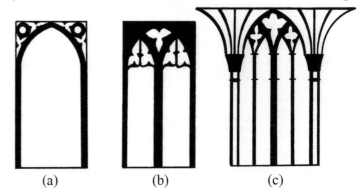

(a)   (b)   (c)

The evolution of the arcaded form:
(a) The arched form as a tracery element in a square-framed bay.
(b) Solid spandrels giving an arched form to a square-framed bay.
(c) An arched bay with vaulting covering the spandrels

number of distinct phases. Initially, the arch appeared only as a tracery element in square-framed screens. Next, solid spandrels were introduced to give an arched form to each of the lights (as at Cascob in Radnorshire). The final step saw the coving of the rood-loft brought down to hide the spandrels, and the coving thus evolve to become a groin vault. At Old Radnor the spandrels, which are hidden to the west behind the vaulting, are carved to the east. Where the vaulting springs both to the west and to the east (as it does at Bosbury – see illustration on p.209 – and Dilwyn in Herefordshire) the spandrels could be dropped altogether. In most counties the arcaded type is rarer than the square-framed type. The exceptions are Devon and Cornwall, where almost all of the screens are of the arcaded type.

The groin vault (as seen at Old Radnor, Bosbury, Dilwyn as well as throughout the West Country) was a significant innovation, for it brought to a state of pleasing unity the formerly distinct rood-loft and rood-screen. For the first time the loft, rather than appearing as a mere appendage to the screen, seemed an organic development of it. The decorative potential of the vault was not lost on screen-builders. By the second half of the 15th century relatively simple rib vaults had given way to elaborate lierne vaults; and the ribs themselves, once plain, had become richly moulded and carved. The enrichment of the vault often came at the expense of the tracery below. At Old Radnor, for example, the tracery has been reduced to an ornamental fringe, which relates more strongly to the vault above than to the screen below (the same applies at Aymestrey in Herefordshire). In the case of the elaborately vaulted rood-screen at Mobberley in Cheshire, meanwhile, the tracery has been omitted altogether.

It is important to acknowledge that within Britain the groin vault was a feature of English-built screenwork only. Lofts of Welsh origin were never vaulted, but instead employed a flat soffit or horizontal coving. It is true that vaulted lofts survive in a handful of Welsh churches (at Montgomery in Montgomeryshire; Usk in Monmouthshire; Llanrwst and Gresford in Denbighshire; as well as Old Radnor), but all are English imports. The groin vault, together with the continuous intermediate standard (i.e. which extends unbroken from the sill up to the head-beam), are two of the clearest signs of an English-built screen. Horizontal coving, on the other hand, is not unique to Wales, and is also a feature of lofts in the south and west Midlands, Gloucestershire, north Somerset, Wiltshire, and Oxfordshire.

The developments below middle rail height during the 15th century were perhaps less dramatic, but are significant nonetheless. The wainscot, which had been left entirely plain during the 13th century, and had been only modestly ornamented during the 14th century, became greatly enriched. Two main types of carved decoration were used (often simultaneously). The first of these was blind decoration (sub-divisible into applied carving, and carving 'in the solid'). Blind decoration began to appear in the 14th century (at Guilden Morden in Cambridgeshire for example) and involved the application of carved details (often congruent with the main tracery heads above) to the head of each bay of the wainscot. Linenfold panelling (found at St. Weonards and Sutton St. Nicholas in Herefordshire, and at Shelsley Walsh in Worcestershire) was also popular. The second type of carved decoration was openwork, in which the wainscot was pierced with a design that echoed or replicated the tracery above.

In most screenwork of the 15th and 16th centuries the wainscot is divided into bays by struts known as muntins. Sometimes these form purely structural elements, deployed in such a way as to provide support to a long middle rail prior to the insertion of boarding. Used thus they may correspond visually with the other vertical elements in the design to a greater or lesser extent. At Llanbister in Radnorshire, for instance, no effort has been made to align the muntins with the mullions above (or with any other elements in the composition). However, at Llangwm Uchaf in Monmouthshire the mullions form carefully orchestrated elements in a consistent overall composition. Here, the design is divided vertically throughout by continuous lines that extend from the muntins of the wainscot, via the screen mullions and the ribs of the loft coving, up to the muntins of the loft parapet.

One further component vital to the appearance of the screenwork of the 15th and 16th centuries is colour. Its importance to the medieval builder and furnisher of religious buildings (not to mention its impact on the medieval churchgoer) is all too easily forgotten now. Too many churches have been scoured of their original colour and gilding, or have had their wall paintings hidden beneath layers of whitewash. Meanwhile, other surviving work has simply faded over time, losing forever the bright complexion of its youth. Nonetheless, rood-screens and lofts, pulpits and font-covers, walls and roofs; even stalls, pews and lecterns, were all the subject of often extravagant polychrome and gilt embellishment. The effect when lit by candlelight can only be imagined at now.

Two areas in particular – East Anglia and the South-west – are justifiably celebrated for the painted decoration of their screens.

Wales and the Midlands have less to show, and when figure painting is encountered it is generally substandard. The medium for the paint used on screens (and other church woodwork) was generally oil; though occasionally (and especially in East Anglia) a kind of tempera made from fish glue was used. The dominant colours were red, green, and blue, always deployed in their brightest and purest forms, and generally in accordance with strict principles (often deriving from heraldry). Black, white and gold were also used; the latter generally over a red ground. In applying the paint, large areas of a single colour were generally avoided. Instead, colours would alternate across the design (for example the panels of a wainscot); or a chequerboard composition might be used, as with the celure at Almeley in Herefordshire or the loft coving at Beguildy in Radnorshire. Reds and greens were commonly used for the screen itself; blue and gold for the coving; and white, or black and gold in a barber's pole design for the ribs and uprights. Gilding was applied to figures and carved trails, but was sometimes replaced by yellow pigment on the backs (i.e. the eastern faces) of screens to save money.

In the South-west and East Anglia figure painting was (and still is) commonplace, and has provided ecclesiologists with a rich area of subject matter in its own right.[14] Here, it will suffice to say that there are a number of significant differences between the screen-painting of the two regions, and that the quality is invariably at its highest – the draughtsmanship at its most refined – in East Anglia. Besides figure painting, gold stars sometimes speckled the blue of loft covings; and foliage and flowers (the latter often stencilled on for ease and consistency) climbed uprights and bloomed against the flatter surfaces. In the Victorian era and during the 20th century colour was reapplied to many screens, particularly in Devon. Whilst the quality and accuracy of this work varies greatly,[15] the garishness – the 'touch of the fairground'[16] – of many recent efforts may recall the original spirit of late medieval colour schemes more accurately than at first seems likely; for the goal of the medieval painter was a pronounced lavishness of effect somewhat too rich for current sensibilities.

During the 15th century, as the skill and status of the woodworker grew, so did the resources lavished on rood-screens. The fitting (together with the Rood overhead) became the paramount component of the church interior, and in most parts of the country its design and decoration informed that of the rest of the church's woodwork. Thus, in Devon, Cornwall, and the Midlands, the pulpit and benches would typically form, together with the screen, a closely matching set of fittings. Even in East Anglia, where such coordination was rare, the various pieces generally corresponded in their proportions and use of line. By the second half of the 15th century the churchgoer can have been in no doubt as to the enhanced status of the carpenter, for his wares now filled the church, right up to the elaborate arch-braced and hammer-beam roofs overhead.

The carpenter's work from this period shows him making decisions about the construction and decoration of rood-screens (and other fittings) both appropriate to the timber used in their construction, and without undue reference to the stonemason. So it was, for example, that he began to use mortise and tenon joints, and to discard dowelling as a means of framing up screens and lofts. As his skill and knowledge increased so did his self-confidence and, inevitably, his ability to express himself with a voice clearly and distinctly his own. As Frederick Bligh Bond characterises it, 'They [the woodworkers] could think and feel, as it were, in the material they were working. Their best products are instinct with vitality'.[17]

With the bursting of the dam, rood-screens began to flood with carved decoration. Wainscot panels and loft parapets were trimmed with blind tracery and fretwork, lights were richly traceried, framing members were variously carved and moulded, and head-beams and bressumers were given carved trails, or fringed above and below with top- and drop-crestings respectively. The decoration could be abstract or geometric, with curved edges or straight, and might feature foils and cusps; or be figurative and include, along with humans and animals, undulating trails of vine, oak, water-leaf, hawthorn and pomegranate.

In Devon in particular this carved enrichment can tend toward the excessive. At Swymbridge, Lapford and Plymtree, for example, no surface has escaped untouched. Carving is piled upon carving, and the choked surfaces, and thus the underlying structures, have all but disappeared from view. In spirit and appearance this encrusted superabundance recalls the stonework of the late Decorated era (seen, for example, in the sedilia canopies at Hawton in Nottinghamshire). Such wood carving is generally of a very high standard, but its deployment is too often undiscerning. With no plain surfaces to punctuate the composition, the eye of the onlooker is never permitted to rest; the richness of the feast leading to a visual indigestion rarely experienced with the sparely carved screenwork of East Anglia.

Although the carpenter initially followed the lead set by the mason, in the 15th and 16th centuries the opposite scenario sometimes prevailed. The rood-screens at Compton Bassett in Wiltshire and Totnes in Devon are virtual copies in stone of screenwork existing elsewhere in wood. Indeed, when painted, both would have been virtually indistinguishable from their wooden counterparts. Although there are hazards associated with such an approach, (not least of which is the fragility of delicate or lacy forms carved in stone) it is a testament to the skill of the mason that he was able to manage it at all, let alone with the success he achieved. Despite this apparent inversion, it would be wrong to imagine that the stonemason's place in the hierarchy of craftsmen was now below that of the carpenter. Instead it remained high, and when the carpenter drew up alongside, the relationship between the two was frequently symbiotic in nature, with each drawing inspiration from the other.

Despite the parity of status enjoyed by mason and carpenter, stone screens were vastly outnumbered by wooden screens during the 15th and 16th centuries. There are three main reasons why this was the case. The first concerns the availability of appropriate materials. In such districts as Devon and Somerset, Norfolk and Suffolk, and the Welsh borderlands, stone of a suitably tractable nature was at a premium. Wood on the other hand was plentiful. Secondly, not only was wood more abundant (or at least accessible) it also proved more democratic: most villages had their own carpenter (but not mason), and the craft was thus familiar to, and practiced by, more people. Thirdly, stone screens were not generally designed to take a rood-loft, and whilst wooden screens were easily altered to accommodate such a fitting, stone screens were not. Other factors may also have played a part, including the relative ease with which a wooden screen could be updated, or even replaced.

Interestingly, in one part of the composition of screens – namely the tracery heads – the woodworker never stopped referring to the products of the mason. Just as the screens of the 13th century (such as those at Stanton Harcourt in Oxfordshire and Kirkstead St. Leonard in Lincolnshire) borrow the rounded shafts and trefoil heads of contemporary window design, so too does the intricate panel or grid tracery of later screens derive from the window designs of that era. Perpendicular window tracery of the 15th and 16th centuries differs from the Decorated tracery of the 14th century in a number of fundamental ways. Where Decorated work relies heavily on curves and ogees, and thus is animated and even flamboyant, Perpendicular work (first seen in a fully resolved state in c.1350 in the chancel of Gloucester Cathedral) takes as its basis rectangular forms. These are divided and subdivided vertically and horizontally to form a grid. The effect is coolly rational; stern rather than playful.

This grid composition is clearly seen in the tracery of rood-screens during the 15th and 16th centuries. In the arched screens of the South-west the tracery is contained above the height of the springing of each arch. This compartment is then divided up by pointed, ogee or cusped arches that spring from the mullions between the standards. Next, the composition is variously subdivided to give a pattern of cusped forms; most notably the classic Perpendicular lights. These formed the essential building blocks of both solid and openwork carved decoration on screens throughout England for almost two centuries. As with window design of the period, motifs seen during the Decorated era were not altogether discarded. Thus it is that ogees, trefoils and quatrefoils, for example, still appear; though crucially they are always contained within the grid that forms the underlying framework of the design, and are never permitted to range freely across the design (as they do at Cropredy in Oxfordshire). Cusping and then sub-cusping the initial rounded or pointed arch was also popular in the 15th and 16th centuries: where the cusps met, little carved Tudor roses were sometimes held in place. Tracery of this type can be found at Canon Pyon and Burghill in Herefordshire.

In general terms the tracery of the Midlands and East Anglia conforms to the principles described above, though with certain exceptions. For example, the tracery of Midland screens tends to be simple and boldly modelled, as befitting the general design of screens here. In East Anglia the bays are often narrower, and the tracery heads shallower. Furthermore, the greater restraint generally shown with carved decoration here, combined with the greater emphasis on painted decoration, often sees tracery playing a less significant role in the overall design (as is clearly the case at Attleborough in Norfolk).

A further technique used throughout the country (but especially in East Anglia) was to vary the thickness of the tracery, or to apply one element over the top of another; to model the tracery heads in such a way as to give them a more sculpted appearance. The thicker (or applied) element was often in the form of a crocketed ogee arch or pinnacle: a motif and a usage common to stallwork of the period. This 'modelled' tracery can be seen in several Lincolnshire churches (for example in Fishtoft, Burgh, and Addlethorpe) but is occasionally found in the Midlands and also in Wales (on the loft parapet at Bettws Newydd in Monmouthshire). The tabernacle work which further added to the depth and richness of loft parapets in the 15th and 16th centuries also appears on rood-screens (for example at Hitchin in Hertfordshire).

In the South-west, the Midlands and East Anglia the tracery is almost always regular from bay to bay across the screen. However, in a significant number of Welsh screens and lofts (particularly those from the Newtown centre) the tracery pattern varies from bay to bay. It seems that the presence in screens of this type of square-headed bay inevitably led designers away from the sub-divided arches and cusped forms of screens with arched bays. However, as to the variation from bay to bay – seen most memorably at Llananno in Radnorshire – the designers clearly believed that visual richness lay not in the unity brought about by repetition, but in the vitality that comes from variety. This diversity is carried (in blind form) up into the panels of the loft coving above. The motifs themselves reveal the debt owed by the makers, not only to Newtown School (and thus Welsh) forms, but also to Perpendicular designs from across the border in Herefordshire.

Regional Variation in Screenwork

A survey of the woodwork of the 15th century reveals plainly for the first time the operation of regional and local variation. In terms of regional variation in its broadest sense it has been suggested that the country be divided lengthways into three distinct schools or traditions, 'by means of lines drawn from Dorset to Cumberland, and from London to the Tyne'.[18] These regional schools are referred to simply as the Western School (which subdivides into the South-west and Wales), the Midland School, and the Eastern School. Ignoring for now localised variation within each region (and the dynamics of influence between the three) it becomes evident that certain broad regional characteristics exist, and that no form of late medieval woodwork demonstrates these more clearly than church screenwork. These distinctions become conspicuous when comparing rood-screens archetypal for each region:

THE WESTERN SCHOOL (THE SOUTH-WEST): BRADNINCH, DEVON

The rood-screen at Bradninch is long and low, and stretches across the church to span side aisles and nave. These characteristics, together with its deep cornice and the wide arches of its arcade, give it a pronounced horizontality. The framing members (most notably the standards and middle rail) are carved with foliage, and are variously moulded. This feature, together with the treatment of the vaulting and cornice, means that much of the underlying framework is disguised or hidden altogether.

Bradninch, Devon

The wainscot panels show both carved and polychrome decoration. Each is painted with a squat, characterful figure,[19] framed above with a cusped ogee arch. The middle rail is interrupted along its length by the intermediate standards, which run unbroken from the sill up to the head-beam. The wide bays above the middle rail are subdivided by mullions, and the heads filled with panel tracery (of A-type – an identifiable design found in many Devon churches). The fan vaulting of the missing rood-loft springs from attached shafts extending up the western faces of the standards from sill level. The vault itself, which is complex and decorated with blind-tracery, spreads to both the east and west. Above this runs a heavy, 'frowning'[20] cornice, comprising three carved trails divided by half-rounds, with top- and drop-cresting.

Throughout, the carving is naturalistic and of a high quality, and is clearly the work of experts. If the overall design has a weakness it is that the decoration can seem excessive; and this, when combined with the low height, heavy cornice and brash colouring (carried out in 1853), leads to an effect that is rather heavy and overwhelming. Here, as in all screens of the Western School, line is subordinate to surface texture.

THE WESTERN SCHOOL (WALES): LLANWNNOG, MONTGOMERYSHIRE

The rood-screen and loft at Llanwnnog are of modest dimensions and comparatively humble character, and well befit the small and humble church in which they stand. Here, the method of assembly is immediately apparent. Indeed, nowhere in Britain is post and beam construction more frankly acknowledged than in Wales. Where arches and curves rule at Bradninch, straight lines and right angles dominate at Llanwnnog.

Below the middle rail the wainscot panelling is entirely devoid of carved or painted decoration. The low middle rail itself runs through unbroken between the wall and door standards. Above, in place of subdivided bays with arched heads and regular tracery, are undivided bays with squared heads and irregular tracery (formed by the mullions meeting the head-beam at right angles). Overhead, in place of fan vaulting, there is horizontal coving divided up by ribs and bosses to give rectangular panels. These panels have applied blind tracery that corresponds with the tracery heads. The bressumer forms a cornice with two carved trails and cresting. Above this rises the mutilated loft parapet.

The screenwork at Llanwnnog, despite appearing to share little with the spectacular screen at Bradninch, exhibits certain traits that reveal the pair to be cousins. In appearance the screenwork of Llanwnnog is squat and heavy, and although nothing like as long as that of Bradninch, shows the same clear horizontal emphasis. Where the affinity is at its most explicit, however, is in the carved decoration; and specifically in the undulating foliage trails that run along the bressumer. More broadly, the carving shows the naturalism and energy that are the hallmarks of the Western School. The additional quality of variation from bay to bay is a wholly Welsh characteristic, however, and emanates from the Welsh screen-carvers' near matchless instinct for invention.

THE MIDLAND SCHOOL: THENFORD, NORTHAMPTONSHIRE

The epithet 'typical' is least appropriately applied to the screenwork of the Midlands, for here most screens are the work of local carpenters, and rarely is it possible to identify more than one screen by the same hand. The rood-screen at Thenford, like many in the Midlands, is restrained in both its design and use

Llanwnnog, Montgomeryshire

Thenford, Northamptonshire

of ornament: the serviceable result of unassuming but effective craftsmanship. If it can be said to relate to the screenwork of one of the other schools it is the Western, and specifically the Welsh, for it has the sturdy rectangularity of a Welsh screen, and is massively framed up with thick timbers (arched screens and fan vaults being the exception here[21]).

The screen's wainscot (although renewed) is entirely plain. In an echo of Welsh screens the middle rail runs through uninterrupted between door and wall standards; and the mullions – two forming three bays to the south, and one giving two bays to the north – are dowelled into this heavy, chamfered rail. The heads to each bay are cusped, and the spandrels pierced with trefoil forms. The head-beam is also heavy and is subdivided horizontally to give a number of parallel faces. One of these evidently housed a vine trail (pieces of which have been re-used in the pulpit). The undulating openwork trail over the head-beam is unusual, and represents inventive fancy on the part of the carpenter. The brattishing that tops the screen is a later addition; possibly (and certainly typically) Victorian.

THE EASTERN SCHOOL: ATTLEBOROUGH, NORFOLK

The rood-screen and loft at Attleborough are strikingly different to those described above. They stand in a typically lofty East Anglian church, and are themselves of typically lofty proportions. Although the screen and loft extend across the side aisles as well as the nave, the insistent horizontality of Bradninch is not at work here. Rather, the composition has an attenuated verticality.

The wainscot panels in the lower half of the screen are blind-traceried, but only very faintly do they retain their original painted decoration. The middle rail above is interrupted by the intermediate standards, which extend from the sill up to the head-beam, to form a series of tall, narrow bays (these are arched; but elsewhere in East Anglia – most notably in Lincolnshire – the heads to each bay are often square-headed, and sometimes wider). East Anglian screens feature the finest figure painting in the country. At Attleborough three bays to either side of the chancel arch (this being an architecturally divided church) are blind and feature the lovely, slender figures typical of the region.[22] With colour the principal tool of decoration, the tracery that tops each bay has been reduced to a dainty fringe.

The loft above is narrow; partly because the narrowness of the bays has restricted the spread of the vaulting to the north and south, and thus to the west. Interestingly, not only is the head-beam hidden here (as at Bradninch), but so too is the bressumer

Attleborough, Norfolk

to the west. Instead, the vault extends to meet a 'floating' arcade that mirrors that to the east, only is slightly higher. This allows the vaulting to be more easily seen from the west. With no visible bressumer, there is no cornice and no horizontal beam housing carved trails. The loft parapet is also painted (this time with various Arms) in a restrained colour scheme of red, blue and white. The upper part of the parapet is pierced with openwork, and topped by the thin rail.

The composition as a whole is light and elegant; strong in overall design terms, with line given priority over surface texture. Carved decoration plays only a minor role, and where it does appear is lithic in quality and devoid of the naturalism and invention seen in the west of the country. Here, the means of construction are not as frankly acknowledged as they are at Thenford or Llanwnnog, but are more so than at Bradninch.

When any of the three regional schools – the Midland, the Eastern or the Western – is examined in greater detail, further levels of variation quickly become apparent. One crucial factor informing the variety (or otherwise) of screenwork in a given area is that of workshop source. In the South-west, Wales, and East Anglia a number of workshop centres operated. Some were small and distributed their products locally, while others were much larger, exporting a range of church woodwork further afield. Inevitably, the workshop system resulted in screens with shared features occupying geographically disparate churches; and has led to a degree of consistency across counties such as Devon and Somerset. Elsewhere (most notably in the Midlands), large workshops were less abundant, and screen-building seems to

have been a small scale enterprise carried out by non-specialists and more often than not village carpenters. This in turn has led to a lack of consistency across such counties as Oxfordshire and Northamptonshire.

In accounting for the appearance of an individual screen a multitude of factors must be borne in mind, each operating at a greater level of detail from the one before. In accounting for broad regional characteristics – for example the differences between a screen in Wales and a screen in East Anglia – issues to do with race, history, and church type are clearly of import. On a county level – for example why a screen in Suffolk differs from one in Kent – such factors as parish size and wealth, or proximity to a workshop centre come into play. On an individual level – for example why the screens of two neighbouring churches differ – the particular characteristics of the work of a local carpenter, the whims of the person commissioning him, or basic inter-parish one-upmanship might prove decisive. Certainly, this dynamic – we can call it improved copying – informed much of the vibrancy that ensued. The dynamics of influence and their modes of transmission are hugely complex, and operate at all these levels simultaneously: between regions, between counties, between parishes, and even between neighbouring churches. It comes as no surprise then that church screenwork is at its most diverse along the borders between the three principal schools of woodwork; and that it is especially varied along the Welsh borderlands, and in Bedfordshire, Cambridgeshire, Derbyshire, Dorset, east Somerset and Northamptonshire.

The dynamics of influence were further enriched by sources from abroad. This was a negligible quality prior to the last quarter of the 15th century, but was to leave an indelible mark on the screenwork of the 16th century (both prior to and following the Reformation). Foreign influence generally operated in one of three ways. Firstly, imported work (for example carved wooden chests from Flanders) provided native carvers with new sources of design. Secondly, foreign craftsmen arriving in England would themselves be employed on commissions. Finally, often through travel, English craftsmen would encounter foreign woodwork *in situ* and become conversant in its construction and design; or be commissioned to produce something similar to that seen abroad by a patron who had travelled there. The main sources for foreign influence on British woodworking were France (specifically Brittany), together with Italy and Flanders.

Design and detailing of an alien character can be discerned in a number of churches in England, but perhaps nowhere is it more pronounced than at Coleridge, Brushford and Colebrooke in Devon. The screen at Colebrooke is particularly interesting, for its flamboyant tracery is remarkably similar to that of St. Fiacre-le-Faouet in Brittany, suggesting that Breton craftsmen may have been employed in the county. The decorative shafts found at Thame and Charlton-on-Otmoor in Oxfordshire, and at Llandinabo, Foy, and Staunton-on-Wye in Herefordshire, also show the influence of French Renaissance design. Elsewhere, the friezes on the head-beams at Llandinabo and at nearby St. Weonards, incorporating as they do mermaids, dolphins, arabesques and other lively confections, are typical of work belonging in date to the first quarter of the 16th century (and, of the screenwork of the southern Marches, are the ones that owe the clearest debt to Renaissance work). The spectacular screens at Carlisle Cathedral (Prior Salkeld's screen, and that dividing off St. Catherine's Chapel) also show the influence of French Renaissance design. Flemish design accounts for other English church woodwork, including the screen at Lullingstone in Kent, and the stalls of St. George's chapel, Windsor.

Foreign influence was not restricted to timber screenwork, and neither was it a one-way process: the great stone screen that stands west of the Lady Chapel of Trondheim Cathedral, in Norway, is strikingly similar to the stone rood-screen at Stebbing in Essex. Trondheim Cathedral is known to have been built either by English architects, or by others conversant in English architecture, as is evidenced by other aspects of the design of the building.

The adoption of foreign design can be seen as an always incomplete appropriation of elements, rather than the substitution of one language of design for another. In the case of late medieval screenwork the result was a lively admixture of local Gothic and external Renaissance motifs, more or less successfully combined. We will never know, especially given the new and growing influence of foreign design, how church screenwork would have evolved had the Reformation not intervened. However, during the 16th century the carpenter was at the height of his powers, his craft had entered a phase of unparalleled richness and inspiration, and it seems certain that the second half of the 16th century would only have added greatly to the riches bestowed during the first half.

MURAL PARTITIONS

Whilst it is clear that the primary course of development saw the chancel wall pierced with a single and ever more expansive archway, this was by no means the only course taken. Broadly speaking, a secondary course of development saw the central archway remain small, but further openings pierce the wall to either side. Crucially, the wall here forms the sole partition; the lack of a wide void removing the need for additional forms of demarcation, such as timber screens.

Although mural partitions represent a course of development of secondary import, their origins can be traced back to the 7th century (to the churches of the Kentish group), and their evolution charted up until the Reformation in the 16th century. Indeed, the stonemason's pre-eminence, which was not seriously threatened by the carpenter until at least the 13th century, makes the various treatments of the chancel wall a significant part of the story of church screenwork in Britain.

The desire to variously pare away the chancel wall was triggered by a fundamental shift in liturgical practice. By the 12th century elements of the service, most notably the Act of Consecration and the elevation of the Host, had been partially demystified, and it was no longer deemed necessary to conceal them from the congregation. However, to bring about this liturgical opening up of the service, it was first necessary to effect a literal opening up of the sanctuary. As we have seen, one way to do this is simply to enlarge the chancel arch. However, another way is to create a wall with more apertures through which the sanctuary might be viewed.

In their two-volume work *Roodscreens and Roodlofts*, Frederick Bligh Bond and the Rev. Dom Bede Camm identify four types of mural partition deriving from the chancel wall. For each one they describe the distinguishing features, and suggest a possible lineage from the earliest precedents through to independent screen types of the 15th and 16th centuries. The initial type identified by

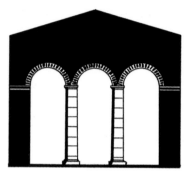

The choir-arcade at Reculver (7th-century Kentish group)

Bond and Camm is the triple arcade, first seen in the churches of the Kentish group (most notably at Reculver). The choir-arcade here was pulled down in 1806, but is known from a drawing made just prior to its demolition. From this it is clear that the arcade consisted of three, pillared arches of equal height and width. Other early triple choir-arcades, such as the one at Brixworth, had a central archway that was both higher and wider than the flanking archways.

The triple arcade virtually disappeared between the 7th century and the 12th century, but in the 13th century and subsequently it reappeared, albeit intermittently, throughout England. At Wool in Dorset is a triple choir-arcade of identical pointed arches, which dates from the 14th century. In appearance it is closely related to the arcade at Reculver. Here, the wall above the arches is

The blind arch arrangement at Little Hereford, Herefordshire

solid; however, the spandrels between the arches of a related choir-arcade – the fine example at Westwell in Kent (erected in the 13th century but later heightened) – are pierced. In this case the arches are trefoil-cusped, and the central arch is slightly taller than those to either side. At Capel-le-Ferne, also in Kent but dating from the 14th century, is a triple choir-arcade featuring a large window-like opening above the central arch, possibly serving both as a frame for the Rood, and as a hagioscope designed to enable those in the rood-loft to see the high altar below. A similar configuration (whose archway is blind) can be seen at Little Hereford, in Herefordshire.

Already at Capel-le-Ferne much of the chancel wall has been pared away; the next step (which transformed the wall into what is more recognisably a screen) saw the wall above the arcade dispensed with altogether. This arrangement can be seen at Welsh Newton in Herefordshire (see page 257; though here a wooden tympanum once filled the void above the arcade). This type enters the mainstream, as an imported screen to fill the void beneath a chancel arch, at Bottisham in Cambridgeshire. It also reaches a point of delightful resolution at Stebbing (14th century) and Great Bardfield (15th century), both in Essex. In each case, the chancel archway is essentially fenestrated with a highly wrought

triple opening: a composition that unifies three arches within a single arch, and thereby echoes the concept of the Father, Son and Holy Ghost unified as a single God. The triple arcade is also a feature of arguably the finest stone rood-screen in Britain, the stunning example at Compton Bassett in Wiltshire.

It is almost certain that the flanking arches of the triple choir-arcades outlined above (excepting Stebbing and Great Bardfield) originally contained solid cancelli screenwork. This feature allies this mural partition type with the second identified by Bond and Camm, in which the outer archways are filled to a height of four feet (or thereabouts) with a solid stone wall. An early precedent for this type is the sanctuary screen of the church of St. Januarius in Naples, which dates from the 3rd century. Here, the flanking archways contain marble slabs. In England a similar arrangement probably existed at St. Pancras, Canterbury (another church belonging to the Kentish group of the 7th century); which itself is echoed at Ashley in Hampshire, where a rounded chancel arch is flanked by rounded openings that appear as scaled-down versions of the central archway. It is possible that these openings are later than the *c*.1200 chancel arch, but in spite of this the comparison with St. Pancras remains a valid one.

The partition at Ashley, Hampshire

In later medieval examples the wall infill of the outer arches becomes an integrated element in a coeval design (in other words a part of the original fabric, as opposed to an imported fitting). However, such arches retain the appearance of having been, at one time, open to floor level, and the partition in totality as having derived from the triple choir-arcade. A fine example of this type exists at Bramford in Suffolk. Here the inner mouldings of the arches are returned across the sill of the wall, while the shafts are carried down to the floor. This latter feature makes the wall infill seem a later addition, when in reality the entire fabric belongs to *c*.1300. From the 12th century onwards it was common practice to place subsidiary altars immediately before these screen walls. Although no such altars survive, piscinae in the walls to either side of the chancel entrance – such as those at Winterbourne Monkton in Wiltshire or at Scawton in Yorkshire – testify to their former presence. Mural partitions of this type find a resonance in mainstream timber screenwork. The double screen at Llanelieu in Breconshire, as well as exhibiting paired triple arcades, also possessed altars at one time, which stood against the timber fence infill of the outer arches.

The third type of mural partition identified by Bond and Camm is closely related to the second, but does not take for its starting point the triple choir-arcade of the basilican-type church, but rather the chancel wall of the Saxon church. Here, in order to open up the sanctuary, holes were simply punched through the wall to either side of the chancel entrance, to form windows, or hagioscopes. At first these hagioscopes were fairly crude: the openings at Baulking in Berkshire (flanking a chancel arch of *c*.1200) are simple rectangles; while at Bracebridge in Lincolnshire the openings do not match one another and are not even of the same date. In both cases the emphasis is utilitarian rather than decorative.

Later, the type begins to exhibit greater refinement. At Curdworth in Warwickshire the Norman chancel arch is flanked by fenestrated openings that date from the Decorated era. In other churches the wall to either side of the chancel arch is pierced more than once. At Winterbourne Monckton in Wiltshire, three trefoil-cusped openings flank a fairly wide chancel arch. The mural partition at Sandridge in Hertfordshire (now mutilated) has a two-light window over the chancel arch, as well as a three-light window to either side. The conclusion of this line saw the wall above disappear altogether, and the partition become recognisably a screen, as at Highway in Wiltshire and Nether Compton in Dorset.

The partition at Bracebridge, Lincolnshire

The fourth and final type of mural partition identified by Bond and Camm also exhibits the triplicity of the other types listed above, but with one crucial difference: here the flanking archways are blind. The type has an early prototype in the chapel of the Blessed Martyrs at Nola in Southern Italy (which dates from the 4th century). Here, to either side of the chancel entrance is a blind

The partition at Scawton, Yorkshire

arch, or niche, containing frescoes or mosaics. This arrangement recurs at Hauxton in Cambridgeshire (where the archway is Norman but the recesses are later), at Otterborne in Hampshire and Shoebury in Essex. In the latter instance the niches, which date from the 13th century, extend down to the floor, giving space for altar backs. At Scawton in Yorkshire, meanwhile, are a pair of round-headed niches pierced by smaller hagioscopes. This blind arch type reaches a point of resolution in certain later screens, such as the example at Ranworth in Norfolk. Here the screen fulfils the role both of transparent chancel barrier and solid reredos to the altars once set against the chancel wall to either side of the archway.

Plate 1 Beguildy church, Radnorshire: Parker's drawing of the screen and loft coving

Plate 2 Heyop church, Radnorshire: Parker's drawing of the door-head tracery of the rood-screen

Plate 3 Newtown, Montgomeryshire: Parker's drawing of the gilt openwork above the vine borders, 1828

Plate 4 Newtown, Montgomeryshire: Parker's drawing of two compartments of tracery

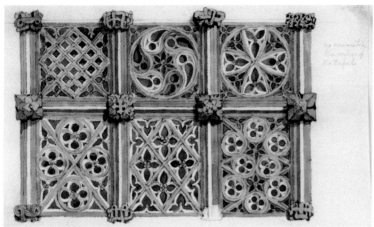

*Plate 5 Newtown, Montgomeryshire: Parker's drawing
of panels from the underside of the loft*

*Plate 6 Newtown, Montgomeryshire: Parker's drawing
of the door-head tracery, with a detail of the fringing*

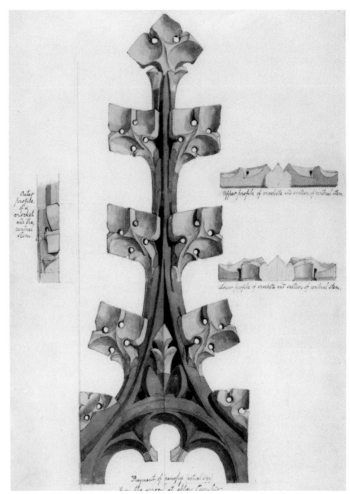

*Plate 7 Abbey Cwmhir, Radnorshire: Parker's drawing
of fragments of the screen, then in Newtown church*

Plate 8 Llananno, Radnorshire: Parker's drawing of the rood-screen and loft, 1828 (note the lack of figures)

*Plate 9 Llanelieu: Veranda of posts
and the complete tympanum overhead*

*Plate 10 Hereford Cathedral: The painted stone screen
to the Audley Chapel*

Plate 11 Strensham, Worcestershire: Rood-loft, now forming west gallery

(Strensham lies just outside the southern Marches, as defined for the purposes of this book, but its painted decoration makes its inclusion here highly instructive)

Plate 12 Usk, Monmouthshire: Brightly painted chancel portion of screen

Plates 13 to 16 Llangwm: Detail of loft coving (top left); details of screen head-beam, showing water-plant trail and blind top- and drop-cresting (top right); and details of 'planted on' wainscot blind tracery heads (bottom)

MINOR SCREENS

As churches grew in size and sophistication, so screens were employed in other locations, besides at the entrance to the chancel. The growing demands made upon church interiors, combined with a recognition of the flexibility of screens, made this appropriation to a variety of new roles inevitable (in an echo of the pattern of development followed in early basilican churches). Of the minor screens found in parish churches, by far the most abundant are the parclose screens. Less numerous (though still forming distinctive screen types) are the presbytery and tower screens. Aside from these three archetypes, screens performing a variety of other roles can be found. Indeed, whenever there was a need to partition off or to enclose an area within a church, screens were invariably used. At Gwernesney in Monmouthshire, for example, a pair of screens has been used to create a font enclosure at the west end of the church (see photograph on p.275). The adaptability of parochial screenwork is confirmed by the numbers of screens that have been re-located to perform roles for which they were never intended.

As well as being by far the most numerous of the minor screens, parclose[1] screens are also invested with the greatest liturgical significance, because they were essentially used to form small chapels. The practice of erecting altars subsidiary to the main altar was both ancient and widespread, and in order to fence off these altars timber or stone screens[2] were employed. The resultant chapels are known as parclose chapels, or simply 'parcloses'. Such chapels were almost unknown prior to the

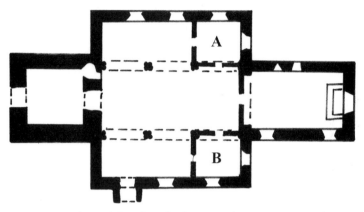

Aymestrey: Plan of the church showing the easternmost bays of the side aisles screened off to form parclose chapels (A and B)

middle of the 13th century, but had become abundant by the end of the 15th century. They were usually dedicated to a saint and were maintained by the parishioners or, in the case of chantry chapels, by guilds or private individuals (in order that Masses for their souls, and readings, might be said in perpetuity).

There is no standard configuration for a parclose chapel or its screens, and the fittings were usually adapted to the existing fabric (and not vice versa). In terms of location, parclose chapels were typically erected at the east end of side aisles. A common way to create the chapel was to box in the easternmost bay of the side aisle, by erecting a screen between the final two piers of the nave

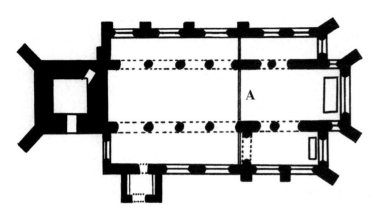

Old Radnor: The rood-screen extending straight across the aisles to form chapels flanking the chancel (A)

arcade, and between the penultimate pier and the north or south wall of the church (as at Aymestrey in Herefordshire). In other churches different configurations existed. In undivided churches with side aisles that extended eastwards to flank the chancel, the rood-screen would form the chapel's western limit and a parclose screen would then be erected to separate the chapel from the chancel next door (as at Old Radnor in Radnorshire).

Occasionally, so as not to encroach on the rights of parishioners, the chantry chapels of private individuals would be added as extensions (often transeptal in form) to existing buildings. Such chapels generally remained the property of the donor (or his or her heirs) and were screened off essentially to maintain the legal rights of the founder. The north chapel at Lydbury North in Shropshire takes this form, and is partitioned off from the nave by

a screen with a high middle rail and unusually narrow openings (it should be acknowledged, however, that this represents an appropriation of an existing transept, and not a brand new extension). St. Mary's church in Chipping Norton, Oxfordshire, has no fewer than four chantry chapels.

In larger churches (in which there were often a number of private chapels) the parclose chapel was sometimes a substantially free-standing structure, whose association with the fabric of the church itself was considerably less pronounced. The Garstang Chapel at Cirencester is an example of the type. It was created by erecting two screens at right angles to one another: one extending from the east wall of the south aisle, and the other from its south wall. It was formed in c.1430–1460 by a family of wool merchants, and contains an altar dedicated to St. Edmund of Canterbury. On the western screen the Garstang arms alternate with the family's trademark.

The degree to which the design of a parclose screen corresponded with that of the adjacent rood-screen varied greatly. At one end of the scale is the exceptional case of Dennington in Suffolk, where the parclose screens represent a seamless continuation of the rood-screen and its associated loft into the side aisles. In this large church the side aisles extend only as far as the chancel arch, and do not continue on to flank the chancel as they might in a Devon church. In order to form a pair of parclose chapels the rood-screen, having spanned the chancel, could not merely continue straight across to the side walls, but instead had to advance westwards up the nave for one bay before heading north and south once more to meet the side walls of the church. The solution is an elegant one. If it has a weakness it is only that it does

Aymestrey: Parclose screen

little to express the hierarchical differences between the main and subsidiary altars (something that separate and distinct rood and parclose screens do).

In other churches, while there are obvious differences between the rood-screen and the parclose screens, it is clear that the fittings are coeval and have been conceived as a matching set. At Aymestrey[3] in Herefordshire, to either side of the tall and exquisite rood-screen, are two near-identical parclose chapels. Here the hierarchy of spaces has been carefully judged by the screen builders and is beautifully articulated by the screens. The lofty rood-screen carries the best and most abundant carving (notably in the cornice, which has a trio of fine carved trails) and is evidently the principal screen here. The parclose screens are more modest in both their scale and ornamentation, and serve to introduce themes that are brought to fruition in the rood-screen.

The majority of parclose screens do not correspond closely with their associated rood-screens (indeed, a number of them are not even coeval with their rood-screens). There are several reasons why this might be so. As the pre-eminent screen within parish churches the parochial rood-screen was subject to changing fashions in a way that the more utilitarian parclose screen was not. Many rood-screens were either substantially altered or replaced altogether in the second half of the 15th century. This was a costly process (particularly when local pride and inter-parish rivalry were motivating factors). It is likely, therefore, that while the rood-screen was often updated or replaced, the less glamorous parclose screens to either side were simply left untouched, or at best only modestly altered.

In some cases, the use of a different workshop centre for the rood-screen as compared to the associated parclose screens may account for variations in the quality and appearance of a church's screenwork. While the more prestigious commission for the rood-screen and loft might be awarded to a well-known regional workshop centre, the job of making a modest parclose screen may have gone to the local carpenter. Either (or both) of these factors may account for the variations between the rood and parclose screens found at Bishop's Frome and Dilwyn in Herefordshire. In both cases the differences in style and execution between rood-screen and parclose screens are marked, and in both cases the screens are certainly not coeval (let alone by the same hand).

On very rare occasions, the parclose screens enjoy a greater prominence than the associated rood-screen. This is noticeably the case at St. Weonards in Herefordshire (see photograph on p.248). Here, the rood-screen (although substantially renewed) is modest in size and occupies the comparatively dark entrance to the chancel. The parclose screens, however, are much more substantial, and occupy the well lit eastern bay of the north aisle. They are sophisticated pieces belonging to the early 16th century, with linenfold wainscot panels and a head-beam decorated with applied carvings of Renaissance character (the latter clearly updated a Gothic vine trail, parts of which survive on one of the other screens).

If the parclose chapel was not parochial in origin, but instead was endowed by a wealthy private individual or guild, then this too might lead to the creation of a fitting that surpassed in decorative terms the rood-screen of the church. The guilds in particular were often fantastically wealthy, and were responsible for the sumptuous enrichment of many church interiors. In the southern Marches, the chapel of the Palmers' Guild at Ludlow is a case in point.

The Palmers' Guild was founded in *c.*1250. By the early 16th century it had 4,000 members nationwide and an extensive portfolio of property and lands. As well as putting money into the rebuilding and upkeep of the church, the Guild paid subscriptions to priests for the reading of prayers and Masses on its behalf. By the 15th century, as many as 10 priests were being employed at Ludlow by the Guild. The greatest legacy of the Palmers' Guild is the chapel of St. John the Evangelist in the north chancel of St. Laurence's church. As well as containing fittings of the very highest quality (including a rare Tudor altar canopy, fine monuments and stained glass) the chapel is divided from the north aisle by a highly-wrought parclose screen that both outshines the choir screen standing to the south and is by some margin the finest of Ludlow church's five late medieval screens.[4]

At the Reformation (specifically, following the 1547 Chantries Act) the chantries were suppressed, their endowments confiscated and their screens dismantled. The Palmers' Chapel escaped relatively unscathed. In 1551 the Guild was dissolved and a number of alterations were made to its chapel at Ludlow (including, for example, the whitewashing over of its frescoes). When the properties of the Guild were handed over to Ludlow Borough Corporation at the Guild's dissolution, this was done on condition that its charities be preserved and a Preacher and Reader be retained. This agreement may have helped to secure the future of the Palmers' Chapel. Whatever the true reason for the survival, the extremely unusual retention of such a fitting as an altar canopy hints at the general resistance to dismantle this chapel and remove its superb fittings. Elsewhere, the founders of chantry chapels (or their heirs) asserted their legal right to the fabric and used them as private pews; an act that helped to preserve many other fine chantry chapels around the country.

A number of other reasons may account for the survival of those parclose chapels that did not belong to private individuals or guilds. Firstly, the lack of a perceived association with the Rood appears to have guaranteed the indifference of all but the most zealous Reformers. Secondly, a timber parclose screen is both an effective and relatively inexpensive way of annexing off a portion of a church. Indeed, their fundamental utility meant that their removal (just like that of the rood-screens in undivided churches) was a perverse act certain only to damage that church's ability to function properly. Thirdly (and this relates to the Victorian restorers in particular) parclose screens are less intrusive upon the earlier fabric of a church than are rood or chancel screens.

Compared with the parclose screen, the presbytery screen represents a far rarer screen type. This was infrequently placed between the sanctuary and the choir in larger churches. Illustrations exist of the presbytery screen that once stood in Brecon Cathedral (see illustration on p.179; parts of which now enclose the St. Keynes chapel), and a delicate screen of this type that once stood in St. Davids Cathedral in Pembrokeshire. Presbytery screens were occasionally employed in parish churches. Francis Bond claims that one stood at Colchester in Essex, and at both Brilley and Michaelchurch in Herefordshire.[5] If the type was not widely used it was because the far simpler device of a stepped difference in floor level was deemed adequate to mark the division between sanctuary and choir in most cases. The Reformation, which saw the laity encroaching for the first time into the chancel, triggered the erecting of altar rails; a fitting that was quite unknown prior to the Reformation.

The last of the recognised screen types is the tower screen. This type, although also rarely encountered, can claim some antiquity, as it echoes the narthex screens found in early Christian churches. These latter partitions divided the people's portion of the church into a western narthex for those yet to be baptized, and an area east of this for those already received into the Church. A number of early Saxon plans show evidence of such a division. Although such a usage became obsolete, screens were occasionally erected in this location to serve other purposes. In some instances they supported western galleries (for singers certainly, but also perhaps for bell ringers or an organ) and may represent a precursor to the Elizabethan and Jacobean galleries erected to house choirs after the demise of the rood-loft. A number of churches, mainly in the eastern counties, retain tower screens, including Addlethorpe and Heckington in Lincolnshire, Brightlingsea in Essex, and Harlestone in Norfolk. In the southern Marches, Llywel has a western tower screen (see photograph on p.193), though this represents the post-Reformation appropriation of the original rood-screen (in order to create a vestry).

A significant amount of late medieval screenwork, although remaining in its original church, no longer stands *in situ*. Many rood-screens, rather than being destroyed, were retained and the material re-used elsewhere in the church. That those responsible for this were willing to do so should be celebrated, for this expedient helped to preserve much fine screenwork. After all, the rood-screen was not in itself offensive to the Reformers (although its figure painting might be) and was rarely offensive to parishioners. It was simply marred by a misdiagnosed association. A compromise, therefore, was to rid the screen of its perceived association by removing it to another part of the church. In the mainly Victorian church at Moreton-on-Lugg in Herefordshire, parts belonging to the original rood-screen have been re-used to box in the organ at the back of the church. Meanwhile, at Eardisland in the same county, the rood-screen now stands at the west

Moreton-on-Lugg: Screenwork re-used to box in the organ

end of the nave, having been re-located on at least three separate occasions during its lifetime.

There are notable instances of parishes resisting demands to remove or destroy rood-screens (particularly in Wales) in open defiance of the Reformers. Besides being a simple expression of independence, such defiance speaks eloquently of the pride felt in fittings that were added to churches at great trouble and expense. Although the obvious decorative appeal of rood-screens must have fuelled the reluctance in many quarters to have them taken down, it may have been their utility, or more precisely their potential for re-use, that persuaded parishioners at least to retain the parts of a dismantled screen. In less well-off parishes in particular, the notion of completely destroying such a fitting, whatever its associations, was clearly unthinkable.

As well as being removed to other parts of the same church, rood-screens (or parts thereof) were sometimes re-used in completely different churches. In c.1500, a fine rood-screen and loft was erected in St. Mary's church in Newtown, Montgomery-shire. Due to flooding, however, this church was abandoned in the 1840s, and a new church built in 1843–7 to designs by Thomas Penson. Much of the old screenwork from St. Marys was re-erected in this new church in 1856, before being taken down again in 1875. In 1909 the surviving pieces were re-used once more, this time in the construction of a parclose screen in the north aisle, and to line the sanctuary (cf. Cwmdu in Breconshire). Such a history is not atypical: a new church, a desire to recover elements from the old church (both for their intrinsic beauty, and to evoke a sense of continuity), a debate about how appropriate the fittings from one era are for a church belonging to another, how

best to incorporate them; concluding in a compromise of sorts that guarantees the survival, however incomplete, of an old screen.

Occasionally, screens were able to survive even their removal to a new church completely intact. Such was the happy fate enjoyed by another rood-screen and loft from the Newtown workshops. In 1876–7, the old church at Llananno was completely rebuilt on the site it had occupied for centuries, beside the river Ithon in Radnorshire. Amazingly (given this almost ideal opportunity to discard it) the rood-screen and loft from the old church were faithfully re-erected in the new single-chamber building. The act even required a slight lengthening of the rood-screen and loft to ensure that both would fit snugly into the slightly wider new church. On another occasion, the screenwork from Chirbury Priory, although mutilated and divorced from its monastic context, was re-erected in a substantially complete state in the church at Montgomery.

Along with the substantially complete survivals, there are also the fragmentary. Often, the only evidence that a screen (or screens) once stood in a church is the small portion of original fabric, stripped of its dignity and proper context, nailed up in a dark corner as a sort of curio. At the Reformation (and in subsequent centuries right up until the present day) pieces of screenwork were discarded in vestries, towers, back rooms, and graveyard storage sheds. Laziness, pity, or the belief that the piece in question might, at a later date, be of some use or interest may account for such careless retention. Whatever the reason, years later a fossicking churchwarden finds a length of vine trail under a bench, dusts it down and puts it on show at the back of the church. As ever, the discovery in a church of such a fragment is both a cause for sadness – because no more of the screen has survived – and gratitude, because there is anything at all left to see.

Fragments of vine trail survive at Redwick in Monmouthshire (on a window ledge) and at Talgarth in Breconshire (at the back of the church). Fawley in Herefordshire (see photograph on p.223) and Llanfigan in Breconshire each have a pair of standards with the adjoining arch braces supporting a length of head-beam; the former at the back of the church, the latter in the side aisle. Disparate pieces of screenwork have been put on display at Ledbury, Lea and Staunton-on-Wye in Herefordshire; loft vaulting at Ledbury, tracery heads at Lea, and a collection of pieces from a variety of dates at Staunton. Very occasionally, pieces find their way into museums or the hands of private collectors. For example, fragments of the screenwork from Llangurig in Montgomeryshire survive as a small domestic screen in the dining room at nearby Glansevern House.

Of the fragmentary screenwork found in the churches of England and Wales, though, none is perhaps more tantalising than that belonging in the isolated church of St. Melangell, which stands amid the Berwyn hills in Montgomeryshire. The pieces in question are from a carved trail, and depict the legend of St. Melangell and the Hare. This magical story has its origins in the 8th century. The Prince of Powys and his men were out hare hunting, when they chased a hare into a dark copse. On reaching the wood, the huntsmen found their dogs agitated and unwilling to enter, so they made their way carefully into the heart of the copse on foot, where they discovered a young girl praying. Nestling in the folds of her dress was the hare. One of the huntsmen raised his horn and was about to blow, when the instrument became stuck to his lips.

When he heard of this, Brochwel, the Prince of Powys, was convinced that a miracle of some kind had taken place. On learning that the girl had lived alone in the copse for fifteen years, he granted her land at Pennant, and here she founded a church and convent. The surviving parts of the carved trail depict the figures of Melangell, Brochwel, the huntsman with the horn stuck to his lips, together with the hare and some of the hounds. Figure carvings on late medieval screenwork are exceptionally rare (to say nothing of the unique subject matter) and the loss of this rood-screen and loft is an especially grievous one.

Elsewhere, fragments of screenwork were not merely put on display, but put back into use; sometimes as a part of a new screen (e.g. the carved trails on the modern screen at Michaelchurch Escley in Herefordshire) and sometimes as a part of another fitting entirely. A piece of carved trail now ornaments the altar table at Llandegley in Breconshire. A number of fine pieces from the cornice and coving of the rood-loft at Llanspyddid in the same county have been re-used to form a decorative sounding board over the church's pulpit. At Llanvair Waterdine in Shropshire, the altar rail employs an array of extraordinary carved pieces from what must have been a spectacular rood-screen and loft.

Framing members from late medieval screenwork were used at Michaelchurch-on-Arrow in Radnorshire to support the reredos on the east wall of the chancel (and are still in place). A number of blind tracery panels and lengths of carved trail have been used to ornament two cupboards in the vestry at Rockfield in Monmouthshire. The south-east transept of Hereford Cathedral houses an unusual portable pulpit that incorporates boarding (pierced by quatrefoils, and probably from a loft parapet) framed up between the original muntins. At Kenchester in Herefordshire, horizontal elements (a bressumer and head-beam) now form vertical components of the church's structural timberwork. Perhaps the most fantastical re-use of screen material was the Rev. John Parker's now-lost 'Tower of Babel' pulpit, made for his own church at Llanmerewig in Montgomeryshire.

THE ROOD-LOFT

Hear you, then, the voice of your brothers and sisters, deep as the seas, and timeless, as restless, and as fierce ... Sing then, Son of Man, and know that in your voice Almighty God may find his dearest pleasure. How Green Was My Valley; Richard Llewellyn

By *c.*1500 the majority of parochial rood-screens in England and Wales supported a gallery known as a rood-loft.[1] This comprised a platform with parapets to the east and west, and was generally accessed via a staircase cut into the wall of the nave. The dimensions of rood-lofts varied greatly. Like the rood-screens below, some spanned only the nave and were relatively short. Others, however, spanned the side aisles as well as the nave and were of prodigious length.

The depth of the loft platform was typically five or six feet.[2] However, the rood-loft at Minehead in Somerset was eight feet deep, while those at Axbridge and Winsham in the same county occupied the full depth of the space beneath the crossing tower. The rood-loft at Yetminster in Dorset extended east-west for the whole of the first bay of the nave, and north-south to span both side aisles. Rood-lofts of prodigious size are rare but not unknown in Wales. Reputation has it that the loft at Llandderfel in Merionethshire could hold 60 people. Conversely, many rood-lofts (particularly in East Anglia) were just three feet deep or less. As a general rule the rood-lofts of the late 15th century and early 16th century tend to be narrower than those of an earlier date (for reasons which are discussed below).

The rood-loft could be supported in one of three ways. Firstly, a sturdy beam – or bressumer – was embedded into the nave walls parallel to, and west of, the head-beam of the rood-screen. Floor joists were then added between the two beams, and a plank floor laid on top. The soffit belonging to this type of rood-loft might be flat, as at Partrishow in Breconshire or Foy in Herefordshire, or coved; steeply, as at Beguildy in Radnorshire, or shallowly, as at Burghill in Herefordshire.

Llangeview: The hefty bressumer that supports the rood-loft, embedded in the nave wall

In churches with a chancel arch (such as Partrishow) the rood-loft would usually extend only to the west of the screen.[3] In undivided churches, such as Llanwnnog in Montgomeryshire, however, a second beam was inserted to the east of the head-beam, and a floor laid between it and the bressumer. Given that the bressumer was rarely supported at any point along its length (St. Margarets in Herefordshire is one exception) and that long timber beams are prone to sagging, this format is really only suitable for churches with a comparatively narrow nave. For this reason this method of construction is widely found in Wales.

The second way to support the rood-loft was through the use of vaulting; a feature that evolved from the coved soffits characteristic of earlier lofts. The vaulting would typically spring from attached shafts – or bouttels – between each bay. Vaulted screens are commonly found in undivided churches, and the vaulting usually extends both east and west of the supporting screen. The main structural advantage of a vaulted screen is that the bressumer can be supported along its length by concealed braces within the vaulting, and can thus be of almost unlimited length (there being little risk of sagging). The vaulted form is most abundant in Devon; a county that is also home to the longest church screens in Britain.

In the case of some East Anglian lofts – Attleborough in Norfolk is a good example – the vaulting does not meet a bressumer, but instead continues down again to meet corresponding cut-off shafts that front the loft parapet. Vaulting, with its enormous decorative potential, suited taller rood-screens (e.g. Aymestrey in Herefordshire) as the intricacies of the fan or lierne patterning on the underside of the rood-loft might thus be more clearly seen by worshippers in the nave.

The least common way of supporting the rood-loft was to raise a second beam upon a veranda of posts to the west of the

Bosbury: Fan vaulting hiding the braces supporting the loft to both east and west

Middleton in Shropshire: a bouttel shaft capped with a crown-like form, from the top of which spring the vaulting ribs

rood-screen, and to slot floor joists between the head-beams of each. Planking could then be laid over the joists to give a flat floor (and a flat ceiling to the underside of the rood-loft). Llanelieu in Breconshire is the prime example of this 'double screen' type (see plate 9). Its western 'screen' precisely echoes the form of its eastern one. The configuration has certain advantages, particularly in undivided churches (of which Llanelieu is an example). For example, the bays to either side of the central doorway can be boxed in with wainscot boarding to provide small recesses (or encloses) for subsidiary altars.

Another significant way in which rood-lofts differ from one another is in the treatment of their loft parapets. These were typically four feet high and, as with the rood-screen below, usually divided up into bays by muntins which generally did not correspond with the mullions of the rood-screen.[4] The muntins

could be plain, as at St. Margarets, or elaborate (featuring offsets or pinnacles), as at Sutton-on-Trent in Nottinghamshire. They could be thin, as at Warfield in Berkshire, or thick, as at Llanwnnog (western face in particular). Occasionally the parapets were plain-boarded (as at Edington in Wiltshire and Cascob in Radnorshire – see photograph on p.163). However, more often than not they were decorated, either with carved or painted work. At Cotes-by-Stow in Lincolnshire, Compton Bassett in Wiltshire, Llanegryn (western side), Besford and Leigh in Worcestershire, and Warfield in Berkshire, the parapet in each case has applied decoration or blind tracery that corresponds with the treatment of the wainscot below, and is not pierced.

The majority of rood-loft parapets, however, were pierced to some degree with openwork carving. This might be of a comparatively simple and regular type, in the form of an arcade

Llanwnnog: Wide loft muntins

Bettws Clyro: The open arcade, cf. *Hereford cathedral*

(or layered arcades) perhaps, as at Oakley in Bedfordshire, Derwen in Denbighshire, Sheringham in Norfolk or Bettws Clyro in Radnorshire. However, it could also be elaborate, as at Southwold in Suffolk and Atherington in Devon,[5] and occasionally irregular, as at Llanegryn and Llanwnnog (eastern side in both cases – see photograph on p.47).

At Partrishow in Breconshire the lacy openwork of the parapet has the character of Perpendicular window tracery or fretwork (and was used by the architect Seddon as a model for his restoration of the rood-loft at Llangwm in Monmouthshire; see photograph on p.281). Elsewhere, applied carvings – typically ogee heads and crocketed pinnacles, foliage and scrolls – were

Montgomery: Constructed with no visible bressumer, and with muntins with offsets and crocketed pinnacles

pegged to the parapet, generally against a pierced loft front (as at Avebury in Wiltshire, Bettws Newydd – see photograph on p.272 – and Montgomery). At Atherington in Devon and Flamborough in Yorkshire the applied decoration of the loft parapet in each case is in the form of elaborate tabernacle work. This has provided the rood-loft with both a series of canopied niches (narrow at Flamborough and broad at Atherington) for carved figures, and a pronounced three-dimensionality.

The display of representations of the saints formed an expedient appropriation of the loft parapet (although the role of the rood-loft was never primarily as an iconostasis). In Britain during the 14th and 15th centuries there was an increase in the cult of the saints – *hagiology* – and with it a desire to honour saints by placing their images in prominent locations within churches. As applied to late parapets, these representations could be carved or painted. The 25 carved figures on the loft front at Llananno are replacements (see photograph on p.169 and note their absence on plate 8), but probably give a good idea of how many rood-loft parapets would have looked, with figures occupying their own canopied niches across the entire width of the loft front.

The rood-loft parapet at Strensham, which now stands at the back of the church, is ornamented with 23 painted (rather than carved) saints (see plate 11). Other rood-loft parapets, such as those at Llanfilo in Breconshire and St. Margarets in Hereford-shire, were also once decorated with figures (although these, in both cases, were almost certainly carved). An unusually high number of images – 69 – is recorded as having once inhabited the western parapet of the rood-loft at Yatton church in Somerset. The rood-loft at Attleborough in Norfolk provides a fine example of a painted rood-loft parapet. However, here it is coats of arms and not saints that decorate the loft front. The top part of the parapet is pierced, giving to this already elegant loft still greater finesse.

The rood-lofts at Cotes-by-Stow and Sleaford in Lincolnshire feature canted middle projections; a feature also found at Lullingstone in Kent and Hullavington in Wiltshire (the latter demolished in 1917). The purpose of these projections has not been ascertained. Suggestions have included: a housing for the organist's seat (Vallance), or for the organ itself or for choristers (Bond and Camm), or even a pulpit (Francis Bond). Further to these, it may be conjectured that they formed a kind of minstrel's gallery for soloists (either musicians or singers). Any or all may be correct, but the feature remains the exception and not the rule. The rood-loft at Montgomery has a projection upon its eastern parapet, but this probably relates to its former incarnation as part of a monastic pulpitum. Western rood-loft parapets are generally uninterrupted by such projections.

The treatment of the eastern parapet of the rood-loft also varied greatly. In decorative terms it could be relatively plain, as at Llananno; or richly ornamented, as at Llanegryn. Carved trails are often seen, even when the parapet is otherwise plain. Typically, the panelling of eastern parapets is narrower, and may be separated by flat muntins of variable width. The boarding used is often thinner than that of the western parapet and is sometimes pierced, particularly in the upper half of the parapet. This is the case at both Llanwnnog and Llanrwst. If the boarding of the rood-tympanum reached to the floor of the rood-loft there was clearly no need for an eastern parapet.

In terms of broad regional characteristics rood-lofts display features, both visual and structural, that correspond with the rood-screens they surmount. So, a typical Welsh rood-loft (e.g. Llanwnnog) is stout and squat in appearance, modest in size, square-framed in construction, and shows an emphasis on surface texture rather than line. The carved decoration tends to be varied, imaginative and of a high quality, and generally incorporates the carved trails and crestings found on the rood-screen below. Vaulting is entirely absent (except in that screenwork of English origin) and flat or coved soffits abound. The rood-lofts of Devon (e.g. Atherington) exhibit many of the same Western School characteristics and, if anything, display even greater levels of carved enrichment. They are almost always much longer than Welsh rood-lofts (as befitting the aisled churches they tend to occupy) and are usually arched and vaulted.

The rood-lofts of the Midlands owe more to the Western School than the Eastern. They are generally unpretentious, sturdy and functional. They are rarely of great length and may be coved or vaulted. The carved decoration, too, tends to the Western School type, but is rarely so lavish. The rood-lofts of East Anglia (e.g. Attleborough) are usually less deep, taller, more elegant, and possess narrower bays. They are generally vaulted and lack the prominent bressumers and cornices of Devon. There is an emphasis on line rather than surface texture. Carved decoration is used sparingly, forms regular patterns, and is often more lithic (and less naturalistic) in character. The painted decoration of East Anglia is also highly distinctive, and tends to be of unrivalled finesse.

The origins of the rood-loft, just like those of the rood-screen, can be traced back to remote antiquity, and again to the basilican churches of Continental Europe. From an early date, fittings known as 'ambones' were erected to one side (or both sides) of the choir enclosure. Ambones are essentially large, marble pulpits designed to accommodate a number of persons, and from which readings (sometimes religious, sometimes secular) were delivered. Italy in particular is rich in early ambones. The earliest may be the ambo in the church of the Holy Ghost in Ravenna, which dates from the 6th century. Over time, the fitting evolved in relation to the choir screen. As the screens grew in height, so the ambones were raised up with them. Often they were carried in part by the screen itself, and would project westwards from its top. Ambones were a standard fitting in Italian basilican churches until the 13th century. A late surviving ambo, dated 1249, stands in the Basilica of St. Pancras in Rome.

The resolution of this line of development esentially saw ambones extend from north to south for the length of the choir screen, thus forming a continuous gallery. This feature later took the French name *Jubé* (after the first words of the blessing: '*Jubé Domine benedicere*') and became common in European cathedrals from the middle of the 13th century onwards. The partition was typically pierced by a central doorway, but sometimes had triple openings or, less frequently, a pair of openings. From the 14th century onwards Italian ambones were supplanted by pulpits.

In England the Jubé has its truest counterpart, not in the parochial rood-loft, but rather in the pulpitum of monastic, collegiate and cathedral churches. The pulpitum is essentially a solid partition, formed either from a single wall or from two separate walls. Like the Jubés of the Continent, English pulpita generally have a single central doorway (as at Canterbury and

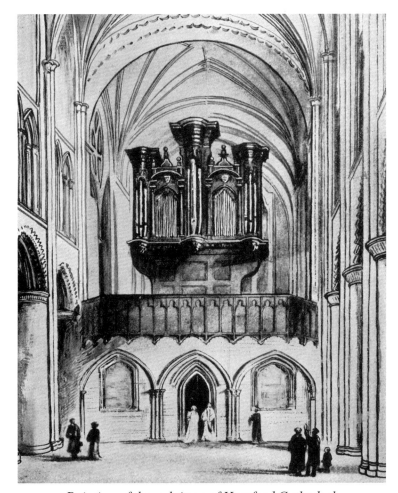

Painting of the pulpitum of Hereford Cathedral, demolished in 1841

Wells). The use of paired walls allowed for a pulpitum of great depth, often extending to a whole nave bay (as at Norwich Cathedral). The primary role of the pulpitum was to enclose the choir at its western end, and to divide this compartment from the nave beyond. In this way it usually forms the backing to the return choir stalls on its eastern side. The gallery of the pulpitum was adapted for a variety of uses. Pulpita, like the ambones of Italy, were generally constructed from stone.[6] However, a number of timber examples survive, including those at Carlisle Cathedral (*c*.1460), Hexham, and Manchester Collegiate.

There is little doubt that the pulpitum was in general use in larger churches long before the parochial rood-loft became established in parish churches. Pulpita may even have been a feature of English cathedrals in the 12th century. Gervase writes of a pulpitum (or an equivalent fitting) existing at Canterbury Cathedral prior to 1174, while a Romanesque example stood in Ely Cathedral until its demolition in 1770. Certainly, from the second half of the 13th century, pulpita were in use throughout England and Wales. The pulpitum should not be confused with the rood-screen typically found one bay to the west of the pulpitum in larger churches. Most such rood-screens were made of wood and have not survived. St. Albans is the only cathedral to retain its rood-screen, but this is made of stone.

Given the enormous influence wielded by the larger churches over their humble, parochial cousins, it might be assumed that the rood-loft and screen represent an unmediated and direct appropriation of the pulpitum. However, this is not the case. The pulpitum had no physical relationship with the Rood in larger churches (the Rood was carried above the rood-screen to the west), whereas the rood-loft clearly did have a physical relationship with the Rood in parochial churches. The pulpitum essentially formed a deep and solid choir screen, whereas the rood-screen generally formed a transparent single wall at the entrance to the chancel. Although the pulpitum was used as a singing gallery, this was one of its lesser functions. One of its major functions, however, was as a platform – a pulpit – from which to preach. The opposite is the case with the parochial rood-loft: the usage as a singing gallery formed a primary function, while the usage as a pulpit was of only minor import.

It would be wrong to suggest that there are no detailed similarities between pulpitum and rood-loft. Organs and altars, for example, were housed in both, and just as altars were occasionally placed to either side of the central doorway of rood-screens, so it was with pulpita. Essentially, however, it seems that the appearance of the rood-loft in parish churches had more to do with a recognition of the general utility of a raised gallery (both to gain access to the Rood and as a platform for singers), rather than a desire to directly replicate the pulpitum and its *modi operandi*.

As well as being a later development than the pulpitum, the parochial rood-loft also came after the parochial rood-screen. Because of this, existing screens were either adapted to take the fitting, or were taken down so that brand new rood-screens and lofts, which were fully integrated both structurally and visually, could be erected in their stead. This integration resulted in the phrase 'rood-loft' evolving to denote both the loft and the rood-screen below; a shift that hints at the pre-eminence gained by the rood-loft itself as a fitting. The precise date of the first parochial rood-lofts is not known, but there is no substantial evidence for their existence before the second half of the 13th century. Rood-stair doorways of approximately this date are still visible at both Thurlby and Colsterworth[7] in Lincolnshire. Documentary evidence for rood-lofts existing in the 13th century is provided by the 1297 inventory of church goods for Pelham Furneaux in Hertfordshire, which records 'a large staircase leading to the rood-loft is wanting in the body of the church'.[8]

Often, only the rood-stairs or their access doorways serve as reminders of the rood-loft that once was. However, it should be borne in mind that the earliest rood-lofts were often accessed by ladder, and that such a loft, representing a lesser disruption to the fabric of the church, might leave us with no trace of its presence once taken down. For this reason the lack of a rood-loft or its associated doorways and stairwell should not be taken as conclusive evidence that the church never had a rood-loft (it also leaves open the possibility that rood-lofts were in use prior to the second half of the 13th century).

The primary function of the parochial rood-loft has long been the subject of debate. It is worth saying, first of all, that no authority ever prescribed the addition of the rood-loft to parish churches (and, for that matter, none ever sanctioned its removal): the fitting evolved, as did the later desire to rid churches of it. Of the many possible uses put forward for the rood-loft, two remain the most compelling: firstly, that it was designed to allow ready access to the Rood; and secondly, that it was designed to provide a raised gallery for groups of singers and musicians. The available evidence suggests that access to the Rood may have been of primary import in the case of the earliest rood-lofts, but that the provision of a singing gallery

may have motivated the near universal adoption of the fitting subsequently. What is certain is that the rood-loft proved itself every bit as versatile as the rood-screen below, and that it was adapted to both of the uses described above, and a number of others besides.

Although the rood-loft essentially derives its 'rood' prefix from its proximity to the Rood (rather than from any didactic or mystical relationship with it) a practical relationship did exist between the two. From an early date, far from being left alone having been set up over the entrance to the chancel, the rood-figures were variously attended to. This might occur infrequently, perhaps to veil the rood-figures at certain points in the religious calendar; or on a weekly or even daily basis, to clean the figures or to maintain the various lights associated with the figures.

The consolidation of the two fittings – rood-loft and Rood – occurred when the Rood was transplanted from the independent rood-beam to the top beam (which later came to be known as the rood-beam) of the loft parapet. For Bond and Camm, the part played by the Rood in the rood-loft's inception and development is central. Their belief is that the rood-loft was primarily designed to support the Rood and house an altar of the Holy Rood, and that the fitting was given a broad floor to enable the faithful to pay homage before both. Set against this is the fact that a ladder (which often provided the means of accessing the rood-loft before mural stairwells became commonplace) would seem suited only to limited use, and not to the heavy traffic of regular worshippers.

There is certainly no doubt that subsidiary altars were located in rood-lofts (thus forming parclose chapels of sorts). The physical and documentary evidence for their existence is both abundant and conclusive. Such a use may seem unlikely, but was entirely consistent with the prevailing instinct to exploit the space within churches by compartmentalising their interiors. Early documentary evidence for rood-loft altars comes to us in the form of the records for Tavistock church in Somerset. These detail money paid in 1392 for rushes to lay before the altar of the Holy Cross in the rood-loft.

Although no rood-loft altars survive *in situ*,[9] physical evidence for their existence does, most notably in the form of piscinas. These are sometimes found high up in the east wall above the chancel arch, or in a nave wall to the north or south. The presence of this feature in a number of churches proves not only that altars existed in rood-lofts, but that Masses were said before them. Rood-loft piscinas survive at Wigmore, Burghill and Ross-on-Wye in Herefordshire. Meanwhile, at Little Hereford a piscina can be seen over the chancel arch, next to an arched niche (originally for the Rood – see photograph on p.52). The altar here was dedicated to the Blessed Virgin Mary, and evidently occupied a central location in the rood-loft. At Buckland in Gloucestershire, meanwhile, an aumbry (a small cupboard) that once served the rood-loft altar survives intact.

Given that Masses were celebrated in rood-lofts, it seems reasonable to suppose that readings or sermons were also delivered from rood-lofts during the ordinary Masses that took place in the main body of the church. This, too, has been much argued over. Once more the associated rood-stairs are cited as material evidence both for and against such a usage. For Vallance, the reading of the Gospel during Mass could not have taken place in the rood-loft because: 'the steps are so remarkably narrow, steep, and even dangerous that it is inconceivable that a priest or deacon in Mass vestments could have scaled their dark and tortuous ascent with convenience or any sort of decorum'.[10] As well as the lack of documentary evidence for this usage, Vallance points to the would-be anomaly of the entrance to the rood-stairs usually occupying the laity's portion of the church – in other words the nave – rather than that reserved for the clergy, namely the chancel.

On the other side of the debate stand the two Bonds – Francis and Frederick Bligh – together with the Rev. Dom Bede Camm. Francis Bond points out that the presence of altars in rood-lofts meant that the priest had to scale the stairs at certain times anyway, and if it was deemed unsuitable for him to do so in his vestments, 'he might vest in the loft'.[11] However, he does agree with Vallance that there is a lack of documentary evidence for such a use. Bond and Camm, too, are certain that rood-lofts, particularly early on, were indeed used as pulpits. They go on to record three Devon churches in which the rood-loft was used as a pulpit: West Alvington, Malborough, and Blackawton. However, in all three cases the evidence points to this being a Post-Reformation appropriation of the rood-loft.

Other compelling evidence against the later use of rood-lofts as platforms from which to preach comes in the form of nave pulpits, from which most sermons were delivered from the second half of the 15th century onwards. A number of records exist for coeval rood-lofts and nave pulpits (for example, at Nantwich in Cheshire), which begs the question, 'why preach from the rood-loft when you have a pulpit in the nave?' Nave pulpits were becoming abundant by the end of the 15th century and an edict of 1547 calls for pulpits to be erected in all churches that were yet to acquire one. Ironically, Post-Reformation pulpits often re-use elements from Pre-Reformation rood-lofts (the pulpits at Raglan in Monmouthshire – see photograph on p.286, Thenford in Northamptonshire – see photograph on p.47, and Widford in Oxfordshire all incorporate such material).

Of the available evidence for the primary function of the rood-loft, the most compelling relates to its use as a singing gallery. In the late 13th century in particular, church music grew rapidly in popularity and became increasingly elaborate. Prior to this, singing in churches had involved little more than a duologue between the priest and a respondent (typically the clerk). However, with the introduction of part-singing, there evolved groups of singers and, for the first time, church choirs. The rood-loft presented an ideal place to locate these singers. The numerous advantages of such a gallery, high up at the head of the nave, are self-evident. In order that the choir begin singing at appropriate points during the service, squints were sometimes cut into the rood-tympanum so that a member of the choir could monitor the progress of the officiating minister in the chancel below. Formal squints pierce the tympanum at Bettws Newydd in Monmouthshire, while those at Llanelieu in Breconshire have been cut somewhat haphazardly through the rough planking of the tympanum.

Whilst very few rood-lofts survive today, a great many of their attendant staircases – or *vyses* – do. The rood-stairs and doorways that survive in Lincolnshire alone, for example, indicate that more than 100 rood-lofts once graced the county's churches. Rood-stairs display a variety of configurations. Early rood-lofts were often accessed by a wooden ladder or steps from the nave (most of which have now perished), but later lofts were generally accessed by mural stairwells. This latter fitting developed in the 15th century and many still survive. Mural staircases were sometimes added in the form of a newel turret to the outside of the building (as at Borden in Kent, and Long Melford in Suffolk) but usually entailed the excavation of the walling at the east end of the nave. An unusual configuration can be seen at Llanwnnog in Montgomeryshire (see photograph on p.139). Here, the stairs are open and run at 45 degrees against the wall of the nave.[12]

Rood-stairs are found on the north side of the nave more often than on the south, and are occasionally found on both the north *and* south sides (for instance, at Eccles, Standish, and Wigan in Lancashire, and in a number of Devon churches). At St. Margarets in Herefordshire (see photograph on p.244) and at Totnes in Devon the lower rood-stair door opens from the chancel, rather than the nave; while at Lydbury North in Shropshire it opens from the north (Plowden) transeptal chapel. At Honiton in Devon and Winchester in Hampshire, access to the rood-loft is via a door in the outside of the church. Sometimes the

Llandefalle: Rood-stairs leading off the nave

mural stairwell was added later, but often it was incorporated into the fabric during the initial building of the church. The rood-stairs were generally furnished with plain oak doors at floor and rood-loft level.[13]

The worn state of many sets of rood-stairs suggests frequent and repeated use, and supports the belief that rood-lofts were in regular and prolonged use by groups of people, possibly singers. As Francis Bond puts it, 'No tramp of gospeller or preacher could have worn the steps of the rood staircases to the state we so often find them in'.[14] As well as singers, rood-lofts were evidently used by musicians, including organists (a usage which echoes that of the pulpitum in larger churches). Numerous sets of parish records refer to the locating of organs in rood-lofts. In 1473, Walter Abraham was paid seven shillings 'for making a seat in le Roode-lofte, when playing on the organys'.[15] According to Bond and Camm, who were writing in the first years of the 20th century, medieval rood-loft organs survived 'until lately'[16] at Tong in Shropshire and at Old Radnor in Radnorshire.

The use of the rood-loft to house singers and musicians was acknowledged by Elizabeth I during the Reformation. Far from demanding their destruction, however, she explicitly states in an Order of 1561 that rood-lofts be carefully taken down and re-erected at the west end of the nave (the actual word used more than once is 'transpose'). Unfortunately, these instructions were often wilfully misinterpreted by certain renegade Bishops intent on forging a spurious link between the Rood and the rood-loft; a policy calculated to make rood-lofts the legitimate targets of their reforming zeal. Bishop Hooper was one such myth-maker. He oversaw the dioceses of Gloucester and Worcester, and

his Injunctions of 1551 and 1552 represent some of the most brazen provocations to religious vandalism framed during the Reformation in England. Just as access to the Rood was both a reason for the erecting of rood-lofts and a cause of their downfall, so it was with singing and music. For the Puritans, the elaboration and sensual pleasure that characterised such activities were abhorrent, and formed a significant catalyst for further depredations.

Rare examples of late medieval rood-lofts surviving in the form of west galleries can be seen at Strensham in Worcestershire (plate 11) and Mamhilad in Monmouthshire (see photograph on p.285). That so few survive in this form reflects both the credible nature of the perceived link between the Rood and the rood-loft (and thus how deserving the rood-loft was of complete removal), and the widespread misinterpretation or ignorance of certain Orders relating to their treatment. In later years, particularly during the 17th, 18th and 19th centuries, west galleries began to reappear in parish churches, built from scratch to once again house groups of singers and musicians. Such an arrangement can be seen at Abbey Dore in Herefordshire and Berkeley Castle in Gloucestershire. At Bishop's Cleve (also in Gloucestershire) an especially fine Jacobean west gallery of c.1640 survives. Interestingly (and happily), the rood-lofts at both Flamborough and Attleborough in Norfolk, which were removed to the west end of the church after the Reformation, have since been re-erected in their original positions at the entrance to the chancel.

Rood-lofts that survived the initial onslaught of the Reformation were adapted to a variety of new uses during the Post-Reformation era. One of these was as a pew for school children, or wealthy or influential members of the community. The practice of creating private pews (generally in the nave) was especially popular during the 17th century[17] and affords perhaps the ultimate example of the compartmentalisation of the church interior. Such pews were often highly elaborate structures,

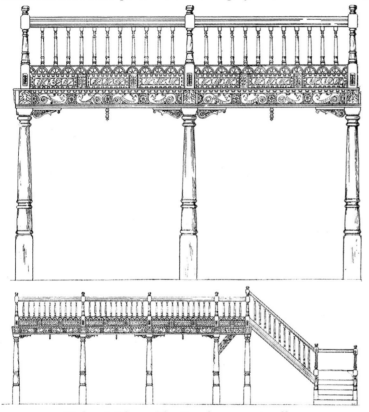

Bishop's Cleve: The Jacobean west gallery

occasionally canopied or roofed (as at Stokesay in Shropshire). The obvious kudos of a pew of this type in an elevated situation made this an obvious adaptation for the fitting. Numerous documents relating to the use of rood-loft pews during this era survive. None however is perhaps as memorable or poignant as the case of the elderly lady from Bradninch in Devon. As the last rightful incumbent of the rood-loft pew here, she would scale a wooden ladder prior to the start of each service in order to reach her seat.

In the centuries following the Reformation, rood-lofts continued to be taken down, sometimes for the most unexpected reasons. Archdeacon Thomas, writing in *Archaeologia Cambrensis* in 1903, describes the events that may have resulted in the removal of the rood-loft at Welshpool church in Montgomeryshire: '... a petition to the bishop for the removal of the loft in 1728–38 alleged that a great number of the very common sort of people sit in it (under the pretence of psalm singing) who run up and down there; some of them spitting upon the people's heads below'.

There is one further intention of the screen-builder that will strike the visitor when confronted with a rood-loft: namely that it be lovely to behold. As well as being carved and pierced, rood-lofts were invariably richly painted and gilded. Even where resources, financial and otherwise, were limited, the rood-loft was often the most lavished upon church fitting. It is demonstrably the case that, with Welsh screenwork in particular, the decorative emphasis shifted over time from the rood-screen to the rood-loft above. Thus, where the rood-screen at Llananno in Radnorshire (excepting its tracery heads, which should be read as belonging to the rood-loft in any case) is a relatively modest fitting, the rood-loft overhead bristles with carved decoration. With this in mind, it is important to avoid falling into the trap of concluding that a modest surviving rood-screen would once have supported only a modest rood-loft. In Wales in particular a plain surviving screen of a late date (such as the one at Llandefalle in Breconshire) would almost certainly have supported a very fine and elaborate rood-loft; the decoration by this date – c.1500 – being concentrated not on the rood-screen, but on the rood-loft above.

Such was the expense lavished on rood-lofts in otherwise modest parish churches that some commentators have been quite unable to accept that such fittings were originally intended for the buildings they find them in. The oft-repeated and generally misguided refrain has been that the fitting was removed to the church from some Abbey or other at the time of the Dissolution.[18] Llanegryn church in Merionethshire affords the perfect instance of this. Here, inside a small and humble structure of the 13th century, stands a very fine rood-screen and loft of c.1500. The guidebook gives the popular account of how these fittings came to be in this church:

> ... the Rood Loft and Screen came to Llanegryn from Cymer Abbey at the time of the Suppression of the Monasteries by King Henry VIII in 1536. Tradition says that it was carried overnight by the monks. Llanegryn being at the time well isolated and unlikely to be visited by Henry's snoopers, the monks housed their famous screen at Llanegryn, and who knows – hoping one day to return it to their Abbey. How the Loft was brought to Llanegryn remains a mystery – perhaps a short route

over the mountains, or maybe by sea from Llanelltyd and up the Dysynni river to a spot opposite the village of Llanegryn.[19]

The writer of this guidebook – one W.R. Hughes – whether because he thought this explanation fanciful or simply because he liked the idea that his community could claim the credit for such a glorious creation, goes on to write, 'For decades experts have told us the above legend, but I like to think at times, at least to muse, that the screen was carved and the loft built in this old village. Surely there were craftsmen who were geniuses in the area in the 13th, 14th and 15th centuries'.[20] He is right to challenge tradition, for there can be no doubt that these fittings were constructed specifically for Llanegryn church (and not Cymer Abbey). He is partly right too about the quality of local Welsh craftsmanship, though in all probability the screenwork at Llanegryn was not produced in the village but rather in a regional centre, possibly on the Lleyn peninsula to the north-west.

Today, only 26 substantially complete late medieval rood-lofts survive *in situ* in England and Wales. The southern Marches is comparatively fortunate in boasting ten of their number:

Herefordshire	St. Margarets
Breconshire	Llanfilo
	Partrishow
Monmouthshire	Bettws Newydd
	Llangeview
	Llangwm
	Mamhilad (as west gallery)

Montgomeryshire	Montgomery
	Llanwnnog
Radnorshire	Llananno

Lesser portions of rood-lofts (including re-located and re-used pieces) can be found in a great many churches. For example, J. Charles Cox and Alfred Harvey[21] list more than 100 churches in which the loft coving still survives (as at Wingerworth in Derbyshire, Burghill in Herefordshire, and Manorbier in Pembrokeshire).[22] Occasionally the parapet of a rood-loft was retained and re-erected on top of the rood-screen. Such a configuration can be seen at Cascob in Radnorshire and Southwold in Suffolk (now on top of the parclose screen in the latter case). For the southern Marches, the greatest loss in terms of rood-lofts has unquestionably been the spectacular example at Newtown (pieces of which line the sanctuary of the new church).

THE REFORMATION

He that hewed timber afore out of the thick trees:
Was known to bring it to excellent work.
But now they break down all the carved work
Thereof with axes and hammers.
Psalm lxxiv. 5-6

Today, the word 'Reformation' has acquired a kind of apocalyptic precision: there was an old order called Catholicism, then seismic events took place, and after the dust had settled there was Protestantism. For religious buildings and their fittings the events seem equally seismic; the sense being that there was a sudden maelstrom of destruction, which left the monasteries in ruins and the churches stripped of lovely and precious things, including their rood-screens. The reality is, suffice to say, far more complex. The destruction was a long drawn out process characterised by confusion, reversals of policy and the inconsistent application of a steady stream of often contradictory orders, acts and injunctions. The picture often painted of orgiastic vandalism carried out by mobs with flaming torches turns out, for the most part, to be a myth. Furthermore, the blackest days for medieval screenwork are not to be found in the 16th century, but rather in the 19th century.

The English Reformation is full of contradictions. It forms a part of a wider pattern of upheaval to the Western Church and yet was essentially an insular process triggered by an extreme act of State. In religious terms, the source of the Reformation was a growing discontent with the Catholic Church, and specifically with what were seen as abuses of its powers (such as the sale of indulgences). In Germany, Switzerland and France, Reformers such as Martin Luther (1483–1546) and John Calvin (1509–1564) rejected the political and religious authority of the papacy in Rome, subscribing instead to the fundamental authority of the Scriptures. Salvation, they argued, was attained through faith and not through grace received in the sacraments (through transubstantiation) or other rites of the traditional Church.

Although the message of the European Reformers was clearly heard in England, and was taken up by such prominent figures as the churchman Thomas Bilney (c.1495–1531) and the Bible translator William Tyndale (c.1494–1536), support for Reformist beliefs was initially restricted to university students and those with foreign connections. Furthermore, English Catholicism, far from being a religion that had run its course, or about which there was simmering national discontent, was alive and well, retaining full command of the loyalty of the English people.

The catalyst for the English Reformation was the failure of Henry VIII to secure papal annulment for his first marriage (to Katherine of Aragon). Rome's procrastination regarding Henry's divorce led the king to reject papal authority in England. In 1534, a series of Acts of Parliament was passed that severed administrative, financial and judicial links with Rome. One of these, the Act of Supremacy, bestowed upon Henry and his successors the title, 'the only supreme head in earth of the Church of England'. Theoretical justification for Henry's actions was manufactured by Thomas Cromwell and took the form of propaganda material, which attacked the papacy and sought to give a wider religious legitimacy to the break with Rome.

In the context of religious buildings and their contents, the monasteries were the first to suffer. The Annates Act of 1534 gave to the Crown (as the successor to the Pope) the Annates of each benefice.[1] This was followed in 1536 and 1539 by Acts authorising the dissolution of the monasteries. The process saw lands confiscated, lead and other materials stripped from buildings, valuable items including copes, altar frontals, staffs, plate and jewellery packed off to London, and less valuable items including furniture, linen and household goods auctioned off on site or given away. Once again, the motive behind this assault was not religious, but in this case political and economic. Henry had a long-term policy of extending the sovereignty of central government, he wanted to secure a new endowment for the Crown and he needed funds to cover losses from his ineffectual foreign policy.

It was during this period that items once belonging to monasteries found their way into parish churches. The items sold off by the church commissioners often included woodwork, such as benches, stalls and screens, which could be re-used in religious buildings that had yet to be targeted by the Crown. Although certain items in parish churches (particularly rood-lofts) have, on occasion, been wrongly identified as monastic in origin, there can be no doubt that a huge number of fittings found in parish churches did indeed once belong in a nearby monastery. Thus, the eastern screen, rood-loft, stalls, canopies and misericords now in the church of St. Nicholas in Montgomery once stood in Chirbury Priory in Shropshire; and the set of stalls at Leintwardine in Herefordshire came from Wigmore Abbey in the same county.

After the monasteries, the focus of the campaign shifted to the parish churches and their contents. In 1538 the religious shrines, together with images which were deemed to be, in the words of the Royal Injunctions, 'abused with pilgrimage or offerings', were targeted. In September of that year Roods began to come down. At first only those deemed to be attracting peculiar levels of veneration were removed (i.e. those that were themselves the objects of worship, such as the miraculous Rood at Gillingham in Kent). However, within a matter of years it was to be all Roods.

Much of this work was not Henry's doing but that of his chief minister, Thomas Cromwell. Henry was a traditionalist at heart and remained vehemently opposed to the Reforming Movement. He hated Luther and disagreed with many of the ideas coming out of Germany and Switzerland. The pace of religious change being forced through by Cromwell even prompted Henry, in April of 1539, to reiterate his belief in all of the key doctrines and practices of the old religion. However, Henry's need for religious justification for his plundering, and his resultant need of a strong Reforming voice at the centre of both government (in the form of Cromwell) and the Church (in the form of Thomas Cranmer) had effectively released the genie from the bottle.

This pattern, of the Crown trying but failing to variously moderate the Reforming movement in England, is also seen in the reign of Queen Mary, who tried to restore the country to Catholicism; and even during the reign of Elizabeth, who remained a keen advocate of ritual, to the dismay of her bishops. Ultimately though, efforts to rein in the Reformers or control the pace of change largely failed, and the confusion caused by short-lived administrations issuing contradictory instructions was exploited by Reformers who often, though not always, outlived the monarchs they had come to serve.

The key year during the English Reformation for parish churches and their fittings is 1547, the year of Henry's death. Acts passed in this year brought about the dissolution of the guilds and chantries. Most of these were located in parish churches and once again, just as with the monasteries, everything passed to the Crown: land and property was forfeit, treasures were taken and less valuable items sold off or given away. For the hard-line Reformers, though, this was not enough. The pace of change was still too hesitant and too intertwined with political manoeuvrings. Much to Cranmer's frustration, for example, Henry had reneged on a commitment to issue an order for all Roods to be pulled down, because (according to another of the king's advisors) it would not play well with certain European heads of state with whom Henry was hoping to have dealings. The death of Henry and the accession to the throne of the boy king Edward VI, however, gave the Reformers the perfect opportunity to strike.

During Edward's minority, England was essentially controlled by a powerful cabal, which included the staunchly Lutheran Protectors, Somerset and Northumberland, Thomas Cranmer as Archbishop of Canterbury, and Nicholas Ridley, the Bishop of London. In 1547, a new Order of Council appeared erasing the former distinction between images that were and were not in themselves objects of veneration, and demanding that all images be totally 'extincted and destroyed'. This encompassed not only Roods, but also wall paintings, statues and stained glass. Rood-figures were generally taken down and burned or broken up, wall paintings were limewashed (an act that ironically served to preserve them) and statues were, quite literally, defaced. Only when it came to stained glass was there a marked resistance to the Order (glass being, at the time, hugely expensive). In 1552, with the publication of the second Book of Common Prayer, orders were given to remove all images still in place.

The close proximity of the rood-loft to the Rood – for Reformers the most prominent and abhorrent of images – seemingly made its persecution inevitable. However, it cannot be too strongly emphasised that the Rood had no relationship with the rood-loft, beyond that of simple physical proximity. Roods had existed centuries before the rood-loft had been devised, and the utility of rood-lofts was recognised long after Roods ceased to be. Furthermore, even when the Elizabethan Order of 1561 appeared, no effort was made by the Crown (at least explicitly) to preface it with any theoretical religious justification. The responsibility for manufacturing a mystical and didactic link between the two fittings lay mainly with others, often from within the Church.

One such figure, Bishop John Hooper, held the dioceses of Gloucester and Worcester. In anticipation of orders to the effect from central government, but with a total absence of legal authority, Hooper issued his Injunctions in 1551 and 1552 calling on parishioners to pull down rood-lofts in which, according to him, 'superstition, idols, images or other provocations to idolatry have been used'. There can be no doubt that the enrichment of loft-fronts with images of the saints, be they painted or carved, was seized upon by the likes of Hooper. For, in this way the rood-loft echoed the Continental iconostasis (such as that found at Torcello in Italy) and did indeed appear to be an accessory to idolatry. The fact that certain physical accoutrements – such as the lights associated with the Rood[2] – were also attached to the rood-beam, can only have given further credence to this manufactured association between Rood and rood-loft.

Whilst rood-lofts were coming down in one part of the kingdom they were still going up in others. Just three years after Hooper had called upon his flocks to pull down rood-lofts in the dioceses of Gloucester and Worcester, Bishop Bonner was saying precisely the opposite in London. His Injunctions of 1555 demanded that a rood-loft be erected in any church that did not already have one.

In this period of confusion and upheaval rood-screens, too, began to suffer. As well as carrying images upon their wainscot panels, there was, by the early 16th century, a high degree of synergy between rood-screen and loft. For the Reformers this factor seemed to implicate both parts, not just the loft, in the crimes of the Rood above. The attacks did not always result in the screen being pulled down, but often took the crude form of the scratching off of the faces of the figures on the wainscot. This type of damage can be seen in the West-country and East Anglia especially, where screens were often enriched with such figures. It has been argued that the conspicuous nature of this vandalism – the display of a clearly violated image, as opposed to its careful erasure – was in itself a significant statement; a kind of public insult, lest the profanity of the old religion be forgotten.[3]

It is important to recognise that, contrary to the picture often painted, the English Reformation was rarely characterised by frenzied vandalism or spontaneous popular iconoclasm. As J.J. Scarisbrick notes, 'The impression derived from churchwardens' accounts is that altars, roods and rood-lofts, statues and holy-water stoups and so on were taken down in Edward's reign, put back in Mary's and taken down again after Elizabeth's accession without great drama or disorder ... England never produced the scenes of mob violence and iconoclasm witnessed in much of Reformation Germany, France, the Low Countries'.[4] In a graphic example of just how deliberate the work to strip church interiors could be, two men had to be paid to take down the rood figures and the statues and paint over the Last Judgement and the rood-loft at Ludlow. Two men also took seven days to remove the altars from the same church: possibly more time than it took to erect them in the first place.

It is also clear that many people were uncomfortable with having to deface and strip churches, whatever the justification. It was recognised by some (including the archbishop of Canterbury, John Whitgift) that despite the popish associations of a given fitting it was still sacrilegious to despoil a church and take away things already promised to God. It was also, transparently, a manifestation of greed. This unease was reflected in the instructions given to the commissioners whose job it was to personally remove items from churches. They were told to act with extreme circumspection, and it is known that a number felt great discontent about what was being asked of them.

Besides this unease, many members of the laity were also unhappy about the loss of wealth to the Crown (in a period of growing poverty for parishes). By the time the order went out in 1549 to return inventories of church goods, a great deal was being done to ensure that the wealth of churches (or some of it at least) might remain within the parishes. The inventories were a barely disguised shopping list of items still to be looted, as well as an acknowledgement that church possessions were 'going missing' before the Crown could lay its hands on them. The Crown was right to worry. It has been shown[5] that throughout the country items were being sold off to ensure that the parish and not the Crown were the beneficiaries of any sales.

In some instances, items that were sold off were simply retained by the buyer, then sold or given back to the relevant church at a later date, particularly during the Marian restoration. Mary did everything in her power to reinstate Catholicism, its practices and its trappings, and during her reign (1553–1558) many parish churches reinstated whatever fixtures and fittings had escaped the looting and destruction of the previous administrations. This included, in several cases, their medieval screens. The rood-screen at Foxley in Norfolk, cut down to wainscot level during the reign of Edward VI, had its upper half reinstated in the reign of Mary. The screen still stands today, the metal strap plates fastening the standards back together clearly visible. The rood-loft from the church of St. Nicholas in Warwick was taken down in 1548 and sold off two years later. However, the buyer kept the pieces safe and when Mary ascended the throne, the pieces were bought back by the churchwardens and the loft re-erected. Likewise the rood-loft from Morebath in Devon was taken down in 1551, kept safe by parishioners, and put up again in 1555 (only to be taken down again in 1562). Brand new rood-lofts were even erected during this period, including one that survives to this day, at Hubberholme in Yorkshire (erected in 1558).

Other items were 'donated' into the safe-keeping of, for instance, a leading local family. William Clopton, whose family had been largely responsible for the building and fitting out of the spectacular church at Long Melford in Suffolk, bought up many items from the church during this period. In the 19th century, one of these – an image of the Virgin and Child – was found undamaged beneath the floor of the church. Clopton was clearly attempting to preserve this and other items, and it is known that the churchwardens at the time were willing accomplices.

The Marian restoration ultimately failed because Mary's reign was too short-lived to secure the comprehensive reintroduction of Catholicism; because sympathy for her efforts was blunted by her unpopular marriage to Philip of Spain; and because in religious terms Protestantism had become too pervasive and hydra-like to effect a complete reversal. For churches and their fittings, too much damage had been done and too much already lost. It was no good ordering that a church, stripped of its finery and robbed of its wealth, be refilled with the elaborate fittings and treasures it once contained. Destroying a statue, a Rood or a rood-loft would always be easier, quicker, cheaper than replacing one: and so it proved.

The religious reversal of Mary was itself reversed with the accession of Elizabeth in 1558, and the restoration of Protestantism. The following year a new Act of Supremacy re-established the monarch as the head of the church, confirming Elizabeth as 'the only supreme governor ... as well in all spiritual or ecclesiastical things or causes'. However, the reversal was a slow process for the new queen, requiring the dismantling of the Catholic episcopate, patient diplomacy in Parliament, and the placating of religious conservatives. In the end, the Elizabethan Settlement can perhaps be characterised as a compromise, albeit one heavily weighted in favour of Protestantism.

With the religious make-up of England now essentially resolved, Elizabeth set about untangling some of the confusion surrounding the organisation of churches and their contents. On 10 October 1561, an Order of Council appeared that dealt in detail with rood-lofts and the screens they surmounted. The Order includes the following lines:

> For the avoiding of much strife and contention, that hath heretofore risen among the Queen's subjects in divers parts of the Realm, for the using or transposing of Rood-lofts ... in every parish church. It is thus decreed and ordained, that the Rood-lofts, as yet, being at this day aforesaid untransposed, shall be so altered, that the upper part of the same, with the soller be quite taken down unto the upper parts of the vaults and beams running in length over the said vaults, by putting some convenient crest upon the said beam towards the church, with leaving the situation of the seats (as well in the Quire as in the Church) as heretofore hath been used.
>
> Provided yet, that where any Parish, of their own costs and charges, by common consent will pull down the whole frame, and re-edifying again the same in joiners' work ... that they may do as they think agreeable, so it be to the height of the upper beam aforesaid.
>
> Provided also, that where in any parish church the said rood-lofts be already transposed, so that there remain a comely partition betwixt the chancel and the church, that no alteration be otherwise attempted in them, but be suffered in quiet. And where no partition is standing, there to be one appointed.[6]

The Order is revealing for a number of reasons. It seeks to deal with the screenwork of parish churches alone, and begins by acknowledging the discord and confusion that had characterised the treatment of their rood-lofts, citing this as the catalyst for the Order. At no point does the Order set out a coherent rationale for the changes prescribed. It does not seek, for example, to make explicit why screenwork should be so altered. In terms of the changes prescribed, these are unambiguous and clearly defined. The rood-loft (as we now understand it) should be taken down to the height of the top of the vault[7] – specifically the bressumer – and an ornamental cresting placed there in its stead. If the whole screen and loft is dismantled, then a new screen is to be put up to the height of the bressumer of old. The Order goes on to make it quite clear that no harm should be inflicted upon the screen itself, and that if there is no screen standing at the entrance to the chancel then one must be erected here. At no point does the Order permit the destruction of screenwork; the tone is measured and the text speaks only of alteration and transposition.

Whilst these instructions were often carried out to their letter and spirit, more strongly iconoclastic (or ambonoclastic) figures than the queen still took it upon themselves to wilfully misinterpret them. Thus, whilst the rood-loft at Hemingbrough in Yorkshire's East Riding was taken down, to be replaced by a 'convenient crest', elsewhere certain bishops were exhorting those in their charge to go much further than the Elizabethan Order strictly allowed. For this reason, in spite of the detailed and prescriptive nature of the Order and its moderate tone, rood-lofts and even screens continued to be lost.

In the second half of the 16th century, the Puritans' hatred of singing gave the purges renewed impetus. The then-bishop of Worcester (Edwin Sandys) is known to have hated rood-lofts precisely because they formed singing galleries. His real motive behind demanding their removal was not, as he claimed, a desire to stamp out idolatry, but rather to strangle the voice of church choirs.[8] Bishop Ridley, who was in charge of the diocese of London, was another who vigorously sought the removal of rood-lofts. As well as having a keen iconoclast in charge of the diocese, the inhabitants of what was essentially a trading port were already well attuned to Protestant ideas from abroad, and particularly to those arriving from the Hanseatic ports of Germany. As a result

of the thoroughness of the purges here during the Reformation, London lost virtually all of its medieval screenwork (including all of its rood-lofts in 1560).

For church interiors, a marked characteristic of Elizabeth's reign was the replacement of images with words. The early Reformers had sought to unravel the mysteries of the liturgy by producing vernacular translations of the Scriptures, thereby democratising to some extent the Word of God. During the Elizabethan era, words, together with the Royal Arms, replaced what had previously been the most prominent and potent image in churches; namely the Rood. The wall above the chancel arch was whitewashed and in its place religious texts were set up. An Order of 1560 specified that these include the Creed, the Lord's Prayer and the Ten Commandments (or Decalogue). In churches

Lydbury North: An example of the replacement of images with words

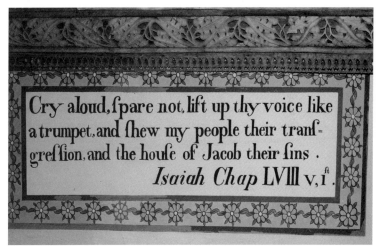

St. Margarets: Sentences painted below the rood-loft

with a tympanum, this fitting was often retained precisely because it made an ideal hoarding upon which to place such texts. A fine set survives at Lydbury North in Shropshire, dated 1561. Other Biblical texts – known as sentences – were painted on the north and south walls of the nave, often within modest borders. A set of these survives (albeit in a refreshed state) at St. Margarets in Herefordshire.

The general aim to democratise worship and demystify the liturgy also had profound consequences for the relationship between the two main spaces within each church – the nave and chancel – and the organisation of these spaces. Broadly speaking, changes during the 16th century saw the clergy spending a greater

Llandegley: Carved trail attached to the altar table

part of the service in the nave, and the parishioners encroaching into what had previously been the *sanctum sanctorum*; namely the chancel.

In 1550, stone altars were abolished, to be replaced with wooden tables. During the communion, the table would be moved from against the east wall of the sanctuary and placed in the middle of the chancel, with its narrow ends pointing east and west. In this way the communicants could kneel at all four sides. One such table, at Llandegley in Radnorshire, is somewhat provocatively ornamented with a carved trail from a rood-screen or loft. Aside from the removal of stone altars, the chancel (according to the 1559 Prayer Book) was to remain unaltered; a policy affirmed in 1561, with an instruction specifying that a partition remain between the chancel and the nave.

By the 1570s, Catholicism had become a minority religion, with most of its practices and trappings all but expunged. The process of its replacement with Protestantism as the national religion had not been instantaneous or straightforward, but drawn-out and painful, taking the better part of four decades. The legacy of the Reformation, however, was huge. For church design, it formed a guiding dynamic of overwhelming potency for some two and a half centuries. As a period in English history, it is perhaps the mirror in which we see ourselves most clearly, as a nation, staring back.

THE POST-REFORMATION HISTORY OF CHURCH SCREENS

The Church's Restoration
In eighteen-eighty-three
Has left for contemplation
Not what there used to be.
From *Hymn* by John Betjeman

Although the Elizabethan Order of 1561 did very little to avert the destruction of rood-lofts, it did secure, at least in the short term, the future of the rood-screen (or simple chancel screen as it now was). During the immediate post-Reformation era it was seen as a grave matter indeed if a church had no chancel screen, and the authorities were usually quick to punish those responsible for the illegal removal of a screen. Thus, when the chancel screen at Bungay church in Suffolk was removed during Elizabeth's reign, the act cost the two churchwardens their jobs, and the parishioners were made to put up a new screen at their own cost.[1]

The Visitation Articles of several bishops and archbishops during the second half of the 16th century and the first half of the 17th century, are full of enquiries as to whether an appropriate screen divides the chancel from the nave in the churches of their dioceses. Thus, the Bishop of Norwich, Richard Montagu, asks in 1638: 'Is your chancel divided from the nave or body of the church with a partition of stone, boards, wainscot, grates or otherwise? Wherein is there a decent strong door to keep out boys, girls, or irreverent men and women?'

By now the chancel screen had lost many, though by no means all, of the idolatrous associations that might have put its continued existence in jeopardy. Shorn of the iconostasis-like rood-loft and the mysterious figures of Christ, Mary and John, the fitting was now surmounted by the royal arms (or those of an archbishop or a leading family, as at Abbey Dore in Herefordshire); and as such was now firmly grounded in the real world. Some screens retained figure paintings on their wainscots, but for most (and in the eyes of both the Crown and the Church) the screen was now a partition, pure and simple: an entirely appropriate fitting that did no more than express the extent of the nave and preserve the sanctity of the chancel beyond. For most, this factor meant that to remove it was to profane the church.

Although very little screen-building took place in the Elizabethan era – one gets the impression that shock at recent events had frozen such activities into a numbed stasis – the last quarter of the 16th century and the first half of the 17th century witnessed a revival of sorts. One of the catalysts for this may have been a nostalgia for familiar things that might provide some affirmation of the continuity of religious life. During this era, the

Abbey Dore: Screen surmounted by arms

screen-friendly advocacy of such figures as William Laud was instrumental. Laud was archbishop of Canterbury from 1633 to 1645, having been made the bishop of St. Davids in 1621, of Bath and Wells in 1626, and of London in 1628. This status gave him a platform from which to broadcast his belief in the fundamental import of chancel screens, and to influence their construction.

The screen-building that took place during this era bears little relationship to what had gone before. Just as in religious terms the Reformation had seen diverse elements from home and abroad seemingly cast up into the air to land again in a completely different order; so it was with church screenwork. When the Reformation struck, the most notable innovation then colouring the development of church screens was that of Renaissance design. Renaissance motifs, such as putti and arabesques, started to appear on church screens midway through the first half of the 16th century (for example, at Llandinabo in Herefordshire, in the chancel screen there of *c*.1530). However, by this stage, the adoption of Renaissance design was still selective rather than comprehensive, and screen-builders were still finding their way with the new language. Screen-building was thus entering a period of transition prior to the Reformation, with Gothic forms gradually being superseded by those from abroad. When it came, the Reformation served only to exacerbate the state of flux being experienced by the craft. Although at no point during the Reformation was the building of screens actually stopped, there is no doubt that the evolution of the chancel screen was profoundly affected by it.

Llandinabo: Renaissance sea-monsters and arabesques

In terms of basic design and construction, the chancel screens of the immediate post-Reformation era tend to follow the format of their rood-screen forebears. The lower half of the screen still consists of a solid wainscot, and above this still runs an open arcade topped by a head-beam. The main compositional difference in post-Reformation screens is that occasionally the first arcade (typically to head-beam level) might be surmounted by a second arcade topped by a further beam. A memorable example of this two-tiered form is the spectacular chancel screen at Croscombe in Somerset.

In stylistic terms, however, post-Reformation screens are dramatically different to their predecessors. There was a clear recognition on the part of screen-builders that the Gothic, as strongly redolent of the old order, was suddenly no longer acceptable (and besides, stylistically it had become outmoded). In its place came a curious hybrid of Renaissance and classical elements, showing only the faintest vestiges of pre-Reformation design. With some screens, such as those at St. John's church in Leeds (1634) and Yarnton in Oxfordshire (c.1610), this intermingling resulted in screenwork that is, although striking and finely crafted, often florid and stylistically muddled. The parclose screen at Yarnton, for example, has mullions and engaged half-mullions in the form of classical fluted columns (each complete with entasis) on tall pedestals, and is topped by a head-beam in the form of a deep entablature. Elsewhere, however, the upper half of the screen is a riot of Renaissance-inspired decoration and Elizabethan strapwork, scrolls and pinnacles.

At Abbey Dore in Herefordshire, classical elements take precedence, the surfaces are left freer of carved decoration, and the result, though hardly

Croscombe: The towering chancel screen

Yarnton: The aisle screen with its wealth of strapwork

sympathetic to its context, is at least bold and fairly consistent. With such screens one has to look very closely for any surviving elements of pre-Reformation design. At Abbey Dore, each light has a trefoil head, albeit unlike any found in Gothic work. At Kedington in Suffolk, in a surprisingly plain screen of 1619, the lights comprise cut-off mullions with drop finials and paired arabesques, which together give a kind of ogee head to each. At Geddington in Northamptonshire the screen now across the south aisle (of 1618) has intersecting tracery and three trefoils enclosed in a large circle, giving it the appearance of a Perpendicular window.

Vowchurch: Turned balusters (echoing a feature of the 13th century)

In an echo of some of the very earliest ecclesiastical screenwork, many post-Reformation screens employ turned balusters as mullions. These can be found at both Abbey Dore and Vowchurch (1613), and correspond strikingly with those at Stanton Harcourt in Oxfordshire and a number of other screens of the 13th and 14th centuries. Elsewhere, the mullions of post-Reformation screens show great variety and invention. At How Caple and Monnington-on-Wye in Herefordshire, twisted posts (and, in the case of How Caple, arches) appear, echoing those of Bernini's Baldacchino in St. Peters, Rome. Elsewhere, an admixture of Renaissance and Elizabethan design, together with the fanciful and unfettered inventiveness of the carver, has led to some of the strangest architectural woodwork ever produced. At Slaidburn in Yorkshire the mullions, which are square in cross-section, taper towards the bottom and are topped by ionic scrolls. Each face is elaborately carved with a variety of figurative and non-figurative elements.

How Caple (left) and Monnington-on-Wye (right): Twisted balusters

Whilst the erecting of chancel screens after the Reformation is easily accounted for, the raising of the occasional rood-loft seems extraordinary. However, not only were a number erected in the 17th century (primarily as singing or organ galleries), the parapet of one at Rodney Stoke in Somerset still survives in its original location at the head of the nave. The west gallery at East Brent in Somerset was originally erected before the chancel there in 1635, and a chancel screen and loft were put up at Sandon in Staffordshire in 1686.

As a rule, though, the 17th century (and especially its second half) saw rood-lofts suffer huge net losses, particularly during the Puritanical purges of the Commonwealth under Cromwell. Here, once again, rood-lofts were the victims of their association with another fitting: in this case the organ, which was often located in the loft. On 9 May 1644, an Order was made demanding that organs be removed. This, allied to the Puritans' dislike of singing and music, seems to have led to further mischievous and unwarranted damage to pre-Reformation screenwork. The Jacobean love for elaborate private pews probably ensured that more rood-lofts were not lost during the 17th century, as did the transposition of a number of lofts to the west end of churches (e.g. Strensham in Worcestershire). The Order of 1644 also reiterated the demand that images be defaced, and much of the damage done to wainscot figure-paintings, especially in the South-west and East Anglia, can be attributed to this period.

After the excitement and upheaval of the 16th and 17th centuries, England in the 18th century was characterised, in religious terms at least, by considerable sloth and apathy. Neo-paganism, religious scepticism and a mounting indifference to church and religious heritage saw church attendance dropping and more and more churches falling into disrepair. For new churches, innovation (both of style and arrangement) rather than continuity characterised much new development, and was often informed by shifts in fashion or quirks of individual taste. Chancel screens continued to be built during the 18th century, but in nothing like the numbers needed to replace those being lost, and still less in a particularly coherent or clearly defined style.

Surviving chancel screens from the 18th century include the simple example at Mardale in Westmorland, with its two tiers of turned balusters, and the handsome screen at Walden (St. Pauls),

Rodney Stoke: The extremely rare post-Reformation rood-loft parapet

in Hertfordshire. Although no screens from the 18th century survive in the southern Marches, a number of west galleries do, including at Croft and King's Caple in Herefordshire. Iron screenwork, more often associated with the 19th century, began to appear in the 18th century. The Staffordshire churches of Tamworth and Penkridge contain iron screens of *c*.1750 and 1778 respectively, both made in Holland. However, in the 18th century, examples of the removal of church screens are far easier to come by than are instances of new screens being put up. In a striking case of officially sanctioned (though wholly illegal) destruction, archdeacons in Yorkshire oversaw the demolition of some 71 church screens in a period of just 17 years, in the first half of the 18th century.[2]

A number of factors seem to have accelerated the rate of destruction in the 19th century. Firstly, (and ironically) the Gothic revival brought with it a desire to strip church interiors back to an idealised state of unblemished architectural purity, and to purge them of clutter. Even Augustus Pugin, a trenchant advocate for the retention of medieval screenwork, was dismayed by the state of the churches. In his *A Treatise on Rood Screens*, Pugin writes:

> Cheap magnificence, meretricious show, is the order of the day; something pretty, something novel, calico hangings, sparkling lustres, paper pots, wax dolls, flounces and furbelows, glass cases, ribands, and lace, are the ornaments and materials usually employed to decorate, or rather disfigure, the altar of sacrifice and the holy place. It is impossible for church furniture and decoration to attain a lower depth of degradation.

For Pugin, however, the list of undesirable contents emphatically excluded screens, which, 'form an essential part of Catholic tradition and reverence, and that no church can be complete without'.

Unfortunately, for many other proponents of the Gothic revival, medieval screenwork did indeed count as a non-original and obtrusive fitting, and Pugin's passionate and articulate pleas went largely unheeded. Just like the Reformers of the 16th century, the Gothic revivalists of the 19th century used the time-honoured justification of the aspiration for 'authenticity'. Thus, just as the extreme German Protestant Martin Bucer had invented the idea that ancient churches were round with an altar in the middle in order to justify open and congregational worship; so the Gothic revivalists invented the idea that Gothic churches were pared down temples to architectural purity in order to serve similar ends.

Examples of the destruction and loss of late medieval screenwork during the 19th century are almost too numerous to mention. In some areas the scale of the losses is breathtaking. Bond and Camm report that during this period, 'In Cornwall nearly every screen was sawn down to the level of the rail beneath the lights'. In the course of the latter stages of the 18th century up to the end of the 19th century, more than 80 screens disappeared in Devon alone. Crossley and Ridgway give an account – by no means exhaustive – of the losses from Radnorshire and Montgomeryshire churches during the 19th century. For Radnorshire, the pair note that, 'Of thirty or more screens existing at the commencement of the 19th century, less than half remain even in fragmentary form'.[3] For Montgomeryshire, they write:

At the turn of the century, 1799–1802, Llandysil was demolished; the splendid screen at Llanidloes — as fine as Newtown — was pulled down in 1816; Machynlleth in 1827 ceased to be a cruciform church, and its various screens and stallwork were destroyed. In 1836 Llangurig was pulled down and the screen given away piecemeal to anyone desiring a relic. Llanwddyn disappeared at a restoration in 1847, and Newtown, the finest of them all, was pulled down when a new church was built, and the remains of it are scanty.[4]

Besides the justification of architectural idealism, a further excuse for the demolition of church screens and other fittings came in the form of the legacy of dilapidated churches inherited from the 18th century. This legacy led to an almost unprecedented period of church restoration, demolition and rebuilding in England and Wales. A survey of Radnorshire churches carried out by the Royal Commission in 1910–1911 lists all of the churches rebuilt, demolished or drastically restored in the county. It concludes that, 'There are in all fifty-two churches in the county of which twenty-eight have been entirely rebuilt, eight others drastically restored and pulled about, being thirty-six out of fifty-two, leaving sixteen churches not completely spoilt'. By the middle of the 20th century, according to the same body, Monmouthshire had lost eight of its ancient churches, 13 others had been drastically restored, and a further 38 had been completely or partially rebuilt. By the same date, 21 churches in Montgomeryshire had been drastically restored and a further 28 completely or partially rebuilt. The vast majority of this work took place in the 19th century.

In many cases the need for renovation or complete restoration was beyond question. However, many restorers took little account of the organic nature of churches, asserting instead that such buildings should form the record of an imaginary slice of time, rather than the rich accretion of centuries of change that was their reality. Neither did this form of restoration value many of the fixtures and fittings of the medieval church. These were often seen merely as non-authentic encumbrances; things that got in the way, both literally and metaphorically, of the essence of the architecture and the distilled experience of worship within it. Where in the past church officials had often been the catalysts for the pulling down of screens and lofts, in the 19th century it was frequently architects. To name a few names, Sir George Gilbert Scott, George Street, John Pearson and William Butterfield were all guilty of the removal of early screenwork in the course of their restorations of churches.

The prevailing attitude during the 19th century, namely that chancel screens were not objects to be valued, meant that many screens were lost as a result of seemingly harmless activities. For instance, many already dilapidated screens were further damaged during harvest festivals, 'whereby', Aymer Vallance rails as only he can,

> an irresponsible, if zealous, band of amateurs, unskilled in the handling of hammer and nails, string and wire, for affixing wreaths and such-like vegetable embellishments, is let loose in the church to do its worst, year by year ... The utter futility, nay vulgarity, of presuming to gild the lily — the fact that ancient screenery is of itself so choice and exquisite an ornament that nothing is needed to improve

it, and that no transitory decking can possibly succeed in decorating it — does not seem to occur to them.

With a screen reduced, through years of neglect and casual damage, to a creaking shadow of its former self, it comes as little wonder that the remedy was usually complete removal rather than sympathetic and expensive restoration.

Fortunately, (and not a moment too soon) the 19th century also witnessed the first stirrings of an appreciation for, and cherishing of, medieval church fittings. Besides Augustus Pugin, with his theoretical *A Treatise on Rood Screens*, there were others who took a more hands-on approach. The Rev. John Parker, provoked both by an aesthetic appreciation for church woodwork, and a desire to record for posterity material that was being lost all the time, made numerous drawings of screens and lofts. His superb draughtsmanship and detailed written notes form an invaluable record. Another writer, the architect Thomas Talbot-Bury, also made illustrations of rood-screens and other church fittings for his 1847 work, *Ecclesiastical Woodwork*.

Elsewhere, other enlightened architects were doing much on the ground to preserve and retain valuable church screenwork. In 1878, John Seddon, the architect of Hoarwithy in Herefordshire, completed a sympathetic reconstruction of the spectacular rood-screen and loft at Llangwm in Monmouthshire. The work took Seddon two years, and involved him taking as his working source the screen and loft at Partrishow in Breconshire. Seddon also found traces of original pigment and used these to inform an unusually restrained colour scheme (for the period). The resultant screen and loft must be seen as essentially a product of the 19th

Llangwm: An unusual case of enlightened Victorian restoration

Canon Pyon: An overly large crest surmounting the screen

century, yet evident here is a real commitment to accuracy, both of design and spirit, on the part of Seddon.

Unfortunately, for every example of a sympathetic restoration, there are at least ten examples of heavy-handedness. When instances of the latter are encountered one has to weigh this damage against the fact that the screen was allowed to survive at all. Thus, although David Walker's restoration of the rood-screen and loft at Llanwnnog in Montgomeryshire cannot be called especially sensitive, just prior to the restoration Glynne described the rood-loft here as 'rather rickety';[5] a factor that could easily have seen the whole lot pulled down. Likewise, the drastic work carried out to the screen at Usk in Monmouthshire is heavy-

handed, but at least much of value still survives. The restoration here saw the screen's proportions ruined and its appearance made very odd when it was illogically re-assembled over a dwarf-wall and the nave portion of it was garishly painted. Again, at Bishop's Frome and Brinsop in Herefordshire the Victorian reconstruction of the rood-screen in each case is muddled, but done in such a way as to incorporate a large amount of original material.

A popular Victorian twist was to add cresting to the top of a chancel screen (in what must be unconscious adherence to the Elizabethan Order of 1561, which demanded the addition of 'some convenient crest' to the head-beam of a chancel screen following the removal of the rood-loft). Victorian crestings tend to be too big for the screens they surmount (in that the scale of the motifs used does not usually correspond with that of existing elements on the screen, such as the tracery). This is certainly the case at Canon Pyon and Brinsop in Herefordshire. However, sometimes a modest cresting can be an entirely appropriate way to visually link a collection of essentially disparate screens, as has happened at Ludlow in Shropshire.

Elsewhere, whilst any remnants of the original colour scheme were generally pickled off and the screen varnished or painted brown, the restoration work was often discreet and sensible, resulting in no more than the like-for-like replacement of missing parts, such as tracery elements and mullions. The rood-screens at Leinthall Starkes and Tedstone Delamere in Herefordshire both show relatively discreet and sympathetic interventions. In the context of sympathetic restoration, the example of the rood-screen and loft at Llananno in Radnorshire is particularly heartening. Not only were the fittings carefully taken down and re-erected in the new church in 1867, but the missing carved figures from the parapet were brilliantly recreated by Boulton of Cheltenham in *c*.1880. We will never know how accurate these figures are, but in their style and their spirit they are entirely in keeping with other figure carving of the 16th century.

As well as retaining some medieval screens and pulling down countless others, the Victorians also designed and built their own church screens. Many of these are of metal, including the extravagant Skidmore screen for Hereford Cathedral (now in the V&A) and the far humbler parochial screens at Little Birch in Herefordshire and Rockfield in Monmouthshire. This last county, Monmouthshire, has an unusually high number of screens dating from the 19th and 20th centuries: here, at least 20 churches contain metal or wooden chancel screens from this period.

While the metal screenwork of the Victorian era may not be to everyone's taste, it is at least distinctly of its time. The wooden screens of the 19th and 20th century, however, often appear only as lifeless shadows of their pre-Reformation forebears. For, where the screen-carver of the 15th and 16th centuries worked with a chisel and gouge, trusting his eye and sacrificing exactitude for overall effect, the screen-carver of the 19th and 20th centuries worked with mechanical tools, and would not permit the human hand to be seen in his carving. As John Parker recognised, 'There is in Gothic work a graceful negligence as to mechanical exactness, like the free and hasty touches of a good painter. The effect of dazzling richness is injured by extreme precision'.[6] Since the Reformation, screen-carvers have generally ignored these words and the approach they describe, to the great detriment of their products.

Llananno: The superb carved figures of c.1880

During the 20th century, losses of medieval church screenwork began to fall sharply, new screens were occasionally erected, and the restoration of early screens continued. Although there are few examples of screenwork of real merit from the 20th century, a number exist. The Art Nouveau screen at Llanvaches in Monmouthshire is interesting for its response to a contemporary aesthetic movement; the screen at Michaelchurch Escley in Herefordshire is boldly carved and likeable; while the rood-loft and Lady chapel screen at North Cerney in Gloucestershire are good pastiches of medieval work (see photograph p.24). In terms of restoration, the work of W.D. Caröe should be highlighted. His heroic efforts resulted in the saving from collapse of the church at Partrishow in Breconshire, and the sensitive restoration of its interior and fittings, including its delicate rood-loft. Caröe also completed important restoration work at a number of other Breconshire churches, including Llanfilo (which also has a fine rood-loft) and Brecon Priory. Elsewhere, whilst the general standard of screen restoration work was improving, muddled work occasionally still took place; for instance at Llansantffraed in Monmouthshire.

The first half of the 20th century also bore witness to a relative explosion in the amount being written on the subject of medieval church woodwork (and screenwork in particular). Some writers, such as F.E. Howard, were architects by profession; others, such

Llansantffraed: Huge crocketed finials attached to the head-beam

as the Rev. Dom Bede Camm, came from within the Church; others still were writers and ecclesiologists. All shared a belief that medieval church woodwork, as a field, merited serious analysis, and that churches – as places that everyone had free access to – contained previously untold treasures that were in urgent need of more wide-spread acknowledgement and appreciation. Advances in photography meant that such books could be enriched with high quality images, able to persuasively testify to the aesthetic quality and workmanship of the fittings. Between them the likes of Crossley, Ridgway, the two Bonds, Camm, Vallance and Howard forced people to look once again at things they had always been familiar with, but to which they had only, on rare occasions, thought to attach real value.

During the 20th and 21st centuries, the loss of pre-Reformation screenwork has slowed to a trickle. This is not to say that the damage and losses have dried up completely, for old screenwork suffers intermittent damage and loss even now; but the valuing of such fittings is now general, and most church screenwork enjoys a degree of statutory protection under listed buildings legislation

Little Birch: The Victorian chancel screen

and faculty jurisdiction.[7] In one respect if no other, however, the loss of even a single rood- or chancel screen remains intolerable: Queen Elizabeth's Order of 1561, which states in the clearest possible terms that 'there remain a comely partition betwixt the chancel and the church' has never been repealed; and thus technically remains binding to this day.

THE WELSH MARCH

Whatever else may come to pass, I do not think that on the Day of Direst Judgement any race other than the Welsh, or any other language, will give answer to the Supreme Judge of all for this small corner of the earth.' Gerald of Wales, *The Description of Wales*

The coinciding of two entirely distinct schools of woodworking – the Western and the Midland – cannot alone account for the variety that defines the church screenwork of the southern Marches. Other broader factors informed the dynamics of artistic interplay that operated in the region, including both the wider cultural differences and the troubled political relationship that existed between England and Wales from the arrival of the Normans up until the Reformation. It is only by examining these wider contexts that it becomes possible to explain why, for example, the cross-border transmission of influence was so lacking in reciprocity; why English screen builders were prepared to draw heavily on the work of their Welsh counterparts, while Welsh screen builders looked almost exclusively to their own for precedents and inspiration. The mixing of divergent cultural and political traditions was made all the more potent because it took place, not across a simple border between England and Wales, but in a Welsh buffer zone ruled and administered by English feudal barons.

Today, the phrase 'the Welsh Marches' retains only a geographical sense, and a vague one at that. Indeed, when people talk of 'the Marches', often they are not referring to Wales at all, but to certain counties on the English side of the border, most notably Herefordshire and Shropshire. Historically, however, the Welsh March[1] had a shape that differed significantly from that understood by the term today. Furthermore, the term originally covered, not a benign and indistinct geographical region, but rather a highly unstable geopolitical land cluster, whose western boundary (if not its eastern one) ebbed to and fro with almost tidal regularity.

The basic configuration of this territorial cluster was well established by the early years of the reign of Henry I (1100–1135).[2] From its pinched, northern end, which incorporated the fringes of latter-day Flintshire, Montgomeryshire and Shropshire, the March widened out to encompass most of Radnorshire, Breconshire, Glamorgan and Monmouthshire, along with some of Herefordshire, before narrowing once again and bearing west to take in southern Carmarthenshire and almost all of Pembrokeshire.

The instigator of the March was William the Conqueror. Having swept imperiously through England in the 11th century, William's heavy cavalry foundered among the Welsh hills. This prompted a tactical rethink, which resulted in lightly armed foot soldiers based in a series of castles along the border being used instead to repel attacks and pursue Welsh raiders. These castles, whilst offering a refuge from Welsh attack, were easily bypassed, however, and their construction did not achieve the desired goal

Map showing the Welsh March

of stabilising Norman control in the region. Furthermore, the Normans were unable to commit the resources, both financial and military, that might have secured a complete or lasting conquest. If the Welsh were to be subdued, another remedy had to be found.

William's solution to the Welsh problem was one of containment.[3] Up and down the border he installed powerful, feudal barons – the Lords Marcher – whose semi-autonomous lordships (eventually about 150 in number and administered from Chester, Shrewsbury and Hereford) taken together effectively formed a *cordon sanitaire* between his kingdom and those of the Welsh rulers to the west. These Anglo-Norman barons, once installed, set about adding to their lands with incursions into Wales in the 11th and 12th centuries. William fitz Osbern, appointed Earl of Hereford in 1067, was one such figure. Having consolidated his border holdings with castles at Hereford, Wigmore, Clifford and Ewyas Harold, he pushed deep into south and west Wales in search of further territories.

Other familiar names also begin to resonate during this era, including the Mortimers of Wigmore, one of whom was to become the self-styled 'Earl of March'. Elsewhere, the de Lacy family held lands in Shropshire, Herefordshire, Gloucestershire and Worcestershire, as well as in the border district of Ewyas. Bernard of Neufmarché acquired estates in Herefordshire and built a castle and established a borough at Brecon. Hugh of Avranches gained Chester, Roger of Montgomery held Shrewsbury, and Robert fitz Hamon, Glamorgan.

Despite the installation of these barons by an English king it should be understood that the March never became a part of England. Nor was it ever strictly a no-man's land between England

and Wales: it remained instead a part of Wales. For this reason, the territories placed under the control of the Marcher lords became known as *Marchia Wallie* (or Marcher Wales), while those remaining in Welsh hands were known as *Pura Wallia*.[4] Wales was thus divided into two spheres of influence; one controlled by the Norman lords, the other by the Welsh princes. Of the latter, the most important figures are Llewelyn ab Iorwerth and Llewelyn ap Gruffydd, both of whom were princes of Gwynedd. They were able to bring all of the Welsh dynasties under their control, and Llewelyn ap Gruffydd was even able to force the English king, Henry III, to acknowledge both his territorial gains and his title, 'Prince of Wales' in 1267 (thus the use of the word 'Principality' to describe *Pura Wallia*).

As befitting the tangled nature of Marcher history, territorial gain was not always secured by force of arms; nor indeed did the Marcher lords automatically come from outside Wales. The relationship between the two cultures in the region, therefore, was not entirely dichotomous. Occasionally, lands were bestowed upon a Welsh chieftain. Alliances, generally through marriage, also saw some lands peacefully inherited. Given the obvious tensions that characterised relations between the Welsh and English, alliances of this type can seem incongruous. However, as Percy Jones points out, 'No racial or social inhibition stood in the way of such marriages'.[5] Thus we find that Llewelyn ab Iorwerth married Joan, the illegitimate daughter of King John; one of Llewelyn's daughters married a Mortimer, and all of Glyn Dwr's daughters married English knights.

For the English kings, the Marcher lordships proved a mixed blessing. Although they formed an effective firewall against the Welsh, the independence and exceptional powers enjoyed by their ruling barons afforded them significant immunity from the Crown. This caused great discomfort to successive English kings, for although the Marcher lords were subjects of the king of England, because the March itself was not a part of England it was not constrained by the English system of government. Neither was this independence restricted to administrative organisation; it also expressed itself in a legal system almost wholly divorced from that of England. The Marcher lords had their own courts in which the Law of the March was administered ('Welsh Law as seen through Norman eyes', as John Davis phrases it[6]).

If the March was characterised by its autonomy and cultural diversity, it was also characterised by its volatility. Given the complexion of those running both *Marchia Wallie* and *Pura Wallia* this can come as no surprise: most were, first and foremost, warlords after all. Nor was conflict restricted to aggression directed towards the Welsh. The Marcher lords were not averse to the odd internecine struggle. With male primogeniture the accepted mode of succession (following the English model) the precarious balance of power in the March was easily upset by the failure to secure a direct male heir. Precisely this situation arose in 1314 with the death of the earl of Gloucester. The subsequent partition of the lordship of Glamorgan shattered the fragile equilibrium of the region. For the combative and jittery Marcher lords the division of these lands represented a serious threat to the balance of power in the March and war was triggered. This sucked in much of the southern March in 1321–22, before spilling over into England. What had begun as a Marcher quarrel in Wales quickly became a full-blown English civil war, leading ultimately to a royal victory and a significant realignment of forces. The episode illustrates perfectly both the incendiary nature of the March and the repercussive quality of unrest in the region.

The March's status as a *cordon sanitaire* was effectively nullified by the Edwardian subjugation of Wales in the late 13th century. The 1284 Statute of Rhuddlan divided Wales between the Principality (land now directly controlled by the Crown) and the remaining semi-autonomous Marcher lordships. The loss of their original *raison d'être* did little to reduce the power or influence of the Marcher lords. On the contrary, with *Pura Wallia* – and thus the Welsh princes – now subdued, the threat from the west had all but dried up. With this distraction (not to mention drain on resources) removed, the Marcher lords were able to focus their energies on converting 'vague lordship over men into precise lordship over land'[7].

The Edwardian conquest was consolidated in two ways: rural colonisation and urban settlement. The former saw the widespread displacement of the Welsh to the poorer, upland regions of Wales. This land held little appeal for the English invaders. They were drawn instead to the fertile, lowland areas in the south, which comprised significant areas of river pasture and meadowland, well suited to both arable and livestock farming. The land in these parts could also be defended adequately (an important consideration given the widespread resentment caused by its usurpation).

In reality, being displaced to the uplands proved relatively unproblematic for the Welsh, for they were already familiar with farming in such areas. As pastoral farmers, they had tended large herds of cattle among the hills, bringing them down to over-winter

Partrishow: Lost high in the hills

at lower altitudes, before heading back to the upland pastures for the summer.[8] Ironically, the displacement of many Welsh to the upland areas may account, at least in part, for the survival here of several spectacular rood-lofts. For those commissioners given the job of hunting down such fittings, many of these churches, tucked away high in the hills, must have seemed all but inaccessible (if they even knew of them). Furthermore, the tensions that existed between England and Wales would surely have made the task of journeying to some remote and hostile village an especially onerous one: better to let sleeping dogs lie perhaps. Whatever the reasons, some of the finest rood-lofts in the Marches – such as those at Partrishow or St. Margarets – are found in hillside churches that remain relatively inaccessible even today.

As well as rural colonisation (and displacement) the partial conquest of Wales was consolidated by urban settlement, specifically in the form of 'planted' towns. The typical pattern for the establishment of a Norman town began with the construction of a motte-and-bailey, initially with a wooden keep. In time, this would be replaced by a more permanent stone castle and a borough would be developed in its shadow, often taking the form of a linear settlement strung out between the castle and a gateway. Usually a church would also be constructed. The new town would act as a local service centre for those garrisoned at the castle. The Normans were the first to plant towns in Wales, but Edward I was also a keen advocate of the policy. Roughly 80 towns were established in Wales between 1070 and 1300. In the southern Marches, Monmouth was one of the first towns to be built by the Normans in Wales. New Radnor is also a planted town, probably laid out at the end of the 13th century.

The Welsh March, as a separate and distinct entity, came to an end in 1489. With the power of its lords drastically eroded, the lawlessness, autonomy and unaccountability of the region no longer tolerated by the Crown, and in an era of European nation-states, it had become a glaring anachronism. By the late 15th century the number of lordships had shrunk to a handful and many were held by absentee landowners. Great swathes of the March now lay in the hands of the king, and consequently the administration of the area increasingly accorded with that of the Principality. The logical conclusion to this process – namely the unification of March and Principality, and the assimilation of all Wales into the English governmental system – was duly confirmed in Henry VIII's Acts of Union (1536–43).

To the shires created on the English pattern following the Edwardian conquests – which included Anglesey, Caernarvonshire, Merionethshire and Flintshire to the north – were added the new shires of Denbighshire, Montgomeryshire, Radnorshire, Breconshire and Monmouthshire to the east. The singular administration of the March, coupled with the restless geopolitics of the Principality beyond, had made Wales a shifting and indistinct entity by the 15th century; the March itself denying the Welsh the satisfaction of a clear demarcation between themselves and the English. One consequence of the unification of March and Principality (and an ironic one given that the intention was also to unite England with Wales) was the creation of just such a line of demarcation in the distinct border formed where the English counties met those of Wales. As A.D. Carr notes, 'the union legislation of 1536 and 1543 did not so much unite Wales with England as unite Wales within itself'.[9]

For Wales, the imposition of the March represents one more chapter in a history dominated by conflict, invasion and attempts at the subjugation of her people.[10] Throughout this history, the characteristic that expresses itself again and again is a nuggety and implacable resistance to external forces and influences. Thus it is that it took roughly 200 years to fully subdue the Welsh, compared with the five or so it took the Normans to yoke the English. Thus it is also that the 'invasions' of Wales have been, for the most part, incomplete campaigns: witness the fact that Wales was never fully Romanised; or that when the Romans withdrew, Wales was the only part of the Western Roman Empire not to be immediately overrun by other invaders, including the Saxons; or again that the Viking assaults were successfully repelled.

This geopolitical background has profoundly informed Welsh national identity. With such fluid territorial organisation, the importance of culture as a means of expressing nationhood has been fundamental. Tellingly, some of the most turbulent periods in Welsh history have coincided with seminal phases in her literature. The 11th and 12th centuries, for example, saw the transcription of the *Mabinogion*, a collection of prose tales described as, 'among the finest flowerings of the Celtic genius and, taken together, a masterpiece of our medieval European literature'.[11] The oldest surviving manuscript in Welsh, the *Black Book of Carmarthen*, dates from the 12th century; and court poetry, composed and performed by the *gogynfeirdd*, also flourished.

The Welsh language itself received a boost with the imposition of Protestantism in the 16th century. A group of Welsh Protestants and humanists successfully argued that the people of Wales could not be converted without a Bible all there could understand. As a result Elizabeth I assented in 1563 to the Act for the translation of the Scriptures. The translated New Testament appeared in 1567,[12] the complete Bible in 1588[13] and Welsh became the only non-state language in Europe to yield a translation of the Scriptures within a century of the Reformation. The future of both Protestantism as the national religion and Welsh as the national language was effectively secured. With Welsh as a spoken language well established, Welsh as a literary language was bolstered by the new dictionaries and grammars produced during this period. In this way the fate of other Celtic languages, such as Cornish and Manx, was avoided.

Elsewhere, wood-carving, and specifically ecclesiastical screen-carving, afforded the Welsh a notable further opportunity for self-expression. Not only was wood more widely used in Welsh churches than in those of England – a factor governed both by its abundance there and its low cost as a material – its aesthetic potential was seized upon more readily and realised with far greater freedom in Wales. Thus it was that by the end of the 15th century, the parish churches of Wales had become the repository for an aesthetic language written out, not with pen and ink, but with gouge and chisel; one that provided Wales with an artistic legacy that was 'as congenial an expression of Welsh medieval aesthetics as a *cywydd* or an *englyn*' (forms of verse).[14]

The Church in the Southern Marches
Little is known about the origins of the early Church in Wales: documentary evidence is non-existent or unreliable, and of pre-Norman buildings we are left with virtually no trace. What we do have – and this certainly indicates Christian usage – are roughly

Partrishow: Carving as an expression of Welsh medieval aesthetics

102

450 inscribed stones, dating from the 5th century up until the 11th century. In their design, many betray links with Ireland and the European mainland. They attest to the presence in Wales of a brand of Christianity related to that of other Celtic-speaking lands, such as Ireland, Scotland and Cornwall, from at least as far back as the 6th century. Worship of certain Celtic saints, too, links the Church in Wales to these lands. Dyfrig, the first of the Celtic saints, can be identified at Henllan (latterly Hentland on Wye in Herefordshire) as far back as the second half of the 5th century. The Celtic influence is also clearly discernible in the tradition of the through-church in Wales and in the carved decoration found on Welsh screenwork.

Prior to the Norman invasion Roman Christianity, widely accepted in England, was widely resisted in Wales. It was not until 768, when Bangor became the first to conform, that Roman Christianity gained a toe-hold in Wales. St. Davids had followed by 928, but it was only after 1107, following the example set by Urban,[15] that the formal submission of the Welsh bishops was secured and the Welsh dioceses were at last incorporated into the province of Canterbury (in England, the promise of obedience to Canterbury had taken place almost 40 years earlier, in 1070).

When the Normans arrived in the 11th century they found a Welsh Church that seemed to them diverse, isolated and hampered by a backward and archaic diocesan structure. As Walker puts it, 'the *clas* [or abbey] church struck no chord of experience or memory [for the Normans]. It was not obviously related to the church with which they were familiar. It did not match the monastic foundations which they took for granted'.[16] The closest equivalent to the Celtic *clas* church in England was the Saxon minster church; a type of monastic mother church, examples of which could be found at Bromyard, Ledbury, Leominster and Stoke Edith in Herefordshire.

For the Normans, the imposition of a unified religion in Wales was another tool with which to consolidate conquest. This led them to actively seek the establishment of monastic settlements in Wales; particularly by the Benedictines, whose severe brand of religious practice seemed to offer an ideal antidote to the divergence and perceived ill-discipline of the native Church. By 1150, helped by endowments from France, the Benedictines had established 17 priories and cells in Wales. With Norman support other orders, including the Augustinians and the Cistercians, were also persuaded to settle there.

The military orders also had a discernible presence in the southern Marches; most notably at wild and unforgettable Garway, where the Templars established a church. The offset

Garway: An impregnable tower

tower of Garway has massively thick walls and, like that of nearby Ewyas Harold, is redolent of fortification and borderland insecurity rather than benign religious practice. The Hospitallers also held land in Wales (in both north and south Wales) associated with their establishment at Halston in Shropshire.

By *c.*1200, the structure of the Welsh Church was beginning to accord more strongly with that of England, a legible hierarchy was in place and the relevant boundaries, rights and privileges had been set down and formally recognised. Throughout the Middle Ages church personnel in both Wales and England essentially occupied one of two tiers (so polarised, they have been called 'two nations'[17]). Generally, those in the top tier were drawn from the educated upper classes, and had experience in royal government (the archbishops of Canterbury and York, for example, were both royal servants by training). In the lower tier was the parochial clergy, responsible for 9,000 or so parish benefices in England, and a further 750 in Wales. Their ranks were swelled by people drawn from the poorly educated lower classes.

The role of the top tier of churchmen was only by definition a pastoral one. In reality, the administration of law may have been of greater import. As John Thomson puts it, 'the language of Episcopal chancery tended to depict the bishop less as a shepherd of souls and more as a judge who corrected offenders'.[18] This legalistic tendency was especially significant during the Reformation when certain bishops (such as John Hooper of Gloucester) spent much of their time making pronouncements and issuing injunctions concerning the treatment of rood-screens. That these were adhered to by the laity suggests that the legal role of the episcopate was widely accepted.

Poverty was a characteristic shared by the clergy in both England and Wales, but the Welsh Church, echoing Welsh society in general, was particularly encumbered by it. The pattern was established in the 12th and 13th centuries with the robbing of church lands by Norman settlers. In 1294, the Welsh Church (by then under the control of Edward I) was taxed for the first time, siphoning off still more of its wealth. Furthermore, Edward, for his part, was not averse to rewarding his officials with some of the richer livings to be had in Wales: a policy which formed part of a wider campaign to moderate both the powers of the Marcher lords and their influence over the Church. Even by *c.*1450, with the Church in Wales undergoing an economic revival of sorts, the total wealth of its religious houses was less than that of Glastonbury in Somerset, while the richest of the Welsh bishoprics – St. Davids – was worth considerably less than that of Carlisle or Chichester in England.[19]

By the 15th and 16th centuries, patterns of church patronage – such a critical factor in the appearance and fitting out of churches – had shifted decisively, and the era saw a democratisation in church construction, improvement and embellishment. The wool trade and a rise in the cost of labour following the Black Death partly account for this shift in patronage. As F.E. Howard comments, 'The merchant was at least as great a man as the soldier, and was beginning to rival the great landholder as a patron of the arts.'[20] Even commoners and the parochial clergy found the wherewithal to build and improve churches. In the southern Marches, Thomas ab Ieuan, a vicar in Brecon, gave generously to the building and fitting out of several local churches, including Brecon Priory. Elsewhere parishioners themselves set about raising funds for the

De Scta Crucis, tall de Henle die ven'is pxt ant fm sci michis Anno rr E tercii (sc'do)		
Johnes le telor	.	ijs.
Johnes (Mortua)	.	xijd.
Willms Lucas	.	iiijd.
Galfridus Sely	.	viijd.
Th de (Culh'm)	.	iiij.
Walts Moryon	.	vijd.
Will de Selne	.	ijd.
Galfridus de Mourton	.	xijd.
Henr	.	vj.
Will	.	xijd.
Henr atte Steplond Phure		ijs.
Adm Clemenc	.	vid. xijd.
Henr le coupe	.	vjd.
Wills le Reade	.	vjd.
Henr Tovey	.	vid. xijd.
Ric Bevane	.	iiijd.
Joh Altesor	.	iiijd.
Rog'us Aleyne	.	vjd.
Rob. Brown	.	vjd. 1vs.
Th Nichole	.	xijd.
Th Huberd	.	xxd.
Willms Dreu	.	xijd. 1vs.
Henr Reede Phure	.	vjd.
Joh atte Wyfold	.	vjd.
Willms le Granger	.	vjd.
Walt. La .	.	xiid. 1vs.
Th le Wastover	.	iiijd.
Johnes de Hurle	.	vjd.
Endorsed		
Walts Lucas	.	xxd.
Adm. Lea	.	vjd.
Johnes ate Wyfold	.	vjd.
Pistator	.	xiiijd.
Augi la Geneve solu.		vjd.
Walts Morion solu	.	vijd.
		Sm xxjs. id.

repair of their church, or left monies in wills and in the form of legacies and bequests.

Elsewhere, other sources and other motives informed change. In England, wealthy guilds (such as the Palmers' Guild in Ludlow) were responsible for the often lavish enrichment of churches.[21] The 15th century was also characterised by a rise in the popularity of pilgrimages. As well as travelling the well-trodden routes abroad (to the likes of Santiago de Compostella) pilgrims also

Left: A parchment roll from the reign of Edward III containing a list of benefactors to the Rood at Henley-on-Thames, graphically illustrating both the democratisation of church embellishment, and the eagerness to put money into the purchasing of the Rood in particular

visited sites in Britain. The popularity of these sites, with their shrines, relics, sacred images and Roods, gave further impetus to the building and improvement of churches, for much of this work was paid for by the pilgrims themselves. Thus it was that worshippers would pay homage to the *Crog Aberhonddu* (the Cross of Brecon), or the important local shrine over the border at Chester and make donations during their visit. On the whole, though, the 15th century was not one characterised by intense religious devotion, and other factors undoubtedly informed much church building and embellishment during this era, including civic pride, self-aggrandisement, and inter-parish one-upmanship.

For churches, the 15th century also saw the rise to near-universal prominence of the rood-screen and rood-loft in England and Wales. However, the importance of this particular fitting relative to the architecture of the church in which it stood differed greatly between England and Wales; a factor which, when unpicked, largely accounts for their divergent screen-building traditions. In both the domestic and religious spheres England could boast, by the later Middle Ages, a distinctive native architecture. It may have shown regional variation, but it was the result of nationwide cultural interplay and was not stymied by insular builders or patrons, or by an economy of means. Informing this architectural style was a vocabulary of recognisable design elements, including chancel arches, hood moulds, string courses and window types at once traceable from district to district.

Church screenwork on the other hand (in the Midlands at least) was often the product of a local carpenter for whom the job to make and carve a church screen might represent a one-off commission. Although there was a degree of cross-fertilisation the lack of a workshop structure distributing products of a consistent design led to diverse screenwork that conformed only loosely to recognisable types. With Midland church screenwork there is no sense of the jealous guarding of the purity of a woodworking bloodline. Rather, Midland screen-builders saw their products as essentially utilitarian rather than decorative, and were suitably pragmatic when it came to their sources. In the southern Marches the English screen-builders, had they had any care for aesthetic loyalty, would surely have turned to the east for inspiration. However they did not. Recognising the comparative weakness of woodworking as a craft in counties such as Staffordshire and Warwickshire, they generally turned instead to the west, and the screenwork of Wales, for inspiration.

Conversely, to the means called upon to express a coherent sense of Welsh national identity, architecture cannot be added.

Kemeys Commander: Simple, local design

This had profound implications for church screenwork in Wales, greatly accounting for its insularity. It has been persuasively argued that medieval Wales essentially lacked a distinctive native architecture,[22] because domestic building was local in both its materials and builders, and because it was produced with an economy of resources and with very little interplay between one district and another. This unadorned and highly localised character, lacking a clear national language of design or detailing, was reflected in church building, and may account for 'the absence of a chancel arch, a rugged and often shapeless arcade and the avoidance of strings, buttresses and mouldings'.[23] Recognising that church architecture was not a vital repository of national identity, Welsh builders were happy to borrow heavily from England. Thus it is that Gresford in Denbighshire for example, arguably the finest late medieval parish church in Wales (and a Welsh church as opposed to one planted by the English), has been described as 'the perfect Cheshire church in Wales'.[24]

The lack of architectural style in Welsh medieval building may in turn partly account for the freedom and inventiveness of Welsh screen-carving, and surely yields a strong argument for the refusal to permit English influence to be felt here. The craft of screen-carving – in the absence of a distinctive architectural style – afforded a precious opportunity for national self-expression. The workshop system, meanwhile, meant that artistic interplay between districts could take place and a native aesthetic could be maintained; one that had to remain free of external influences if it was to remain truly distinctive and truly Welsh.

THE SCREENWORK OF THE SOUTHERN MARCHES

Often there is a touch of Welsh genius to be found wedded to the more sober and solid achievements of the English craftsmen, a fascinating alembic of thought and artifice used to excellent purpose which has left an unmistakable mark upon its products. F.H. Crossley & M.H. Ridgway

In their construction the rood-screens of the southern Marches (and Wales in particular) generally consist of four main posts and three beams, which together form a sturdy and adaptable framework with a strongly rectangular appearance. The horizontal members comprise (from the bottom up) a sill, middle rail and head-beam. The vertical members consist of two wall standards, two door standards, a series of mullions in the upper half of the screen and muntins in the lower half. The joints used are usually mortise and tenon, fastened with wooden pegs. These basic components are common to rood-screens on both sides of the border, though in England the main verticals of the wall and door standards are sometimes accompanied by continuous intermediate standards in between (for instance, at Aymestrey, Bosbury and Dilwyn in Herefordshire). These latter screens are all vaulted and of arched form, making them less rectangular in appearance.

The Sill

The sill of the rood-screen always lies at floor level. Although it may span the width of the nave unbroken, more often it is punctuated by the doorway (which is always located in the middle of the screen, giving a sill of two equal lengths).[1] Occasionally, continuous sills lie hidden beneath later floors (as at Culmington in Shropshire and at Burghill in Herefordshire), or have been cut through at a later date (as at Llananno in Radnorshire). Sills are not usually moulded, but tend to be either squared or chamfered (even when the screen is otherwise elaborately carved). The sill at Llangwm in Monmouthshire is an exception. Its western face has been carved with flattened trefoils contained in a series of triangular compartments. As well as providing one of the four sides of the outer framing of the screen, the sill typically carries a continuous groove for the boarding of the wainscot above. It may also have mortise holes for the wainscot muntins (if these are constructional and not 'planted on' to the wainscot panels purely for decorative effect).

The Head-beam

The uppermost beam of the rood-screen is the head-beam (sometimes called the top-beam). In the case of Welsh screens of an early date this is usually a massive timber beam, its ends typically, though not always, embedded into the nave walls to the north and south. Occasionally the head-beam stops short of the wall and its weight is taken solely by the wall standards, as at Pixley in Herefordshire; or, on rare occasions, is supported upon corbels, as at Gwernesney in Monmouthshire.

Monumental and severely unadorned head-beams of an early date can be found at Merthyr Cynog, Llandeilo'r Fan, Llanelieu and Llanfigan in Breconshire, and at Pixley and Stretford in Herefordshire. The head-beams in these cases are variously chamfered: sometimes to give a flat face, as at Llandeilo and Stretford; and sometimes to give a big quarter-round, as at Pixley. Mouldings, where they exist, are rudimentary: Llanelieu, Lanfigan and Merthyr Cynog share simple quarter-rounds between fillets, Stretford has a half-round terminating at either end with a crude leaf form, while Landeilo shows a round moulding upon its eastern face (below the chamfer) that corresponds with a hollow on its western face. Pixley and Merthyr Cynog also share a curious serrated moulding, prefiguring the drop-cresting popular on later screens, but here carved in the solid.

As a part of the framework of the rood-loft above, head-beams often show blocked mortise holes in their western and top faces for the missing parts of the loft framing. Those punctuating the western face are for the joists of the loft floor, while those in the top face are for the framing members of the eastern loft parapet or tympanum (often a groove will also be found here, for the accompanying boarding). The screen at Merthyr Cynog has filled mortise holes along its western face, together with holes and a slot in its top face for the missing loft tympanum. With later head-beams, so as not to interrupt the face upon which carved trails would be set, the floor joists would be slotted, not into the middle of the western face, but into the top of that face.

Later on, the head-beam became less massive as the wood-worker's understanding of his material grew and he sought for greater delicacy of effect. As well as an actual reduction in bulk, the once-ungainly beams were enlivened by carved trails. Where once the head-beam jutted out over the screen, it was now almost flush with the screen or it curved in to meet the top of the screen. The trail was rarely carved directly onto the face of the beam, but in openwork from planking, which was then fixed to the head-beam. In order that this work could be seen to best effect (i.e. with plenty of shadow detail giving depth to the modelling) the trail would often be convex in cross-section, then set against a concave moulding on the head-beam. Such a configuration is immensely effective, and results in the head-beam appearing lighter and less ungainly.

The delicacy of the treatment of the head-beam could be enhanced by the addition of top- and drop-cresting (as at St. Margarets in Herefordshire). Occasionally, the decoration of the head-beam was updated, as it was in the parclose screen at St. Weonards in Herefordshire, where a Gothic vine trail has given way to applied work of Renaissance influence. In vaulted screens, such as those at Aymestrey, Bosbury and Dilwyn in Herefordshire, the head-beam is entirely hidden by the vaulting and as such requires no decorative treatment.

The apparent 'double head-beams' at Withington and Elton in Herefordshire are in fact nothing of the sort. In both cases it appears that, following the dismantling of the rood-loft, certain beams from the rood-loft – including the bressumer or top-beam – were re-used to give the screens a re-configured cornice. Crestings, generally too big for the screen, were also added to head-beams to provide a decorative 'crown' to the screen following the dismantling of a rood-loft (as a result of the Elizabethan Order of 1561 and in the 19th century). Such crestings can be found at Canon Pyon, Brinsop and Bishop's Frome in Herefordshire. Sometimes brattishing also tops the head-beam, as it does the middle rail (for example, at Brecon Cathedral).

The Middle Rail

Between the sill and head-beam runs the third of the horizontal members: the middle rail. The term is something of a misnomer, as the middle rail almost never comes midway between the sill and head-beam. The typical Welsh middle rail (e.g. Cascob's in Radnorshire) is set well below the mid-point. In the case of the low screens of Wales, this may have had more to do with maintaining the proportions of the screen than with any issues to do with religious usage. In England the opposite may have been the case. During the later Middle Ages, shifts in religious practice led to the partial demystification of the chancel, which in turn led to the development of rood-screens of greater transparency. The simplest way to achieve this was to lower the height of the solid portion of the screen (the wainscot). Thus, at Aymestrey the height of the wainscot is just one quarter that of the rood-screen.

The treatment of the middle rail differs fundamentally depending on whether the screen is of English or Welsh origin. In the latter case the middle rail always runs unbroken between the wall and door standards (unless the screen is an English import). In the former case, however, the middle rail is usually broken by continuous intermediate standards that extend unbroken from the sill up to the head-beam. This rule brings into question whether the one-time presbytery screen of Brecon Cathedral was in fact made in Wales or, as its punctuated middle rail would suggest, England.

In broad terms, the middle rail followed a similar evolutionary path to that of the head-beam. Thus, early middle rails are often plain and unduly massive (e.g. Pixley's in Herefordshire) or are chamfered.[2] Later middle rails tend to be of more compact cross-section and to exhibit a wide range of decorative treatments. Sometimes, the middle rail is carved to return the mouldings of the standards and mullions in the top half of the screen, or to return those of the standards and muntins in the wainscot (at Llandefalle in Breconshire it is carved to do both). In the parclose screen at St. Weonards in Herefordshire, the attractive reeding of the middle rail marries up with the standards only (here the mouldings of the mullions and muntins are not returned by the middle rail).

At Llananno and Bosbury the middle rail has a flat channel between chamfers, seemingly to house a now-lost enrichment (though there is no evidence for this). Carved decoration, where it does appear, is almost always carved in the solid. Thus, at Dilwyn and Aymestrey the western face of the middle rail carries a series of four-petalled flowers in square compartments. At Canon Pyon the flower or leaf forms are of a similar character, but are contained within the triangular compartments formed by a continuous zig-zag. Occasionally, the middle rail incorporates an openwork component, sometimes between two solid rails. The screen at Brinsop, although much altered in the 19th century, features a series of roses held by cusps within squares, thus giving a band of openwork quatrefoils. This is flanked by solid rails; the upper one strongly reminiscent of that found at Llanegryn in Merionethshire (which is also a double rail enclosing an openwork component). Double rails of this type can be found at Ludlow and Bettws-y-Crwyn in Shropshire, and at Old Radnor in Radnorshire. At Little Malvern in Worcestershire a unique (to the southern Marches) stepped middle rail exists; the higher parts affording privacy to the choir seating beyond).

The Standards

The typical Welsh rood-screen has four main posts: two wall standards and two door standards. The wall standards are generally framed up between the head-beam and the sill. However, an early configuration saw the wall standards extend up to the wall plate and tie-beam overhead, thus becoming integrated with the roof timbers and the skeleton of the building itself. This configuration exists at Pixley and Stretford in Herefordshire, and at Disserth, Bettws Clyro, Aberedw, and Michaelchurch-on-Arrow in Radnorshire. The wall standards are usually moulded upon their inner faces only, in order to match the design of the mullions

Characteristic uprights of the southern Marches: cross-sectional views of a typical standard (left) and mullion (right). With slight variations such mouldings can be found at Middleton, Aymestrey, English Bicknor, Shelsley Walsh, Ludlow, Culmington, Lydbury North, Llanvair Waterdine, Eaton Bishop, St. Weonards, Tedstone Delamere, Stoke Lacy, Moreton-on-Lugg, Burghill, (& etc.)

and the muntins. Their western and eastern faces almost never carry any decorative treatment. Those at Withington and Yatton in Herefordshire are exceptional, for the western side of each is carved with attenuated Gothic loop lights.

Whereas the eastern and western faces of the wall standards are usually left plain, those of the door standards often carry an attached shaft known as a boutell. These often spring from bases at floor or sill level and can be rounded or squared. On screens that are not surmounted by a rood-loft, the boutell shafts often terminate in a crocketed pinnacle (as at Stretford) or, in the case of a squared shaft, have one or more offsets. In vaulted screens, the fan vault springs from a cap topping the boutell (as at Dilwyn and Bosbury). The screen at Michaelchurch in Herefordshire has the highly unusual feature of rounded shafts on the inner faces of the door standards, rather than on the western or eastern faces. This appears to have been done as part of a refurbishment programme that also saw matching shafts attached to the inner faces of the mullions of each light.

Squared shafts can be found on the door standards at Trostre (eastern and western faces), at Kemeys Commander (western face only) and at Bettws Newydd (eastern face only), all of which are in Monmouthshire. The rood-screen now at Llangurig, a copy of the original, has the extremely unusual feature of a carved trail running up the western faces of the door standards. A similar treatment appeared at Newtown in Montgomeryshire. Here, the boutells carried an ascending twisted leaf and berry design. Carved figures survive on the door standards at Dilwyn (as bases in the form of fierce heads) and at Vowchurch in Herefordshire (at the top of the standards in the form of Adam and Eve). In early screens the door standards are sometimes severely plain, as at Pixley and Llanfigan, where two huge curved timbers have been carved to give a cave door-like entranceway.

The Mullions

Between the wall and door standards, rood-screens have vertical subdivisions in the form of mullions above middle rail height and muntins below. The mullions divide the screen up into bays, the number partly dependant upon the width of the screen. Thus, the tiny rood-screen in the divided church of Gwernesney has just two bays flanking a central doorway of four bays, while the expansive rood-screen in the undivided church of Canon Pyon has eight bays to either side of a central doorway of four bays.

For mullions, a wide variety of mouldings is found, and often the design used upon the western face does not correspond with that found upon the eastern face. Early mullions tend to have flat or hollow chamfered corners, while later ones tend to be thinner and to employ (often in combination) ogees and half-rounds, divided one from another by fillets. The inner faces of mullions often carry a groove into which the tracery heads would be slotted; the remainder of the channel down to the middle rail being taken by thin mouldings. Sometimes the slots for the tracery heads would be cut right through the mullions, as at Gwernesney (in the parclose screen now at the back of the church), echoing the treatment found in some screenwork of the 13th century.

The most unusual mullions in the southern Marches are those at Llandinabo and Foy in Herefordshire. They owe a conspicuous debt to French Renaissance design, and are exceptional for not being uniform across the screen (those at Llandinabo are of four designs; those at Foy are of three). Indeed, the mullions at Foy are not even uniform for the whole of their length, but change design midway up.

In Welsh rood-screens each bay (as defined by the mullions) is almost always square-headed and is usually quite narrow. In English screens, however, the major bays described by the standards are often arched and sometimes then subdivided (typically into three lights) to give the appearance of a Perpendicular window. Such a configuration can be seen at Bosbury and Dilwyn. The rood-screens at Old Radnor and Aymestrey also have arched heads, but these are narrower and are not subdivided by mullions.

The Muntins

The final vertical elements in the composition, the muntins, also show a wide variety of configurations. They are sometimes used structurally, as integral parts of the framework of the screen. In this way they can support a long and heavy middle rail (as at Llanbister in Radnorshire). Elsewhere, they are used merely as decorative elements and are 'planted on' to the wainscot. Used in this way, they tend to be deployed to line up with the mullions above. However, even when they do line up, they may not correspond in terms of design. Thus, at Burghill in Herefordshire, the slender and delicately-moulded mullions are in line with, but do not match, the wide and flat muntins below. Visually, there is clearly some merit in using muntins that correspond perfectly with the mullions above (as they do at Llangwm). However, again and again in Welsh screenwork this was not done. With the decorative emphasis coming above middle rail height, and specifically upon the rood-loft, the screen-builder may have decided that he should concentrate his efforts on these areas, perhaps calculating that a hierarchical treatment of enrichment was desirable as it would help to draw the eye upwards.

The mouldings used for muntins echo those found elsewhere on the screen. Simple chamfers are frequently seen, as are half-rounds, hollows and ogees (in a variety of configurations). The muntins of the rood-screen at Lydbury North in Shropshire are extremely unusual. They consist of two mouldings side by side, each consisting of paired ogees. Those belonging to the screen at Eaton Bishop and the portable pulpit at Hereford Cathedral, which are related to the standards at Yatton and Withington, are also highly unusual, incorporating as they do very narrow Gothic loop lights. Very occasionally, the wainscot of a rood-screen will have no muntins at all, just plain boards, as at Stretford in Herefordshire.

The Wainscot

Wainscot treatments vary in the southern Marches, but typically the gap between the sill and the middle rail is filled with plain panelling, usually consisting of boards inserted vertically and butted flush together. Where carved decoration does appear it is sometimes carved in the solid; as at Llangasty Tal-y-Llyn in Breconshire, Shelsley Walsh in Worcestershire, and at Aymestrey, Sutton St. Nicholas and St. Weonards in Herefordshire (the last four of which feature linenfold panelling). Elsewhere, the decoration is planted on. At Llangwm (albeit in a heavily restored screen) and at Old Radnor and Eaton Bishop, the blind tracery heads of the wainscot correspond with the openwork tracery heads above. At Dilwyn, Bishop's Frome, Stoke Lacy and Staunton-on-Wye in Herefordshire, and at Alfrick in Worcestershire, small

cusped spandrels survive, carved with a range of leaf and flower designs.

In the southern Marches, wainscot panels are only very rarely pierced. At Bosbury three bays to either side of the central doorway contain elaborate openwork panels (however, this screen was considerably meddled with in the 19th century, and this may represent a later configuration). The wainscot of the rood-screen at Lydbury North has a series of lovely, small openwork panels featuring cusped diamond shapes holding small flowers, essentially forming quatrefoils. At Llandinabo in Herefordshire a series of small squints in the form of Gothic loop lights punctuate the wainscot just below the middle rail. The importance of wainscot panelling to the coherence of a screen becomes strikingly apparent when this panelling is removed. This has been done at Dilwyn (with both the rood and parclose screens) and at Pixley. The result in both cases has been catastrophic, with the screen's legibility as a partition all but destroyed, and the visual composition thoroughly undone.

The Tracery

The tracery heads found in the southern Marches show immense diversity (where they do not, for example, in Devon and Somerset). They are usually uniform in their design across the screen, but occasionally vary from bay to bay (as they do at Llananno, and at Llanwnnog and Newtown in Montgomeryshire). Sometimes the heads are carved upon both sides, as at Tedstone Delamere in Herefordshire; and sometimes upon the western face only, as at Leinthall Starkes in the same county. The tracery and its motifs can be big and bold, as at Montgomery in Montgomeryshire and at Aylton; or small and fine, as at Llangwm.

Although a wide variety of tracery designs can be discerned, the vast majority draw from a surprisingly modest palette of motifs and elements. There are three principal arch forms used within tracery heads: the rounded arch, the pointed arch and the ogee arch. In addition, there is the trefoil, quatrefoil (variously formed) and circle, the Gothic loop light (sometimes double-headed), cusping and sub-cusping, and finally a range of foliage-based elements, including crockets and flowers. By variously drawing from this palette almost inexhaustible variety is possible.

In Welsh screenwork the tracery heads were always carved as separate panels for each bay, before being set into grooves in the mullions and the underside of the head-beam. In the screenwork of some Midland counties the tracery heads are formed from a continuous plank slotted through the tops of the mullions. Although the tracery heads should usually be 'read' as a part of the composition and embellishment of the rood-screen, occasionally they have been deployed in the service of the rood-loft above. This is certainly the case with the screenwork of Llananno and Llanwnnog, where the tracery heads form a decorative fringe, or drop-tester, beneath the loft. That the tracery should be read in this way is made clear by the composition of the loft coving, which echoes the tracery heads in blind form. At Old Radnor in Radnorshire, the frilly and shallow tracery serves to draw the eye to the lierne vault above.

The Rood-loft

Screens of Welsh origin (and some English screens showing strong Welsh influence) are not vaulted, but instead employ coving; sometimes of a shallow pitch, as at Llananno and St. Margarets; sometimes of a steeper pitch, as at Llangwm, Beguildy in Radnorshire, and at Kenderchurch and Eyton in Herefordshire; and sometimes very deep, as at Burghill. At Partrishow in Breconshire and Foy in Herefordshire a flat soffit is employed. Loft coving is generally divided up into panels by a lattice of ribs, with carved bosses at the junctions. The panels were occasionally carved (as at Llananno and Llanwnnog), and were generally painted (as at Beguildy). Screens of English origin – such as those at Ludlow, Usk in Monmouthshire, Old Radnor, Bosbury, Dilwyn, and Aymestrey – are variously vaulted, with the vaulting springing to the west only (at Aymestrey), or to both the east and west (at Bosbury). Some fragments of a vaulted screen survive at Ledbury in Herefordshire.

The beams associated with the rood-loft (where this fitting survives) share many characteristics with those of the rood-screen. Like the head-beam of the rood-screen, the lower of the two western beams of the loft – the bressumer – is usually embedded into the nave walls to the north and south. However, additional support is occasionally found in the form of wall posts on corbels (as at Llangwm and Withington), or full length posts (as at St. Margarets and Burghill). In all four cases, curved spandrels have been used at the junction of post and beam. These are usually carved and carry a continuation of the drop-cresting that runs along the underside of the beam.

Carved spandrels can also be found at Fawley and Aylton in Herefordshire, and at Bronllys and Llywel in Breconshire. The bressumer (and thus the rood-loft coving) at Burghill is supported upon four posts, which have elaborately moulded western faces, but flat backs. The bressumer at Bettws Newydd and St.

Margarets is supported by just two, the latter encrusted with fine tabernacle work and having niches for now-missing statuettes. The bressumer at Llanelieu also has four posts equally spaced, thus mirroring the arrangement of the rood-screen to the east. The arch braces found here (and at Llanfigan and Merthyr Cynog in the same county) are clearly structural, but prefigure the carved spandrels found on later screens.

In churches where the rood-loft has been removed (and occasionally in churches where the screen below has also gone) the bressumer sometimes survives. This is the case at Pipe and Lyde in Herefordshire, at Langattock Lingoed in Monmouthshire, and at Shelsley Walsh. Of all the beams associated with the rood-screen and loft, the bressumer was generally the most heavily enriched, so its occasional retention is perhaps understandable. The bressumer at Llangwm, for instance, has three carved trails divided one from another by two further delicate bands of enrichment (giving five altogether) and is fringed with both top- and drop-cresting.

Often, when such a beam is retained it is re-set in a new position and is then misidentified as a rood-beam. Identifying a beam that has been removed from its original context can be done by examining the distribution of mortise holes in the faces of the beam. By doing this it becomes possible, for example, to identify the two beams now forming wall posts at Kenchester in Herefordshire as the bressumer (north wall) and the head-beam (south wall). Mortise holes in the top of a beam and in its eastern face – for the loft parapet and the floor joists respectively – make it certain that the former beam was once a bressumer. Mortise holes in the underside and in the top of the western face – for the

screen standards and the floor joists respectively – make it certain that the latter beam was once a head-beam. At Little Malvern there never was a rood-loft and the beam over the screen here is, for once, a genuine rood-beam (as evidenced by the sizable mortise holes in its top face for the three rood-figures).

The top- or rood-beam of the rood-loft generally corresponds with the bressumer below, but may not be quite so deep or heavily enriched. Between these two beams the loft parapet (like the wainscot of the screen below) comprises a series of muntins that frame up the panels in between. The loft muntins may or may not correspond, in either their design or distribution, with other vertical elements in the composition. At Llangwm, all of the vertical elements – the screen muntins and mullions, the coving ribs and the loft muntins – line up precisely. At Llanfilo in Breconshire none of these elements line up. Like screen muntins, loft muntins display a wide range of treatments. One unusual feature is the application of carved strips of decoration to the chamfers of the muntin. Such an arrangement can be seen at Llangwm, and probably once existed at Partrishow in Breconshire. Related to these are the attached triangular buttresses on the loft front at Llanfilo.

The panels of the loft parapet might receive either painted or carved decoration. Carved decoration is commonly in the form of openwork (as at Llangwm, Bettws Newydd and Mamhilad in Monmouthshire, and at Partrishow and Montgomery). At Partrishow the whole panel is given over to extremely fine Perpendicular grid tracery; at Mamhilad sturdy tracery heads (doubtless once matching those of the screen below) are employed. At Bettws Newydd and Montgomery both openwork and applied carving is employed. Sometimes the loft front is not pierced at all (as at Llananno, St. Margarets and Cascob). At Llananno, applied carving, including tabernacle work and figures, is employed to luxuriant effect. Painted decoration, in the form of a series of saints, survives at Strensham in Worcestershire, and may have graced the parapets at St. Margarets in Herefordshire and Cascob in Radnorshire.

The treatment of the eastern parapet of the rood-loft (as at Llananno and Llanwnnog) is usually similar to that of the western parapet, though less elaborate (in terms of both the enrichment applied to the beams and the parapet front). Llanegryn in Merionethshire provides a rare instance of an eastern parapet that is far richer than the western parapet. The top-beam of the eastern parapet was sometimes used as the rood-beam, thus locating the rood figures directly against the tympanum. At Llanelieu, this beam carries the mortise for the foot of the missing Rood. The Rood seems to have occupied a corresponding beam at Bettws Newydd.

Colour

Although colour still plays an important role in the screenwork of East Anglia and the West-country, the same cannot be said of the southern Marches. Here, virtually all has been stripped off and not replaced. One exception is the screen at Usk. This extends across both the nave and the north aisle, and here the nave portion has been brightly re-painted (as part of the unforgiving restoration of the screen in the 19th century; plate 12). The aisle portion, which contains more original fabric than the nave portion, has been left untouched. The screen at Llangwm features some modest re-colouring, added by its restorer, Seddon, and apparently based on traces of original pigment. The lavish paintwork of the rood-screen at Newtown, which included a series of saints, was finally pickled off in 1875, but was in a fairly complete state as late as 1829.

Elsewhere, the stone screen to the Audley chapel in Hereford Cathedral is unusual for retaining much of its late medieval scheme, which incorporates depictions of Christ and various saints and Apostles (plate 10). Saints also dominate the loft front (now at the west end of the church) at Strensham in Worcestershire. The colour decoration at Llanelieu, with its stencilled flowers and pink ground, is nothing like so sophisticated, yet remains unforgettable. Some original colour also survives on the fragments at Weobley and Llanfigan, and some later gilding on the screen at Gwernesney. The coving at Beguildy and the celure at Almeley share a chequerboard design with bold Tudor roses, much of it original work. The most colourful of all southern Marches screenwork – the Gilbert Scott choir screen for Hereford Cathedral – belongs to the 19th century and now stands in the V&A in London.

Provenance and Origin: Wales

In Wales (as in England) efforts to understand the provenance of rood-screens and to chart patterns of influence have been severely hampered by the loss of roughly 90% of Britain's late medieval screenwork. While some interrelated screens can still be found, other screens exist as standalones, marooned in lonely hillside churches. The story of church screenwork, once intricate and comprehensive, has become sketchy and incomplete. With an unbroken narrative lost long ago, ecclesiologists have had to try to piece together the story from a dwindling supply of complete screens and scattered fragments.

In this regard, Wales has been especially well served by two ecclesiologists in particular. In 1943, Volume XCVII of the Welsh academic journal, *Archaeologia Cambrensis* carried the first in a series of papers on Welsh screenwork, by Fred H. Crossley and Maurice M. Ridgway. The first piece, a detailed introduction to the subject, was followed at regular intervals by papers analysing the screens of each of the Welsh counties in turn. The series concluded in 1962 (almost 20 years after it had begun) with a paper discussing border influences and featuring a distribution map of Welsh screen types.

Through their research, Crossley and Ridgway found that church screens in Wales often came from one of two principal sources. Firstly, there were the major workshop centres, whose considerable output of clearly identifiable products was distributed widely and without regard to district. The best example of this type is the Newtown centre in Montgomeryshire, whose products survive in at least four counties, as far north as Daresbury in Cheshire, and as far south as Llananno in Radnorshire. Secondly, there were a number of minor workshop centres, whose output was modest and whose distribution and influence was essentially local. One such group of closely related screens originating from a minor centre can be found in Denbighshire, in the churches at Clocaenog, Gyffylliog, Llanelidan, and Llanrhudd.

A significant number of screens do not fall readily into either of these two categories. The rood-screens and associated lofts in the churches at Partrishow and Llanfilo in Breconshire, for example, have no obvious relations in Wales or England. This can mean one of two things. The screen and loft in question may once have belonged to a group sharing identifiable characteristics, but is now the only example left of its type (the others having gone unrecorded, or been destroyed or mutilated beyond recognition). The second explanation is that the screen in question may be a genuine one-off; the singular product of a woodcarver, or group of woodcarvers, who were insufficiently influenced by existing work to create something identifiably related to other screens.

In Wales as a whole, Crossley and Ridgway identified 13 Welsh screen types.[3] Outside the southern Welsh Marches, the richest area for screenwork is north Wales. Here the pair identified three main groups. Besides the Denbighshire type mentioned above, they also discovered notable clusters in the Dee Valley in Merionethshire and on the Lleyn Peninsula in the north-west. The Dee Valley group (which includes examples in Montgomeryshire) comprises nine screens: at Llanfor, Llandderfel, Tal-y-Llyn, Gwyddelwern, Llanfrothen and Llandrillo in Merionethshire, and at Pennant Melangell, Meifod and Trelystan in Montgomeryshire. The defining characteristics of the group are their deep middle rails and semicircular panelled wainscots with patterned squints. The screens are dispersed over a fairly wide area, suggesting that they came from a larger workshop centre of some import. The Lleyn Peninsula group includes the rood-screens at Llanengan, Llanbedrog, Llanarmon, Llanaelhaiarn, and an outlier in the form of the rood-screen and loft at Llanegryn in Merionethshire to the south. The defining characteristics of this group include continuous uprights extending unbroken from the sill to the head-beam, a lack of intermediate mullions, wide bays, and elaborate drop-cresting in place of tracery heads.

The richest area for identifiable church screenwork in Wales is the southern Welsh Marches. Here, Crossley and Ridgway discovered no less than eight distinct screen types. The most important of these is the Newtown or Montgomeryshire type, examples of which can be found at Llanwnnog, Newtown, Llanidloes, and Bettws Cedewain in Montgomeryshire; at Llananno, Llanbadarn Fynydd, and Llandegley in Radnorshire; at Daresbury and Runcorn in Cheshire, and at Downton in Herefordshire. The ten examples of screenwork from the Newtown centre share a pronounced rectilinear construction, and have plain wainscot panels divided up by constructional muntins, often aligned with the mullions above.

However, it is not for these characteristics that the screenwork from this centre – including that found at Newtown itself, Llananno and Llanwnnog – is famed: it is for its decorative treatment. The enrichment of this screenwork is focused in three main fields: the tracery heads, the soffit panels beneath the loft, and the carved trails. Of these, the most significant are the tracery heads and soffit panels. For, whilst the carved trails are not dissimilar to those found in the West Country, the tracery heads and soffit panels, with their free and wilfully inconsistent treatment, are entirely without echo in England (or indeed, elsewhere in Wales). Adding significantly to the importance and appeal of the work from this centre is the very high quality of much of the carving.

Of the screens and lofts from the Newtown centre, those at Llananno in Radnorshire and Llanwnnog in Montgomeryshire are substantially complete. The screenwork at Newtown in the same county and at Llanbadarn Fynydd in Radnorshire is mutilated, but enough survives to give an idea of how it must once have looked. Fragmentary remains survive at Daresbury in Cheshire and Bettws Cedewain in Montgomeryshire; while the screens and lofts that once stood at Runcorn in Cheshire, Llanidloes in Montgomeryshire, and Downton in Herefordshire are known only from records. Evidently, the Newtown workshop represents a major centre for church screenwork, producing a significant quantity of work and distributing it widely throughout Wales, and even into England.

Allied to the screens of the Newtown centre is a clutch of three screens belonging to a minor Montgomeryshire type. The screen at Llangurig is a Victorian reconstruction of 1878, from drawings of the original screen by the Rev. John Parker in 1828. However, fragments of the original screen survive at Glansevern House, Berriew. The screen at Llangynyw survives in something like its original form, while over the border in Shropshire the screen at Llanyblodwel has been much restored. The group displays a blend

Bronllys: The carved spandrels

Bettws Clyro: Wall-post extending above the head-beam

of characteristics including some elements apparently drawn from the Newtown palette, and others typically found in Herefordshire and Gloucestershire screenwork.

Also allied to the screenwork of the Newtown centre are the screens at Llywel and Bronllys in Breconshire. Their construction is characterised by a bressumer supported by a triple arcade. Neither screen is anything like as ornate as the Newtown screens further north, but both retain attractively carved foliate spandrels. The wall standards at Llywel are distinctive, and are related to those at Llanbister in Radnorshire. They each have a boutell that halts some way below the beam and is topped by a moulded cap. The screen at Llywel survives in mutilated form, but the screen at Bronllys is substantially complete. Both screens now stand at the west end of their respective churches; Llywel's beneath the tower arch.

Moving south, a cluster of closely related screens has been identified in Radnorshire; at Aberedw, Disserth, Michaelchurch, Bettws Clyro, Cregrina, Llandegley and Pilleth. The screens belonging to these churches are distinguished by their wall-posts, which extend from the sill up to the roof line (specifically to the wall-plate or tie-beam). In their construction they have links

with the screenwork of the Breconshire and Cardiganshire groups described below. The screen at Aberedw is perhaps the best surviving example of the type. However, those at Llandegley and Cregrina are also substantially complete. The screen at Bettws Clyro survives in a mutilated form, while parts only survive at Disserth and Michaelchurch. Nothing remains of the Radnorshire screen that once stood at Pilleth. The tightness of the cluster would suggest that this screenwork may have originated from a lesser or local workshop centre.

Heading south into Breconshire, a small group of closely related screens exists, in both spirit and appearance as far removed from the Newtown type as it is possible to imagine. The group comprises Llanelieu, Llanfigan, Llanlleonfel, and Merthyr Cynog in Breconshire, and is allied to a separate group

Llanelieu (top) and Merthyr Cynog (bottom): Characteristic arch-braces

in Cardiganshire to the west. The screens of this group are double-screens, each with a simple three-bay screen accompanied by its twin a few feet to the west. Originally, the resultant veranda of posts would have supported a rood-loft overhead. Beneath, to either side of the doorway, wainscot panels once enclosed side altars. Each of the screens was very simply constructed, with heavy timbers solidly braced. The nature of their decoration is especially striking, for they appear to have received very little in the way of carved decoration, and were painted instead.

Of the four examples that have been identified in Breconshire, the double-screen at Llanelieu is the most complete. As well as its veranda of posts, the pinky-red painted rood-tympanum survives intact overhead, decorated with white flowers and with the ghost of its long-lost Rood still visible. The related screen at Merthyr Cynog is nothing like so complete, but retains enough material to put its association with that of Llanelieu beyond any doubt. At Llanfigan, only the door standards and a portion of the head-beam survive (however, again this is enough to confidently place it within the group). Of the other Breconshire screen known to belong to the group – Llanlleonfel – nothing now survives. To the west, three screens of a distinct but closely related type are known to have existed in Cardiganshire, at Llanddeiniol, Llangeitho and Llangwyryfon. All were also double-screens, but had carved decoration in the form of spandrels and tracery.

Moving south, Monmouthshire is home to a small but significant cluster of related screens at Bettws Newydd, Kemeys Commander, Mamhilad and Trostre (the latter inexplicably overlooked by Crossley and Ridgway). All share a strongly rectangular construction and have distinctive, if slightly crude, carved ornamentation. The tracery heads, which are unusually

Trostre: Characteristic tracery heads of the Monmouthshire group

deep and thick, have tall Perpendicular lights; while the loft panels, too, are pierced with grid tracery and have 'planted on' canopies. The head-beams are enriched with dense (and rather heavy) carvings, and have a long cavetto moulding upon their eastern side. The most complete example of this type (indeed, the most complete set of rood furniture to survive anywhere in Wales or England) is that found at Bettws Newydd. Here, the screen, loft and tympanum all remain in largely unadulterated form. At Mamhilad, the loft survives as a west gallery. The screens at nearby Kemeys Commander and Trostre have been much renewed, but are still reasonably complete. Fragments of another screen belonging to this group survive at Dingestow Court (forming part of the chimney-piece in the hall).

Of the remaining screenwork of Welsh construction, two other churches – at New Radnor in Radnorshire and at Llandefalle in Breconshire – can be said with certainty to contain related material, both sharing a distinctive scissor tracery. The screen at New Radnor is no more, but parts of it (including several of the tracery heads) have been incorporated into the altar rail in the new church. The screen at Llandefalle, however, is substantially complete. Fragments of another screen of this type are kept at Christ College in Brecon. The scissor form is also employed in the outermost tracery heads at Partrishow, in the door-head at Llanwnnog, and at Llangynyw in the same county.

Aside from the Welsh screens that conform to the types listed above, there exist in Wales a number of rood-screens of English origin and construction. Grouping them together is natural, but it should be acknowledged that whilst some of these screens are clearly related, others fall into the group for no other reason beyond the fact of their essential Englishness. More than half of the screens of English manufacture in Wales are to be found in the southern Marches. Outside the region, three survive in north Wales, and three in south Wales. In the north, the rood-screen and loft at Llanrwst are especially memorable, while to the north and west, English screens survive at Aberconwy and Clynnog Fawr in Caernarvonshire. In Glamorgan in the extreme south of Wales, there are three screens with features linking them to the screenwork of Somerset: at Llantrithyd, Porthkerry and Cardiff (St. John).

Of the eight screens of English origin and construction in the southern Marches, four are entirely unrelated: those at Montgomery, Old Radnor, Michaelchurch-on-Arrow and Usk. Three of the remaining four – at Beguildy, Heyop and Cascob in Radnorshire – are closely related and bear comparison to those over the border at Kenderchurch and Eyton in Herefordshire. The distinguishing features of this group include the tracery heads and, in the case of Beguildy, Kenderchurch and Eyton, the pitch of their loft coving.

Provenance and Origin: England

Although most Midland screens were not produced by specialists functioning within a workshop system, in the Marches it is possible to identify a number of screens that correspond so closely with one another that a shared workshop source seems certain. The most notable of these groups is the one consisting of Aymestrey in Herefordshire, Hughley in Shropshire, Gresford in Denbighshire, and Astbury in Cheshire. The wide geographical spread of these screens points to a significant workshop centre. This centre may have been located in or near to Ludlow in Shropshire.[4] From their

120

design and construction it is certain that the screens are of English manufacture, for their distinguishing features include continuous intermediate standards and elaborate lierne vaulting or coving. However, their carved decoration not only displays the influence of Welsh carving, it may even have been produced by Welsh craftsmen working in an English workshop. Crossley and Ridgway suggest that other woodwork, including the screens and stalls at Aberconwy (Caernarvonshire), Chirbury (now at Montgomery), Wigmore (now at Leintwardine), Ludlow itself and Tong in Shropshire may also emanate from this workshop centre.[5]

Further evidence for a Ludlow (or at least Shropshire) workshop centre is provided by the middle rails and standards of a number of screens in Shropshire and beyond. The middle rail type seen at Ludlow itself (on the Palmers' Chapel screen), Bettws-y-Crwyn, Lydbury North and Middleton, is highly distinctive.

The design, carved in the solid, features a series of encircled quatrefoils spaced apart, with a string undulating over and under, and curved teardrop-shaped leaves in the resulting spandrels. This design is found nowhere else in the southern Marches. The standards at Ludlow (on both chancel aisle screens) together with those at Lydbury North and Astbury in Cheshire are also highly distinctive, moulded as they are with a central round flanked by smaller half-rounds. If this screenwork does not represent the work of a single workshop, it is at the very least an extremely specific example of cross-fertilisation.

Moving south into Herefordshire and Worcestershire, the screenwork at Lea, Bishop's Frome, Dilwyn and Stoke Lacy, together with that found at Alfrick in Worcestershire, is linked by the employment of highly distinctive 'planted on' wainscot

Lydbury North: Distinctive Shropshire middle rail design

Stoke Lacy: Carved 'planted on' wainscot spandrel found in a number of Herefordshire churches

spandrels. The spandrels contain serrated leaf forms, sometimes with further serrated forms or flowers overlaid. The curved edge of each spandrel is cusped, with the central cusp foliate in form and the outer ones generally terminated by little three-petalled flowers. The central cusp is sometimes filled with a serrated leaf form or flower. The spandrels correspond so closely from church to church that a single workshop source – if not a single craftsman – may have been responsible for their production.[6] In their workmanship and setting out, the middle rails at both Dilwyn and Canon Pyon may also be the work of the same carver or carvers.

Stoke Lacy: Tracery head found in a number of Herefordshire churches

In the case of three of the group – Bishop's Frome, Stoke Lacy and Lea – the work is also linked by the use of corresponding tracery heads. The design is an effective one and shows two principal variants. In the first (and simpler of the two) a pointed arch, variously cusped, is bisected by the crocketed pinnacle of an ogee arch below, which has flower cusps. In the second variant, paired loop lights, one on top of the other, are contained in the sides of the tracery head. In their general design these tracery heads conform to a type also found in Gloucestershire, Wiltshire and north Somerset. The design can also be found over the border in Wales (for example at Michaelchurch-on-Arrow and Beguildy in Radnorshire).

Intriguingly, the screen at Stoke Lacy also possesses a highly distinctive carved trail of a type found in only two other churches in the southern Marches: at St. Margarets and Michaelchurch Escley on the Welsh border. The design features a straight stem, from which leaves sprout at intervals above and below, and about which a stylised leaf or flattened stem (in the form of a continuous ribbon) spirals (see photograph below). The examples at St. Margarets and Michaelchurch are virtually identical, and being in churches that are located so close to one another, there seems no doubt that both originated from the same workshop, and probably the hand of the same carver.

Stoke Lacy: Carved trail similar to that found at St. Margarets and Michaelchurch Escley

The example at Stoke Lacy, however, is not identical to the other two. The trail zig-zags rather jarringly, the leaves (which are of a different design) do not fill the spaces in the same way and small fruit of some kind sprout from between the leaves. If this trail is of Welsh manufacture it surely does not originate from the same workshop as the other two, but is more likely to represent a copy of the design by another carver (possibly English). From its design it seems likely that the screen as a whole was imported from closer to the Welsh border, and that the illogically planted-on wainscot spandrels did not originally belong to the screen (as is clear from the mouldings of the standards and the lack of muntins).

Also in Herefordshire the screenwork at Yatton, Withington, Hereford Cathedral (in the small portable pulpit) and Eaton Bishop is linked through its use of highly unusual and distinctive upright elements, carved with tall and narrow Gothic loop lights. This design can be seen in the wainscot muntins at Hereford and Eaton Bishop, and in the standards at Yatton and Withington. The feature is so uncommon and the workmanship so analogous that a common source is a very real possibility. On the wall in the south chancel aisle of Hereford Cathedral is also an arcade of interlocking cusped ogee arches, similar to that surviving at tiny Bettws Clyro in Radnorshire.

Yatton and Withington are also strongly related to one another, and to the chaotically re-assembled screen at Aylton, in their use

Right: Distinctive narrow loop lights between panels of trefoils on the wainscot at Eaton Bishop (top) and quatrefoils on the portable pulpit at Hereford cathedral (centre left), and between tracery at Withington (centre right) and Yatton (bottom)

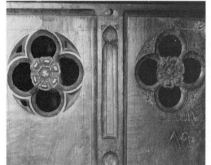

of a type of carved spandrel occurring at the junctions of standard and head-beam. The design has a number of variants, including encircled trefoils, quatrefoils and mouchettes. The big and generally simple motifs are highly distinctive, and make a single workshop source, especially in the case of Withington and Yatton, a real possibility. The lack of delicacy and the more obviously Decorated nature of the motifs would tend to support a date before c.1450 for the work. The fragments at Fawley also feature boldly

Aylton: Spandrel similar to those at Withington and Yatton

carved spandrels, but these are blind rather than pierced and are less refined still. Furthermore, these spandrels are essentially arch braces with chock infills, suggesting a date nearer to that of the screen at Pixley (or the Breconshire double-screens): possibly the second half of the 14th century.

Although the fine rood-screen at Old Radnor has no obvious relations in the southern Marches, it is certain that it originated from a Gloucestershire workshop centre (and one of some import). The much altered parclose screen at Cirencester features the same Tudor-headed forms and distinctive vine trail, and is clearly related to that found at Old Radnor. According to Crossley and

Ridgway this workshop centre, possibly located in Cirencester itself, supplied ecclesiastical woodwork to Gloucestershire, Herefordshire and Worcestershire, and its influence is discernible in a number of Radnorshire churches.[7]

Sources and Influence

In their discussion of the regional schools of woodwork, Howard and Crossley note that, 'The Midland is the style of the normal English race, the Western is leavened by the Celts and the Eastern by the Danes'.[8] Whilst it seems somehow self-evident that Welsh church screenwork bears the imprint of Celtic design, it is generally easier (and perhaps more appropriate) to speak of the influence of a broad language and spirit of design, rather than of a direct appropriation of motifs.[9] For Lloyd and Jennifer Laing, Celtic art, 'is an art in which naturalism in the classical sense is largely absent, and in which pattern predominates. It is an art which delights in curvilinear forms, in intertwining lines, in ornament which is often ambiguous.'[10] In spirit, Celtic art tends to be dynamic and exuberant, virile and alive.

All of these characteristics are abundantly evident in the carved trails found on the head-beam of Welsh rood-screens and the bressumer and top-beam of Welsh rood-lofts. These trails have

First century ivy-trail found on the gilt-bronze mount from Elmswell in Yorkshire

specific precedents in the form of the running-dog pattern found in much early Celtic art and the running scroll motif found in later Celtic art. The most important difference is in the scale of the motifs and in their usage. Thus we find a tiny undulating ivy-leaf trail on a gilt-bronze mount of the first century[11] (see illustration opposite) that is strikingly similar in its design to the carved trails found on Welsh screens. Interlacing and knot-work – which become gloriously inventive and intricate in the metalwork, stone crosses and illuminated manuscripts of the Celtic renaissance era (*c.* 400–1200) – are especially well seen in the Newtown School water-plant trails at Llananno in Radnorshire and Newtown itself in Montgomeryshire.

Dragons (which generally appear as Wyverns on Welsh screens) are found throughout Celtic and Germanic Dark Ages art, most numerously on swords and scabbards of the 4th century BC onwards. In this context they appear in affronted pairs, often in the form of a lyre scroll (a curly S-shape) or a C-scroll. Dragons of this type survive in Celtic 'Sword Style' work in Hungary, France and England.

Although nothing like so striking, the 'triskele' – an almost ubiquitous motif in Celtic art – is also found on

The triskele found throughout Celtic art

Llananno: The intricate water-plant trail on the back of the head-beam

Stoke Lacy: Triskele forms as flower whorls

125

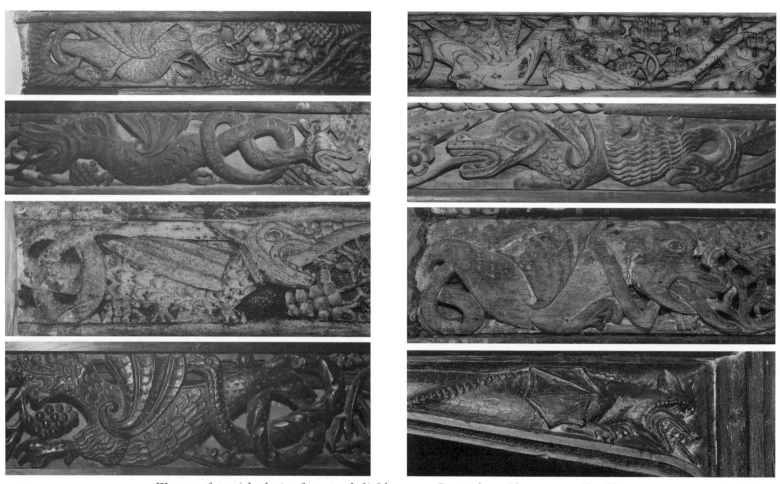

*Wyverns from (clockwise from top left) Llananno, Partrishow, Llanwnnog, Llanfilo,
Dilwyn, Newtown, Llandefalle and Llanwnnog*

much late medieval church screenwork. It is thought that for the Celts the motif had magical significance, though the precise symbolism has been lost. Certainly the number three has great significance both in the context of Christian art and Welsh culture (Welsh poems were often composed in sets of three, called Triads), so the appropriation of such a motif is perfectly understandable. However, there is no compelling evidence that the use of the triskele upon late medieval screenwork is anything other than a recognition of its formal geometrical qualities. Whether symbolic or not, the motif frequently forms the central whorl in small carved flowers; as at Lea, Bishop's Frome, Llanvair Waterdine, Alfrick etc. It also appears in much larger openwork form within one of the spandrels at Withington.

With a legacy of Celtic design, the Welsh screen carvers could perhaps afford to be insular. Sources of design lay all about them in the form of inscribed stones and crosses (such as those at Nevern and Carew in Pembrokeshire). Some carvers, or at least their patrons, may have been familiar with the exquisite work to be found in the pages of illuminated manuscripts. Religious commissions may also have placed other examples of Celtic workmanship in the path of the screen carver, such as church plate, croziers or jewellery; all of which were dazzlingly ornamented. The Welsh belief that this Celtic style was *their* style – one that differentiated them from the English – accounts in part for the pervasive and enduring influence of Celtic design in Wales, and there is no question that for the Welsh the spirit of Celtic design resonated strongly.

As we have seen, Welsh screen carvers proved remarkably resistant to the influence of English screenwork, both in terms of its construction and detailing. When an English-type screen is found in Wales – as at Aberconwy, Gresford, Michaelchurch, Usk and Old Radnor – it is invariably a direct import from England into a border settlement with strong links to England. Tellingly, even the presence of such a screen in their very midst did little or nothing to persuade native screen builders to borrow from the design of such screens. This insularity even precluded foreign influence from entering Wales via Devon and Somerset, and this despite the fact that these counties shared the same Western School background as Wales (and thus many constructional and decorative characteristics). Thus it was that the foreign influence so clearly seen at Colebrooke,[12] Marwood, Atherington, Holbeton, Swymbridge (etc.) in Devon, is never discernible in Wales. Llandinabo and Foy, just over the border in Herefordshire, are the closest examples, but these are exceptional even in the English Marches.

Foreign and specifically Renaissance design was just beginning to affect English screenwork when the Reformation struck. Even in the case of Midland School screenwork – a long time bastion of indigenous design – it is found; and not only in post-Reformation screenwork. In Oxfordshire, the screen mullions at both Thame and Charlton-on-Otmoor, which feature the same playful and varied surface treatments as are seen at Llandinabo and Foy, are clearly informed by Renaissance design.

Although English screen design had a negligible impact on Welsh screenwork, the influence of Welsh screen design is widely felt in churches on the English side of the border. This influence expressed itself in one of three main ways. Firstly, the entire screen – its construction, design and detailing – might be Welsh;

as in the case of St. Margarets in Herefordshire and Daresbury in Cheshire. Secondly, the screen might be of Welsh construction but have English detailing, as is the case with the screens at Burghill in Herefordshire and Gresford in Denbighshire.

Thirdly, the screen itself might be English in construction, but betray in its detailing and carved decoration the clear influence of Welsh screenwork. This is the case, to varying degrees, in a large number of screens on the English side of the border. The use of carved trails along the bressumer and head-beam is perhaps the most conspicuous and abundant sign of this influence. However, it is clear that whilst English carvers were happy to borrow from the designs and motifs of their counterparts, they were not always as comfortable in their handling of them. The trails found at Stoke Lacy in Herefordshire, Tong in Shropshire and at Rendcomb and Fairford in Gloucestershire are clearly informed by Welsh work, but are thinner and less fluidly modelled; less naturalistic than the trails found on Welsh screens.

Another distinctly Welsh feature variously taken up by English screen builders was the denial of complete uniformity across the screen; a feature seen most noticeably in the tracery heads of the screens at Llananno and Llanwnnog, where repetition for its own sake has given way to riotous variety and the formation of enrichment akin to a decorative fringe. In undiluted English screenwork, such bay to bay variety is never seen. However, it has evidently informed the design of the screens at Blore Ray in Staffordshire, Astbury, Barthomley, Cheadle and Malpas in Cheshire, Northenden in Lancashire and Hughley in Shropshire, all of which have been subject to Welsh influence.

Foy: Standards showing Renaissance influence

The following are some of the carved elements found on rood-screens and lofts (many in the form of trails). The list is far from exhaustive and it is important to acknowledge that the motives behind the use of a given form are rarely straightforward; they are perhaps never governed by symbolism alone, and may not be governed by symbolism at all. Whilst the depiction of meaning may have been fundamental for one screen carver, for another this factor may have been incidental to purely decorative motives.

In the case of carved trails, although certain plants are clearly identifiable – such as the vine – others are not. The use of generic plant types used purely for decorative effect should not be discounted. The 'serrated leaf' type decoration, for example, takes diverse forms and is often shaped to fit into the compartment it inhabits in a given design. The budding 'crocket' enrichment so characteristic of the Decorated era also appears widely on screenwork, particularly in the form of 'planted on' ogee gables with crocketed pinnacles and in crestings. Again, the vegetation here is essentially generic rather than specific.[13]

Vine

The vine is a continually recurring motif in Christian art and architecture, and is by far the most common plant form used in carved trails. Vines and grapes symbolise the Eucharistic wine (the blood of Christ) and in early Christian art Christ himself: 'I am the vine, ye are the branches: He that abideth in me, and I in him, the same bringeth forth much fruit: for without me ye can do nothing' (*John* 16: 5).

Oak

The oak was appropriated for symbolic purposes long before its use in Christian art. It represents steadfastness and endurance, especially in the face of persecution, and thus obliquely refers to Christ. The oak was also one of the trees believed to have provided wood for the Cross. Although nothing like so commonly found as the vine, it exists on a number of screens in the southern Marches, including those at Llanfilo and Bettws Newydd.

Hawthorn

The hawthorn, like the oak, is rich in symbolism (much of it non- or pre-Christian). For Christians, the crown of thorns worn by Christ was made from Hawthorn and the plant is thus redolent of the Crucifixion. Hawthorn trails are fairly unusual, but exist at both Partrishow and St. Margarets.

Pomegranate

The pomegranate is a symbol of the Resurrection; a usage that may derive from Greek mythology (Persephone was able to periodically return from the underworld after eating a Pomegranate seed). For church screenwork the pomegranate has additional significance. It was the badge of Katherine of Aragon, whose ill-fated marriage to Prince Arthur in 1501 is commemorated on a number of rood-screens and lofts in the Marches. Arthur was given Ludlow Castle as a wedding present and made Lord of the Marches, so his connection with the area is a strong one.

Water-plant

The water-plant or water-flower is found on many Welsh rood-screens and lofts, particularly those from the Newtown workshops. Its symbolism (beyond that of the obvious water as life metaphor found for example in *Revelation* 21:6: 'I will give unto him that is athirst of the fountain of the water of life freely') is obscure. If the water-plant can be identified as a water lily, then its connotations may include purity (after the water nymphs of Greek mythology, which give to the plant its genus: *Nymphaea*) and the Resurrection (from its ancient symbolism of rebirth, which derives from the way it closes up at night to reopen again each morning).

Dragon

Dragons, and specifically Wyverns, often terminate the carved trails on rood-screens and lofts. In Christian art the dragon symbolises evil generally and Satan specifically. *Revelation* 12:9 says: 'And the great dragon was cast out, that old serpent, called the Devil, and Satan, which deceiveth the whole world: he was cast out into the earth, and his angels were cast out with him.' The Wyvern found in Wales (though not exclusively here) has distinctive characteristics: 'so doth the Wiuerne partake of a Fowle in the Wings and Legs ... and doth Resemble a Serpent in the Taile'.[14] The tail in the form of a serpent not only recalls Satan's form in Eden, but also the amphisbaena: the fabled two-headed serpent of the ancients able to move in either direction (thus symbolising inconstancy).

Rose

The rose was an early Christian symbol, appearing in Roman catacombs and possibly denoting paradise. Later it became strongly associated with the Virgin Mary. The Tudor rose, which features the white rose of York over the red rose of Lancaster, is emblematic of Henry VII (1485–1509). Other flower types also appear on rood-screens and it seems clear that decorative considerations often dictated the size and number of petals.

Green Man

Green man figures appear on several screens in the southern Marches, including those at Bronllys and Kenderchurch (in the spandrels) and at Llanvair Waterdine. The figure appears widely in European art and is a pagan symbol with Celtic forebears; specifically perhaps the *Derg Corra* — the 'man in the tree' of Celtic mythology, or the Celtic deity *Cernunnus*. Its various appropriations down the ages have invested it with a wealth of meanings relating to nature, fertility and growth etc. In Christian symbolism, a vine sometimes emanates from the mouth of the figure, thus referring to Christ and notions of regeneration.

Trefoil and Quatrefoil

Ubiquitous elements in Gothic art and architecture, the trefoil can symbolise the three-in-one unity of the Holy Trinity (and is a simplification of three interlocking circles). The quatrefoil can represent the four Evangelists: Matthew, Mark, Luke and John.

Dating Church Screenwork

The vast majority of surviving pre-Reformation church screenwork dates from the second half of the 15th century and the first quarter of the 16th century. Indeed, in their exhaustive survey of the rood-screens and lofts of Devon (the richest county in England for late medieval screenwork) Bond and Camm were able to show that most surviving Devon screens were erected between 1470 and 1520,[15] (and that almost nothing belongs to a date earlier than the 15th century). Screens and lofts, as the pre-eminent church furnishings (and those from which the other furnishings, such as pulpits and benches, took their cue) were especially subject to fashion, local patronage and the expression of civic pride. For these and other reasons (including the need for their adaptation to take rood-lofts) they were intermittently updated or entirely replaced. Consequently, of the screens that survive, we are left with very few from the 14th century, and still fewer from the 13th century.

With notable exceptions, late medieval screenwork was left unsigned and undated by its makers. The middle rail of the rood-screen at Mobberley in Cheshire carries the maker's name, Mr. Peter Acton, together with the date, 28th May 1500, but this is exceptional. In the southern Marches, wall plaques adjacent to the post-Reformation screen at Vowchurch name the patrons of the screen as the children of Thomas and Marget Hill, together with the date of its construction: 1613. The inscription on the rail at Llanvair Waterdine reveals that the screen was put up by Sir Matthew and Meyrick Pichgar of Clun. Although no precise date is given, the appearance of the name of the priest betrays a rough date of between *c.*1485 and 1520 for the screen.

The general qualities of the screenwork of the 15th and 16th centuries as compared with those of earlier screenwork include greater all round finesse, the use of smaller and more delicate forms and motifs, thinner framing elements, and rectilinear or grid (i.e. Perpendicular) compositions rather than curvilinear (i.e. Decorated) compositions. By this era the turned baluster as mullion, so beloved of the earlier craftsman, had given way to ogee-, hollow- or round-moulded uprights, and the head of the screen as a single continuous board had given way to the individual tracery head. The rood-loft had become universal, and even though missing from all but a handful of rood-screens, has everywhere left its mark. Certain motifs found in contemporary window design, such as the ubiquitous Gothic loop or grid light, are widely found. Gone is the discomfort with the handling of wood so evident in the monumental rood-screen at Pixley in Herefordshire, to be replaced by confident understanding of the material, expressed most strikingly in a wealth of carved ornament.

Of the other means of dating church screenwork, a useful one is the presence on the screen of the pomegranate. This was the badge of Katherine of Aragon, whose short-lived marriage to Prince Arthur in 1501 is thus commemorated at Conway, Llananno, Llanfilo, Llangynyw and Llanwnnog. The presence of the pomegranate thus confirms a date in the early 16th century for the screen or loft in question. Wills and churchwardens' accounts, where these survive, occasionally record dates and donors, and whilst the date of the putting up of a rood-loft or screen may not be recorded, the date of its subsequent removal may still be. Thus, the churchwardens' accounts for St. Edmunds church in

Salisbury talk of 'the pullinge downe the Roodloffte' in 1561/62; while those for nearby St. Thomas's church record the 'taking downe of the roode loffte and the setting on of the creste' in 1561[16] (in fulfilment of the wishes expressed in the Elizabethan Order of the same year).

MONTGOMERYSHIRE

LLANGURIG, ST. CURIG

Llangurig church stands in a circular churchyard beside a headwater of the Wye and consists of a nave and chancel, north aisle and chancel aisle, and a west tower. St. Curig, whose life is depicted in the church's stained glass, founded a *clas* (a Celtic mother church) on the site in the 6th century. Although parts of the building date from the 15th century or earlier, most of the fabric, including the stained glass, belongs to the comprehensive restoration (or rebuild) carried out in the 19th century.

The screen that now divides the chancel from the nave also belongs to the 19th century and is loosely based on the original of the late 15th century, and specifically upon drawings executed by the Rev. Parker in 1828.[1] Although it represents a conscientious response to the original rood-screen, in neither its workmanship nor its composition does it tell us much of value about its predecessor. Not only is the workmanship mechanical in execution and somewhat lifeless in effect, but (for example) the bays to either side of the doorway number five, rather than the three of the original. The only old work in the current screen is a single foliage trail.

Parker describes the old rood-screen's central arch (i.e. its door-head tracery) as 'the ne plus ultra of gothic richness'[2] and from his and other evidence, both physical and documentary, it is clear that this was once a screen of great beauty and distinction. In its original form it had three bays to either side of a central doorway, with each bay divided by mullions dowelled into the middle rail.

The standards ran through uninterrupted between the sill and the head-beam and unusually their centre mouldings were enriched with a delicate trail of running ornament; all of which (mouldings and trail) were returned over the heads. At each junction a berry or small leaf was inserted. This arrangement corresponds with that found at Llangynyw and Newtown in the same county.

The uniform tracery heads of the old screen each had a cusped arch overlaid with an ogee gabled and crocketed head (essentially forming a small hood or canopy of niche-work). To either side the design contained light grid tracery and further crocketed gables terminated below by a pendant. This recalls work of the Gloucester-Hereford type. The door-head tracery was especially rich, and comprised five circles variously filled, with grid lights between, free tracery infilling, all framed between the Tudor arch of the doorway and a band of drop-cresting below.

Surmounting the screen was a rood-loft which once extended across both the nave and the side aisle (*cf.* Newtown). This had a flat soffit and was supported to the west upon four posts with arched braces springing from their heads. Unfortunately, whilst Parker's drawings are explicit in part, they are less detailed when it comes to the appearance of the wainscot, the western parapet of the loft and certain aspects of the decorative scheme. The stairs to the rood-loft are not mentioned by Parker, but are referred to by Glynne.[3]

The screenwork of Llangurig was dismantled in 1836. The story of what happened next is taken up by a contemporary

*Llangurig: Pair of fine tracery panels,
now part of a screen wall at Glansevern House*

Llanmerewig church stands quite alone among fields on a hillside to the east of Newtown. It belongs mainly to the 19th century and has a number of curious but engaging features, not the least of which is a narrow tower with a gabled roof carried on corbels. Much of the work (particularly to the interior) was carried out under the direction of the Rev. John Parker, who was rector here from 1827–44.

Llanmerewig: Motley assortment of fragments worked into the new screen

The current screen, with its lancet openings to either side of a central doorway, was erected in 1892. It incorporates fragments from the original rood-screen of the 15th century. The early woodwork is hard to identify, but

observer: 'the churchwardens, who must have been ignorant of its value, allowed anyone who expressed a desire to become possessed of samples of the tracery to carry away specimens, so that literally, bit by bit, it disappeared, and not a vestige of it was left'.[4] Five of these pieces, all finely carved tracery panels (and including the door-head piece mentioned by Parker) were used to form a small screen wall in the dining room of nearby Glansevern House (a private residence) where they survive to this day. The screen in its original form has no obvious surviving counterpart.

the cusped quarter-circles framed up in the corners of the door-head together with the crocketed finials beneath and the carved spandrels look suspect. They seem to have been shoehorned into the scheme, and the effect is jarring and illogical. Pieces from the old screen were also used by Parker to create what Richard Haslam describes as, 'a fantastic Tower-of-Babel-like pulpit'.[5] Unfortunately this was destroyed and is known only from a drawing in the National Library of Wales. The current pulpit has a narrow, pierced vine trail – but this is of metal.

LLANWNNOG, ST. JOHN

This single-chamber building stands in a raised circular churchyard in the middle of the village. The fabric incorporates much medieval stonework, but was heavily restored in the second half of the 19th century. Although we should be grateful that the church's rood-screen and loft survive at all, it must be noted that the loft in particular has suffered a number of insensitive and destructive alterations in recent centuries.

The rood-screen here, just as at Llanfilo and Partrishow, seems incidental when compared to the rood-loft overhead (for photograph of full screen and rood see page 47). This is designedly the case (although the difference in status would have been more pronounced when the loft parapet still retained its original form and decoration). The screen consists of five bays to either side of a central doorway, which takes the space of two bays. The standards each have a double ogee moulding and (in the case of the door standards) a boutell. The mullions that divide the bays are dowelled into a sturdy and low, chamfered middle rail. The plain wainscot beneath is divided up by muntins bearing no relation to the mullions above. Thus, where each half of the screen above middle rail height is divided into five bays, each below is divided into eight. Sadly, only the tracery heads to the north survive. These are well carved (on both western and eastern faces) with free all-over patterning of three different designs; a feature shared with the screen at Llananno in Radnorshire. Each of the heads is bisected by a small cusped ogee arch. The door-head tracery, with its band of diamond-shaped quatrefoils, was once fixed below the bressumer to the west of its current position, between the western posts that once

supported the rood-loft. In its design this tracery is allied to that found at Llanderfalle and Partrishow in Breconshire, and in its effect forms a deep fringe of drop-cresting for the loft (indeed, it should be read as an ornamentation of the rood-loft rather than of the rood-screen below).

The slightly coved soffit under the rood-loft springs to both the west and the east from the top of the enriched head-beam. It is worth noting that the vertical ribs of the soffit relate not to the bays of the screen below but to the loft parapet above, again emphasising the decorative pre-eminence of the rood-loft at this date. To the west the soffit is ceiled with square, fretted panels,

Llanwnnog: Parker drawing of open woodwork in the chancel screen in January 1828. The drawings can be compared with the top two photographs overleaf

135

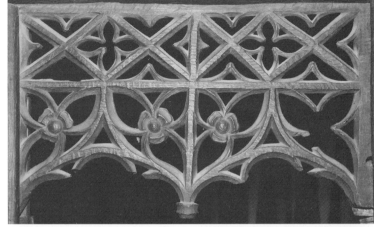
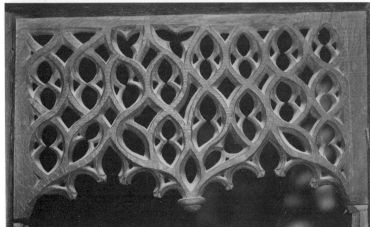

*Llanwnnog: Three of the surviving tracery panels, each with free all-over patterning,
and the re-set door-head tracery with head-beam above (bottom right)*

Llanwnnog: Panels of applied carving on the loft soffit, framed above by the bressumer and below by the head-beam, and with tracery heads forming a fringe below

Llanwnnog: Detail of eastern parapet of loft, which, unlike the western, survives in something like its original form

Llanwnnog: Finely carved Wyvern on the head-beam (closely related to those at Newtown) beneath mismatched top-crestings

again similar to those at Llananno (but lacking their variety). These have bosses and monograms at the intersections. The eastern side has plain panelling divided up by ribs.

The biggest disappointment at Llanwnnog is the condition of the western loft parapet. This was once lavishly and delicately enriched with niche-work. In its setting out it was clearly similar to Llananno, having, according to Glynne, a series of sculpted figures alternating with plain panels. Between 1871 and 1899, however, 'its delicate niche-work was swept away as if it had been so much dirt and cobwebs'.[6] The replacement panels of the 19th

century are of a strange design and have an alien appearance. The loft parapet should be the culmination of the decorative scheme, but Victorian dissolution has resulted in something of an anti-climax. The rebate cut across the muntins two-thirds of the way up would have held the hoods to the niche-work, and is one of few clues to the loft parapet's original appearance.

The eastern parapet fared much better. It comprises a series of 20 panels divided by flat muntins, each panel perforated with tracery of two different designs. These panels recall those found at Llanrwst (Denbighshire), Llanegryn (Merionethshire), and Llanengan (Caernarvonshire). At one time the western bressumer of the loft was supported upon two moulded posts; an arrangement reminiscent of that found at Bronllys (Breconshire), Beguildy (Radnorshire) and Burghill (Herefordshire). As well as the head tracery (which has since been removed to the east) there was also

Llanwnnog: Wyvern on the bressumer of the rood-loft, below a spiralling leaf trail

Llanwnnog: Rood-stairs

a deep drop-cresting, some of which survives at the bressumer's northern end. Originally, this would have continued down the edges of the curved spandrels of the moulded posts. The eastern bressumer was also supported by two posts corresponding with the door standards, but these were unmoulded (like those at Aber Conwy in Caernarvon).

The rood-screen and loft at Llanwnnog are considerably enriched by a number of interesting and finely-carved crestings and trails of running ornament. The western face of the head-beam of the screen features a water-plant trail issuing from the mouth of a Wyvern (one of two). These also appear at Llananno in Radnorshire. The western bressumer has a good vine-leaf trail below, and one of serrated leaves about a central stem above (this is 'raguly' twisted — a stylised, undulating form deriving from heraldry). The rood-beam has lost all but a tiny fragment of its enrichment. On the eastern side the head-beam features a closely twined and deeply serrated leaf trail. Unusually, the bressumer is decorated with an oak trail (abundant in acorns) and over this, one of pomegranate (which confirms a date of post-1501 for the fitting). This latter appears again, though in a different form, on the rood-beam. Of the various crestings, the one over the western head-beam, with its plaited lower band, is especially good.

The stairs to the rood-loft are also noteworthy. Lofts were usually accessed via mural stairwells hollowed out of the wall; the rood-stairs themselves often being of spiral or dog-leg form. The staircase against the north wall of the nave at Llanwnnog, with its massive oak steps arranged in a straight flight, is entirely open and is reminiscent of the ladder-type staircases that gave access to early rood-lofts. Although these stairs were originally open, it appears that for a time they were blocked up, or at least boarded over. In a letter to Aymer Vallance, one W.M. Dodson notes that, 'The stair-case was found at the restoration built into the wall'.[7]

MONTGOMERY, ST. NICHOLAS

The hillside town of Montgomery lies above the Severn valley close to the Shropshire border. Its church occupies an elevated site at the top of the town, and is of single-chamber form with transepts projecting to north and south, and a tower at the end of its north transept. Apart from its fine roofs, which date from the 15th or 16th centuries, most of the fabric belongs to the 13th century. Restoration work in the 19th century included the rebuilding of the tower and south porch.

The screenwork (and much of the other woodwork within) is of uncommon interest, partly because most of it was never intended for this church. For once, the oft-stated but generally mistaken belief that a given church's late medieval rood-screen and loft were imported from a nearby monastery at the time of the Dissolution[8] turns out to be perfectly correct. Three miles away just within Shropshire (but formerly within Montgomeryshire) was the Augustinian priory of Chirbury. At the Dissolution, the screen (now the eastern screen at Montgomery), together with the rood-loft and the stallwork was all brought to, and set up inside, the church. The stalls are identical in their design to those at Leintwardine in Herefordshire (which originally came from Wigmore abbey) and are similar to those at Ludlow in Shropshire. The Montgomery set features a lively (if mutilated and incomplete) set of misericords.

The eastern screen (if in its pared down and skeletal state it can still be referred to as such) was backed by the pulpitum at Chirbury priory and enclosed the choir there. In this context transparency was not called for and the screen would have been both panelled and carved. In its design and construction it incorporates (and is a continuation of) the choir stall bays set against the north and south walls of the choir. The stalls were re-set against the screen at Montgomery, minus their panelling and canopies in order to afford views through to the high altar (but not on the south side where they would have blocked access to the rood-stairs). The doorway is framed by *riddel* posts, which once supported a projecting pulpit at Chirbury (and from which curtains were hung). A few scraps of carved decoration survive, including buttresses and pinnacles on the posts, two fine panels (one with a quatrefoil enclosing a Tudor rose) to either side of the doorway and a handful of small, carved bosses high up.

The loft overhead also comes from Chirbury, but it is unclear whether it formed the parapet of the pulpitum there or an independent fitting. It had to be shortened to allow its insertion at Montgomery, for the choir at Chirbury was slightly wider. The loft parapet is divided into 24 elongated heads by buttressed pinnacles. Below, the loft front overhangs dramatically and there is apparently no bressumer (*cf.* Attleborough in Norfolk, see p.48). The panels here once had pendant carvings, but these have disappeared.

All of the woodwork removed from Chirbury priory is English in origin, and the loft in particular seems glaringly un-Welsh. However, the western screen at Montgomery is of Welsh construction, it was made for the church and it almost certainly occupies its original position at the entrance to the chancel. It consists of five bays to either side of a central doorway, which takes the space of two bays. The head of each bay has a repeated design of big, cinquefoil tracery. The central doorway, meanwhile, features an ogee with semi-circles to either side and grid tracery

Montgomery: Parker drawing of the screen, March 1831.
He included the note: 'The tracery of [the] central arch and the comparts. of the side of it are gone,
but are restored in the drawing from the five which remain at the North side.
The Gothic desks are now very much obscured by modern pewing, which has been omitted also'

above. The mullions that divide the bays are dowelled into the middle rail, which runs through unbroken between wall and door standards in the familiar Welsh manner. The door standards have elaborate crocketed pinnacles upon their western faces. The wainscot panels and muntins below are missing, and the space below the middle rail has been boarded over.

The two screens enclose areas to either side of the central doorway which have been put to a variety of uses down the ages. Archdeacon Thomas records that 'Between the two [screens], at the base, is an open space, now occupied as a ladies' choir, but formally appropriated as pews'.[9] It seems likely that these areas were used for high status occupants during the 17th century, in an era when

Montgomery:
Detail of rood-loft parapet

Montgomery: Screen doors
– a Jacobean addition

canopied box pews were *du jour*. The Jacobean carved doors in the west screen also belong to this period. The rood-loft itself was also used as a high status pew, probably at the disposal of the local manor.

Taken together, west screen, east screen and rood-loft form a slightly discordant and unlikely triumvirate. However, the saving and re-use of the woodwork from Chirbury priory, together with the retention of the screen at Montgomery, remain acts of unusual sympathy and foresight.

NEWTOWN, ST. DAVID

The new church of St. David replaced the old church of St. Mary whose ruins still stand silently beside the river Severn to the north. St. Marys was abandoned midway through the 19th century due to flooding. The new church was completed in 1847 and consists of a nave with clerestory, north and south aisles, chancel, north porch and west tower. It is a large, brick-built structure, loosely Gothic in style, and with a profusion of plain-

Newtown: A trio of luxuriant trails, including the vine and pomegranate, over one of the two door-heads

glazed lancet windows which serve to give it a pronounced verticality and to flood its interior with light.

Inside, numerous pieces from the rood-screen and loft from old St. Marys have been variously re-erected to form a small parclose chapel at the east end of the north aisle (which houses a canopy over the altar within) and to line the walls of the sanctuary. The woodwork is startling in its variety and includes several carved pieces of almost unparalleled finesse. Only at Llananno in Wales and a handful of churches in England can anything be found to compare with this carving for quality or inventiveness.

We are fortunate to have a number of comprehensive descriptions of Newtown's rood-screen and loft. These descriptions (which date from the 19th century and the early 20th century) are invaluable, for they record the various metamorphoses, both major and minor, endured by the screenwork during this period. Although the accounts differ in their details they are consistent in their praise for the quality of the fittings. Richard Fenton writes that, 'The Rood-loft, as to carving, gilding, and painting, is perhaps the most perfect thing of the kind in the kingdom'.[10] The Rev. John Parker, when referring to the carved panels of the rood-loft (plate 5), is even more effusive: 'this mutilated and ruinous fragment is in itself a world of Gothic art, a magazine of original and exquisite patterns, all of which, when it was entire, were disposed in such

Newtown: Range of carved panels from the loft soffit (cf. Llananno and Llanwnnog) lining the sanctuary in St. Davids

Newtown: Detail of the exceptional water-plant trail that once graced the head-beam

Newtown: An especially fine Wyvern (note the various surface treatments, including feathers and scales etc.)

a way as to satisfy the taste and feast the eye of the spectator, with the highest luxuries of workmanship and colouring'.[11]

Originally, rood-screen and rood-loft stretched some 42 feet across the entire width of the old church, to span both nave and south aisle (a characteristic more commonly associated with the screens of the South-west). The standards ran unbroken from the sill up to the head-beam, with the intermediate mullions dowelled into the middle rail. The mullions were painted with a ribbon-twist of colour (like a barber's shop sign) and followed closely the setting out of the main standards. Each of these was enriched upon its eastern and western faces with a boutell, ascending up which was a trail of twisted leaf and berry (like the one that graced the old rood-screen at Llangurig). This moulding plus decoration was returned over the heads of each bay. To either side of each boutell the standards also featured an ogee moulding divided by quirks. The head-beam carried a spectacular and deep water-leaf trail (portions of which survive in the new church) and was fringed above with a cresting of pellet and seaweed design, and below with cabling completed with a series of trefoils

below. In one of Parker's drawings it appears that the wainscot below was decorated with linenfold panelling (as at Llangwm in Monmouthshire, St. Weonards in Herefordshire and Shelsley Walsh in Worcestershire).

The screen had two doorways; one opening into the nave and the other the south aisle. Both door-heads contained elaborate tracery, and were framed by straight Tudor arches above (plate 6) and drop-cresting below. One head contained four circles with wheel tracery; the other head ten circles of diminishing size filled in with quatrefoils or foliated cusps holding a central rose. The screen bays each contained double ogee-arched heads and tracery displaying a wealth of free and formal designs, which made delighted and ingenious play of circles, quatrefoils and wheels in particular (just as Llanwnnog and Llananno; plate 4). Many of these survive in St. David's church.

The rood-loft's western soffit contained 85 open traceried panels in a double row, similar to the layout found at Llanwnnog and Llananno. Some of these designs (which now decorate the sanctuary wall in the new church) are identical to those found at

Newtown: Detail of the dazzling seaweed cresting now fixed over the altar in St. Davids (see also plate 3)

Newtown: Canopy in the parclose chapel, which gives some idea of how the loft would have looked

Daresbury in Cheshire. The panels were framed by ribs and had carved bosses and monograms at their intersections. The soffit ran unbroken across the width of the church. Where the screen was punctuated by the arcade that ran between nave and side aisle, the soffit continued in front of the pier (again, a treatment more often associated with the screens of the South-west).

The original appearance of the rood-loft and specifically of the loft parapet is less clear. However, it seems that the parapet featured not carved figures in the niches, but painted ones. Of these, eight defaced panels (one of which apparently depicted St. George and the dragon) were recorded by Parker in 1832. At this time much of the original colour still remained intact, including the faded remnants of blue, red, purple, brown and gold pigments, (prompting Parker to imagine the screen's original 'dreamy,

shadowy brightness'[12]). The loft parapet also featured elaborate tabernacle work and was framed by a bressumer below and a rood-beam above, both enriched with trails of running ornament. These incorporated twisted and serrated leaf designs, together with flower, vine, pomegranate and seaweed trails, and the now-familiar dragons from whose jaws the trails issued forth. The screen and loft both had fine top- and drop-cresting; one of the finest fragments of which is now fixed over the altar in the new church. The rood-loft, as well as housing singers, also supported an organ.

Like so much church screenwork, that belonging to Newtown has been mutilated by degrees over time. So, when Glynne

145

Newtown: Detail of the bressumer trails,
with three of the tracery heads below

stood before the screen in 1810 the loft seems to have been substantially complete. However, when Parker did the same in 1829 the rood-loft had gone, to be replaced with the panels of the loft soffit. These had been misappropriated to form a new western parapet for the rood-loft. Of this arrangement Parker writes, 'The dislocation of these panels gives to the whole screen such an awkward effect, that until the spectator becomes aware that they were not originally so placed, he would be likely to condemn the work altogether as a specimen of barbaric pomp and gorgeous clumsiness'.[13] These misguided alterations must have been carried out sometime between 1824 and 1829.

Subsequently it appears that some of the screenwork was re-erected before the apse (or as a reredos) in the new church, only to be taken down once more and placed in the cellars of the rectory when a larger chancel was added in 1875. In 1909 the pieces were taken out of storage and used to construct a parclose chapel and, in the case of 55 of the soffit panels and some of the trails of running ornament, to panel and line the sanctuary. Sadness at the mutilated state of what was evidently a spectacular rood-screen and loft, bright with colour and alive with carving, must be tempered once again by gladness that so much of the original fabric survives. The misappropriation of late medieval screenwork, whatever form this takes, is always preferable to its loss.

SHROPSHIRE

BETTWS-Y-CRWYN, ST. MARY

The church stands in a beautiful and remote spot in the hills above the Radnorshire border. It consists of a nave and chancel in one, a south porch and a bellcote. Most of the fabric belongs to the Victorian restoration of 1860. The roof is characteristic of the area, having collar-beams on arch braces, with wind-braces forming quatrefoils. The nave contains an especially satisfying set of pews, cut from thick timber and with simple trefoil bench ends.

The rood-screen has evidently undergone substantial alteration during its lifetime, and the possibility that it was not originally intended for this church cannot be discounted. Furthermore it has a close and intriguing relationship with the Palmers' screen at Ludlow. Like the Palmers' screen it consists of three double bays to either side of a central doorway, which takes the space of two double bays. The door and wall standards, together with the four intermediate standards, all extend from the sill up to the head-beam. The standards are original (albeit with some replacement woodwork at floor level) and are elaborately moulded with hollows, rounds and half-rounds. The screen is subdivided above middle rail height by mullions that correspond with the muntins below. The mullions have similar mouldings to the standards, and all but one is original. The condition of many of the uprights (due to the vagaries of time and woodworm) is quite poor, so it is particularly satisfying to find these timbers retained.

The double middle rail consists of a much renewed central band of cusped openwork squares (in effect, quatrefoils), flanked above and below by narrower enrichments carved in the solid. On the north side, the upper of these comprises a length of encircled four-petalled flowers, two-thirds of which is old work. The lower band is the more distinctive of the two and consists of the same flowers, this time with the gaps between filled by little leaf forms. This unusual design is, once again, very similar to that found at Ludlow, (and at Lydbury North). To the south, the enrichments to either side of the central band of openwork feature a double scallop design, all of which is old work. The middle rail treatment to the east, both in its design and in the percentage of new work

Bettws-y-Crwyn: Much-altered rood-screen, stripped of its vaulting

Bettws-y-Crwyn: Subdivided and round-headed
Perpendicular tracery light of exceptional quality

incorporated here, is identical to that to the west. Below middle rail height the wainscot boarding is new. However, the sill on which the screen stands is original. This portion of the screen has seen a great deal of alteration. The middle rail (as evidenced by the Palmers' screen and others) should not be this high, and the suspicion here must be of a Victorian re-composition (at Usk the Victorian restoration of the screen resulted in a lifted middle rail and a similar peculiarly 'un-medieval' composition).

The upper parts of the screen have also seen a great deal of alteration, and provide the strongest evidence for this screen's possible status as an alien fixture. Above the very fine tracery heads, the screen has been shorn of its vaulting and loft; a factor adding to the odd appearance of the screen. Originally, the vaulting would have sprung from the standards at a height half way up each tracery head. The gaps between the rounded arch of each head and the renewed head-beam (actually a tie-beam) would have been hidden by the vaulting (*cf.* Ludlow). At this point there is an obvious problem: given that the tie-beam is roughly at the height of the missing loft floor, there is surely not enough room for a loft and its parapet above (without these cutting into the eaves). For this reason, if this is not an alien fixture, then the screen has been raised in height (which is not impossible, given the additional woodwork to the standards at floor level).

Another question mark hangs over the tracery itself. This quite clearly belongs to the early 16th century. Each head consists of an ogee arch below, with its point stretching up to a quatrefoil beneath a pointed arch above. This gives two compartments, each of which has been filled with delicate Perpendicular panel tracery. The top spandrel contains a trefoil. These tracery heads

Ludlow, Palmers' Chapel screen: the relationship between the tracery and vaulting, showing how the screen at Bettws-y-Crwyn would have looked

are carved upon both faces, and seven of the eight are original. This distinctive design is almost exactly replicated at Ludlow (even to the stepped, battlemented horizontal elements), yet the tracery at Ludlow appears much later and could certainly be Victorian. Is it possible, therefore, (also given that it appears to be alien) that the screenwork now in Bettws-y-Crwyn once belonged in Ludlow, and that it was removed to this little church at the time of the coeval restoration of both churches in 1860? In other words, was the Ludlow screen 'refreshed' with new woodwork; and the original tracery heads, rather than being discarded, used to make the partition at nearby Bettws-y-Crwyn? After all, the

arch-restorer of late medieval woodwork, George Gilbert Scott, oversaw the restoration of Ludlow in 1859–1860. Scott is not named as the restorer of Bettws-y-Crwyn, but is known to have worked on the restoration of more than 500 churches during the 19th century.

CULMINGTON, ALL SAINTS

Culmington church is memorable for a number of features; the most prominent of which is its extraordinary spire. This begins its ascent as a standard broach spire, but after a short distance suddenly becomes an open framework of lead struts. The only concession this makes to the broach spire portion below is in its continuation of the lines of the former. The rest of the church consists of a nave and chancel in one. The fabric belongs mainly to the 13th and 14th centuries, but the walls contain a quantity of herringbone stonework that attests to earlier origins. Inside, the roof is also memorable: it has straight braces supporting collar-beams, and double-curved windbraces.

The rood-screen within has been partially renewed and is of considerable interest. It has five bays to either side of a central doorway, that takes the space of three bays. The standards and mullions carry matching ogee and cavetto mouldings. The standards are original, but the mullions contain some new work. These latter are dowelled into a middle rail, which has a squared top but is chamfered below. The wainscot is plain-boarded with no muntins (again some of this is new work). The sill is now obscured by later flooring, but is likely to be original. The uniform tracery heads, carved upon both sides, are also original. The design features a pointed arch, cusped and sub-cusped

*Culmington: Detail of tracery heads and head-beam,
the latter with unique leaf trail and attached top-cresting*

below, with the spandrels also cusped to give trefoil forms. The
mouldings of the mullions are returned over each head. Half of
the door-head tracery is replacement work.

The carved trail on the west face of the head-beam is arguably
the most interesting feature of the screen, and is extremely
unusual. Each compartment formed by the undulating trail is
filled with a foliage form, in appearance like the fanning out of
the veins on the underside of a leaf. This trail has been partially
renewed. The east side of the head-beam has a flat face between
half-rounds above and below. This face may have carried a carved
trail, but now houses a series of 11 little carved bosses (which
may originate from the soffit of a rood-loft). The top of the head-
beam has mortise holes for the rood-loft above. In the south wall

of the church, just before the screen, is a tiny door giving access
to the rood-stairs. Above this, there is an equally tiny door that
once opened onto the loft floor and through this door can be seen
a minuscule window to light the stairwell. To the west of this is
a larger rectangular window, presumably inserted to throw light
onto the Rood itself.

Llanvair Waterdine, St. Mary

Llanvair Waterdine stands right on the Radnorshire border, closer
to the churches of Beguildy and Heyop than any in Shropshire.
The church was rebuilt midway through the 19th century, and
consists of a nave, chancel and south porch. The original stone
roofing slates were re-used to pave the path when the church was
re-roofed.

The interior offers very little, and the church no longer
possesses a rood-screen at the entrance to its chancel.
However, the altar rail contains perhaps the most tantalising
and extraordinary collection of screen fragments to be found
anywhere in the southern Marches. Figure carvings are extremely
rare in late medieval screenwork, but in the modest remains at
Llanvair Waterdine there survives a spectacular array of human
and animal figures, both real and imagined, together with a
mysterious text and a number of unusual and significant pieces
of carved foliage enrichment.

The altar rail consists of a top rail, a sill and eight mullions
framed up between. The mullions are well moulded to both the east
and west with a sequence of quarter-rounds and quarter-hollows,
and each one is fronted with a half-round. These mouldings are
returned both over and under each bay to the west, but only over

150

each bay to the east (the sill being simply chamfered on this side).

The top rail on the north side has three distinct portions of carved trail, but has been composed to ensure that a continuous, undulating trail runs along its length. At the northern end of the top rail is what might be a stylised vine trail (though the vegetable forms are clearly different to the more obvious grape bunches further along). Moving south, the next section features vegetable forms that have every appearance of corn on the cob. In the midst of these is a dragon. Moving south again, there is a more traditional rendering of the vine, with a lion at its northern end.

The sill on the north side is also divided into three lengths of enrichment. At the northern end is a trail corresponding with that above, but with a bird at its northern end. Next comes a series of little square flowers and overlapping leaves; and south of this an oak trail with big acorns. The northern door-post has a trail

Llanvair Waterdine: Detail of altar rail –
vine trail and the mysterious text

Llanvair Waterdine: Detail of altar rail, from top to bottom –
a scene from a hunt; a characterful lion; a lively dragon

similar to that found at the northern end of both the top rail and the sill. This also features an elongated dragon and a figure with its hands up. Opposite this, the south door-post has a full-length woman over a three-quarter length bearded man.

The top rail and sill to the south, like those to the north, are also formed from three lengths of enrichment. The trail at the northern end of the southern half of the top rail has further exotic vegetable forms (which also have the appearance of corn on the cob). Also carved here are a deer and a hare (the latter beautifully rendered from above, as if lying in a 'form'). Moving south there are further unfamiliar forms: a depiction that looks something like peas in a pod, and finally a trail that matches the middle length in the northern half of the top rail.

The sill on the south side contains perhaps the most remarkable depiction to survive here: that of a hunt, with four dogs chasing a stag. Next to this comes a piece that comprises a series of square, foliage bosses (whose centres are of two different designs), and finally one featuring a series of very long serrated leaves. These leaves also appear on the top rail to the east (as does a green man with long serrated leaves coming out of his mouth at the northern end upon this side). The eastern face of the southern door-post features one large sun and three further smaller suns (or flowers?) of a similar design below; the eastern face of the north door-post has an undulating trail with single leaves in each compartment.

The part of the top-rail that closes over the entrance carries a piece of text, apparently in Arabic, which was eventually deciphered by the late Celtic scholar Sir John Rhys. It reads: 'Sir Matthew and Meyrick Pichgar of Clun set it [the screen] up for ten pounds together.' The appearance of the name of the priest –

Matthew – indicates that the screen was erected sometime between 1485 and 1520. The workmanship and invention is of a high order throughout, and the pieces clearly belonged to a quite glorious rood-screen and loft. No precedent exists for this work (save for Llangasty Tal-y-Llyn) and it may be that the screen was a one-off, produced (or at least carved) by an exceptionally gifted Shropshire artist. The screen was demolished in 1853.

LUDLOW, ST. LAURENCE

Gracing one of the loveliest of all English towns and visible for miles around, St. Laurences fully deserves its unofficial title, 'The Cathedral of the Marches'. As befitting such a large church it has a fairly complex building history, with the first church appearing on the site at the end of the 12th century. Today, very little survives from before *c*.1300 and the building's character is essentially Perpendicular (with a number of significant Decorated features).

As it now stands, the church consists of a nave, choir, chancel, side aisles, chancel aisles (forming chapels), a vestry, south porch and crossing tower. The interior west of the crossing is broad and lofty. At its east end it divides into a number of compartments, which contain between them a collection of church fixtures and fittings to rival any in England. The choir stalls have superb misericords (of the mid-15th century). The Palmers' Chapel on the north side contains fine woodwork and the lovely Palmers' and Annunciation (or Golden) windows. There is also a fine east window and chancel roof, an interesting collection of monuments, and no less than five late medieval screens.

The choir screen at Ludlow has the character of a monastic pulpitum. The decorative emphasis here is not given to its western

Ludlow: West side and underside of choir screen, showing the elaborate net of ribs that forms the vaulting, and the flattened pendant bosses

upper one with big, curly leaves. Running along the top of the screen is a top-cresting over a frieze (which matches that of the chancel aisle screens to the north and south). The ceiling is lierne vaulted, and is divided into eight square bays with elaborate pendant bosses at the intersections. The short corridor beneath this ceiling is panelled to both the north and south, and has some blind tracery. The eastern side of the screen is taken up with the stallwork of the choir.

face, but rather to its vaulted ceiling. The screen consists of one bay to either side of a central entranceway, which takes the space of four bays. Each outer bay is divided below middle rail height into two bays, and enriched with blind tracery heads. The high middle rail carries a frieze of quatrefoils within squares, while above the middle rail each single bay has a cinquefoiled head. The big standards are well moulded with ogees and rounds, and have, upon their western faces, squared then rounded boutell shafts with caps. From these spring the vaulting. Above are two carved trails of similar width; the lower one a vine trail and the

Ludlow: Generous but flattened spread of the vaulting of the south aisle screen

The south chapel screen is memorable chiefly for the unusually generous spread of its vaulting. This screen is divided into three major bays of four lights each (the central bay forming the doorway). The standards are well moulded (again with rounds, half-rounds and ogees) and are very similar to those at Lydbury North. They carry rounded boutell shafts topped with caps from which the vaulting springs. The plain wainscot is framed up between a huge chamfered sill and a middle rail; the latter returning the mouldings of the standards above and below. The tracery above, though expansive, is relatively simple. In line with the springing of the vault, each of the four lights belonging to the bays has a simple trefoil head. Above, these lights divide again to give pointed and cusped Perpendicular lights; the spandrels above containing quatrefoil and trefoil forms. The mullions are ogee-moulded, and the central one in each bay carries a half-round, both to echo the boutell shafts of the standards, and to link in with the vault above.

The vaulting of the south chapel screen has been noticeably flattened east to west, but the effect remains light and elegant. The bressumer to the west has a carved trail consisting of crinkly, spreading leaves between half-rounds. A frieze of quatrefoils within squares has been added to the top of this beam to give a degree of visual continuity across the three aligned screens at the east end of the nave and aisles. Below runs most of the screen's original drop-cresting. The corresponding beam to the east has a curved face between half-rounds (doubtless for a carved trail) and three-quarters of its original drop-cresting.

The screen to the north (or Palmers') chapel is especially fine, and together with the other fittings here (most notably the rare altar canopy) dates from the second half of the 15th century. It consists of three double bays to either side of a central doorway, which takes the space of two double bays. The standards are very similar to those of both the south chapel screen at Ludlow and the rood-screen at Lydbury North. The mullions, which are ogee-moulded, also match those of the south chapel, and throughout the screen the mouldings are returned over and under the bays both above and below middle rail height. The wainscot is decorated with blind tracery heads, each with a pointed arch over a cusped ogee arch. This has given two compartments, each containing a

Ludlow: Vaulting of the north (Palmers') chapel screen: how Bettws-y-Crwyn's screen might have looked with its vaulting in place

flower held by cusps (essentially forming two quatrefoils) and two spandrels, each containing a leaf form.

The double middle rail has a pair of carved trails with encircled four-petalled flowers. These flowers are spaced out to accommodate a running trail that undulates over and under, to give compartments each containing a leaf. This design is also very similar to that found at Lydbury North and Middleton, and it seems likely that all three screens originated from the same workshop centre. Between the middle rails is a series of quatrefoils with foliate cusps, (similar to those found at Kinnersley in Herefordshire). With the principal bays divided to give two lights

Ludlow: Cornice of north (Palmers') chapel screen, showing finely carved, paired vine trails

per bay, there are six tracery heads to either side of the central doorway. Each of these contains dense grid tracery over an ogee arch. The door-head is elaborately cusped and sub-cusped, and has spandrels carved with Tudor roses and foliage.

The tight but attractive lierne vaulting of the screen springs from caps topping the boutell shafts that front each standard. The bressumer carries two vine trails; the upper one deeper than the lower. Above this is the frieze of quatrefoils within squares found on the other screens, and below is a drop-cresting. The eastern side of the screen corresponds with the western, except for two differences. Firstly, the tracery heads have not been carved on this side; and secondly, the vaulting has been extended here. This latter seems to have been an afterthought, for a fringe of drop-cresting divides the original vault from a new portion that is set out quite differently. Two vine trails also appear on this side.

The screens to the north and south transepts are clearly related. The north screen now encloses the organ and consists of 13 bays, with a two-centred arch doorway taking the space of three bays. Rather than having distinct standards and mullions, the screen is divided by identical uprights that extend from the sill up to the head-beam. These have squared buttresses with offsets at middle rail height, and terminate in a second offset halfway between the middle rail and the head-beam. Lengths of an unusual (and low) middle rail, consisting of a hollow face containing one little foliate boss (or patera) per bay, are dowelled between these uprights. The wainscot has blind spandrels carved with foliage and flowers that terminate the cusps below. These are similar to those found at Bishop's Frome and Stoke Lacy etc. in Herefordshire. The simple mouldings of the uprights are returned over each bay, and a trefoil head tops each bay. The door-head has a two-centred arch with carved spandrels, and a rail matching that of the middle rail below. The head-beam has a deep trail of crinkly leaves. Above this a narrower face between half-rounds. This may also have housed a trail at some point.

The south transept screen differs from the north in a number of details, and appears to contain later work. It consists of four bays to either side of a central doorway, which takes the space of four bays. The spacing of the bays here is wider than that of the north transept screen. The middle rail is higher, and the wainscot below has blind tracery. This screen does have mullions dowelled into the middle rail. These are big and simply moulded with quarter-hollows along each edge. The carved trail is similar to that of the north transept screen, but may be new work. To the south, this beam has a flat face between half-rounds. At one time this evidently housed a further trail.

LYDBURY NORTH, ST. MICHAEL

Lydbury North has one of the oddest exteriors of any church in the southern Marches. Its walls are part-rendered, and its tower is held upright by a motley collection of buttresses. Inside, apart from the screens and the tympanum, there is a roof with arch braces supporting collar-beams, a pleasing collection of Jacobean box-pews, and an interesting font. The church consists of a nave, chancel, transepts (the southern one with a schoolroom above), a south porch and the west tower. The fabric belongs to the 12th and 13th centuries, but was altered and restored in both the 17th and 19th centuries.

The rood-screen has been greatly altered (certainly in the early 17th century, to judge from its tympanum) but retains much old work and is of great interest. It is clearly related to the screenwork at Ludlow and elsewhere. It consists of three bays to either side of a central doorway, that takes the space of two bays. The four intermediate standards extend from the sill up to the head-beam, and lengths of middle rail are dowelled between. All of the standards are well moulded, with a distinctive cross-section that matches that of the standards of the Palmers' screen at Ludlow. To either side of the foremost round, there are half-rounds and then ogees. Each central round belongs to a boutell shaft with a cap from which a fan (or lierne) vault once sprang. The eastern mouldings of the standards are similar but devoid of the two half-rounds (also, the boutell shafts here are not topped with caps).

The square-cut middle rail shows three mortise holes in its top face per bay for the mullions that once subdivided the design above middle rail height. The front of this rail carries a carved

frieze with an undulating trail, encircled quatrefoils and curved leaves: again, this is very similar to that found on the Palmers' chapel at Ludlow. The most interesting features of this screen, however, are to be found below middle rail height. Here, the wainscot is divided into narrow bays by very unusual muntins, each featuring two raised mouldings formed by paired ogees. Between these, three delightful openwork panels occupy each principal bay formed by the standards. The design appears to be a uniform pattern of four-petalled flowers and quatrefoils, but in fact these much restored panels are not quite uniform. The sill below is original but is encased in new timber. The fretwork tracery heads in the top of the screen are all new. The new head-beam has a curved face to east and west, with big bosses to the

Lydbury North: Huge hoarding painted with Decalogue, Creed and Lord's Prayer, occupying the space vacated by loft and tympanum

west. The rood-screen was repaired again in 1908; a factor that certainly accounts for some of this new work.

Over the rood-screen (and filling the space once occupied by the rood-loft) is painted the Decalogue, the Creed and the Lord's Prayer. As well as being a fine example of this once common post-Reformation feature, the work is also signed and dated: Charles Bright, Churchwarden, 1615. The Decalogues are supported by the head-beam below and a huge tie-beam above, and have been plain boarded to the reverse. In the north wall, the door that once opened onto the rood-loft can be seen (now behind glass), whilst in the north (or Plowden) chapel are the original rood-stairs.

The north chapel is divided from the nave by a relatively simple (and more clearly utilitarian) parclose screen. This has unusually narrow bays above middle rail height, and there is no evidence that these were ever topped with tracery. The standards are moulded with ogees and hollows; the mullions with ogees only. The head-beam is moulded with two half-rounds, the high middle rail is squared above and chamfered below, and the sill on which the screen stands is original.

MIDDLETON

Tiny Middleton church stands close to Middleton Court and an adjacent farm. It dates from the 12th century and consists of a nave, chancel, north porch and bellcote. It was comprehensively renovated midway through the 19th century.

For such a modest structure, the church contains an unusually interesting screen and loft. Although it incorporates a great deal of early work, as configured it is as much a creation of the 19th century as of any earlier period (*cf.* Llangwm in Monmouthshire).

The screen consists of three bays (the outermost ones blind) to either side of a central doorway, which takes the space of two bays. The standards are moulded in familiar fashion, with a round to the west and ogees to the east and west. The rounds belong to boutell shafts, each topped with a distinctive carved cap (very similar to those found at Lydbury North) from which springs the fairly intricate lierne vault of the loft. The standards also have grooves running up their inner faces, presumably for the tracery and moulded strips below.

The heavy middle rail carries a frieze of encircled quatrefoils upon its western face. These are related in their design to those found on the middle rails at Lydbury North and Ludlow (except that here, serrated triangular leaves, rather than curved leaves,

Middleton: Rood-screen and renewed loft

157

fill each compartment along the design). The middle rail has a groove running along its upper face. It is quite possible that in the course of alterations during the 19th century the middle rail was inverted, and that this groove once held in place the wainscot boards. Below, the wainscot now has new boarding and new tracery; the latter having two trefoil-headed lights (cusped between) below an ogee arch, with encircled quatrefoils in the spandrels. The new muntins and grooved sill below are chamfered.

Middleton: Crown-like boutell cap, with the vaulting ribs springing from the top

The pointed arch tracery heads are cusped and sub-cusped, with flowers terminating several of the cusps. The design is a delicate one carved upon one side only, and some of the heads have been damaged. The door-head, composed of the same components, is also damaged. Over the door there is a pair of interlocking back-to-front 'Ns'. The bressumer that terminates the vaulting to the west incorporates three carved trails. The uppermost, with two leaves and a diamond-shaped form to each compartment, may be new work. The middle one is a pomegranate trail, and is old work. The lower one features two leaves and a little flower per compartment, and is also old work.

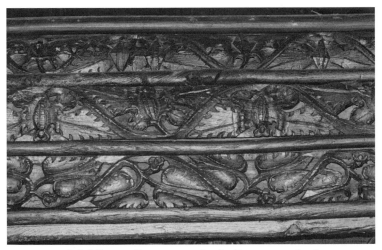

Middleton: Bressumer, including water-leaf and pomegranate trails

The loft parapet above appears to be all new work (with the possible exception of the very wide, flat muntins). Between these are six openwork panels: two with trefoils, two with quatrefoils, and two with a pair of spiralling dagger forms. The top beam is ornamented with a very unusual vine trail, which (rather bizarrely) has been attached so that it faces straight down. The design consists of a triple leaf and two bunches of grapes per compartment, with a stem running straight through, and an undulating trail forming each compartment: it is not well carved. Viewed from the east, it is clear that the 'loft' serves no functional purpose as it now stands, but is merely intended (along with the screen below) to enrich the interior of the church. No access to the original rood-loft is now visible.

RADNORSHIRE

ABEREDW, ST. CEWYDD

The exterior of St. Cewydds is memorable for its north porch, whose timber-framed gable end features a huge quatrefoil and two trefoils over a rugged, foiled truss. Inside the porch are tiered benches once used by mourners during wakes. The main body of the church consists of a nave and chancel (of the 14th century) and a west tower.

Once in the nave, the view eastwards is dominated by the cage-like screen which encloses the chancel. This fitting started life as a standard Radnorshire-type rood-screen in the late 15th century, and was originally surmounted by a rood-loft and tympanum. Together, these fittings would have completely walled off and enclosed the chancel, essentially forming a two-chamber structure. At some later date the loft and tympanum were taken down, and in the 17th century the screen was extended upwards with two tiers of wavy balusters.

This vertical extension entailed significant alterations to the original rood-screen. In order to raise the lintel over the doorway, the head-beam was cut through and a portion of this beam was lifted and re-mortised into the renewed door standards. To either side of the central doorway the screen is divided into seven narrow bays above the middle rail and six below. The tracery heads (each composed of a cusped ogee arch over which is a row of four grid lights each holding a rose) have been turned back to front, so that the carved sides now face eastwards into the chancel. In the process the mullions were also reversed and now stand upside down,

dowelled into a renewed middle rail. The mouldings used include ogees and half-rounds and are indicative of work belonging in date to the late 15th century. Above this are two tiers of wavy, fretwork slats. These are very similar to the slats found on the renewed loft front at Dolwyddelan in Caernarvonshire (though it seems highly unlikely that those at Aberedw originally formed a later balustrade to the loft parapet – there are simply too many of them). The tie-beam spanning the church at roof-springing level has also been re-faced with new woodwork.

Aberedw: The striking, cage-like screen, which dominates the view eastwards

Before being altered the screen appears to have had a comparatively low elevation; a factor that may have prompted the raising of the head-beam over the doorway. The middle rail, on the other hand, is unusually high and has been fixed above the half-way point between the sill and the head-beam (typically it would be fixed only one third of the way up). The head-beam, although mutilated, still retains the groove into which the tympanum was fixed. At either end the screen is framed by wall standards that extend from the sill up to the tie-beam overhead. This distinctive feature can also be found at Bettws Clyro, Disserth and Michaelchurch-on-Arrow in Radnorshire, and it once existed at Cregrina in the same county.

Nothing now survives of the rood-loft, but it seems likely that its bressumer was either fixed into the north and south walls of the nave, or was supported upon corbels or even upon an arcade of posts (as at Llanelieu in Breconshire). Aside from the tracery heads, there is little evidence of carved decoration and it has been suggested that colour, in the form of painting and gilding, was the chief mode of ornamentation here (again, as at Llanelieu).[1]

BEGUILDY, ST. MICHAEL

The church of St. Michael is a large, single-chamber structure which occupies an elevated site amid houses and farm buildings in this small village. Much of its fabric belongs to the late 15th century, but like so many other Welsh churches it was comprehensively restored in the second half of the 19th century.

The rood-screen and loft coving within are of great interest, not least because they represent a very rare instance of the operation of English influence upon Welsh screenwork (indeed, the fittings may originate from an English workshop source, for they are clearly related to the screenwork at both Kenderchurch and Eyton in Herefordshire).

The screen has seven bays to either side of a central doorway, which takes the space of four bays. The head-beam is moulded with hollows, half-rounds and an ogee (this latter to link it with the mullions below). Neither the head-beam nor the bressumer was intended to carry a carved trail.

The middle rail runs through unbroken between wall and door standards. This feature is characteristically Welsh, yet the rail, together with the sill and the muntins, is chamfered: a characteristic of many Midland (i.e. English) screens. In addition the tracery heads (whose west faces only are carved) are of a familiar Herefordshire-Gloucestershire type. Each tracery head features a cusped ogee arch, with the space above divided to give

Beguildy: Tracery heads of a type found in Herefordshire (e.g. at Stoke Lacy)

Beguildy: Rood-screen and loft coving looking west (see also plate 1)

a narrow grid light to either side of a traceried and pointed arch. The door-head is composed of four quatrefoils fringed by cusped foils, and is especially good. The tracery heads, middle rail and wainscot are all very similar to those belonging to the rood-screen at Heyop, just five miles to the south-east. These two screens, together with the one at Cascob (also in Radnorshire) display the same ogee-moulded members in their framing, making it just possible that all three may have originated from the same workshop centre.

Over the rood-screen, the steeply pitched coving of the rood-loft springs to both the east and the west. The western coving has been renewed, but its bressumer is supported upon the original posts that still stand one bay north and one south of the central doorway. The middle rail and wainscot below originally branched off at right angles to the west to meet with these posts, thus forming encloses for the side altars. Posts such as these once supported

Beguildy: Green man boss

the bressumer at Llanwnnog and can still be seen at Llanelieu in Breconshire (albeit in an earlier form). The attached spandrels with their serrated leaves are original; however, the drop-cresting below the bressumer is new. It replaces the more delicate original known only from drawings done by the Rev. Parker in 1830.

The eastern coving is substantially complete and retains much of its original carved and painted decoration. It consists of 20 panels in two rows, divided by ribs and carved bosses (including a fine Green Man) at the intersections. The panels are decorated with large, Tudor roses and the painting is executed in bluey-grey and white, with the roses themselves delineated in black.[2] In 1945, 18 out of the 20 panels still retained their painted decoration.[3] That number has now dropped to 13. The screen, having no trails of running ornament, relied heavily on painted enrichment for decorative effect.[4]

BETTWS CLYRO, HOLY TRINITY

This small, single-chamber chapel is not easily found. It stands quite alone among sheep-strewn fields in the hills above Clyro, and is hidden from the road by a thick strand of woodland. The structure was rebuilt in 1878–9, but retains a roof dating from the 14th century and parts of its old screenwork.

Although fragmentary, the surviving screenwork here is of unusual interest, for it belongs in date to the late 14th or early 15th century and incorporates a substantial part of an early and rare loft parapet. As it stands today the fitting consists of two wall standards which, like those of Aberedw, Disserth and Michaelchurch, extend from the sill up to the wall-plate of the roof. Although peculiar, this method of construction is entirely reasonable, for the wall standards are effectively braced between the sill and the roof principals, giving a sturdy frame in which to build up the screenwork and tympanum overhead. The ogee moulded wall standards each have an attached boutell, terminated by a cap and a plain brace where they meet the head-beam. The top of the head-beam has five mortise holes for the tympanum

Bettws Clyro: Parapet Detail

(now lost) and another series of later mortise holes which may once have held in place the parapet of a post-Reformation singing gallery. The lack of any mortise holes in the underside of the beam suggests that there was never a fence screen filling the void below the rood-loft. This is quite possible given that this was always a modest chapel (possibly domestic) and never a parish church. The beam may have been used as a rail from which to hang a Lenten veil.

The old parapet front has been set up on the top of the head-beam. It consists of 12 openings, cusped over and under. The mullions do not frame each bay (as they do in screens of the late 15th or early 16th century) but rather split half way up to join with the tracery. The moulding used has a centre fillet with two quarter-rounds, and runs seamlessly throughout both mullions and tracery. The design is not an invention of the wood carver but essentially of the stone mason, and is strongly indicative of a date of origin sometime in the late 14th or early 15th century.

CASCOB, ST. MICHAEL

The church occupies a memorable setting in an isolated hillside village. All around, nature seems on the point of reclaiming this churchyard. St. Michaels consists of a nave, chancel, south porch and west tower (built upon an artificial mound). The fabric belongs to a number of eras, but most notably perhaps the 14th and 15th centuries. The inevitable restoration of the 19th century was uncharacteristically restrained here (only the reredos betrays any Victorian heavy-handedness).

The screen within is of five bays to either side of a central doorway, which takes the space of three bays. The wainscot has two constructional moulded muntins dividing its plain panelling to each side of the doorway. The middle rail runs through

*Cascob: The plain but pleasingly moulded screen
and loft parapet*

163

between wall and door standards. The standards are pleasingly moulded with a series of rounds and hollows. Between are four intermediate mullions to each half of the screen, this time ogee-moulded to both east and west. Each bay has a semi-circular head made up of paired spandrels. These are carved in the solid with serrated leaves, and are almost certainly not coeval with the screen (though they may still be early). Carved spandrels such as these are characteristic of work belonging to the early 16th century, and though perhaps not as fine as the open tracery heads that may once have graced each bay, in their form they neatly echo the semi-circular arches of the door-head (which is original). The grooves for the original tracery heads can still be seen in the sides of the mullions, but no such groove exists in the head-beam. This is because the original head-beam and the loft soffit were removed to be replaced with the bressumer (which shows in its eastern face the joist holes for the loft floor) and the loft parapet overhead. At one time a tympanum would have filled the void above the screen (and enclosed the rood-loft on its eastern side).

The fine mouldings that characterise this screen are continued in the muntins of the loft parapet, which is divided into 15 panels. Each muntin has been moulded with a boutell flanked by hollows and ogees. The uncarved panels between may have been painted with figures of saints (as at Strensham in Worcestershire). The lack of any carved trails upon either the bressumer or the top-beam suggests that once again coloured rather than carved enrichment may have been pre-eminent here. Originally, a soffit projected westwards to the bressumer, which may have been supported on four posts with curved spandrels (as at Beguildy). No rood-stairs survive, suggesting that the fabric of a mural

access was lost during restoration, or that access was via a ladder or timber staircase, later removed. The mouldings used at Cascob (along with those found at Beguildy and Heyop) reveal the debt owed by these screens to Herefordshire work of the same period. Aside from the obvious material alterations, the screen has been carefully renewed in places, particularly on its southern side.

CEFNLLYS, ST. MICHAEL

Although Cefnllys church is remote even by Welsh standards, this was not always the case. Once there was a medieval borough here, enclosed by an elbow of the river Ithon and watched over by the precipitously sited Castell Cefnllys high above. Now the castle is ruinous and the houses have all gone. Foundations and footpaths still shadow the fields, but this is a place of birdsong and memory now.

Cefnllys: The rood-screen with its renewed tracery heads

164

In 1893, in an effort to force worshippers to attend the new church in Llandrindod Wells the Archdeacon had Cefnllys church unroofed. The story is taken up by the *Christian Pictorial* of 2 August 1894: 'It must not however be supposed that this ruthless demolition has really inflicted any serious inconvenience on the great majority of people, the attendance having been little more than nominal. Indeed, it is no uncommon thing for the officiating clergyman to be seen on a Sunday morning riding along in view of the church, to ascertain whether any of the neighbours were wending their way in that direction, and if not, turning his horse's head and hastening home again!' This drastic policy was later reversed and the church received its current hammerbeam and curve-braced roof in 1895, preserving the fittings within including the rood-screen of *c*.1500.

Two years open to the elements and 500 years of usage have not surprisingly given the rood-screen a weathered appearance. New woodwork was added to the head-beam, the panelling and the heads of each bay; and woodworm is everywhere apparent. The screen has six bays to either side of a central doorway, which takes the space of two bays. The low middle rail runs through and is very simply moulded, with three of its corners chamfered. Dowelled into this are mullions moulded with half-rounds and hollows. The standards too have corner chamfers, and the door standards each have a boutell surmounted by a cap (as at Beguildy and Bettws Clyro etc.) The wainscot is plain and has muntins that do not match up with the mullions above. Some of the muntins are constructional, others are not. The tracery heads have been replaced with fretwork panels of the crudest workmanship. The ruggedly carved head-beam has a hollow, a half-round, and

an ogee to the west, and may have carried a single trail of carved ornament upon both its eastern and western faces. The top of the head-beam retains mortise holes, probably for the tympanum.

CREGRINA, ST. DAVID

St. Davids stands in a circular churchyard, and consists of a nave and chancel of different dates. The fabric belongs to the 13th century or earlier, but was rendered and whitewashed midway through the 20th century. There are very few straight angles at Cregrina: the chancel is not aligned with the nave, and the screen that divides the two leans from the perpendicular in care worn fashion, its wainscot planks spilling out like cards from a deck.

*Cregrina: The sturdy little rood-screen
at the entrance to the chancel*

The rood-screen is small but its framing is stoutly constructed from disproportionately massive timbers. It consists of just three bays to either side of a central doorway (that takes the space of two bays) and was once framed by sizeable wall standards which extended from the sill up to the tie-beam (as they do still at Aberedw, Bettws Clyro, and Disserth). The disappearance of these wall standards means that the screen no longer fits as it once did. The bays have tracery heads whose western faces only are carved. The pattern is repeated and consists of a rose-cusped ogee head filled with grid tracery above. The door-head tracery once consisted of a series of grid lights with a quatrefoil to the centre. Each door standard has a buttress terminating in a crocketed pinnacle. This feature, together with the square blocking of the mullions where they meet the middle rail, echoes the setting out at Michaelchurch (though without the refinement). The head-beam has mortise holes for the soffit of the rood-loft, and a continuous rebate for the tympanum.[5] The massive timbers, rugged carving, and the presence at one time of wall standards that extended up to the wall-plate, all indicate a relatively early date for the screen; if not in the 14th century then possibly no later than the middle of the 15th century.

DISSERTH, ST. CEWYDD

The church stands next to a caravan park beside the river Ithon. It is unusually interesting both inside and out and has benefitted greatly from being overlooked by the restorers of the 19th century. As Richard Haslam notes, 'The church stands very much as a Victorian architect, called in for advice, might have found many of the Radnorshire churches'.[6] The exterior, with the exception of the superb west tower of $c.1400$, is whitewashed. The rest of the fabric belongs to the 15th century. The interior is a time capsule that has remained little altered since about 1700. The whole body of the church (but for the flag-stone floor bisecting the nave) is filled with box pews, variously inserted between the middle of the 17th century and the early 18th century.

Of the original screen only the wall standards now survive. These extend from the sill up to the tie-beam overhead (as at Aberedw and Bettws Clyro). Mortise holes in the wall standards and sill betray something of the screen's original form. It once had eight narrow bays (with tracery heads) to either side of a central doorway (that took the space of three bays) and stood butted into the western halves of the wall standards. Above the height of the screen the chamfers of the wall standards die out to leave a slot decorated with semi-circles.

In 1945 the wainscot, middle rail and a shortened door standard still remained on the north side, along with the sawn off end of the head-beam (moulded upon its western face with two half-rounds) in the north wall. The wainscot was plain boarded. The middle rail and door standards were unmoulded but for plain chamfers, and the head-beam had half-rounds and no trails of running ornament. No carving or tracery survives. The tie-beam once supported the tympanum. Below was the rood-loft, which was supported upon the head-beam and extended to the west only. The survival of these few fragments owes much to the intervention of F.E. Howard (of *English Church Woodwork* fame) who carried out repairs to the church.

HEYOP, ST. DAVID

Heyop enjoys a tranquil, valley setting. Its church, which belongs to the late 19th century, stands on the fringes of the village, on a site once occupied by its predecessor of the 15th century. The current structure has a nave and chancel in one and a little west tower topped by a broach-spire. Perhaps because of the single-chamber form the old screenwork was re-erected in the new church, thus maintaining the division between nave and chancel.

The mellow-timbered screen is closely allied to that of nearby Beguildy, though is nothing like so complete. It features the same ogee mouldings to the standards and mullions, and the same plain middle rail and wainscot below (the middle rail and the wainscot muntins are both simply chamfered). The western faces of the door standards have buttresses with offsets and shaped bases. The head-beam is moulded to the east and the west but is more elaborate than Beguildy's, with a wealth of hollows, rounds and ogees (like the head-beam at Beguildy it was never intended to take carved trails; see plate 2). The tracery heads are also similar to those at Beguildy. Much of the original woodwork

Heyop: Related to Beguildy but less complete

has been painstakingly restored, with old fragments carefully re-inserted wherever possible (the tracery heads and eastern faces of the mullions are cases in point). The door-head tracery and the cross overhead (buttressed by a reversed version of the door-head tracery) are both modern.

LLANANNO, ST. ANNO

The wonder of Llananno is that such a modest building could possibly contain such riches. The church was built in 1876–7 to replace the old church that had stood on the same spot beside the Ithon. The earlier building is described in a manuscript of 1818 by Jonathan Williams as 'a small antique structure consisting of a nave, chancel, porch and low tower'. The exterior of the new church offers little to excite the visitor, and nor would its interior but for the late medieval rood-screen and loft, which were carefully re-erected in the new church. This act, which nowadays might be taken for granted, shows an unusual degree of enlightenment for the period. As Crossley and Ridgway put it, the screenwork 'has survived the vicissitudes of the rebuilding of the church when an excellent opportunity was offered for its destruction, for to the modern mind it is an obstruction with a faint odour of superstition hanging about it'.[7]

This masterpiece of joinery and decorative carving is the work of the Newtown School of screen-carvers, and is arguably the finest piece of substantially complete church screenwork remaining in Wales. Of the other surviving work produced by the School only the incomplete screen at Daresbury in Cheshire and the numerous but misappropriated pieces of the rood-screen and loft at Newtown can compete with it for quality, invention or variety.

The current church is wider than the old one, and the screen and loft within have been lengthened by two bays and new woodwork inserted to ensure a proper fit. The screen now consists of five (rather than four) bays to either side of central doorway, which takes the space of two and a half bays. The wall and door standards extend from the huge, raised sill up to the head-beam above. The sturdy middle rail into which the mullions above and the matching muntins below are dowelled has a flat channel that may once have contained a carved trail. The various framing members are moulded with a series of half-rounds, with those belonging to the mullions being returned across the heads of each bay, and the foremost moulding of the standard meeting with the bottom half-round of the head-trail. The wainscot panels are plain.

The distinctive tracery heads are of six different designs, each consisting of a double arcade filled above with a delightful, free patterned tracery (carved upon both faces). This tracery is of an identical type to that found at Llanwnnog in Montgomeryshire and, but for the replacement panels, is cut from a single board which has been slotted through the mullions. The superb door-head features spandrels each of which contains five tracery wheels that diminish in size as they near the apex. The flat arch formed below has drop-cresting. The tracery heads bear no relation to window tracery, but instead form a lacy fringe whose intricacies can be enjoyed in silhouette against the whitewashed, east wall of the chancel. This decoration marks the downward extension of the decoration of the rood-loft, and specifically of that belonging to the loft coving.

The head-beam retains its original trails of running ornament upon both its eastern and western faces. To the west is a leaf and flower trail of a design found nowhere else; to the east, a

Llananno: the tracery heads, designed to embellish the rood-loft rather than the screen below

trail described by Crossley and Ridgway as 'probably the finest rendering of the water plant as a decorative motive in existence'.[8] This was originally attached to the west side of the head-beam.

From the head-beam the coving of the rood-loft springs to both the east and the west. The eastern cove has 36 plain panels divided by ribs and bosses; but the western cove (which has 34 panels[9]) gleefully continues the theme of richness and invention set by the tracery heads below. The panels are of at least 17 different designs. These are backed by the loft floor and, in a neat counterpoint to the treatment beneath, it is the pierced form of each panel that is here thrown into shadow, rather than the tracery itself. A number of the panels have been carefully renewed.

Llananno: Rood-screen and loft

*Llananno: Finely carved bressumer featuring a Wyvern (top),
out of whose jaws a vine trail springs (bottom).
The pomegranate trail below confirms a date of
post-1501 for the screenwork*

The eastern bressumer houses a single trail of serrated leaves. The western bressumer has two trails: the lower one is an abstract pomegranate trail (also with serrated leaves) confirming a date of post-1501 for the fitting. The wider trail above is a vine trail, and emanates from the jaws of a Wyvern at the southern end (that occupying the northern end is a later addition).

To the east the loft parapet has plain panels divided by muntins. The top-beam on this side never had a carved trail but was probably ornamented with cresting. The western parapet has 25 canopied niches divided by pinnacled buttresses. Each two-sided canopy has a matching crocketed pinnacle in front, which divides the two crocketed and cusped heads of each canopy. Each niche contains the figure of a saint (carved by Boulton of Cheltenham in *c*.1880). These are well executed, with an appropriate degree of Gothic attenuation. They are tightly packed in and do not draw the eye as individuals, but rather contribute en-masse to an overall effect of encrusted and textural richness. The rood-beam overhead has a fine and deep water-plant trail. Messrs. Crossley and Ridgway report finding paint traces in 1915, and there seems little doubt (given what we know of the screen and loft at Newtown) that Llananno's screenwork was once sumptuously endowed with gilt and polychrome enrichment.

LLANBADARN FYNYDD, ST. PADARN

Like the church at nearby Llananno, that at Llanbadarn Fynydd stands next to the river Ithon and is an essentially Victorian structure of single-chamber plan. It was more fortunate than Llananno in retaining its *c*.1500 arch-braced roof together with one Decorated window. Where it was less fortunate was in the retention of so little of its late medieval screenwork. Today, only the bressumer-beam survives, together with four fragmentary trails of carved decoration which have been variously inserted upon its western face.

In 1829, when the church was visited by the Rev. Parker, other pieces of the screen were still present including a complete tracery head, parts of the head-beam and mullions and the foliage trails still visible today. Some or all of these pieces had been incorporated in a later west gallery, but most were lost when the church was

Llanbadarn Fynydd: The surviving bressumer with lengths of a thin vine trail (top) and water-plant trail (bottom)

restored in 1894 and the gallery taken down. The tracery heads were evidently unusual and fine. The design consisted of two circular quatrefoils each framed by a semi-circle above and a cusped ogee archlet below. They also had small, pierced corner spandrels. The surviving bressumer is well moulded to the west only with hollows and rounds, and has a series of mortise holes cut into its top for the loft parapet. The foliage trails are of three different types: vine, water-leaf (without flowers in this version) and four-petaled flower. The pieces have been fixed into the centre hollow of the bressumer, but could have come from any one of the other beams associated with the original rood-screen and loft. The screenwork here probably originated in the county, but may not have come from the Newtown centre.

LLANBADARN-Y-GARREG, ST. PADARN

The little whitewashed church of St. Padarn stands in a field next to the river Edw. There is little to betray its true date, but it probably belongs to the 13th or 14th century. Inside, an unmoulded timber beam supported at either end by curved braces spans the chamber. Its western face is chamfered and it has mortise holes in its eastern face and its underside. What function it served is unclear. Only two beams belonging to a rood-screen or rood-loft can have mortise holes at right angles to one another: the head-beam of the screen or the bressumer of the rood-loft. For it to have been either of these it must at some time have been turned lengthways through 180°, or rotated, for it makes no sense as it is currently set. The beam now supports a plaster and lath panel that once displayed the Royal Arms upon its western side and a sacred text to the east.

LLANBISTER, ST. CYNLLO

This very unusual church, which dates mainly from the 14th century, derives many of its idiosyncrasies from its setting on a sloping site overlooking the hillside village of Llanbister. It has a tower belonging to the 16th century at its east end (rather than its west end) and no windows in either its east or west walls. Access to the church is gained via first one flight of steps up to the door and then a further flight inside. The floor of the nave is thus almost level with the roof of the south porch. The church is of single chamber form, but the demarcation of the chancel is registered by a further jump in floor levels. It has a west gallery of 1716 and below it an old schoolroom.[10] Also at the west end is an immersion font. One of the church's restorers in 1908 was W.D. Caröe, who also worked at Llanfilo and Partrishow in Breconshire.

The old rood-screen stands on the edge of the raised floor of the chancel. It spans what is a fairly wide nave, and has eight bays to either side of a central doorway, which takes the space of three bays. The wainscot is divided up by constructional muntins that do not match up with the mullions above. The muntins are moulded upon both faces, and are all original save one on the north side. The panelling of the wainscot narrows to the north in order to absorb the slope of the nave floor here. The middle rail features the same flat hollow seen at Llananno (and this too may once have held a carved trail). The mullions are handsomely moulded with ogees, and the door standards with ogees and half-rounds. Each door standard has a boutell with a base and cap (as at Beguildy). The tracery heads are weak copies of those found at Llananno, and were added when the church was restored. The

Llanbister: Wide rood-screen with renewed tracery heads based on those found at nearby Llananno

wall standards are plain but for the rough mouldings and tracery head slots in their inner faces.

The massive head-beam is also plain, but its western face may have been moulded at one time (and the mouldings subsequently chiselled off). It has a groove along its top for the tympanum and it almost certainly supported the rood-loft at one time (which extended to the west only). Due to the considerable width of the nave the western bressumer of the loft may have been supported upon posts originally (as at Beguildy). Given the probable late date of the screen (i.e. *c*.1500) the loss of the rood-loft has robbed the fitting of its richest component. However, the workmanship visible in the forming of the mullions and the door standards attests to the high quality of the fitting in its unmutilated state.

LLANDEGLEY, St. Tecla

Llandegley: Tracery head

This single-chamber church was largely rebuilt in 1876 when its west tower, which is topped by a little broach-spire, was added. Prior to restoration it appears that a loft of some kind (possibly a later singing gallery) surmounted the rood-screen and was accessed via a staircase from the chancel.[11]

The old screen was retained but has been greatly altered. It now stands on a new sill and consists of six bays (rather than five) to either side of a central doorway. The plain wainscot is grooved into the underside of a chamfered middle rail and has muntins that match the mullions above. The tracery heads to the north are original, but those to the south are replacements (so too the door-head tracery). The heads are of two different designs (both of which feature rose cusping) and are carved upon their west faces only (just as at Aberedw). The original work on the north side is cut from a single board which has then been slotted through the mullions (*cf.* Llananno). In its setting out and its mouldings the screen is closely allied to those found at Aberedw, Cregrina and Disserth. A length of boldly carved water-plant trail was cut up and fixed around the edge of the altar table (which belongs to the 19th century, see photograph on p.84). This carving was probably imported from elsewhere, and may be a product of the Newtown workshops.

MICHAELCHURCH-ON-ARROW, St. Michael

Michaelchurch occupies a peaceful site close to the Herefordshire border. It consists of a nave, chancel and saddleback tower (whose roof pitches east-west, rather than north-south). The fabric belongs mainly to the 13th and 14th centuries, but was subjected to a punitive restoration in 1869. The interior is interesting both for the substantially complete screen which still divides the chancel from the nave, and the fragmentary remains of an earlier screen, which have been set up in the sanctuary.

During the restoration the rood-screen was given a new head-beam and wall standards.[12] Originally, the latter would have had pinnacles (as the door standards and mullions still do) but these have been lost. The screen framed by these elements appears

Michaelchurch-on-Arrow: Tracery heads

173

*Michaelchurch-on-Arrow: Door-head tracery
with its richly-crocketed ogee arch*

Welsh in construction, with the standards running through between sill and head-beam, and the mullions dowelled into the middle rail. However, the mouldings on the vertical elements – the door standards, mullions and muntins – are less obviously Welsh. Gone are the familiar rounds, hollows and ogees, to be replaced here with chamfers having buttressed fronts (the standards and mullions feature crocketed pinnacles). The door standards, mullions and muntins meet the hipped middle rail in a series of awkward and distinctive joints. The middle rail is cut to show on the inner face of each door standard, while the mullions end in plain blocks that are wider than the top of the middle rail.

Below the middle rail the screen has a plain wainscot topped by a frieze of round, openwork quatrefoils.

The tracery heads feature big crocketed and cusped ogee arches of a Herefordshire type, which are carved upon their west faces only. These are set slightly proud of the screen on its western side, and form canopies to each bay. Above this and set within the square head of each bay is a series of cusped and crocketed arches, whose crockets rise up into narrow arches which are flanked by small grid lights. The design of the tracery, together with the mouldings on the framing members, makes it not only possible but quite likely that this screen was imported from Herefordshire. Unfortunately, the replacing of the head-beam and wall standards has made it all but impossible to discern the original appearance of the rood-loft that once surmounted the screen.

The current chancel screen almost certainly dates from the early 16th century, but the remains in the sanctuary (possibly placed here to support a reredos) are probably a century older. They belong to a screen of Welsh construction, having wall standards extending from the sill up to the wall-plate of the roof (as they do at Aberedw and Disserth). Above middle rail height the mouldings of the wall standards (which consist of shallow hollows or cavettos divided by quirks) feature four paterae.[13] Above head-beam height the standards each have another mortise; this time for a cross-beam designed to support the Rood and tympanum, as at Llanelieu. Indeed it is possible that these fragments were once components of just such a double screen.

New Radnor, St. Mary

Restoration does not get less sympathetic than this. The old church was completely demolished in the 1840s, and but for the modest intervention of a clerk called Dashwood not one single scrap of the old fabric would have been retained. The new church was completed in 1845 and is described by the RCAMW as having 'no pretence of architectural consideration'.[14] Dashwood's contribution was to suggest that parts of the old screen be kept and worked into the new communion rail. The opportunity to save money (rather than any of the historical fabric) seems to have persuaded the committee overseeing the works that this was a reasonable course of action. Today, 12 tracery heads of two different designs survive in this form.

Prior to the demolition of the old church the Rev. Parker paid a visit and made some brief notes and drawings, once again giving us an invaluable record of a now-lost rood-screen. The old church had a nave with a side aisle to the south. According to Parker, the chancel screen consisted of seven bays to one side of a central doorway, and six to the other. A deep, unmoulded middle rail surmounted a wainscot enriched with blind tracery; the latter having muntins that matched up with the mullions above. Overhead, there was a strong and fairly plain head-beam. The screen continued across the side aisle, and there was a parclose screen spanning the final bay of the arcade between the last of the five octagonal piers and the east wall. The surviving tracery heads are well carved upon one face only. Ten of the heads feature straight-sided arches formed by two members crossing but not reaching the corners, so admitting a cusped light to each side. The lights are cusped below, and are similar to those found at Llandefalle in Breconshire. The other two heads have four cusps rather than two, and open corner spandrels which are also cusped. When Crossley and Ridgway visited in 1945 the door-head and 18 tracery heads survived; some of which then formed part of the reredos.[15]

Norton, St. Andrew

The church, which stands in the middle of the village, was largely rebuilt by Sir George Gilbert Scott in 1868. He added small transepts to an existing single-chamber structure and retained some of the older fabric, including the attractive bell-turret of the 17th century, parts of the roof and the chancel screen.

The screen within has six standards extending from the sill up to the head-beam (instead of the usual four). These form two principal bays to either side of a central doorway. Each bay is subdivided by a mullion dowelled into the chamfered middle rail, which lines up with a muntin below. The quatrefoil-headed lights, the cresting and the wainscot panels are all modern, but much of the framing of the screen is original. The head-beam, the standards and the mullions are all well moulded; the standards each having three boutells, and the mullions plain hollows. The head-beam, which is moulded on both sides, probably never had any carved trails. Flanking the doorway on the screen's eastern side are two old, half bench-ends.

Old Radnor, St. Stephen

The church's very English design, construction and detailing are accounted for by the settling of the western boundary of the diocese of Hereford in the 12th century. This enclosed the border

Old Radnor: Detail of rood-screen

parish of Old Radnor and brought it within the compass of English influence; its patronage passing from the princes of Powys into the keeping of the Mortimer family.

The church, which occupies a lofty hilltop site, is visible for miles around. It fully deserves such prominence, for this is a treasure house packed with good things. The building was substantially remodelled in the 15th century and consists of a nave and chancel, side aisles with chapels, a west tower and a south porch. As well as a complete set of screens, it contains superb roofs, interesting stained glass, a fine organ case of the 16th century (probably the earliest in the British Isles), medieval floor tiles and a font that may date from before the Conquest.

The rood-screen stretches right across the church to span the side aisles as well as the nave. Further east and dividing the chancel from the aisles are three parclose screens (one to the north[16] and two to the south). The central portion of the rood-screen has three bays to either side of a central doorway, which takes the space of two bays. The portion to the south has two bays to either side of a central doorway (again of two bays), while that to the north has four bays, this time with a door at its southern end. Although the screen as a whole is punctuated by the piers of the arcade, the loft coving above projects far enough to the west for this to run unbroken from north to south. The standards all extend from the sill up to the head-beam in typical English fashion, and the bays are wider than those commonly found in Wales.

The rood-screen is elegantly designed and finely carved throughout. The decoration starts in the wainscot. Here each bay is divided into two panels, each topped by a cusped, blind-traceried head. Above are two middle rails[17] with quatrefoils upon their western sides, separated by an open carved frieze of quatrefoils. The shallow tracery heads to each bay are composed of foliated and cusped trefoils, which have rose cusps below and spandrels containing encircled trefoils to each corner. The heads are generally uniform, but show some variation between screen sections.[18] The doorways, which take the space of two bays, each feature a door-head that has a cross-bar supporting a section of standard in order to maintain the regular pattern of the heads (and vaulting) across the whole of the screen. The door-heads have cresting and are filled with rather thin tracery (which may be modern) between the cross-bar and a flat arch below; that

Old Radnor: Parker drawing labelled 'Elevation of a screen in the North aisle'

belonging to the north aisle echoes the tracery above it and has solid spandrels carved with foliage.

The treatment of the tracery heads is necessarily different to the east and west due to the design of the loft vaulting overhead. To the west the bays have Tudor arch-shaped heads framed by ribs which form part of the tierceron vault above. However, to the east the rood-loft was supported over a straight soffit (rather than a vault), as it is at Clynnog Fawr in Caernarvonshire, Hughley in Shropshire and several other churches along the border. This has left solid spandrels in the heads of each bay on the eastern side, each of which has been carved with a serrated leaf design.

The ribs of the shallow vault to the east spring from caps surmounting boutells on the fronts of the standards. At the intersections the ribs have small floral bosses. To the west the soffit has vertical ribs aligned with the uprights below. The soffit to the east has been tilted to such an angle as to ensure that the eastern bressumer is at the same height as the western bressumer, and the loft floor between the two is flat. The carved trails between the renewed top- and drop-cresting of the bressumer are very unusual. Both are versions of a vine trail with highly stylised square leaves, and grape bunches that look like corn on the cob. The lower trail is half the width of the upper one. The vine trail in the north aisle is less unusual.

Although the screenwork at Old Radnor is unusually complete, much has been lost and its appearance was evidently quite different to that which we find today. A rood-loft once surmounted the screen for its entire length (the bressumer still has the mortise holes for the loft parapet) and colour played an important role. A visitor to the church in 1818 writes of, 'The beautiful screen ... painted and gilded, and bearing on it the representations of saints and religious persons, placed in ranges, compartments or niches'.[19] A Victorian restoration clearly saw to this enrichment, and the moving of the organ into the chancel must have resulted in the destruction of one of the two north parclose screens.

The head tracery in the parclose screens (along with some of that in the door-heads of the main screen) has been renewed. It once featured two quatrefoils per head over a cusped ogee arch, rather than the current arched trefoils[20] (this design is of the same Gloucester-Hereford type as that found at Winchcombe). The head enrichments and crestings of the parclose screens are also modern, and at least one doorway has been moved or taken out altogether.

The vaulted screenwork of Old Radnor, encompassing as it does the side aisles, and once featuring painted representations of the saints, recalls that of the West-country. However, the nature of the vaulting, the bressumer trails, and the elaborate middle rail are all redolent of the mutilated screenwork at Cirencester, and there is little doubt that both originated from the same workshop source, possibly in Gloucestershire; a workshop whose products also appear in Worcestershire and Herefordshire.

BRECONSHIRE

BRECON, THE CATHEDRAL CHURCH OF ST. JOHN THE EVANGELIST
Brecon Cathedral nestles on a ridge overlooking the town, its visual impact restricted by its compact size and low tower. Most of the building belongs to the mid-13th and the 14th centuries. However, its lovely Early English chancel was erected in the first years of the 13th century. In both date and appearance it is closely related to the Lady Chapel at Hereford Cathedral. Up until 1923 Brecon Cathedral was a Benedictine priory church and is still adjoined by many of its early conventual buildings.

Before the Dissolution, Brecon priory possessed a notable array of late medieval screenwork. Besides the rood-screen (and its associated fixtures) there was also a presbytery screen, a pulpitum and a number of fence screens. The rood-screen was especially important in priory churches, as it divided the parishioners' nave from the areas reserved for monastic worship. Brecon's rood-screen was evidently wide, and may have incorporated a reredos (like the one at Beverley in Yorkshire, or Gresford in Denbighshire). It probably had doorways to either side of the altar for processions (as at Ewenny in Glamorgan) and certainly had panels decorated with paintings (and possibly carvings) relating to various local guilds.[1] Today, the doorways and corbels high up in the walls of the nave are all that remain of the rood arrangement that once stood west of the crossing. Parts of the presbytery screen survive in mutilated form as the parclose screen to the St. Keyne's Chapel on the north side of the nave. Aside from these vestiges and a few other notable fragments all else is lost.

The renowned late medieval rood arrangement of Brecon Priory, situated high above the rood-screen and loft, consisted of a rood-group and celure (or canopy of honour) overhead. The Rood was flanked by the Blessed Virgin Mary and St. John the Baptist, as well as the figures of the two thieves (as at St. Fiacre-le-Fouet in Brittany) and the symbols of the four Evangelists. The focus of this arrangement was unquestionably the giant Rood itself, variously referred to as the *Crog Aberhonddu* (the Cross of Brecon)

Brecon: Engraving of the presbytery screen in situ *(from a drawing by H.S. Davis) prior to its removal in the 19th century*

or the Golden Rood. In the second half of the 15th century the Welsh bards wrote poems in its honour, and pilgrims, enchanted by tales of its beauty and keen to test its reputation for healing the sick, travelled great distances to see it. For a time the church even became known as the Church of the Holy Rood.

The scale and prominence of the rood arrangement is clear from the positions of the rood-doors and the corbels west of the crossing. The two doors (some eight feet up) would have opened out on to the floor of the rood-loft. Of the corbels immediately above this, those at the front probably supported the rood-beam (which in turn supported the Rood), while those at the back supported the tympanum. The orientation of the corbels higher up suggests the coved form of a celure (however, it is possible that those at the front supported a beam designed to steady the Rood).

It is not known when the Rood and celure at Brecon were taken down. However, the unusual levels of veneration attracted by the *Crog Aberhonddu*, and the widespread nature of its fame, must have made its removal a high priority for the iconoclasts during the Reformation in the 16th century. According to Theophilus Jones,[2] the rood-loft remained in place until 1809, before this too was pulled down leaving behind just the screen. This too was later removed, though the date of this act is not recorded.

Moving slightly eastwards, the corbelling off of the inner mouldings of the western tower arches attests to the presence of a pulpitum here at one time. This was most likely of stone, but no part of it survives today. Moving eastwards again, we reach the eastern tower arch and the location of the presbytery screen of the 16th century. This was taken down in 1862 by George Gilbert Scott during his restoration of the chancel. It was initially re-

erected as a fence screen before the Havard chapel in the north transept, before being moved to its present position in 1921.

The screen comprises six double bays (two double bays are missing). Each bay has a single, plain wainscot panel below the middle rail and is divided by a mullion to give two lights above, each of which is decorated with cusped tracery. Although the screen features the rectangular construction familiar to much screenwork of the southern Marches, it has no obvious kinship with local work. Indeed, a number of its features are decidedly un-Welsh. For example, the standards run unbroken from the sill up to the head-beam,

Brecon: Detail of parclose screen to the St. Keyne's Chapel

with lengths of middle rail dowelled between (in most Welsh screens the middle rail is continuous and all of the vertical elements between the wall and door standards are dowelled into it). The brattishing of the middle rail and the design of the tracery heads also point to an English origin. At one time the hollow-chamfered head-beam housed a single carved trail (from which the pieces re-used in the pulpit may derive). The carved wooden bosses on the wainscot panels and the head-beam once belonged to the late Perpendicular choir roof.

Some notable fragments of old screenwork have also been incorporated into the nave pulpit. These include a narrow band of vine trail, and three panels (once of openwork, but now backed) which may have come from a rood-loft parapet. These panels are finely carved, and are similar in their design to those at nearby Partrishow.

BRONLLYS, ST. MARY

The church of St. Mary consists of a chancel and nave (both substantially rebuilt in the late 19th century) and a squat, detached bell tower possibly of the 13th century. The chief interest of the church's interior is the rood-screen, which dates from the early 16th century and now divides off the vestry at the west end of the nave. In the east wall of the nave, meanwhile, are a number of components associated with the missing rood-loft.

In 1947, the rood-screen still stood at the east end of the nave, eight feet to the west of the chancel arch. If this did not represent its exact position prior to restoration it was probably not far out, for as designed it would have supported the front of the rood-loft. Across the chancel arch there was probably a fence screen, and against the blank parts of the east wall to either side there stood two stone altars. Over the fence screen a tympanum once filled the upper half of the chancel arch. Such an arrangement can also be found at Llywel in Breconshire and at a number of churches in Radnorshire and Montgomeryshire. Today, the door to the rood-stairs and a single loft corbel can still be seen in the east wall of the nave. In the second half of the 20th century (probably before

Bronllys: Robustly-carved spandrels at the intersection of standard and head-beam

1979) the screen was moved to the west end of the church. Its fabric was little altered in the move, though the wall standards were evidently replaced.

The screen itself is massively constructed, and is of three bays with well-curved spandrels at the intersections of standard and bressumer. These spandrels are ornamented with lively foliage carvings. One of these was described by a Mrs. G.F. Dawson[3] in 1909 as having 'a rather spirited head'. This is a green man with leaves springing from its open mouth (see photograph above). Along the bressumer are 12 square paterae, in the form of stylised vine leaves. These are a later addition and conceal mortise holes that once housed the joists that supported the floor of the rood-loft. This being the case the screen faces west as it has always done, and was not turned through 180° when it was moved to the west end of the church.

CWMDU, ST. MICHAEL

St. Michaels is a large and consistent church of the 1430s. It comprises a nave with south aisle,[4] choir and small chancel, and has a battlemented tower at its west end. The church has a number of fine windows, of which the expansive and panel-traceried east window is perhaps the most noteworthy.

Inside, no screen divides the chancel from the nave. However, a significant collection of pieces from a rood-screen (and perhaps loft) of *c.*1500 now lines the sanctuary (*cf.* Newtown). This includes 30 traceried heads, several lengths of vine trail and fragments of cresting. Some of this woodwork has been renewed, but most is original. The carving is generally of a high order, but is especially good in the slightly wider vine trails over the altar. It is not clear whether the 14 trefoil-headed bays that form the arcade of the altar rail (*cf.* New Radnor) also once belonged to a rood-screen or – as is more likely – a rood-loft parapet, though either is quite possible.

Cwmdu: Screen fragments lining sanctuary

LLANDEFALLE, ST. MATTHEW OR MAELOG

The large church at Llandefalle stands on the south-facing slope of a small valley, with only a rectory and a few farm buildings for company. The interior is airy and unadorned, and in typical Welsh fashion consists of a nave, chancel and south aisle. The chancel arch, however, is uncharacteristically large for Breconshire.

The rood-screen survives in its original location and in something like its original form (though minus its rood-loft). It is composed of four bays to either side of a central doorway, which takes the space of two bays. It is constructed of oak that has been allowed to mellow over time to a warm, sandy brown colour. The general composition of the screen is particularly coherent and satisfying, with identical mouldings (completed with a half-round) used throughout and returned over the heads of each bay.

Each bay above middle rail height has a tracery light consisting of a crossed diagonal (or scissor form) cusped below and with each of its three compartments containing an encircled quatrefoil. Only the door-head tracery is new work; the rest is original. The design of the tracery, which is related to that found at Partrishow and several other churches in the county (as well as at New Radnor in Radnorshire) indicates a date of *c.*1500 for the fitting. The head-beam is decorated with a fairly deep vine trail which springs from the mouth of a Wyvern at its northern end. The wainscot panels below consist of paired, feathered boards and are entirely plain. Prior to the restoration of the church the wainscot was hidden by Jacobean pews on the screen's western side. Although the quality of the carving does not match that emanating from the Newtown workshops, in terms of overall design and construction the screen is one of the finest in the southern Marches.

Llandefalle: Fine and substantially complete rood-screen, which in all probability once carried a spectacular rood-loft

183

Llandefalle: Wyvern on head-beam (top) and one of the distinctive 'scissor form' tracery heads contained within well-moulded framing elements. Above runs a flowing vine trail (bottom)

The rood-loft was taken down before 1809,[5] and its original size and appearance are a mystery. In the north wall of the nave are the rood-doors and stairs that once gave access to the rood-loft. The upper doorway is lit by a tiny window. Also in the north wall, mortise holes for beams that no longer survive suggest that a once-narrow loft may have been widened at a later date to form a more substantial gallery, with a span perhaps equivalent to that at Burghill in Herefordshire. The loft would have required additional support at its southern end due to it meeting the open arcade of the south aisle at this point (rather than solid wall). The way the carpenter has halted the moulding of the middle rail short of its southern end suggests that some fabric associated with the rood-loft may once have occupied this position.

LLANDEILO'R FAN, ST. TEILO

The humble, undivided church of St. Teilo stands with a clutch of cottages beside a churning brook that hurries away down a narrow, wooded valley. Much of the fabric of the structure dates from the drastic restoration (or rebuild) of 1873. The interior is interesting both for its screen and for its timber roof: the former belongs to the 15th century, the latter to the 16th century.

The old rood-screen forms the only division between nave and chancel, and though incomplete is arresting both for its absolute plainness and for the massive, almost black timbers used in its construction. As it stands, it consists of four bays to either side of a central doorway. Following the familiar Welsh pattern the mullions and muntins are dowelled into a middle rail that runs unbroken between wall and door standards.

The gigantic head-beam is almost 10 inches square in cross section, and seems disproportionately massive over standards that are 'only' three inches in depth. The beam has been mutilated. Only on its eastern face does it retain its original form, here consisting of two hollows. A series of 11 mortise holes roughly 13 inches apart visible on its western side probably housed the cross-ribs that once supported the floor of a rood-loft. The top of the beam also has a series of mortise holes, possibly for the eastern loft parapet. Crossley and Ridgway believe the beam to be a bressumer, but for this to be the case it must have been swung through 180°. The fact that the underside of the beam does not incorporate slots for tracery heads might at first seem like evidence in support of the bressumer theory, but the mullions do not have slots for tracery either.

In 1946 the screen still had its wainscot panelling (consisting of two plain boards to each bay) and a text on the western face of the head-beam. Both the boarding and the text are now gone. At the time the screen was also 'painted a dull brown, making it difficult to distinguish old from new'.[6] This factor, combined with the complete

Llandeilo'r Fan: The massive head-beam

lack of ornamentation, makes it difficult to date the screen with any confidence. The design of the head-beam suggests that screen and loft were conceived and built as a single, unified structure. This makes any date prior to the middle of the 14th century highly unlikely. However, the clumsy framing up of the screen, whose ungainly proportions are the result of placing a too-big head-beam over too-small uprights (just as at Pixley in Herefordshire) makes it hard to envisage a date later than the midway point in the 15th century. The hollowed face of the head-beam may have housed carved trails (though this is highly unlikely). If anything, such a feature would tend to support an origin sometime in the 15th century, rather than the 14th century.

LLANELIEU, ST. ELLYW

Hidden high in the hills above Talgarth is the lonely church of Llanelieu. It stands at the centre of a round churchyard (more of a field really) protected by an encirclement of trees. The church itself is a single-chamber building of the 13th century. It would be special for its location alone, but is made unforgettable for what survives within. Perhaps nowhere in the southern Marches is it more effectively (or tantalisingly) demonstrated that spectacular rood arrangements once existed in the very humblest village churches.

As it stands today, the double-screen at Llanelieu consists of two matching triple arcades, parallel to one another and six feet apart (see plate 9). These supported a lattice of cross-ribs (some of which remain) over which the floor of the rood-loft was laid. The eastern screen still supports the tympanum, which is made up of two rows of boards half an inch thick. Here, the original

*Llanelieu: Sturdy lattice of ribs
that once supported the loft floor*

pigment survives to an unprecedented degree. The background, mottled with age, is now pinky-red in colour and is speckled with stencilled white roses. The ghost of the Rood (which had a splayed foot) is still clearly visible, as is the dovetail mortise hole into which the foot of the cross was set. There were never any attendant figures: the Rood stood alone. Cut into the tympanum are seven informal squints (four of them quatrefoils) to enable those in the loft to follow the priest officiating in the chancel below. The upper surface of the bressumer of the west screen is pierced with mortise holes for the missing loft parapet. A wooden staircase once gave access to the rood-loft at its northern end, and there may have been another at the southern end, but the damage

caused by the addition of the later pulpit makes it impossible to confirm this. In the north and south walls are two windows designed to light the screen altars and the rood-loft overhead.

In 1869, prior to the restoration of the church, the screenwork was even more complete. The roof over the loft was, according to Glynne, 'coved and boarded'.[7] The celure described by Glynne no longer survives, but a number of support joists belonging to the celure can still be seen among the roof timbers. The bays to either side of the central doorway of both screens were originally wainscoted between middle rail and sill, and the pulpit whose insertion was to result in the mutilation of the western screen had yet to appear. Originally, the small spaces enclosed by the wainscoting to either side of the central doorway would have contained altars, but these had disappeared long before the restoration of 1869.

The screenwork at Llanelieu is the most comprehensive surviving example of the distinctive double-screen type represented by lesser remains at Merthyr Cynog and Llanfigan in Breconshire (and at a handful of churches in Cardiganshire). The type features paired triple arcades with plain braces between the standards and the head-beam, and is constructed from massive, rugged timbers. At Llanelieu the braces spring from mouldings taking the form of a quarter-round to either side of a fillet. This moulding exists on all four sides of the door standards, and is a characteristic found at Merthyr Cynog. Another significant characteristic is the favouring of painted enrichment over carved. At Llanelieu, in contrast to the tympanum behind, the westernmost screen features red, six-petalled flowers stencilled onto a pale ground.

Llanfigan, St. Meugan

The church lies well hidden at the end of a narrow lane, close to a small stream. It has a nave with a north aisle and south porch, a chancel and a west tower. Most of the fabric belongs to a Victorian rebuild. However, the north aisle and arcade may belong to the 14th century.[8] The interior is rather bare and 'scrubbed' and would hold little of interest were it not for the screen fragments now set up in the north aisle.

Llanfigan: The scant but valuable remnants of the double-screen

The modest remains of the old screen consist of two door standards, a doorway arch and a length of head-beam. Although insubstantial these pieces are of great interest, for they evidently belong to the same double-screen type of the 14th century represented at Llanelieu and Merthyr Cynog in the same county. The portion at Llanfigan clearly formed the central bay of the easternmost screen. According to *Archaeologia Cambrensis* the rood-loft was still *in situ* in 1813. However, subsequent restoration work resulted in the dismantling of the screenwork and the mutilation and loss of much original fabric (including the mural rood-stairs).

The length of head-beam is well moulded upon both faces with hollows and rounds. On the side now facing the wall are the mortise holes for the cross-ribs of the rood-loft floor; on the top is the slot for the tympanum. The shortened door standards have shallow buttressing divided by offsets. The moulding of the standards is carried along the edge of the curved braces above, and the archway itself is completed by a small, arched chock at its apex. The standards also show the mortise holes for the middle rail and those for the braces of the neighbouring arches. The surviving screenwork retains much of its original painted decoration, including red and blue with white roses on the head-beam, and a pinky-red (similar to that found at Llanelieu) with climbing foliage and more white roses on the braces. Some of this colouring was partially renewed at a later date.

In 1946, several moulded joists belonging to the loft floor were being stored beneath the tower.[9] They had similar mouldings to those at Merthyr Cynog and Llanelieu (quarter-rounds divided by a fillet) but have since disappeared.

Llanfilo, St. Bilo or St. Milburg

Llanfilo is a small hillside village with far-reaching views over the Black Mountains to the east. Its church stands on a sloping site near the top of the village, and presents a shabby but engaging exterior to visitors. Apart from the eastern end of the nave (which is Norman) most of the fabric belongs to the 15th century or later. One of Llanfilo's restorers in the early 20th century was W.D. Caröe, for whom the screen at Llanfilo was 'of absorbing interest'.[10] Caröe was also responsible for saving the church at Partishow.

Llanfilo: Detail of rood-screen

Despite the restoration of the church, the rood-screen and loft survive in something like their original condition. The small screen fills the chancel archway below the rood-loft and consists of three bays to either side of a central doorway, of three further bays. The middle rail is only three feet above the sill, but this successfully maintains the proportions of the screen. Unlike at Partrishow, the muntins and mullions are aligned here. However, whereas the muntins are unmoulded, the mullions (together with the head-beam and middle rail) are moulded with ogees and half-rounds.

In the top half of the screen the heads of the lights contain paired quatrefoils of the Herefordshire type (carved upon the west face only). Prior to restoration only the bays immediately to either side of the doorway retained their head tracery; the others are replacements. The head-beam is carved with vine trails that spring from the mouth of a Wyvern at its northern end. The beam was cut short at its southern end, presumably to allow space for the memorial of 1792 now fixed to the wall here. In front of the screen there once stood a pair of stone altars, or *mensae*, as at Partrishow. One of these of *c.*1200 was rediscovered in the floor of the chancel.

The little rood-screen seems almost incidental when compared to the rood-loft overhead. The latter both literally and visually overwhelms the screen. From the head-beam of the screen the loft coving spreads five feet to the west and four to the east to give a loft floor nine feet deep. The western coving is now divided by moulded ribs with bosses at the intersections (of which only three are original) to give 33 panels. In a photograph of Llanfilo's rood-screen and loft dating from the turn of the century[11] a number

Llanfilo: Rood-screen and loft

Llanfilo: Detail of bressumer (top) featuring a vine trail over a pomegranate trail, divided by half-rounds and framed between a top-cresting and an unusual blind enrichment (note also the oak carving on buttress foot). Below is a Wyvern

of the vertical ribs seem rather thin, it is not clear whether there are any horizontal ribs at all, and there are certainly no carved bosses.

The western bressumer of the loft is enriched with two trails of running ornament (the eastern bressumer, which is moulded, carried no such enrichments). The upper of these is an elaborate vine trail, while the lower one features a distinctive pomegranate trail (indicating a post-1501 date for the fitting). The western

Llanfilo: Rood-window

bressumer originally rested upon braces at either end, just as at Llanwnnog in Montgomeryshire.

The parapet of the rood-loft is the most-altered part of the ensemble. Originally it was divided into 15 panels, each of which held a carved figure probably beneath a small canopy of tabernacle work. In the first quarter of the 20th century and prior to its restoration the parapet front was plain apart from two attached triangular pilasters. These were fixed in line with the door standards of the screen beneath. In this unadorned state it would have been far more closely allied in its composition to the rood-loft at St. Margarets in Herefordshire, and a lot lighter in its appearance. When Caröe first saw the loft front at Llanfilo there was also a panel fixed to its centre upon which was painted a Welsh Biblical quotation.

Following Caröe's restoration the parapet was divided by four additional triangular pilasters into five principal bays, each framing three of the original panels. It must be acknowledged that these unusual pilasters sit a little awkwardly against the loft front, and do not marry up happily with the bressumer below. In the centre of each of the five main bays are fixed renewed figures beneath very pretty carved hoods. From left to right these are: St. Peter,

Llanfilo: Rood-loft prior to restoration (cf. St. Margarets).
Note loft parapet and missing tracery heads

St. James the Great, the Virgin and Child, St. Luke, and St. Paul. They were carved by Nathanial Hitch between 1926 and 1930, as was the Rood on the east wall of the nave. The two trails running along the top beam of the parapet are also noteworthy. The upper one again features the pomegranate, while the lower employs a rarely-seen motif (in the context of screenwork) – a series of circles enclosing trefoils. Access to the loft is via rood-stairs in the north wall of the nave.

LLANGASTY TAL-Y-LLYN, ST. GASTAYN

The church occupies a glorious setting beneath tall pine trees on the southern fringes of Llangorse Lake. It was rebuilt midway through the 19th century by J.L. Pearson, who was also responsible for the haphazard re-use of parts of the rood-screen and loft (which date from the early 16th century) in order to create a low chancel screen.[12]

As it stands today the screen comprises two sections, each four feet wide and three feet tall to either side of a central entranceway. The wood is a rich, chestnutty brown colour and was clearly treated and varnished in the 19th century to disguise which parts were new and which old. The carving of the screen is wholehearted, if crudely executed and a little unruly. It is also highly unusual. The six individual panels are of four different designs and contain an exotic array of motifs, of which the sharply pointed and serrated pinnacle is the most prominent. What makes the decoration particularly unusual is that most of it has been carved in the solid, as opposed to being applied (a feature it shares with the mutilated screenwork – now an altar rail – at Llanvair Waterdine in Shropshire).

It has been suggested that these panels once belonged to the wainscot of a rood-screen,[13] but with their backing removed another explanation offers itself: namely that they may once have belonged to a loft parapet; particularly if the vine trail beneath is in its original position (for Crossley and Ridgway this once formed a part of the middle rail). Whatever the original deployment of the surviving parts the loss of the complete screen (and loft) is grievous indeed, for this was evidently a fitting of singular and dramatic appearance.

Llangasty Tal-y-Llyn: Detail of the striking screenwork, whose 'carving in the solid' calls to mind that found at Llanvair Waterdine in Shropshire

LLANSPYDDID, ST. CADOG

Llanspyddid lies on the busy A40 to the west of Brecon. The church was erected in the 14th century and is a plain, single-chamber structure. Externally, its appearance is lifted by an attractive south porch, which was fronted in the 16th century with a carved bargeboard.

The old rood-screen no longer stands within, but some fragments of it have been re-used to make a tester, or sounding board, over the pulpit. This canopy is fixed to the wall with curly iron brackets, and is near-black in colour. A length of vine trail has been employed on three sides, while a portion of the panelling of the original loft soffit now forms the sounding board itself. This is divided by moulded ribs to form six compartments

Llanspyddid: Screenwork parts as sounding board

with bosses and half-bosses (carved with leaves and flowers) at the intersections. The fact that so little remains is a tragedy, for the carving is extremely fine; particularly that of the bosses and half-bosses, and the ingeniously plaited stems of the vine trail. It bears comparison with work found at Llananno and Newtown. Although the pieces clearly belong to a screen of the late 15th century, too little survives to relate it with any certainty to other Breconshire screenwork.

Today, the chancel of the church is divided from the nave by a timber screen erected in the 20th century (and typical for its date). The absolute precision of this later fitting, allied to its glossy shallow-relief carving, gives it a lifeless and mechanical quality, and the piece forms a revealing and striking counterpart to the earlier work.

LLYWEL, ST. DAVID

The church of St. David belongs mainly to the late 15th century and retains many of its Perpendicular features. It consists of a nave and chancel, and has a castellated west tower possibly belonging to the 14th century. The interior has the attractive barrel-vaulted roof with moulded ribs and plaster infill found in many Breconshire churches. The church was restored in 1869, at which point the rood-loft was taken down and the screen moved to the west end of the church.

Today, a modern screen stands before the sandstone chancel arch at the east end of the nave. Against the north wall here are the two rood-doors that once gave access to the rood-loft via rood-stairs in the wall cavity. The old screen has been re-used to form a tower screen at the west end of the nave. The screen once measured 25 feet in length, but has been severely curtailed to fit into the 11 foot wide tower arch at the west end. This has played havoc with its proportions, for the screen was never intended to have an arcade of semi-circular arches. These alterations, allied to the indignity of modern, textured glazing, have given it a cumbersome, unfamiliar appearance.

The wall standards and wainscot boards of the screen are modern replacements. However, the door standards, spandrels and bressumer are all original. The door standards feature boutell shafts topped with moulded caps (similar to those found at Llanbister in Radnorshire). The only surviving decoration is in the six spandrels, which spring from small corbels. They are vigorously carved with flower and foliage designs. The bressumer enrichment is now lost. The screen is related to the example that survives at Bronllys and probably also dates from the early 16th century. They both formed the western screen of a pair that once supported the rood-loft (the eastern screens – the ones originally standing beneath the chancel archway – have been

Llywel: Screen
(now beneath the tower)

lost). Both are sturdily constructed from massive timbers and are characterised by four standards supporting a bressumer, having carved spandrels at the intersections.

MERTHYR CYNOG, ST. CYNOG

The church is long and low, and stands in a partly overgrown, circular churchyard at the top of the village. Dating the fabric is not easy, but the stout west tower probably belongs to the 13th century or earlier, and the nave and chancel to the 14th century.

The rood-screen is mutilated but remains in its original location (or something close to it) between the nave and chancel. It belongs to the same Breconshire double-screen type of the 14th century found at Llanelieu, Llanfigan and elsewhere (though is noticeably finer in its workmanship than that of Llanelieu). At one time there was a parallel screen west of the one still standing and the two screens would have supported the flat floor of the rood-loft. The mortise holes for the cross ribs of the loft floor can still be seen in the head-beam. In 1865, the head-beam was decorated with a vine trail, but this enrichment did not originally belong to this screen.[14] At the intersections of post and head-beam are six braces (see photograph p.118), which spring from the moulded shafts of the posts (just as at Llanelieu and Llanfigan). In later screens these essentially structural components evolved to become spandrels, thus presenting the woodworker with a larger surface area upon which to carve.

The middle rail runs unbroken between door and wall standards. This is wainscoted with plain boards. There are no muntins below the middle rail and no mullions above. However, a series of small holes drilled into the top of the middle rail suggest that a metal grille may have been inserted at a later date. At one time the screen would have been painted. In 1946, Crossley and Ridgway found traces of paint on the door standards, 'the colour is faint, showing a powdering of red roses on a coloured background'[15] (again, just as at Llanelieu and Llanfigan).

PARTRISHOW, ST. ISHOW OR ISSUI

Partrishow is unforgettable. The little church stands completely alone on a steep valley side high up among the Black Mountains. Glynne described its setting thus: 'The situation of the church is striking; on an eminence so steep that the latter part of the ascent is more like a staircase, and inaccessible to carriages'.[16] To the south-east are distant views between the hills to the lowlands beyond. The church itself consists of a nave and chancel, with a small chapel to the saint – an *eglwys y bedd* – at its west end.[17] The structure has parts belonging to the 12th, 13th and 14th centuries, and was restored in 1908–9 by W.D. Caröe (who also restored the church at Llanfilo). The interior is packed with interest, for besides the rood-loft and screen there are two early screen altars, a pre-Conquest font and a fine wall painting of a Doom figure on the west wall of the nave. It is unquestionably the rood-loft, however, which first takes the eye of the visitor on entering the church. For the much-travelled Richard Fenton, who saw the church early in the 19th century, it was 'the most perfect and elegant Rood loft now standing in the kingdom'.[18]

Both the rood-loft and the screen are of *c*.1500, and span the entire width of the nave (unlike at Llanfilo, where the screen is confined within the chancel arch). When the screen was erected the two stone altars were already *in situ* and the carpenter was

Partrishow: Rood-screen and loft

Partrishow: Detail of carved bressumer showing Wyvern and vine trail, water-plant, serrated leaves (possibly hawthorn) and drop-cresting

four mullions on the north side. From the head-beam flat coving divided by ribs and bosses (also renewed) extends to meet with the bressumer of the rood-loft.

The rood-loft parapet, with its intricate Perpendicular panel tracery, is arguably the chief delight of Partrishow. Between the head-beam and the bressumer are 18 well-moulded muntins. These divide the loft front into 17 individual bays. Each of these

forced to make slight compromises with his design. Above middle rail height the screen is balanced and regular and has five bays to either side of a central doorway (the outermost bays wider than the other four). However, the carpenter was then left with two awkward gaps below the middle rail, between the door standards and the altars. Instead of inserting a muntin to correspond precisely with the mullion above he simply divided the left-hand space into two equal bays, leaving the right-hand space as a single bay. The tracery in the wider bays belongs to the same type as that found at New Radnor and Llandefalle. Some of the woodwork of the screen has been renewed, including the door-head tracery and the

Partrishow: The tiny rood-window (top right in left-hand image) and one of the two exceptionally rare screen altars: a fixture once commonly found against rood-screens in parish churches

contains a panel of lacy openwork, whose design features an arched head, an ogee arch two-thirds of the way down; and is divided into four vertical strips, which are further subdivided by cuspings throughout. The effect is very beautiful. The bressumer has three stepped trails of running ornament, each wider and more boldly carved as they ascend. A vine trail strung out between two Wyverns fills the uppermost, water-plant the middle, and serrated leaves sprouting from an undulating stem the lower. The head-beam repeats the ogee trails of the bressumer, but has two trails interlinked, giving a series of ovals that have been cusped and ornamented with pairs of roses. The top-cresting above is mostly original (whereas the drop-cresting beneath the bressumer is replacement work).

Talgarth: Fragmentary remnants, comprising loft head-beam and parts of screen head-beam. The carving has the rugged quality of that found at Llandegley but, unusually, is carved in the solid

The rood-loft is accessed via mural rood-stairs in the north wall. A small south window designed to throw light onto the Rood can still be seen; but the tympanum, once fixed over the screen's head-beam and filling the upper part of chancel arch, has gone. Because of this the barrel-vaulted chancel roof with its moulded ribs and plaster infill can be glimpsed through the loft parapet. In 1946 it was apparently still possible to see a faint mark on the wall above the chancel arch where the Royal Arms may once have been attached.[19] The head-beam of the parapet has 18 socket holes for candles upon its top. Unusually, the screenwork shows no signs of ever having been painted.

TALGARTH, ST. GWENDOLINE

This large church consists of a nave and chancel, south aisle and porch, west tower and north vestry. This last, described by Glynne in 1851 as a transeptal chapel,[20] may represent the earliest part of the structure and date back to the 13th century or earlier. The nave and south aisle were rebuilt *c*.1400; the tower is later.

The rood-screen and loft were taken down prior to 1851. Glynne reports that, 'There are remains of a Rood screen in the chancel, and part of the corner of the Rood loft may be seen'.[21] No screenwork remains *in situ*, but at the west end of the south aisle a section of the enriched head-beam of the loft parapet survives, almost 10 feet in length. This has small holes along its upper surface, probably for candles. The underside has mortise holes for the muntins of a loft parapet. The enrichment of the beam consists of two trails surmounted by a trefoil cresting. The lower one is a vine trail, while the upper features the pomegranate, indicating a date of post-1501 for the screen. The beam is supported upon two uprights. These once formed parts of the head-beam of the screen and have mortise holes for mullions, and grooves for head tracery. The wood is dark brown in colour, and the quality of the carving is unrefined and hesitant.

HEREFORDSHIRE

ABBEY DORE, ST. MARY

St. Marys began life as mighty Dore Abbey; a Cistercian monastery built during the last quarter of the 12th century and the first quarter of the 13th century. Two developments in particular have resulted in the building's current distinctive form: the loss of its entire nave, and the gaining of a tower in the 17th century. As it now stands, the church consists of a crossing with transepts, a chancel bounded by side aisles (which form chapels) and an ambulatory behind the east end linking the aisles. None of the monastic quarters associated with the abbey has survived.

The church is now entered via a porch in its south transept. This opens into the lofty, echoing chamber formed by the crossing and transepts. This is closed off to the west by an expanse of wall where once there showed the awesome perspective of the monastic nave. The nave consisted of nine bays and had side aisles. A pulpitum once stood between the second pair of piers west of the crossing. A stone rood-screen, meanwhile, was located in the middle of the fifth bay west of the crossing (the intervening space enclosed a retro-choir).[1] The fascination of the remaining structure lies in its detailing, for here the transition from the stillness of the Romanesque to the dynamism of the early Gothic remains exquisitely caught. In the north transept is a round-headed doorway and elsewhere Norman capitals can be seen; yet the ambulatory is all pointed arches and rib-vaulting, and the east end of the chancel has profusely-shafted piers and soaring lancets overhead.

If the current church can be called singular in its appearance, so can the screen now dividing the crossing from the chancel beyond. Nothing quite like it survives anywhere else in England. It was erected in c.1634 as part of the restoration of the church by Lord Scudamore, and may be the work of the carpenter John Abel[2] (who was also responsible for the old town halls of Hereford and Leominster). It consists of eight bays to either side of a central doorway; the bays divided into sets of four by standards in the form of ionic columns on pedestals (rather than bases). The mullions between are in the form of turned balusters, squared at the top and bottom where they meet the head-beam and the middle rail respectively. Two of the mullions have been cut short and now hang like stalactites.

The middle rail below has been renewed, presumably to cover over the mortise holes. Each bay has a small trefoil head, and here it is possible to discern the faintest echo of the treatment found in pre-Reformation screens. However, the door-head has a pair of elaborately shaped and carved brackets with big Tudor roses, and a grape bunch pendant between. The mullions of the screen correspond with the sturdy muntins below, whose edges are moulded with quarter-rounds. The wainscot is plain-panelled, and the screen to either side of the doorway rests on a simple, chamfered base. The head-beam is in the form of a wide entablature, and is broken by the consoles crowning the columns below. Mounted on the cornice are three cartouches of arms. These show, from north to south: the impaled coat of Scudamore

Abbey Dore: Screen now dividing the chancel from the crossing

surmounted by a coronet, the Royal (Stuart) arms, and the see of Canterbury impaling Laud.

Although the screen is an impressive piece of carpentry, both for its visual impact and its workmanship (and of course it serves an important function here), its lack of sympathy to its setting should also be acknowledged. It is altogether too heavy and self-conscious; its silhouette too busy, for the pure and bounding grace of the chancel beyond.

ALMELEY, ST. MARY

The church consists of a nave and side aisles with chapels to the north and south, and a tower to the west. The church's best features belong mainly to the 13th century: the sturdy and likeable tower is of *c.*1200, and the chancel is lit by a window containing Geometrical tracery.

Almeley: The very rare celure – an extra-decorated canopy of roofing to honour the rood-figures below

The screen now standing beneath the chancel arch is modern. However, the roofing overhead retains a celure belonging to the early 16th century. This once formed a canopy of honour for the rood-figures below, and is an extremely rare survival. The boarding of the celure has been painted with ribs and floral bosses. This boarding comprises some 40 panels, alternately light then dark like those of a chess board. Each panel contains a Tudor rose whose design has been repeated along each diagonal. The painting of the celure has almost certainly been intermittently refreshed.

AYLTON

Aylton church is tiny. It is of single chamber form and has a little bell-turret and a sundial at its west end. The fabric belongs mainly to the 12th and 13th centuries.

The screen inside has been described as 'wildly assembled',[3] and it certainly shows great determination on the part of its creator to make use of a disparate collection of screen fragments whatever the cost in terms of overall effect. As it stands, it consists of a head-beam, standards, loft muntins, a top rail above, two lengths of battlemented rail and a number of boldly carved tracery elements. The remains of the tympanum boarding can be seen overhead, embedded in the roof. Clearly the screen did not always look as it does now, but the possibility that these pieces originally belonged in another church must also be considered.

The door standards are squared below middle rail height, but they are well moulded above, with rounds to each corner. One of the door standards has a slot, possibly for the middle rail. The wall standards are now partially encased by boarding and are hidden by the wall fabric. The wall standard to the north has several mortise holes cut into it, again possibly for the middle rail or other framing members. These posts have every appearance of having once belonged to a much taller screen. The current head-beam started life as a bressumer. It has eight mortise holes for the joists of the loft floor cut into its eastern face. It is well moulded to one side only with a concave face for a carved trail, and a half-round above. Its underside is moulded with two quarter-rounds.

The bressumer supports 11 bays, possibly from a loft parapet. The muntins that form the bays have half-rounds that are returned over the heads. The five central bays each contain a big tracery

Aylton: The bizarre rood-screen, constructed from pieces from a screen and loft, with the remains of the tympanum above

head composed of trefoils (with cusps terminating in small flowers) over a trefoiled arch. The bays to either side contain boarding with paired half-circles cut out to correspond (albeit very weakly) with the neighbouring tracery heads. Above is a beam scooped out to give a hollow moulding along its western face. Again, something is clearly not right here. The muntins do not fit into (or marry up with) the top of the bressumer properly. Also, the rail height is too low for a loft parapet and the five tracery heads appear severely curtailed. It seems likely that these bays do not belong on top of this beam and it is possible that the bays may not even belong to a loft parapet, but simply incorporate tracery heads from a screen within renewed framing. Once again the encasing of a framing member, this time the top rail, is unhelpful.

At the intersections of the standards and the head-beam are four openwork spandrels and four other fragments. Three of the spandrels have encircled trefoils with dagger forms to the corners; two of the three have cusps terminating in roses. The fourth spandrel contains encircled mouchettes. On the outside of the door standards are two cusped pieces with smaller flowers terminating the cusps, and two lengths of battlemented rail. These latter may have crowned a middle rail (*cf.* Brecon Cathedral) or, what is more likely, a head-beam.

Whilst it seems certain that the various tracery pieces belong to the same screen (for across all there is a consistency of scale, workmanship and motif) it is less certain if that screen was intended for this church (although, judging from the tympanum, it is certain that a screen was). The tracery forms seem too big and it is difficult to envisage how they could be framed up in a way that might satisfy the demands of scale and proportion here. The remaining screenwork at Yatton (All Saints) shows how tracery spandrels of this size appear when attached to taller posts in an altogether loftier church (although of course this screen was brought in from elsewhere). A number of the spandrels at Yatton are very similar to those at Aylton, both in their size and design. Although not of openwork, one in particular has the same encircled mouchettes with dagger forms to each corner as found at Aylton.

AYMESTREY, ST. JOHN THE BAPTIST AND ST. ALKMUND

The church stands in a rumpled churchyard next to the road and is entered through a doorway beneath its west tower. This shows onto a nave with side aisles and a chancel beyond. The structure dates from the 12th century, but has been added to intermittently, not least in the early 16th century when it received its parclose screens and its lofty and lovely rood-screen. This latter is closely related to those found at Astbury in Cheshire, Hughley in Shropshire and Gresford in Denbighshire, and it is certain that the four screens originated from the same workshops, possibly in or near to Ludlow. The extent of the geographical spread of the four screens (they occupy four different counties and Astbury is some 80 miles north of Aymestrey) points to this being a major centre.

The most striking characteristic of the rood-screen at Aymestrey is its great height. In East Anglia such a composition would not be so arresting, but in the southern Marches, where churches (and thus the screens within) are usually low or even squat, the form seems one of considerable daring. The screen has three bays to either side of a central doorway, which takes the space of two bays. If the screen were half as tall the bays would seem quite wide. However, its height, continuous standards and low wainscot have given the composition a soaring (though measured) verticality.

The wainscot, although emphatically subordinate in decorative terms to the upper parts of the screen, is both a pleasingly resolved and confidently executed design. The middle rail, broken by the standards, is carved in the solid with a series of folded ribbon and flower designs. The flowers are of a similar type to those found on the middle rail at Dilwyn. The principal bays above middle rail height are halved below by muntins (the mouldings of which are returned over each bay). The wainscot panels have linenfold decoration.

Aymestrey: Rood-screen vaulting and cornice

Aymestrey: Rood-screen vaulting

Aymestrey: Rood-screen

From here, the eye follows the stem-like standards to the point at which, high above the floor, they burst like snap-dragons into the joyous profusion of the tracery and vaulting. The ingenious vaulting starts from octagonal cappings that surmount boutell shafts which front each of the ogee-moulded standards. The ingenuity of the vaulting lies in the fact that it begins as a groin vault above the standards, then takes on a coved form before reaching the bressumer as a groin vault once again. Each bay of the loft coving is served by a number of ribs which meet with the corners of a cross formed by five squares (the ribs well moulded throughout). The central square contains a quatrefoil, while the outer four contain trefoils. Various small bosses, cuspings and crockets serve to further enrich the design. The composition is a lovely one, and forms what is essentially a highly unusual lierne vault. This design is almost identical to that found at Gresford, and is very similar to that of Hughley and Astbury.

The head-tracery, which is uniform (unlike that of Hughley) has the appearance of a series of parted lacy curtains, and is reminiscent of that found at Gresford, Middleton (in Shropshire) and at Old Radnor in Radnorshire. All of the designs are cusped and sub-cusped, and should be 'read' as relating not to the screen but to the vaulting (and ultimately the loft) above. The feature that perhaps most clearly differentiates the Aymestrey screen from its three sisters is the decorative fringe that hangs below the bressumer. This echoes the treatment of the heads to the east, and is what gives to the screen its dripping luxuriance.

The superb bressumer has three finely carved bands of enrichment divided by rounds. The uppermost (and widest) of these is a vine trail proceeding from the mouth of a Wyvern.

Below this, there is what appears to be a narrow vine trail, and below this is a water-leaf trail. The cresting that crowns the screen may have been renewed.

The presence in the church of a complete set of parclose screens coeval with the rood-screen is highly unusual. These divide off the easternmost bays of the side aisles to form two parclose chapels.

Each of the four screens consists of four bays to either side of a central doorway, of two bays. The treatment of the wainscot and middle rail of each corresponds with that of the main screen. The parclose screens are divided up by standards (with corresponding mullions and muntins between) to give bays that are narrower than, but in proportion to, those of the main screen. Ogee mouldings are employed throughout and are returned over the heads of each bay. The head-tracery is of two different designs; one employing an ogee arch

Aymestrey: Detail of parclose screen, of simpler form to rood-screen but sharing linenfold decoration and carved middle rail

below a rounded arch, cusped above and below, and the other a flattened arch below a rounded arch, again cusped but with an encircled quatrefoil between.

The head-beam has just one carved trail – a vine – which has been renewed but is substantially old (and of good quality). The top-cresting, however, may be new. The design and construction of the parclose screens in relation to the rood-screen has been carefully considered, and carried out in such a way as to clearly express the hierarchical differences between the screens. No access to a rood-loft survives.

BISHOP'S FROME, ST. MARY

St. Marys shows Victorian restoration at its most muddled and obtrusive. The nave, north aisle and chancel are decked out with elements variously lifted from the Norman and Early English vocabularies, but here deployed with little understanding or discrimination. Despite the prevailing insensitivity, some of the original parts remain intact, including the west tower (of the 14th century) and the Norman south doorway and chancel arch. In the Mudderfield chapel is a very fine and unusual painted memorial of 1598, depicting a husband and wife kneeling above a skeleton.

Beneath the chancel arch stands a small but appealing rood-screen. It consists of three bays to either side of a central doorway, that takes the space of four bays. Although essentially a creation of the 19th century, it incorporates a number of valuable old fragments and has been put together with some care and sensitivity. The principal framing members – sill, wall and door standards, and head-beam – are all substantially new. The head-beam, however, has been constructed from a number of pieces;

Bishop's Frome: Rood-screen tracery heads

some old, some new. The enrichments of the head-beam are substantially new, but a close examination reveals some notable early fragments. The portion of vine trail over the door-head is old work and has been extended with new carving to the north and south (look in particular at the grape bunches in each portion). Over this is the base of a delicate length of cresting, and above this a length of typically big, Victorian cresting.

Below the head-beam, the tracery heads to either side of the doorway each consist of a crocketed ogee arch with water-flower cusps beneath, and a cusped and pointed arch above. They are of a similar design to those found at Stoke Lacy and Lea, and have probably been renewed. The door-head features four blind tracery pieces, fixed back to back to give two carved faces each. These have foliated and floral cusps below and spandrels containing serrated leaf and flower designs. They originally belonged to the wainscot, and are very similar to those found at Dilwyn, Stoke Lacy and Alfrick. They are of a darker wood and are more highly wrought than those of the wainscot below. The design is also more elaborate, incorporating an extra layer of serrated leaves.

The mullions in the top half of the screen correspond with the muntins below, but unusually they are backed with new wood. It is possible that the mullions were originally ogee-moulded upon both faces, and that they were split length-ways in order to yield flat-backed muntins that could then be fixed against the new boarding of the wainscot (thus showing matching moulded uprights to the west). Eight blind tracery spandrels, similar to those in the door-head, have been fixed to the wainscot; four upon the west face, and four upon the east. Fixed to the east side of the

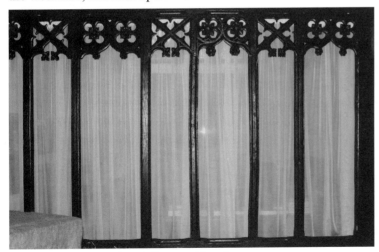

Bishop's Frome: Parclose screen

wainscot are also several fragments of a delicate frieze of squares enclosing quatrefoils and small flowers. A length of this has also been fixed to the underside of the door-head.

The parclose screen enclosing the Mudderfield chapel to the north is jet black. It consists of nine bays framed up between a new head-beam above and a dwarf wall below. The standards and mullions are mostly old and correspond with one another, having edges that are cavetto moulded. The tracery heads are of two different designs; one of a cusped scissor form and the other having encircled quatrefoils. Five out of the nine tracery heads are original. This screen is almost certainly earlier than the rood-screen.

BOSBURY, HOLY TRINITY

Like Abbey Dore, Bosbury church bears witness to the nascent Gothic style. Norman round-headed windows mingle with Early English lancets, while other elements seem caught in a moment of exquisite indecision; the piers and capitals of the nave arcade among them, neither quite managing to make up its mind which style to commit to. The church consists of a clerestoried nave with side aisles, a chancel and south porch. At the east end of the south aisle is the fan-vaulted Morton chapel, erected in *c*.1500. To the south of the church stands a fine, detached tower. Broken free of its moorings it drifts across the churchyard.

The rood-screen, although greatly renewed, retains some old work. It consists of two bays of three lights each to either side of a central doorway. Fan vaulting springs from each of the six standards (to both the west and the east). Everything below middle rail height appears to be new work, including the six tracery panels, which loosely correspond with the tracery heads above. The design consists of two tiers of three cusped ovals (the cusps holding small flowers) over a cusped and foliated arch. The six wainscot panels of the outer bays are plain. The middle rail incorporates some old material to the south, but has been substantially renewed. The six standards (which extend from the sill up to the head-beam) are original. They are densely moulded upon both sides with hollows, rounds and ogees. However, the mullions in between are replacements.

The upper parts of the screen (including the vaulting above) present a number of problems; not the least of which is differentiating old work from new. It will be noted that the arches formed by the vaulting cut slightly awkwardly into the screen's

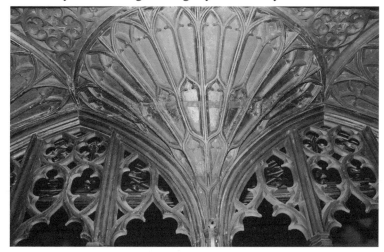

Bosbury: Detail of tracery heads (similar to those at Dilwyn); and the vaulting, which is a more elaborate version of that surviving at Ledbury

tracery heads. These heads (which are similar to those at Dilwyn) consist of cusped ovals over a cusped (trefoil) ogee arch; but the two central flattened quatrefoils are smaller than the flanking ones. Despite the awkwardness here, both the tracery and the vaulting appear to consist of mostly old work. The design of the fan vault, the way the forms of the panel tracery double as the vault rises and spreads, is both clever and effective. The bressumer to both the east and the west is original, and is moulded with ogees and rounds (though the carved trails are replacements). To the west, the bressumer is supported upon short posts resting on the scalloped capitals of the half-piers that begin the nave arcade. No means of accessing a rood-loft survives.

BRINSOP, ST. GEORGE

Brinsop church looks out over a lake and fields to a forested hillside beyond. The setting is a special one, doubtless loved by Wordsworth who visited Brinsop on a number of occasions. The church belongs to the first half of the 14th century and consists of a nave, chancel, north aisle, south porch, and Victorian bell-turret. For such a small church it contains much that is of interest. The Herefordshire School of Romanesque Sculpture is represented here by a tympanum showing St. George, and some lively voussoirs. These pieces all date from the middle of the 12th century. The church also has some fine glass of the 14th century, both in its east window (St. George etc.) and in the upper trefoil of the north-west window of the north aisle, which is occupied by an exquisite seated Christ. Being otherwise undivided within, the church employs screens to demarcate both the chancel at the end of the nave and the chapel at the end of the north aisle.

The rood-screen consists of four bays to either side of a central doorway. The bays are divided by double ogee-moulded mullions, which appear mostly original and correspond with the muntins below. These latter are moulded with hollows and half-rounds, which are returned over each head of the wainscot. The plain wainscot boards are all new, as is the sill on which the screen stands.

The wall standards appear to be original, though both stand detached from the wall (the gap to the north filled, while that to the south is open). The fact that the wall standards do not stand flush with the wall on either side makes it certain that the screen was reconfigured at some date. In the early stages of screen construction, the wall standards were always framed up flush with the wall. As well as being visually unsatisfactory to have

Brinsop: Rood-screen detail

Brinsop: Detail of middle rail, which is very similar to that found at Bettws-y-Crwyn in Shropshire

the posts away from the wall, it also compromises the screen structurally. The door standards do not match the wall standards: their inner faces are unmoulded for that section of each post that meets with the double middle rail. The door standards are thus definitely coeval with the current arrangement of middle rails. However, the wall standards point to another, earlier arrangement. The upper middle rail has upon its western face a trail of quatrefoils within ogivals. This blind traceried beam looks to be new, and is not moulded to marry up with the wall standards (as the band of openwork quatrefoils and the top rail of the wainscot below do). The band of quatrefoils meets the moulded inner face of the wall standard happily on the south side, but less so to the north where the final quatrefoil has been halved. The RCHM[4] suggests that both of the enriched sections of middle rail belong to the end of the 14th century or the beginning of the 15th century. However, it seems that when the screen was restored the upper rail was added (with the corresponding door standards) and the moulding on the wall standards was cut back to allow the insertion of the new rail here.

The tracery heads are of two different designs. The four to the north contain slightly flimsy Perpendicular grid tracery and appear new. These are certainly not of the same date as the squared quatrefoils of the middle rail. The four to the south have rounded arches, cusped below to give trefoil heads, and with foliated cusps and spandrels containing either serrated leaf carvings or openwork cusps holding a tiny leaf or flower. These tracery heads contain some old work. The thin tracery of the door-head, which replicates the tracery to the south, is almost certainly new.

The lowermost mouldings of the head-beam marry up fairly well with the mouldings of the mullions and standards, but this beam has clearly been greatly added to. The blind trail of encircled quatrefoils (similar in feel to the ogival trail below) is new, as are the little square bosses (or paterae) above. It is possible that a single carved foliage trail once ran along the western face of the head-beam in place of these enrichments. The top mouldings suggest that the head-beam is at least partly original. The top-cresting, however, like that of Canon Pyon and Bishop's Frome, is new and too big for the screen it crowns.

The parclose screen that divides the chancel from the chapel to the north is substantially new, though its mullions, muntins and head-beam are original. The parclose screen dividing the north aisle from the chapel contains no old work.

BURGHILL, ST. MARY

This fairly large church occupies an elevated churchyard setting in the middle of the village, and is approached from the south up an avenue of yew trees. It retains work from the 12th, 13th and 14th centuries, but was substantially restored in 1880. It consists of a nave with side aisles, a chancel, south porch and low west tower.

Once inside, the view eastwards is dominated by the rood-screen; or perhaps more accurately by the unusually deep coving that belonged to the rood-loft above. This coving stretches westwards to form an elegant canopy, which is supported upon four tall, moulded posts. The screen below is of five bays to either side of a central doorway, that occupies the space of four bays. The middle rail runs through between heightened standards, which are moulded with ogees and hollows to east and west.

Burghill: Detail of the junction of post and bressumer

Burghill: Rood-screen and loft soffit

These mouldings are also found in the slender mullions that divide each bay above middle rail height. The middle rail and the muntins are altogether heftier, and emphasise the reed-like quality of the mullions above. The muntins are simply moulded with rounds; as is the underside of the otherwise unmoulded middle rail. However, the mouldings are not returned seamlessly over each bay of the wainscot. Instead, the muntins simply (and rather crudely) meet the middle rail at unmoulded junction points. This suggests a later intervention, perhaps in the 19th century when, according to the RCHM,[5] the screen was heightened (and moved eastwards). The wainscot's lack of height is accentuated by the raised flooring that extends the floor of the chancel westwards.

The cusped tracery heads are of an unusual design, and have clearly been renewed. They are reminiscent of those at Canon Pyon (if somewhat flatter). The head-beam carries a blind trail of quatrefoils within ogivals, very similar to that found at Brinsop, but without the trefoil forms between. The mouldings of the mullions are not returned over each bay as one might expect. This feature also points to a renewed head-beam.

The coving of the rood-loft, as well as being exceptionally deep, does not form a regular arc as most loft coving does, but rather a parabola. From being steeply curved at the head-beam of the screen, it has almost flattened out by the time it reaches the bressumer. The coving is divided into 33 panels by ribs, and has renewed bosses at the intersections. The boarding itself also appears to be new. The mouldings of the westernmost horizontal rib match those of the standards and mullions. The bressumer has two finely carved trails: a narrow water-plant trail above, and a very unusual vine trail below that features curious zigzagging stalkage. Above and below are crestings that have been much renewed; the double trail of drop-cresting mirroring the top-cresting of the head-beam below to the east.

The bressumer is supported by four tall posts, plain to the east but moulded with double ogees to either side of a round to the west. The original posts would have been moulded upon both faces, and these must be replacements (and are possibly Jacobean). The easternmost drop-cresting of the bressumer is continued around small arch braces where the posts intersect with the bressumer, at which point they terminate at unusual cusped brackets. The spandrels of the braces contain serrated leaves. The back of the screen contains two modern and inappropriate carved trails, mechanically rendered in a lighter wood and glossily varnished.

Above the screen and coving, high up in the south wall, there survives a trefoil-headed piscina. This indicates that an altar once occupied the rood-loft. It is possible that during the Victorian rebuild this was simply re-inserted higher up, to be visible above the loft coving as a curio. The walls here were evidently rebuilt, as no means of access to the loft – neither doorways nor mural staircases – survives. If, however, this piscina is in its original position, then the loft was much higher up (and the screen much taller) than is the case now. Crossley and Ridgway believe that the screenwork at Burghill may have originated in Wales (or at least that it may have been made by Welsh craftsmen). There is some persuasive evidence for this, including the continuous middle rail, the square-headed lights, the coved soffit and the carving of the trails on the bressumer. What can be stated with certainty is that if it is English work then it is heavily informed by Welsh design and construction techniques.

CANON PYON, ST. LAWRENCE

Canon Pyon is a fairly large church that belongs mainly to the 13th and 14th centuries. It has a nave with side aisles, a south tower and porch, and to the east a chancel and north chapel. The interior is made unforgettable by its south arcade, whose alarming tilt has been halted by the intervention of flying buttresses.

With no chancel arch inside, the division between chancel and nave is signalled by a rise in floor levels and is established by a screen, whose setting at the top of the steps leading into the chancel makes for an impressive sight. It has been considerably renewed, but retains much notable early work. It consists of eight bays to either side of a central doorway, which takes the space of four bays. As well as the wall and door standards, there are also two intermediate standards extending from the sill up to the head-beam, and two uprights of a similar type forming mullions one bay north and one south of the door standards. These latter correspond with the muntins below, but are the only mullions that do. The sill and wainscot panels are new.

The middle rail is carved in the solid with a zigzag that encloses a series of serrated, triangular leaves. This pattern is not quite consistent along the whole of the middle rail: below the outer four bays and in the south door the zigzag is slightly flatter, and not composed of the right angles that appear in the other lengths of rail. A length of almost identical enrichment survives attached to the wall beneath the tower at Staunton-on-Wye. The unusual head tracery (which is faintly reminiscent of that found at Burghill) is new, and matches that found in blind form on the choir stall fronts beyond. The west face of the head-beam carries a vine trail of fairly standard design, strung out between two

Canon Pyon: Detail of tracery and head-beam, with a typically oversized Victorian or 20th-century cresting above

dragons: unusually, the principal wavy stem does not emanate from the mouths of these beasts, as it does elsewhere. The big ogee moulding and cresting above are new work.

Aside from the obvious addition of much new work, it seems that the composition of the screen's various framing members has at some time been altered, presumably during the Victorian restoration of the screen. The new sill, the half standards to either side of the doorway, the inconsistent middle rail and the narrowing of the wainscot bays towards the centre of the screen all point to a rebuild, during which old work must have been lost. The parclose screens appear to be entirely new.

Canon Pyon: Expansive rood-screen standing on the steps of the chancel, and spanning the wide nave

Dilwyn: Detail of standard

DILWYN, ST. MARY

St. Marys is a large church. It consists of a clerestoried nave with side aisles and a chancel beyond, all belonging to the years either side of 1300. The west tower, however, dates from the 12th century, while the magnificent south porch belongs to the Perpendicular era.

The church contains a notable collection of late medieval screenwork, consisting of a tall rood-screen, and parclose screens to the north and south. The former is divided into five principal bays, each one arched and subdivided to give three lights. The wall, door and intermediate standards all extend from the chamfered sill up to the head-beam. The standards are moulded with hollows, rounds and half-rounds. Uniquely, the standards are supported upon carved heads, some grimacing. The muntins of the wainscot do not correspond with the mullions above: each principal bay below middle rail height is subdivided into two bays, rather than three. The wainscot boarding has been removed (greatly to the detriment of the screen as a whole) and the slots for this boarding can still be seen in the sill, standards and muntins. The once-blind tracery forms have been backed with new wood and re-inserted into the heads of each open bay of the wainscot. These pieces, with their foliated cusps and their spandrels containing layered, serrated leaves, are virtually identical to those employed at Bishop's Frome. The four lengths of middle rail are carved in the solid with four-petalled flowers and are original.

The mullions, like the standards, appear to be original also. Attached shafts extend from the carved heads up to caps from which the fan vaulting springs. The Perpendicular grid tracery has been renewed, and is reminiscent of that found at Bosbury. However, the two-centred door-head, with its Wyverns carved to fit the narrow spandrels, is original. The vaulting has also been renewed, and the bressumer with its carved paterae is entirely new (though the cresting above is old work). Gaps between the arches of the tracery heads and those of the vaulting reveal that when the vaulting and head-beam came to be renewed, the builders were unable to match the relative pitches of the two sets of arches. The vaulting should spring from lower down each standard in order to follow the lines of the arches of the tracery heads. At first it may appear that this is simply clumsy or lazy workmanship. However, the builders may have calculated that by allowing the vaulting to spring from further down it would necessarily have extended too far to the west (if the pitch of the vaulting remained the same), thereby carrying the then-unsupported bressumer too far to the west also. The

Dilwyn: Rood-screen

doorway high up in the north wall, the surviving corbels and the two windows above the chancel arch all indicate that the loft was originally considerably higher up than the current arrangement would suggest.

The parclose screens are of an altogether different character. The framing members are unmoulded, except for those belonging to the north side parclose screens, which feature squared then chamfered boutell shafts that terminate in crocketed pinnacles. All of the wainscot boarding has been removed in a perverse echo of the treatment of the rood-screen. The slots for the boarding can still be seen. The tracery heads have been carved rather crudely upon both sides. They are original and of an interesting design: the little *pomme* crosses in the tops of the tracery heads to the south are extremely unusual. The massive, plain framing and the

Dilwyn: Parclose screen tracery heads

chunkier tracery, with its cusped ogee arches point to an earlier date than that of the rood-screen: possibly as early as the first half of the 15th century.

EARDISLAND, ST. MARY

The church stands discreetly amid houses and cottages in this attractive black and white village. It consists of a generous nave with south porch, west tower and chancel. The fabric dates from the 13th and 14th centuries, but was comprehensively restored in 1864. High up at the west end of the nave is an elaborately carved tie-beam.

The screen at the west end of the nave has been moved on at least three occasions during its lifetime, and has clearly been restored more than once. It consists of eight bays to either side of a central doorway, which takes the space of perhaps five bays. The old work includes one of the door standards, parts of the head-beam (note the mortise holes) the unexceptional vine trail, and some fragments in the mullions. These latter, which are moulded with quarter-rounds along each edge, have been painstakingly used as the template for the renewed mullions. The design of the surviving tracery heads varies a little. The basic design consists of a pointed arch divided by a crocketed ogee pinnacle over a trefoil head. However, the spandrels are sometimes solid, sometimes of openwork; the pointed arches sometimes cusped, sometimes not. Everything else is new.

As it stands today the screen is interesting for displaying two divergent approaches to restoration. The painstaking incorporation of tiny fragments of mullion into new work is one of which the Victorians would have approved. Indeed, they

Eardisland: Detail of tracery heads (of Herefordshire type) and head-beam with vine trail

would have gone one stage further and painted the whole screen with brown paint to mask what parts were new and what old. Recently, this approach has been seen by some as fundamentally disingenuous, and frequently efforts are now made to clearly differentiate new work from old. Here, the missing tracery heads could have been replaced by passable copies, but instead the heads have been left empty, or given simplified metal heads. Consequently, the screen wears its age and its alterations with an unusual degree of candour.

EATON BISHOP, ST. MICHAEL
The church stands opposite smart Georgian houses and consists of a clerestoried nave with side aisles, a chancel, south porch and west tower. The west tower is Norman, but the rest belongs mainly to the 13th and 14th centuries. Like so many other large churches it carries the scars and vestiges of other eras. The west wall of the church betrays the roof-line of the Norman nave (as it was prior to the addition of the clerestory); the aisles betray the roof-line of the Early English chancel. One south arcade pier is topped with the stiff-leaves that once graced every pier (until an act of vandalism saw to them in 1885). Eaton Bishop's greatest treasure is without question its collection of *c*.1330 stained glass. This can be found in the east and south-east windows of the chancel, and is characterised by the distinctive combination of greens, browns, yellows and reds, and by the fluidity and empathy with which the figures have been drawn.

The current rood-screen is essentially a creation of the 19th century (perhaps of 1885) but retains in its wainscot some valuable pieces of old screenwork (see photograph on p.123). It consists of three bays to either side of a central doorway, which takes the space of three bays. The chamfered sill and middle rail are new, but dowelled between are four late medieval muntins. These are of considerable interest, for upon their western faces are tall, Perpendicular, blind tracery lights. This distinctive feature is found on screenwork in just three other churches in Herefordshire: at Withington, Yatton and Hereford Cathedral. Most of the blind tracery heads between are early. The design, of a cusped ogee arch with encircled trefoils above, is a familiar one (existing for example in the parclose screen of the Mudderfield Chapel at Bishop's Frome). Some of the flowers within the trefoils or terminating the cusps below have a central whorl of three curved grooves. This design detail can also be found on the screenwork at Lea and Bishop's Frome. The wainscot panelling onto which these heads are fixed is new.

The standards and the mullions are also new, but all correspond with the precedent set by early screenwork found elsewhere in Herefordshire (e.g. at Burghill, Moreton-on-Lugg, St. Weonards etc.), having ogees to the east and west. It is likely that when the screen was rebuilt some old pieces were used as templates for the new woodwork. The main tracery heads are all new, and of a design without precedent in the county: a curved scissor form has given to each a pointed arch, which has been variously cusped, with little flowers deployed throughout. The tracery is a little thin, but the effect is not unattractive. The head-beam is entirely new, and has carved trails to east and west (that to the east has square bosses inserted into the design). The cresting to both the east and west is also new.

ELTON, ST. MARY

The little church stands with its yew trees next to Elton Hall. The setting is a lovely one, with fine views to the west and an intimate valley behind. Much of the church's fabric is Norman, but the windows belong mainly to the 13th century, some of the fittings belong to the 17th century, and the structure as a whole was rebuilt in 1876. The church is of single chamber form and has a Victorian south porch and bellcote.

The rood-screen that forms the only division between nave and chancel has been much altered. It consists of two subdivided bays to either side of a central doorway, which takes the space of three bays. The wainscot is the most obvious legacy of a rebuild of the 17th century, and carries the date 1641 on its reverse. The

Elton: Detail of rood-screen showing double head-beam, finely moulded uprights and renewed tracery heads

standards, which are finely moulded upon both sides with ogees, hollows and half-rounds, spring from the boxed-in wainscot (rather than extending to a sill below), and their half-rounds are returned over each double-head.

Mysteriously, a short length of standard now hangs below the door-head. It is inconceivable that a standard once extended down to the floor in this position, so what is this piece doing here? There are two possibilities: either it was always this length and has always hung in this way from the head-beam, or it was fixed here at a later date. Of the two, the latter seems the more probable, and such an arrangement may have been as a consequence of alterations made to the standards as a whole.

It is possible that the lower portions of some or all of the standards were damaged at one time (perhaps by wet or dry rot, or death-watch beetle). This may have led in turn to the following remedial action: the standards were sawn off below middle rail height to the north, and above to the south, and the lower half of the screen boxed in to renew the partition and disguise the changes made. The standards on the south side were evidently damaged above middle rail height, but those to the north may not have been damaged at all (or may have been less seriously damaged). If this was the case then sawing off the standards from the north of the screen would have yielded new lengths of undamaged timber, which could then be used to repair the standards to the south. It is just conceivable that the piece hanging from the door-head is simply a leftover piece following the completion of this work; one the repairer was unwilling simply to dispose of. A small shield now terminates the piece.

The renewed tracery heads each consist of a cusped ogee arch (with flowers terminating the cusps), below a cusped and rounded arch. The top of the screen has also witnessed much alteration. Two beams now surmount the screen, one on top of the other (*cf.* Withington). These are identically moulded to the west, with a curved face (for a carved trail) and half-rounds. To the east, however, they are different: the upper beam has a deeper curved face between half-rounds, while the lower one has a half-round, a hollow and a slightly convex face below. The upper beam has a series of mortise holes and a continuous rebate to the east. The top beam is evidently a head-beam, but what function the lower beam originally performed is now unclear.

On the north wall, opposite the entrance, is a finely carved panel with the royal arms of Elizabeth I. Such panels (usually painted) were placed over chancel screens in place of rood-figures.

EVESBATCH, ST. ANDREW

Little St. Andrews stands in the hills above Bishop's Frome. It was rebuilt in the 1870s and consists of a nave and chancel, with a timber bell-turret. At the junction of nave and chancel is a tall screen (of sorts). It consists of two wall and two door standards (each moulded with hollow chamfers), which extend up from a plain wainscot. Beneath the head-beam (or, more accurately, the tie-beam) there are a series of ogee arches, cusped below to give cinquefoil heads, and with encircled quatrefoils in the spandrels. This rather vague partition is substantially Victorian, but it is possible that some of the wood-work belonging to the wainscot is Jacobean (and thus coeval with the church's unusual font cover). In its design, Evesbatch's screen is inexplicably similar to the stone screen at Ilkeston in Derbyshire.

EYTON, ALL SAINTS

Like Elton, Eyton is a small church of single chamber form dating from the 12th century. However, its screenwork is finer than that of Elton and has been considerably less tampered with.

The rood-screen has five bays to either side of a central doorway, with the wainscot to each side of the doorway divided into two bays by wide constructional muntins. Wide door and wall standards rise from the floor (there being no sill) up to the head-beam. The deep middle rail runs between, and renewed mullions are dowelled into its top (following the Welsh format). The wainscot is plain-boarded. The various framing members of the screen are simply moulded with hollow chamfers. The uniform tracery heads each have encircled quatrefoils in the spandrels formed by an ogee arch, and have been renewed. The

Eyton: Details of the loft coving (above) which is related to that found at Kenderchurch and Beguildy; and the bressumer (below) showing a narrow water-plant trail over a wider vine trail, and damaged drop-cresting below that

head-beam is plain to the east, but well moulded to the west with a series of hollows and rounds. It was never intended to carry a carved trail.

The coving of the rood-loft springs from the top of the screen. This is divided into 16 square panels by ribs with bosses at the intersections. The boards and bosses have been renewed, but the ribs are original. To the west, the coving meets with a fine bressumer, which has two carved trails divided by half-rounds upon its western face. The lower (and wider) of the two is a vine trail; the upper is a water-plant trail. Some of the bressumer's original drop-cresting also survives.

FAWLEY, ST. JOHN

The old church stands next to a farm, and can be seen ducking down behind a tall hedge at the end of a rough track next to the farmhouse. An origin sometime in the 12th century is betrayed by its altered Norman chancel arch (made into a triple arch in the 19th century) and its Norman south doorway and font.

At the back of the church, propped up against the west wall of the nave, are two standards with highly unusual arch braces. These are all that remains of a now-dismantled screen. The standards are chamfered to the west and carry a square moulding to the east, which terminates in a half-round and an offset. The inner faces of the standards also have small, attached elements consisting of a chamfer between two half-rounds. The braces feature blind encircled quatrefoils. On three out of the four braces, the corners contain dagger forms, while the fourth has a pair of figure of eight forms. These braces, in their ornamentation and size, are very similar to those found at Aylton and, even more

Fawley: screen fragment

strikingly, at nearby Yatton, whose arch braces also display blind decoration. The top of each post has a mortise hole, and the braces have fin-shaped mortises that stand just proud of their tops. These elements framed up with the top-beam. The braces also have little, triangular chocks to keep them solid into the intersections. These posts and braces may have formed the supports for the western beam – the bressumer – of a flat-floored rood-loft, somewhat like those of the Breconshire group of double screens. It is possible that they belong to a similar date (i.e. the 14th century).

Foy, St. Mary

As the crow flies, Foy church stands very close to Fawley chapel. However, because of the Wye, getting from one to the other by car involves a circuitous journey along winding lanes for

perhaps eight miles. The church consists of a nave and chancel, west tower and south porch. It belongs for the most part to the 14th century, but has several components belonging to the 17th century, including its east window (a copy of that found at nearby Sellack) and many of its internal fittings.

The rood-screen inside is a peculiar piece. It belongs mainly to the 17th and 19th centuries, but retains some early parts. It has three bays to either side of a wide central doorway. The wainscot below the simply moulded middle rail has linenfold panelling. Although essentially a Tudor feature, the panels here may belong to the 17th century (as the doors clearly do). The renewed mullions (and half-mullions attached to the standards) are extremely unusual, but not without precedent. They consist of a lower half (hexagonal in cross-section) with one tall Perpendicular light to each face, between a base and a cap. Up to this height, the mullions are uniform. However, their upper halves carry fluted twist, lozenge or scale ornament. The Renaissance screen at Llandinabo, of *c.*1530, has mullions that feature precisely this type of encrusted decoration (though at Llandinabo it extends for the full height of each mullion, giving an effect that is less architectural). Only one other church in Herefordshire contains woodwork of a similar nature: beneath the tower at Staunton-on-Wye are two lengths of upright (half-round in cross section, like the pieces attached to the standards at Foy). These have a pattern of lozenge-shaped leaves very similar to those found a Llandinabo, but are of a width similar to those at Foy, and are topped by short, twisted caps (again like those found at Foy).

The head tracery at Foy is unique to Herefordshire (see illustration on p.128), although something similar can be found at Wolfhampcote in Warwickshire and at Doddbrooke in Devon. Moulded arches vault over the neighbouring mullion either to alight once more on the mullion one removed, or to spring out of the sides of the screen altogether. In doing so, pointed arches are formed over each individual bay. These have cusps that have been obliterated by spiky leaf forms (echoed in some of the mullion caps below). This overlapping of round arches to give intermediate pointed arches was not a new invention. It was widely used to great effect as a blind tracery form in the 12th century (for example in the chapter house at Much Wenlock Priory in Shropshire).

The screen has no massive head-beam, but instead possesses a framing beam that corresponds with the standards. From here a flat loft soffit extends west to meet the bressumer. The soffit is divided by eight ribs that are moulded with rounds and half-rounds, and has half-bosses at the intersections. The bressumer carries a reasonable (though slightly flat) vine trail. Some fragmentary lengths of old cresting are attached to the back of the head-beam. The doors of the screen belong to *c*.1660.

HEREFORD, THE CATHEDRAL

Although Hereford Cathedral must count as one of the minor English cathedrals (for both its size and architectural merit) it is not without its pleasures. Externally, the Decorated crossing tower is pleasingly colossal and features an abundance of paired lights and ballflower enrichment. It lends majesty to the composition as a whole, particularly when viewed from across the Wye. Inside, the north transept (of *c*.1250–5) is startling for the severity of its triangular arches. The Lady Chapel at the east end is less

stern and is light and rich in feel (*cf.* Brecon Cathedral). It dates from *c*.1220 and is animated by a profusion of attached shafts. Of the cathedral's highly disparate screenwork, only the painted stone screen to the Audley Chapel, together with some enticing fragments in the south-east transept, now survive. The great stone pulpitum was demolished in 1841, and the extraordinary Victorian choir screen now resides at the V&A in London.

The stone pulpitum of Hereford Cathedral was located at the west end of the nave, between the final piers before the crossing and beneath the western crossing arch (see illustration p.68).[6] During the 18th and 19th centuries, the cathedral suffered more than most from poorly judged and over-zealous restoration work, and the pulpitum was one of the principal victims. James Wyatt, while working on the rebuilding of the west end in the late 18th century, suggested moving the pulpitum further to the east. However, this plan was dropped, and the fitting remained *in situ* until midway through the 19th century, when first Lewis Cottingham and then George Gilbert Scott saw to its removal, citing the hazardous state of the tower overhead as justification for this act.

The western side of the pulpitum consisted of a blind (or engaged) arcade of three two-centred arches (the middle arch slightly narrower than the two outer ones). A cluster of three attached shafts formed each central pier of the arcade; while single attached shafts formed the outermost ones (the arches springing from capitals in each case). Beneath the central arch was a two-centred doorway beneath a corresponding hood-mould. This gave access to the choir beyond. The door itself was described as of 'Gothic panel work ... The lower stage contains two arches, divided each by mullions into six compartments, with similar tracery in the head'.[7] In each outer arch was a recess, or niche, probably intended for a reredos (there being altars against the pulpitum here at one time). The wooden organ gallery above had a panelled parapet supported upon corbels. This was divided by muntins into 22 blind trefoil-headed panels (18 for the flat front and four to the northern and southern ends, where the parapet turned in at 45°). The appearance of the eastern face of the pulpitum remains a mystery.

Dating the pulpitum is virtually impossible now. All that can be said with certainty is that it was erected sometime before 1686, as this was the year in which the massive organ was placed on top. The plainness of the overall design, however, makes a medieval origin possible (though the wooden parapet may have been a later addition).

Between 1492 and 1502, a small two-storey chapel was added to the south side of the Lady Chapel by Bishop Audley.[8] This was walled off from the Lady Chapel by a painted stone screen, whose fine mouldings divided the composition into nine bays and two half-bays above and below a horizontal division at door-head height (see plate 10). The sill of the screen is in the form of a plinth faced with a series of quatrefoils. Contained within these are flower cusps that alternate with shields of arms (including those of Audley, St. Ethelbert and the see of Hereford). Above this, the principal bays are divided from one another by attached shafts that extend for the full height of the screen. At the height of the door-head the 'stems' of the principal and intermediate shafts split open briefly to enclose a further series of quatrefoils (this time containing what are essentially foliage bosses). Where the bays above and below meet with this decorative band they are cusped to give trefoil heads (for the lower bays) and trefoil feet (for the upper bays). The taller principal bays in the upper half of the screen are topped by crocketed ogee heads, which bisect an openwork parapet course above to give pairs of trefoil-headed lights. The principal shafts are returned over each double-bay by rounded arches and a straight string-course above.

Much of the Audley screen's painted enrichment has survived. Spiral bands of black and white wind their way up the principal shafts and around the door. In the upper range, each panel (except the 17th, which has a shield of St. Ethelbert) contains a figure that stands upon a capital surmounting a column of stylised building parts, and beneath a canopy formed by a tall, crocketed pinnacle. The figures include Christ, the Twelve Apostles, and six further Saints. Christ occupies the 10th panel, and proceeding left (east) from here, we find SS. Peter, Andrew and Bartholomew; while to the right (west) are SS. Paul, Thomas, John the Evangelist, James, Jude and Philip. The bays of the lower range (but for the two double-bays taken by the door and the two taken by the windows) were at one time also filled with figures (including a pope and St. Sebastian). Now, only the two immediately to the east of the doorway survive.

Although all of the figures have been variously defaced and repainted over the years, the screen as it now stands is fairly true to its original appearance. From 1590 until 1840 the cathedral's chained library was kept in shelving erected in the Lady Chapel, and it is just possible that, far from leading to the damage of the screen, this may have helped to preserve the paintwork by reducing the amount of light hitting the screen.

225

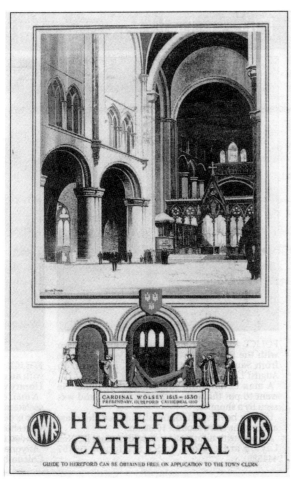

Hereford Cathedral: Railway poster from the first half of the
20th century showing the Scott screen in situ

The doorway of the screen is also noteworthy. Within a deep and well moulded surround (comprising a series of attached shafts that are returned over the door-head) is a two-centred arch in a square head with foliate spandrels. The door itself is framed and divided into four panels by rails and stiles that have been enriched with squared paterae (reminiscent of those on the middle rails at Aymestrey and Dilwyn). The panels contain linenfold carvings and the door is crowned by a superb dragon.

As well as being partly responsible for the removal of the old pulpitum, George Gilbert Scott was also the force behind the creation of the extravagant metal choir screen that stood in Hereford Cathedral for roughly 100 years, up until its removal in 1967. This removal took place despite a high-profile campaign fronted by Nikolaus Pevsner and John Betjemen. The dismantled screen was subsequently sold to the Herbert Museum and Art Gallery in Coventry (presumably because the original maker of the screen – the metalworking firm of Francis Skidmore[9] – was based in the city). The Herbert Museum passed on the screen (and the responsibility for its restoration) to the V&A in London, and in 1999 the dilapidated screen, comprising 13,703 separate pieces, became that museum's largest ever conservation project.[10] This work is now complete, and the screen is a star exhibit once more, just as it was at the 1862 International Exhibition.

To look upon Scott's choir screen now is to look upon an object that almost defies description. Certain words applicable to late medieval screenwork – trefoil, cusp, cresting etc. – still have currency here, but their ability to communicate the reality of this object is almost nullified. In some ways it appears that the screen was not really designed at all; that buried deep in the composition are a series of armatures upon which colours and textures and forms have simply been permitted to burst forth of their own accord in a riotous and uncontainable spectacle. Of course, it was designed and closer scrutiny reveals that, in its underlying format at least, the composition broadly echoes that of most other chancel screens.

The screen consists of two double bays to either side of a central doorway, which takes the space of two wider bays (actually equivalent to three of the flanking bays). Each double bay is surmounted by a pointed arch and divided by an intermediate standard to give two intermediate lights, each of which is topped by a trefoil head. The central doorway has a triangular head in the form of a gable end or pediment. Under this is a pointed arch, and below this a pair of trefoil arches; all larger than those of the flanking bays. Running along the top of the screen is a cornice of sorts (loosely equivalent to the head-beam of a late medieval screen) which continues behind the screen's central gable. The lower portion of the screen consists of a low middle rail and a series of perfectly square 'wainscot' panels.

Encrusted upon every surface, jammed into every space and gap, are forms natural and imagined, formal and informal, straight and curved. Huge Tudor roses fill the pointed arches, Christ hovers in a mandorla over the central doorway, sprigs of plant life climb the steep sides of the gable, cresting is piled upon cresting, and in their restlessness the standards change design half-way up. Such superabundance has readily transmitted itself into the materials and colours used to further enrich the screen. These include cast iron, copper, brass, zinc and wood; mosaics of marble, stone and glass; huge quantities of semi-precious stones; and the whole painted in myriad colours and glowing with gilding.

As a church fitting, this is as far from a utilitarian partition as it is possible to get. It is a show piece; a decorative object designed to floor the goggle-eyed onlooker. However, superabundance, both in terms of texture and colour, was not a new idea midway through the 19th century. The same qualities can be found on any number of late medieval screens in Devon. What is impossible to answer in each case is: to what extent is the creation of such a dazzling object about the glory of God, and how much that of the man who creates it?

In the south-east transept are several valuable fragments, some of which certainly belonged to a late medieval screen. Attached to the east wall are a series of intersecting openwork trefoils. These are reminiscent of those at Bettws Clyro in Radnorshire. It is impossible to say for sure how these were originally deployed (and if, indeed, they actually formed parts of a screen in Hereford Cathedral), but the possibility that they may have belonged to a rood-screen or loft, perhaps of the late 14th or early 15th century, is a strong one. It is also just possible that they once belonged to the pulpitum's eastern face. The small portable pulpit standing in the south-eastern transept is of great interest. Below a rail moulded with an ogee and two half-rounds, are ten panels and eight muntins. Each panel has an openwork quatrefoil holding a small Tudor

Hereford Cathedral: Carved arcade that recalls
that surviving at Bettws Clyro in Radnorshire

Hereford Cathedral: The screen as now restored and displayed at the Victoria and Albert Museum

Hereford Cathedral: The screen, from a drawing made by the Victoria and Albert Museum in 1999

rose. These panels could have belonged to either the wainscot of a rood-screen, or the parapet of a rood-loft. Once again, an early date is a real possibility. The muntins are moulded with Perpendicular lights, and are of a highly distinctive type, found also at Withington, Yatton and Eaton Bishop (all of which are in Herefordshire).

Hereford Cathedral: Small portable pulpit made up of pieces from a rood-screen and loft

How Caple, St. Andrew and St. Mary

How Caple church, like Monnington-on-Wye, dates from the end of the 17th century. The nave, south transept and west tower all belong to 1693–5; only the chancel is earlier. Inside, there is an unusual late Norman font decorated with plant-life and geometrical designs, all rendered in low relief. The stained glass, of the early 20th century, is also unusual. The church is attractively sited above the scoop of a sloping valley.

The screen and royal arms that fill the chancel archway are coeval with the fabric, and make for a strange and memorable composition. Two very tall door standards and two corresponding half (or engaged) wall standards, each with a twisted top third

and squared bottom two-thirds (with small ogee mouldings to each corner), extend from the sill up to the head-beam. To either side of the doorway the screen has a low balustrade, consisting of posts and half-posts that echo the design of the standards, (being twisted above and of square cross-section below). These are dowelled into the underside of the middle rail. The twisted arches (flattened over the door-head) are especially strange. This is perhaps as un-structural and un-architectural as wood can be made to appear. The head-beam is in the form of an ogee-moulded cornice that breaks forward over the door-head (*cf.* Monnington-on-Wye). This occurs almost at the height of the corbels of the chancel arch. The sumptuously carved Arms of William III (see p.29) that surmount the screen retain some of their gilding and are framed by the chancel arch overhead. As an object of utility, this screen has nothing to do with the security of the chancel, and everything to do with the giant emblem it is designed to support.

The screen has evidently been restored and altered during its lifetime. The inner face of each standard has a pair of filled rectangular slots, into which cross pieces of some kind must have been dowelled at one time. The lower parts of the screen – the middle rail and the little twisted balusters – have clearly been renewed (or altered in accordance with other changes, perhaps relating to the filled mortise holes above).

Kenchester, St. Michael

Despite its setting next to a farm, this small church still feels isolated. It dates from the 12th and 13th centuries and is of single chamber form. Inside is an unusual font. It is narrow and cylindrical, and has a shallow hollow in its top, like a birdbath.

Suggestions (by the RCHM) that this may be of Roman origin are given credence by the church's proximity to the Roman town of *Magnis*.

Inside, there are the fragmentary remains of a rood-screen and loft, which have been re-used in a strange and quite unexpected way. Put simply, elements that originally were deployed as horizontals have become verticals. Attached to the wall on the north side of the church is a 'post' that carries a length of vine trail between two half-rounds. The lower part is replacement work. The post has six mortise holes cut into its eastern face. This was clearly a beam at one time, and specifically formed the bressumer of a rood-loft. The mortise holes are for the joists of the loft floor. If this post were to be prised away from the wall, further mortise holes would become visible in what is now its northern face (actually its top face) for the muntins of the loft parapet. The post now attached to the south wall is well moulded along its western face and plain to the east. It has mortise holes both along its inner face and its western face close to the wall. This beam was clearly the head-beam of a screen; the first mortise holes being for the uprights of the screen below, the latter for the joists of the loft floor. The trefoiled

Kenchester: screen fragment

arch-braces and the top beam are new work (though the latter is topped by old timber). This singular arrangement may have been composed during the restoration of the church in 1925.

KENDERCHURCH, ST. MARY

Were it not for the noise and resinous stink of the sawmill below, the setting would be almost beyond compare. The sawmill is real though and from up on its hill the church looks out over a world that has left it far behind. The building consists of a nave, chancel, vestry and bellcote. Most of the fabric belongs to a Victorian restoration of 1871.

Inside, with the possible exception of the Norman font, only the screenwork catches the eye. It has been much renewed but retains some carved work of great interest. As it now stands, the screen consists of five bays (two of which are blind) to either side of a central doorway, that takes the space of seven bays. Everything below head-beam height appears to belong to the 17th century (i.e. coeval with the Jacobean pulpit etc.) or later. The head-beam, however, is characteristic of work of the late 15th century. Its eastern face carries a half-round, and its western face a wide hollow and a half-round. The head-beam is chamfered to both the east and west where it meets the mullions. Above the head-beam to the east are plain, Jacobean panels.

The loft coving, which is divided into 22 panels, is new. The bressumer is original though, and still shows the mortise holes along its top for the loft parapet. The vine trail is of an extremely unusual design. The grape bunches are linked by a completely straight stalk running through the middle of the design. This feature is found at St. Margarets, Michaelchurch Escley, and

231

Kenderchurch: Detail of bressumer (with its unique vine trail) and one of the spandrels, carved with a characterful green man

Stoke Lacy; but the design as a whole is unique in the southern Marches. At either end is a lively (and again very unusual) carved spandrel. Each contains the face of a green man with bristly chin and tongue sticking out; the one to the north being slightly better than that to the south.

KINNERSLEY, ST. JAMES

The church has one of the most memorable church towers in Herefordshire. It belongs to the early 14th century but feels more ancient still, with its arrow-slit windows and lack of either dividing string courses or ornamentation. It is topped by an unusual saddleback roof. The main body of the church may be

a little earlier, and consists of a nave and chancel, north aisle and south porch. The inside of the church is also memorable, not least for its painted chancel and its woodwork. The former was designed by the architect G.F. Bodley, while the latter includes some interesting Flemish relief carvings of *c.*1530.

Before the chancel arch, there stands the base only of a chancel screen. It features a series of unusual openwork quatrefoils upon its western face, and what appear to be bosses topping the sawn-off tops of the standards. These latter are elaborately moulded with paired half-rounds separated by flats (apart from to the west, where the rounds are flanked by half-rounds). Dating the base is difficult, but the considerable amount of Jacobean woodwork in the church makes an origin sometime during the 17th century a distinct possibility.

LEA, ST. JOHN THE BAPTIST

Lea church stands next to a busy main road. Its comprehensive restoration (of 1854) left only the spire-topped west tower largely untouched. It has a nave and chancel, north aisle and north porch. Its great treasure is its *c.*1200 Italian font which consists of a shallow basin, beautifully carved and with a rim decorated with Cosmati (mosaic) work. It is supported upon an oversized capital that tops a column (knotted halfway up), which in turn stands on the back of an elephant whose saddle is also decorated with further Cosmati work. It has been called 'The most surprising font in Herefordshire',[11] but then it would be difficult to envisage a place where such an object would not be surprising.

At the east end of the north aisle stands a partition constructed from pieces from an old rood-screen. Its framing members comprise five standards, two mullions and a middle rail; all moulded with ogees. The sill and head-beam (this latter having a curved face between half-rounds, and a groove along its top) appear original. The second bay from the north side is a door. The spaces between the framing members are taken up with tracery heads and new (and rather thin) boarding. There are six double and four single tracery heads, each employing one of three different designs.

One head design is particularly interesting. It has a rounded arch above (with leaf spandrels) and an ogee arch below whose point stretches up to the apex of the rounded arch. Halfway

Lea: Tracery heads of Herefordshire type

up, there are two further ogees, giving four compartments in all, each with cusps that hold a small flower. The ogee arch below also has cusps terminating in small flowers. Four double heads of this unusual and pretty design survive here. The four single heads, each with its crocketed pinnacle and flowers held in more formal tracery compartments, are also effective and are reminiscent of the heads at Stoke Lacy and Bishop's Frome (but without precisely matching either). The two other double heads are of a more familiar design, and are less delicately rendered than the other heads here.

LEDBURY, ST. MICHAEL

For such a large structure, Ledbury church makes only a modest visual impact. It lies well back from the High Street; its spire terminating the famous, narrow vista of Church Lane, which leads away from the Market House. Ledbury church consists of a long nave flanked by side aisles, a chancel flanked by chancel aisles (forming chapels), a further chapel sprouting from the north side of the north chancel aisle, and a north porch and vestry at the west end. A mighty detached tower topped by a spire stands on the north side of the church.

In date, the church has notable parts belonging to the 12th, 13th and 14th centuries. The Norman work belongs to two separate phases and includes the fine chancel, with its rounded arches and scalloped capitals. The outer north chapel, with its spectacular Decorated windows peppered with ballflower (by the same group of masons who were later to work at Leominster Priory) is of the 14th century. The tower belongs to the 13th century and is topped by a later spire. The interior has much to recommend it, not least a spectacular assortment of monuments.

Sadly, only fragmentary parts of Ledbury's late medieval screenwork survive. At the west end of the north aisle are the heads of three screen bays and the vaulting between; all cut off at the springing point of the vaulting. The heads contain blind Perpendicular tracery and the compartments of the vaulting are subdivided by cusped ogee heads. Two of the caps that once surmounted boutell shafts rising up the lost standards also survive. If this is late medieval work at all then it is certainly of a very late date; specifically perhaps the first quarter of the 16th century. A further fragment of vaulting (now free-standing upside

Ledbury: Fragmentary remains of vaulting and unusual blind tracery heads of a rood-screen of uncertain date

down in the south aisle) does not correspond with the north aisle remains, and could even be Victorian.

LEINTHALL STARKES, ST. MARY MAGDALENE

The church stands beyond the village and is approached down a grassy path bordered by neat hedges. All around spreads an expansive and glorious landscape fringed by hills. The church itself has only yew trees for company, but these have edged ever closer to the east and west end, and now peer in through little windows. The church dates from the 12th century and is of single chamber form with a south porch and a bellcote overhead.

The rood-screen inside forms the only division between chancel and nave: a factor that probably guaranteed its survival.

It has been greatly (though quite skilfully) renewed; almost certainly in the 17th century and again more recently. It consists of five bays to either side of a central doorway, which takes the space of three bays. The standards, well moulded with ogees to the east and rounds and half-rounds to the west, extend from the sill up to the head-beam. The wainscot has been entirely renewed. The middle rail, however, is probably original. To the west it shows a flat face between a half-round above and two rounds below. The mullions dowelled into the middle rail have very similar mouldings to the standards, and also appear to be original. The tracery heads are new work, though of a familiar Perpendicular design of little, straight-sided lights over a cusped and foliated trefoil arch. It may be that some old work was used as a precedent for the design. The heads have been cut from thin

Leinthall Starkes: Rood-screen

234

Leinthall Starkes: One of the thin Perpendicular tracery heads

board (like fretwork) and have been carved upon their west faces only. Replacement strips slotted into grooves in the mullions below the tracery heads suggest that the heads may have been deeper at one time (or that, at the least, some tampering has taken place here). The head-beam above is also new. The tympanum was still *in situ* over the screen prior to 1909.[12]

LEINTWARDINE, ST. MARY MAGDALENE

Leintwardine is a big, sandstone church that consists of a nave with side aisles, a south-west porch tower, south porch, transeptal north chapel, and chancel with north chapel. It has components belonging to the 13th, 14th and 15th centuries, but its windows and chancel in particular betray the heavy touch of the Victorians.

Inside, the choir stalls are interesting, and may have come from nearby Wigmore Abbey. They are high-backed and have panel tracery. They retain, on the south side, several good misericords.

Some old screenwork has been incorporated into the partition (on the other side of which is the organ) at the west end of the chancel north chapel. Whilst some of these fragments certainly came from a screen, it seems possible that other pieces may be associated with the imported choir stalls. Two tall standards, each with a boutell topped by a crocketed

Leintwardine: Tracery head with crocketed ogee arch

pinnacle, support a head-beam moulded with a curved face between rounds (which may have carried a carved trail). New mullions have been dowelled into the ogee-moulded middle rail that runs between the standards. The tracery heads, numbering six and of various designs (and including one odd, triple head), are big and boldly carved. They have applied crocketed ogee heads of a type rarely found on screens but occasionally featuring as canopies on stallwork.

The transeptal north chapel is divided from the north aisle by a modern screen.

LLANDINABO, ST. DINABO

The tiny church stands like a private chapel next to an impressive farmhouse. It was built by a Shrewsbury firm in 1881 and consists of a nave, chancel, south porch and timber-framed bell-turret.

Inside, there is a highly unusual and complete rood-screen, predominantly of Renaissance character and dating from *c.*1530. It has three bays to either side of a central doorway, that takes the space of three bays. The wainscot is divided into four bays to the north and five to the south, and each of its bays is pierced by one or two Gothic loop lights. Taken together these have the appearance of formalised elevation squints. Each standard and mullion in one half of the screen has a twin on the other side. The designs are fanciful and have an encrusted quality. The door standards have interlocking, diamond-shaped, crinkly leaves; the

Llandinabo: The head-beam and tracery heads of the rood-screen, joyously overrun by Renaissance motifs

door side mullions are of a similar design (though here the leaves are smaller and the diamonds straight-edged). The wall side mullions have elongated hexagons and the wall standards have leaves, overlapping as if to simulate feathers or scales. The door standards here are very similar to the fragmentary half-posts at Staunton-on-Wye, and the wall standards are similar to the half-mullions attached to the wall posts at Foy. Similar uprights can be found at Charlton-on-Otmoor and Thame in Oxfordshire.

The tracery is interesting because it reveals an intermingling of Gothic and Renaissance motifs. At first glance, each tracery head, with its fancy, tumbling scrollwork, appears to be wholly non-Gothic in design. However, a closer look reveals that the scrolls spring from one of two cusps beneath each rounded arch. The spandrels, meanwhile, are also cusped to give familiar trefoil forms. Only in the repaired door-head is there a complete absence of the Gothic.

It is possible that the head-beam above once belonged to an earlier screen. Without its frieze and its narrow scrolling lengths of decoration it would have only a flat surface between lengths of moulding above, and a curved face below. These faces may once have housed Gothic carved trails. The blind-cresting just above the tracery heads may have been openwork drop- (or top-) cresting at one time, for it is composed of the same spiky leaf forms found in the pointed arches at Foy. Over this blind-cresting, there are two lengths of ornament, each twisted and beaded, and over this is the spectacular frieze.

The complete absence of plain surfaces in the upper parts of the screen means the eye has no resting-place and tends to dart about bedazzled. However, few screens in the southern Marches repay close scrutiny quite like this one, for here are mermen, scaly sea monsters, mask-like faces with tongues sticking out, prancing nudes sporting periwigs and wings, figures leaping out of cakes (or are they crowns?) – it doesn't really matter: all cavort gleefully across the top of the screen. The design bursts with energy, imagination and humour and is robustly carved. The back of the head-beam re-uses seven cut down linenfold panels. These may have come from the wainscot of an earlier screen (or from this screen before restoration work was carried out to it).

MADLEY, NATIVITY OF THE VIRGIN

This very large church is architecturally memorable both inside and out. It consists of a long nave flanked by side aisles and a polygonal apse beyond. On the north side is the Norman porch; to the south an outer aisle (the Chilston Chapel) and to the west a fine tower. The porch belongs to the 12th century and was once the north transept of a smaller, aisleless church. The rest of the fabric belongs to the 13th century (nave, side aisles and tower) and the 14th century (the outer south aisle and the apse). The unusual apse (with crypt beneath) and the self-assured west tower are the highlights of the exterior. Inside, the apse is a wonderful space. Its east window contains some of Herefordshire's earliest (and loveliest) stained glass, including several roundels of the 13th century.

No rood-screen currently divides the nave from the chancel beyond, but in the north aisle is a parclose screen that encloses a pew of the 17th century. This incorporates several pieces from a screen of the late 15th century, including 17 uniform tracery heads and a wide door-head. The 17 tracery heads are carved upon one face only with a standard Perpendicular design of four loop lights

Madley: Door-head tracery with rank of loop lights, reminiscent of East Anglian work (particularly in its width)

over a cusped ogee arch (the cusps terminating in flowers). The door-head is more unusual. Here, the ogee arch does not reach far enough, and so develops two further rounded heads before reaching the edges. This form is cusped below and has 12 loop lights above, thus corresponding with the other tracery heads. All of the heads are framed up with woodwork of the 17th century (including big, carved balusters topped with pineapple finials).

Overhead, there is a fine beam that is probably coeval with the tracery heads. This is chamfered below and has, upon its western side, a flat face between a half-round below and two little half-rounds and a hollow above (which may have housed a carved trail at one time). Up in the east wall of the aisle behind the screen is an open doorway, and at floor level is another door. These clearly gave access to a rood-loft sometime prior to the dramatic alteration of the chancel-nave junction in the 14th century.

MICHAELCHURCH, ST. MICHAEL

St. Michaels sits beside a pond in the dip of a valley, small and forgotten. It has a nave and chancel in one, a south porch and bell-turret, and dates from the 12th century (though Bishop Herwald may have founded a church here as early as 1056). Its interior is a joy. Few churches have been allowed to mellow and fade like this down the centuries. There is an interesting Norman font

Michaelchurch: Detail of rood-screen showing the turned shafts added to update the screen

and beyond this, beneath a window in the north wall, a small Roman roadside altar. The walls are painted with imitation brickwork, with a flower in each 'brick': a design almost identical to that found at Aston in Herefordshire, and Duntisbourne Rouse in Gloucestershire.

Even with its later additions, the sturdy rood-screen that divides the chancel from the nave is entirely in keeping with the rest of the interior (see photograph on p.27). It has three bays to either side of a wide central doorway. The principal framing timbers – the wall and door standards

and the head-beam – are all simply chamfered. The mullions between do not correspond with the head-beam, and may also be replacement work. There is no sill, and the standards rest upon stone blocks. All of this appears to be early work (i.e. of the 15th century). However, at a later date (possibly the 17th century, given the nature of some of the other furnishings, such as the pulpit) the screen was lightly embellished to bring it up to date and invest it with a little finesse.

This work involved the addition of various attached shafts with moulded bases and turned caps. Those on the inner faces of the door standards support a simple flat-arched door-head. From the tops of those in each of the six bays, there spring pairs of pointed arches; the meeting of the two arches in the centre of each bay terminated below by a turned piece that matches the caps to either side, and has the appearance of a bobbin. The current heads certainly replaced earlier tracery heads. The top of the head-beam has four large mortise holes and a rebate for the loft and tympanum above. Some of the tympanum can be seen protruding from the ceiling overhead (the ceiling is later and almost certainly hides a significant portion of the surviving tympanum). Below the middle rail the screen has plain boarding. The slots for the original wainscot boards can still be seen in the wall standard and underside of the middle rail on the north side.

MICHAELCHURCH ESCLEY, ST. MICHAEL

The church stands in the middle of a large churchyard, in lovely countryside close to the Welsh border. It has a nave and chancel in one, and a south porch and west tower. The main body of the church belongs to *c.*1400, the porch to the 16th century and the

Michaelchurch Escley: Late medieval carved trails
– almost identical to those at nearby St. Margarets
– with later tracery heads

have been a bressumer. It features two carved trails separated by half-rounds upon its western face, and a round and two slight hollows to the east. The upper trail is a fairly standard vine trail, but the lower one is of great interest. It features a central stem that runs straight through the design, spiralling around which is a ribbon of foliage enrichment. This gives small compartments, each of which contains two diamond-shaped leaves branching off the straight stem.

The design is almost identical to that of the lower trail on the bressumer at nearby St. Margarets (which also has a wider vine trail above), and is similar to those found at Kenderchurch and at Stoke Lacy. It is possible that all three trails came from the same workshop source. The top-cresting that surmounts the head-beam at Michaelchurch Escley may also be early; but the woodwork topping the beam on its eastern side is new. Over this beam is another early beam. This has a half-round between two rounds to the west and is plain to the east. It appears to have mortise holes for rood figures and may originally have been a rood-beam.

MONNINGTON-ON-WYE, ST. MARY

The walk to the church is a memorable one. A wide, grassy path curves past woodland and brings the visitor up to a delightful lych-gate next to Monnington Court. Beyond this, and hidden until now, stands the church. Its west tower is Perpendicular, but everything else dates from 1679. This makes it something of a rarity, for very few complete churches of the late 17th century exist in England.

The church consists of a nave, chancel and south porch. Inside, the enthusiasm for twisted balusters is everywhere apparent. They have been deployed in the fronts of the pews, in the pulpit

pyramid-topped tower to the end of the 19th century. Inside, there is a wall painting of *c.*1500 depicting 'Christ of the Trades'. The subject matter was apparently a warning to Sabbath breakers that their tools, if used on a Sunday, could do injury to Christ.

The current rood-screen is a bold and confident piece, erected in 1911. It consists of three bays to either side of a central doorway (also of three bays), and has big ogee arches above and linenfold panelling in the wainscot. In the latter a variety of animals can be found: a horse, fish, duck, dog, fox, pheasant, squirrel, frog and ram etc. The head-beam, however, belongs to the end of the 15th century or the beginning of the 16th century, and may originally

Monnington-on-Wye: Chancel screen detail

and the reader's desk; even in the Arms of Charles II mounted on the north wall. They are also found in the chancel screen. This has four bays to either side of a wide central doorway, and is of a fairly simple design. It is panelled up to middle rail height, and has twisted balusters as mullions above. These support a head-beam in the form of a cornice, which breaks to the east and west (that at How Caple breaks only to the west). The screen at How Caple, which also makes conspicuous use of twisted uprights (and is similar in date), provides Monnington with a striking analogy.

MORETON-ON-LUGG, ST. ANDREW

This modest, Victorian church stands side-on to the road, and has an exterior that promises little to passers by. Its appearance is deceptive though, for within there is much of interest. The interior has been energised by a series of bright mosaic panels (by Salviati) that lines the nave and culminates in a jewel casket of a chancel at the east end. The church has a nave, chancel, north porch and south-west tower. A Norman church evidently stood

on the site (note the window in the south wall of the chancel). However, almost everything here belongs to W.H. Knight's rebuild of 1867.

A little (metal) Victorian chancel screen now stands at the head of the nave. At the west end of the nave, however, the remains of a *c.*1500 screen now enclose the organ. As it stands, it is an engaging piece that consists of eight bays; six facing the entrance and two (or, more accurately, one and a half) returning the screen at its eastern end. The west wall and door standards are original, and have ogees upon their inner faces. The mullions contain new woodwork, but have ogees to match the standards. The uniform

Moreton-on-Lugg: Parts of the old rood-screen re-used to enclose the organ in the 19th century

tracery heads to each bay appear to be original and are carved upon one face only with cinquefoil heads. Running along the top of the screen is a vine trail. This is of reasonable quality only and lacks the pierced detail that would have given to the design the depth of other trails. Below middle rail height the screen contains mostly new work.

PEMBRIDGE CASTLE CHAPEL

This chapel stands in the shadow of 'a relatively well-preserved smaller border castle',[13] and belongs to the 16th century. Its screen, like its other fittings, was imported from outside the county and originated in Essex. It consists of two bays to either side of a central doorway, the bays with simple tracery heads over trefoiled arches and the door-head is cusped below its tracery. The castle is now privately owned and, despite its name, stands some 20 miles from Pembridge itself.

PIPE AND LYDE, ST. PETER

The church stands beside the busy A49 just outside Hereford. Its fabric dates from the 13th century, but was heavily restored by F.R. Kempson in 1874. It consists of a nave, chancel, west tower and south porch. The chancel has an attractive arch-braced roof.

No rood-screen now divides the chancel from the nave, yet by some miracle a sumptuous, late-medieval bressumer has survived. This beam has two carved trails, divided by half-rounds, upon its western face. The upper trail consists of an undulating stem that forms compartments each of which contains a double leaf. The lower (and wider) of the two enrichments is a well curved vine trail with big, square leaves and spiralling tendrils (again

Pipe and Lyde: Detail of surviving bressumer featuring a vine trail of exceptional artistry

coming off an undulating stem). The carving is of the highest quality, but the real achievement here is in the composition itself. The various components of the vine trail – grape bunches, leaves, stems and tendrils – have been deployed to give a regular pattern; a formalised and essentially artificial arrangement, and yet the effect here is unforced, elegant and highly naturalistic.

The beam has a slot in its underside for a now-lost drop-cresting. It appears that the lowermost mouldings of the bressumer (and the cresting) may have curved down at either end to meet similar mouldings on wall posts, so forming spandrels (perhaps similar to those at Burghill). The eastern face of the beam is now hidden behind thin board cladding, making it impossible to see the mortise holes that would confirm this as a bressumer. This beam is now roughly two feet higher up than it was when a part of the rood-loft. Overhead, there is a second, crenellated beam, which supports the framing and boarding of a tympanum.

PIXLEY, ST. ANDREW

Pixley is another small church, like Fawley and Stretford, marooned on a farm far away from any village. It is of single chamber form with a south porch and dates from the 13th century. Its bell-turret belongs to the restoration of 1865.

Pixley: The massively-constructed earliest timber rood-screen in the southern Marches is shown here as it stood in the early 20th century, complete with wainscot panels and more of its loft fabric than it now retains

The rood-screen forms the only division between nave and chancel, and is of exceptional interest. It is almost certainly the earliest timber screen in the southern Marches (the stone screen at Welsh Newton being earlier) and is one of very few screens of the 14th century to survive anywhere in England. It is striking for the extreme massiveness of its framing timbers and for the distinctive nature of its construction. As it stands today, it consists of three bays to either side of an arched, central doorway. The wall standards extend from the sill up to the wall-plate and tie-beam overhead, thus enabling the standards to frame up not only the head-beam, but also the rood-beam above. This is one of the earliest known methods of screen construction, and can also be found employed at Stretford in Herefordshire and (in a more refined form) at Aberedw, Bettws Clyro and Disserth in Radnorshire.

The door standards comprise two giant, curved timbers, with chocks inserted above to give a pointed apex to the arch. This arrangement is reminiscent of the early screenwork of the Breconshire group of double-screens, which includes those at Llanelieu, Llanfigan and Merthyr Cynog. The inner face is chamfered to the east, and is moulded with a quarter-round (or ovolo) to the west. Dowelled between door and wall standards is a huge middle rail; its upper face chamfered to the south. The mullions to the south are original. Those set against the wall and door standards are moulded with quarter-rounds to both east and west, while the two between are chamfered. The two mullions to the north are new and the inner faces of the door and wall standards here have slots, evidently for a horizontal rail of some kind. The upper face of the middle rail has one mortise hole to the north and one to the south. Both of these housed mullions at one time. The head-beam is ovolo-moulded to the west, and has grooves running along its top for boarding. The slightly curved beam overhead has 13 round mortise holes cut into its underside, possibly for uprights that once formed the frame for loft boarding in between. The eastern face of the other beam (slightly lower and further east) is moulded with a groove and an ovolo. Until quite recently the wainscot contained new boarding.[14]

The monumental construction of this screen speaks eloquently of the then-nascent state of the craft of woodworking. The extreme over-engineering of the structure and its lack of carved decoration reveal that neither the potential of the material nor its limitations had yet been fully understood or realised. The result is lumbering and inelegant, but also functional and utterly compelling. Its survival is near-miraculous, and must be due in part to this being an otherwise undivided building.

PUTLEY

Putley church stands beside a pond close to a farm. It was comprehensively rebuilt in 1875, but a smattering of Norman fragments attests to the existence on the site of a much earlier church. As it stands, the church consists of a nave, chancel, south porch and bellcote. Inside at the east end there are stalls with traceried canopies: an unusual feature in so small a church. The low chancel screen dates from the time of the Victorian rebuild, but incorporates pieces dating from the late 17th or early 18th century. It has two bays to the north (plus a further two for the pulpit) and three to the south. The design (all carved in the solid) consists of blank arches and ionic pilasters. The current top board appears to be modern work.

ST. MARGARETS, ST. MARGARET

The church inhabits a magical setting between the Black Mountains and the Golden Valley. It can be reached, with patience and a little luck, via the narrow lanes that knit these hills. The structure dates from the 12th century and consists of a nave, chancel, south porch, and weather-boarded bell-turret. Despite the protestations of its modest architecture and crumbling plasterwork, St. Margarets contains one of the greatest ecclesiastical treasures of the southern Marches.

Inside, a crystalline rood-loft of pale oak illuminates the nave. Such is its crispness it might have been carved yesterday. The rood-screen that once filled the tiny chancel arch below the loft has gone, but was clearly of two narrow bays to either side of a central doorway. There are six mortise holes in the underside of the head-beam: two for the door standards, two for the wall standards, and two (shallower ones) for the mullions. The head-beam has no slots for tracery heads, either because these were originally slotted between the standards and mullions only, or because the screen simply never had any (perhaps due to the extreme narrowness of each bay). The small rood-screen at Llanfilo, standing as it does beneath a not dissimilar rood-loft, gives an idea of how the screen at St. Margarets might have looked.

The head-beam of the screen at St. Margarets is embedded into the north and south walls, and is enriched with an oak trail. The top-cresting is original, but the drop-cresting, which at one time was set back within the chancel arch only, has been brought forward and extended (with the addition of new work) to run the full length of the head-beam. From the top of the head-beam the vertical ribs of the loft coving spring west to intersect with

St. Margarets: Rood-loft boss and Rood-stairs

two horizontal ribs, to give 42 square panels in all. The ribs are moulded with hollows and have 30 carved bosses at the intersections (21 of which are original). The loft coving (and specifically the boarding) was comprehensively restored in *c*.1900.

The loft coving terminates in the back (or eastern side) of the bressumer. To the west, this beam carries two carved trails divided by rounds and is further enriched with a top-cresting and a pair of drop-crestings. The upper (and wider) of the two trails is a fine and naturalistic vine trail. It is original, apart from a two foot length at its southern end. The lower trail is arguably the most interesting of the rood-loft's various trails. It is of a type that occurs at only three other places in the southern Marches: at Michaelchurch Escley, just three miles away, and (in a less similar form) at Kenderchurch

and Stoke Lacy. It has a continuous ribbon of serrated leaf that twines around a horizontal central stem, with two leaves occupying each compartment. The top-cresting here has been renewed, as has the lower of the two drop-crestings. The delicate forward drop-cresting is original.

The parapet front is divided into 19 compartments by chamfered muntins. This portion of the loft is the most altered part of the fitting, having been entirely stripped of its original ornamentation. The face of each muntin has three peg-holes for little buttresses, while the panels between also have three peg-holes, almost certainly for carved figures. There is also evidence that each panel had decorative paintwork. Crossley and Ridgway report finding that, 'In the centre of a number of the panels very faint traces of 4-in. wide five-pointed star (or perhaps a five-petal flower) remain'.[15] The effect of all this carved and painted decoration must have been exceedingly rich.

St. Margarets: Roof-loft post

St. Margarets: Rood-loft

St. Margarets: Detail of bressumer with a vine trail and leaf trail framed up between top- and drop-cresting

The top-beam has a hawthorn leaf trail; a motif employed only infrequently by screen-carvers (e.g. at Partrishow, just across the border in Breconshire). The top-cresting of this beam has been renewed, while the drop-cresting is entirely new and replaces the damaged (but more interesting) original.

The bressumer is supported upon two richly encrusted posts. The front of each post has three faces (each showing one of three different designs) between a series of crocketed pinnacles running up each corner. Just below the loft, there is a pair of crocketed canopies, which may re-use pieces from the loft parapet (*cf.* Llananno). The canopies crown little niches that probably housed statuettes. The new drop-cresting of the bressumer is carried around small leaf spandrels (thus linking the posts with the rood-loft overhead) and halts rather crudely, level with the bottom of each canopy. The eastern face of each post has mortise holes for return rails. These were slotted into the wall standards of the now-lost screen, and fenced in small areas (or encloses) to the north and south for screen-altars (one of which survives in the chancel).

The rood-loft is accessed via a door on the north side of the chancel, and a staircase cut through the east wall of the nave. This meets an upper door that opens onto the north side of the loft. In the loft itself are a set of decaying Decalogues. These were put up in place of the Rood after the Reformation, and comprise the Ten Commandments, the Creed and the Lord's Prayer. A very fine set survives *in situ* in Lydbury North in Shropshire.

Although occupying an English church, the rood-loft of St. Margarets is without doubt Welsh in origin. In both its design and enrichment it echoes the work of the Newtown centre to the north, and in particular the loft at Llanwnnog (though screenwork from this centre generally appears in through churches with no chancel arch). In its construction methods (specifically its triple arcade), the rood-loft at St. Margarets is also distantly related to the incomplete screens of the Breconshire group at Bronllys and Llywel. At St. Margarets the crispness of the carving, the integrity of the structure and the (admittedly recent) equal weighting given to plain and carved surfaces (in contrast to Llananno), make this one of the most satisfying examples of late medieval screenwork to survive anywhere in England or Wales.

St. Weonards, St. Weonard

The village lies on the undulating road that links Hereford with Monmouth to the south. The church belongs mainly to the 14th and 15th centuries and consists of a nave, chancel, north aisle, west tower and south porch. It contains some unusual stained glass, including a panel from the 16th century that may be German[16] (in the nave south window).

Inside, there is both a rood-screen and an attractive parclose screen; this latter fencing off a chapel at the east end of the north aisle and enjoying greater prominence than the rood-screen. The rood-screen has been much altered. Above middle rail height, it now consists of two bays to either side of a central doorway. However, slots in the top of the middle rail show that there were once three mullions to each side, giving four bays to either side of the doorway. Below middle rail height this composition is still honoured: six ogee-moulded muntins (four of them original) divide the wainscot into bays, each with linenfold panelling. The middle rail above is unusual: otherwise plain, its west face is tightly moulded with paired double ogees (giving the appearance of reeding). This rail incorporates some new work. Of the screen's principal framing members, the door standards and the wall standard on the south side are original. The head-beam represents more of a mystery. Its top shows a continuous rebate and yet it appears to be new work. The vine trail (on both the eastern and western faces) also appears to be new.

The parclose screen in the north aisle presents a handsome and regular composition of 14 uniform bays to the west, before turning at right angles and continuing for three bays into the final pier of the arcade, to emerge once again for a further six bays.

The sill on which the screen stands is simply chamfered, but the other framing members are finely moulded. The ogee mouldings upon the western face of the middle rail are continued up and down the standards. The mullions have ogee mouldings and a round to both the east and west, and correspond with the muntins below, which are moulded with a flattened version of the same

St. Weonards: Detail of the vine trail on the head-beam (above), later updated with interlocking serpents (below)

St. Weonards: Parclose screen

design. The tight reeding of these mouldings is echoed in the fluting of the linenfold panels of the wainscot, giving the screen a particularly harmonious appearance.

The head-beam has a flat face between two half-rounds, and has been decorated with applied carvings. The composition is one of interlocking serpents; the undulations forming compartments that contain various fruit, flower and leaf forms. This carved work, like that at nearby Llandinabo, reveals the influence of Renaissance design, albeit in a more measured way. It is possible that this enrichment represents an updating of the screen in the first half of the 16th century: the work may have replaced a standard late medieval trail, such as the vine trail seen elsewhere on the screen. The tracery heads, carved upon one face only, are also unusual and may be coeval with the decoration of the head-beam. They consist of three compartments, each of which has been cusped to hold a flower. The ogee head below is also cusped to take little flowers. The tracery heads at Kedington in Suffolk, belonging to a screen of 1619, share the same characteristic of two almost independent forms meeting in the centre to give an ogee arch.

Access to the parclose chapel is through a door that opens from the east end of the nave. However, the chapel can also be accessed via a door in the screen that now fills the final bay of the arcade. This screen has six bays (two of which are taken by the door) and corresponds with the main portion of the parclose screen, but for the crude vine trail on the southern face of its head-beam.

STAUNTON-ON-WYE, ST. MARY

The church is well seen from the road below, standing on a ridge above the Wye valley. It consists of a nave, chancel, south porch and west tower. The south doorway and the blocked north doorway are both Norman, but most of the fabric is of *c.*1300 or later. The chancel was rebuilt in the 18th century and contains fittings belonging to the 19th century.

Inside, beneath the tower, there is an interesting collection of carved panels and fragments. Some have no connection whatever with late medieval screenwork. There are, for example, a number of Jacobean panels, and there used to be six medallions of the mid-16th century, each showing a head in profile (these were stolen and only one has ever been recovered). The other pieces appear to have come from a screen (or screens) and consist of a strip

Staunton-on-Wye: Screen fragments beneath tower; that at the top related to uprights at Llandinabo and Foy, that below is similar to the middle rail treatment at Canon Pyon

of enrichment, two half-columns, and at least 20 small carved spandrels. Of these, the half columns are the most interesting. They are very similar to those employed at Llandinabo. However, both are roughly six feet in height, so could hardly have been mullions. Their profile shows that they were employed as engaged columns. Both feature interlocking, diamond-shaped leaves and are topped by twisted caps. The thin zigzag enrichment of serrated leaves is very similar to that found at Canon Pyon. The spandrels, meanwhile, clearly formed blind tracery enrichments in the upper corners of wainscot panels. They are similar to those found at Bishop's Frome and elsewhere.

STOKE LACY, ST. PETER AND ST. PAUL

The church stands at the bottom of a swooping dip in the road; an unexceptional structure almost entirely rebuilt by F.R. Kempson in 1863. It consists of a nave, chancel, west tower and south porch. The chancel arch is Norman.

For such an unforgiving Victorian church, the significant (if mutilated) screen within, which belongs to the early 16th century, comes as a great surprise. It is almost certain that it once belonged in another church. As it now stands, it consists of seven bays to either side of a central doorway (the bays to the northern end of the screen having been severely mutilated to take account of the pulpit). The wall standards have been sawn off, but the door standards remain undamaged. They have a wide flat to the east, and ogee-moulded edges. The mullions between are similar, but have much narrower flat faces. They are dowelled into the squared top of the sturdy middle rail. Below, the middle rail appears at first to return the mouldings of the standards over the top of the wainscot, but in fact does not do so precisely on the south side, and does so even less well to the north. The middle rail to the north looks wrong, and is either badly damaged or a later addition.

The head-beam carries a single carved trail: an enrichment of an unusual design that corresponds closely, but for one detail, with only two other such trails in the southern Marches: namely at St. Margarets and Michaelchurch Escley, (on the Welsh border 30 miles south-west of Stoke Lacy). The compartments formed by the twining ribbon of foliage at Michaelchurch and St. Margarets contain two leaves. At Stoke Lacy these are joined by a third element, looking like a fir-cone, but more likely to represent either a grape bunch or an acorn. Another trail, at Kenderchurch, is a more distant relation. Below the carved trail, the mouldings of the muntins (and standards) are returned over each head. The top of the head-beam shows no mortise holes or groove, and may never have carried a rood-loft.

A number of features link this screen to that of nearby Bishop's Frome. The tracery heads have crocketed pinnacles rising out of an ogee arch to

Stoke Lacy: Detail of the mutilated screen

250

terminate at the apex of a pointed arch above. A very similar design appears at Bishop's Frome (and four tracery heads of an identical design can be found in Lea church). In a further echo of Bishop's Frome, the wainscot panels (in this case on the north side) have a number of spandrels attached. No effort has been made here to distribute these in a way that relates to their original role (namely in blind tracery heads framed up between the muntins of the wainscot). They have simply been spared and placed on display here as attractive curios. The lack of any muntins to divide up the wainscot makes it certain that these spandrels did not belong originally to this screen.

One obvious explanation for the similarity between the screens at Bishop's Frome and Stoke Lacy is the intervention of F.R. Kempson. Just two years earlier he was at work on the nave at Bishop's Frome. The appearance of two screens that possess such similar characteristics in two such geographically proximate churches can be no coincidence. This raises a number of tantalising questions. If the screen at Stoke Lacy was brought in from another church by Kempson, which church was it? The tracery heads and spandrels (though not the carved trail on the head-beam), suggest Herefordshire workmanship. And what implications, if any, does this have for the much-reconstructed screen at Bishop's Frome? It possesses similar attributes, and bears no relationship to the earlier parclose screen in that church. Could this also be imported work?

STRETFORD, ST. COSMAS AND ST. DAMIAN

Internally, this is one of the most unusual and engaging churches in the southern Marches. It has two of everything, exactly matched:

two naves divided from two chancels by two hefty screens (or, perhaps more accurately, a nave and chancel with an aisle and chancel chapel next door, handled in an identical fashion). Overhead, supported by the wall-plates and the bisecting arcade is a lattice of giant roof timbers. The fabric of the church belongs to the 12th century (north side), 13th century (arcade and south side), and 16th century (roof, screens and porch). The fittings are modest and include a Norman font and a later shrine (set against the eastern respond of the east arch) to St. Cosmas and St. Damien.[17] The church's modest exterior, with its timber bell-turret and sturdy south porch, gives little hint of its fascinating interior.

Perhaps the most interesting characteristic of the two screens is their wall standards, which extend up to meet a giant tie-beam that crosses over the arcade in the middle of the church. This construction technique echoes that seen at Pixley; and more faintly at Aberedw, Disserth and Bettws Clyro in Wales. The two screens at Stretford are essentially alike (except for details such as the door-head treatment). Both consist of three bays to either side of a central doorway. The principal framing members are formed from huge timbers. The sill is square-cut, the middle rail and head-beam are chamfered, and the standards carry simple quarter-round mouldings. The west face of each door standard has a boutell shaft that terminates just below the head-beam in a crocketed pinnacle. The mullions are also simply moulded, with half-rounds to the west and hollow-chamfers to the east. The tracery heads to each bay (and the blind decoration of the door-head) feature a pared down design entirely in keeping with the character of each screen as a whole. The design of the tracery

Stretford: Hefty rood-screen, whose near identical twin divides the aisle from the chancel chapel

heads relates to those found at Llanwrin in Montgomeryshire. The head-beam at Stretford carries a half-round terminating at either end in a crude leaf form. The wainscot is entirely plain.

It is difficult to overstate the massiveness of the construction of this pair of screens. The mullions that divide each bay above middle rail height are thicker than the standards found on most other screens. The two screens are not merely partitions here, but almost seem to be components fundamental to the structural integrity of the church. No late medieval screens in the southern Marches (given that they also stand in an otherwise undivided church) were less likely to be removed in the centuries following the Reformation than these two.

SUTTON, ST. NICHOLAS

The church stands in the heart of the village and consists of a nave, chancel, south transept, north porch and west tower. Apart from the tower (which was raised in the 16th century) most of the fabric belongs to the 13th and 14th centuries. Inside, there are two especially fine piscinas (one in the chancel and one in the nave) decorated with ballflower and dating from the early 14th century.

The modest screen that divides the chancel from the nave has been so thoroughly meddled with during its lifetime – damaged and renewed, taken down and put back up, varnished and re-varnished – that differentiating new work from old, let alone discerning accurately what its original appearance might have been, is made almost impossible.

As it stands the screen consists of three wide bays to either side of a central doorway, of perhaps one-and-a-half bays. The screen is not contained within the chancel arch, but stands before it. Extending from the squared sill up to the head-beam are two wall standards, two door standards and two intermediate standards (these latter dividing off the outer bays). A chamfered middle rail runs between the standards, and two mullions extend from the middle rail up to the head-beam. The standards and mullions are ogee-moulded in the familiar fashion.

Unusually, the most interesting parts of the screen exist below the middle rail, for the wainscot is made up of linenfold panelling of three different designs, divided by unusual muntins (having small ogee mouldings to either side of a wide flat). Of the three designs, that found on two panels on the north side and one on the south side, featuring a decorative seam that fringes the linenfold,

Sutton: Much-abused rood-screen with distinctive linenfold wainscot panels

is both particularly effective and highly unusual. The two other designs are less effective, and the stylised and angular type found in the outer panels may represent later replacement work.

Above, the head-beam has flat faces between rounds to the west and is mostly old. However, the three short lengths of carving above the door-head – two lengths of cresting and one of a narrow vine trail – appear recent. The tracery heads to each bay consist of a flattened ogee arch, cusped and foliated below, and with six cusped lights (with flowers held by the cusps) above. The design is reminiscent of that found in a number of Radnorshire churches (e.g. Aberedw and Llandegley). The door-head tracery (a flattened, many-cusped arch with encircled quatrefoils and flowers, again held by cusps) has suffered terribly, with the flower cusps that once formed a decorative fringe crudely hacked off. Elsewhere, even the treacly coat of brown varnish cannot disguise where timbers have been sawn through and new woodwork added (e.g. to the tracery heads, the backs of the mullions and the head-beam etc.)

The beam that now spans the nave at the apex of the chancel arch may be a rood-beam. There is no fabric attesting to the presence of a rood-loft (and new timber upon the head-beam of the screen makes it impossible to check for mortise holes). It is tempting to believe that the groove cut into the chancel arch may once have contained the boarding of a tympanum. However, given the date of the arch (early 13th-century), unless the groove was cut later this seems unlikely.

TEDSTONE DELAMERE, ST. JAMES

The church stands at the end of a long path that curves through a hillside field below the garden of a big house. It is a small structure with a nave, chancel, south porch and west bell-turret. The fabric dates from the 12th century but has been much restored. In 1856–7 the chancel was rebuilt by Sir George Gilbert Scott.

Inside, the nave is divided from the chancel by a small *c*.1500 rood-screen of two bays to either side of a central doorway, that occupies the space of three bays. The wall standards have been boxed in, but the door standards are moulded upon both their eastern and western faces with ogees and small half-rounds (the door standard to the north incorporates some replacement work). The mouldings are returned over the heads of each bay. The

Tedstone Delamere: Attractive and partially-renewed little rood-screen at the entrance to the chancel

Tedstone Delamere: Rood-screen tracery head

mullions carry ogee mouldings that match those of the standards. The tracery heads are original, carved upon both sides, and are of a lively and unusual design. Above a cinquefoiled arch with flower cusps, there are compartments formed by rising and intersecting curves. These are filled with little Perpendicular lights that hold flowers or, in the kite forms above, quatrefoil forms. The spandrels have serrated leaves. The door-head has been repaired and some new work inserted. This too is an ingenious design, composed of narrow triangles with encircled quatrefoils (the upper ones have cusps that terminate in flowers) and dagger forms. The head-beam has a cavetto-moulded face above a half-round to the west and new work along its top. Below the plain middle rail is an equally plain wainscot.

VOWCHURCH, ST. BARTHOLOMEW

Vowchurch stands in the midst of the Golden Valley. It has a nave and chancel in one, a south porch, and an attractive timber-framed bell-turret overhead. Most of the structure dates from the mid-14th century, but the bell-turret belongs to *c.*1522 and the church was refitted in the early 17th century. Inside, more woodwork catches the eye: the nave roof has queen-posts and collar-beams over tie-beams; the chancel roof has cusped struts.

Unusually, the church's rood-screen is dated. In the chancel is a diamond-shaped board with '1613' and the Latin phrase *Vive ut postea vivas*. On the opposite wall is a similar board on which has been carved:

> Heare below ly the body of
> Thomas Hill
> ande Marget his wife whose children
> made this skryne

Vowchurch: Adam

255

Vowchurch: Eve

The screen has four bays to either side of a central doorway, and is framed up between giant, chamfered wall standards that extend up to the tie-beam overhead (in a late echo of the early screen framing technique found elsewhere). The sill, middle rail and head-beam, together with the constructional muntins of the wainscot, are all chamfered. Above middle rail height, the bays are separated by turned mullions. The screen is embellished with several crudely-executed, but engaging carvings. The most prominent of these are the figures to either side of the doorway. Locally, these have always been referred to as 'Adam and Eve', (though pears, and not apples, have been carved above their heads). There are also two dragons (with what appear to be horses' manes), Tudor roses (over the door-head and on the east side of the door standards) and, now almost too faint to make out, some further shallow carvings over the door-head. The screen is topped by a triangular pediment.

WELSH NEWTON, ST. MARY

The church stands in the south of the county just three miles north of Monmouth. It consists of a nave and chancel in one, and has a south porch and a little west tower topped by a little stone spire. The structure dates from the end of the 13th century.

The stone rood-screen that forms the only division between nave and chancel is one of the most surprising church fittings in the southern Marches. It is as if a group of pointed arches from a nave arcade had turned abruptly, and chosen instead to wander straight across the church from north to south. This screen is also the earliest in the southern Marches (indeed, it is one of the earliest in England or Wales). It is coeval with the fabric of the church and is thus of *c*.1300. It consists of three pointed arches on octagonal piers; the two outer bays wider than the central bay. The arches are elaborately moulded and, to the west, are framed above by hood moulds. These have

Welsh Newton: Rood-window

Welsh Newton: The rare and early rood-screen, which has the appearance of a nave arcade

been ornamented, albeit in a restrained fashion, with ballflowers (one of the most characteristic motifs of the Decorated era). When employed more numerously – as they are in the aisle windows at Leominster Priory and the north chapel at Ledbury – the result can be very rich. The spandrels between are filled with coursed and dressed (though irregular) stonework. To the west, the screen has a top cornice with ballflower, which matches the hood mouldings below. The apex of each arch has a small bridging piece linking the arches to the cornice.

The south rood-window is both especially fine and unusually large. It would have flooded the lost rood-figures with light, (as it does the plain cross now standing upon the screen). It is a dormer of two lights with a quatrefoil beneath a hood mould.

WEOBLEY, ST. PETER AND ST. PAUL

Weobley is one of Herefordshire's most attractive black and white villages. It has a large church that lingers in the memory chiefly for its very tall north-west tower and spire, which were raised in the 14th century. The rest of the church consists of a nave with side aisles and clerestory, a chancel and a south porch. The fabric dates from the 12th century (though most of the current structure belongs to the 13th and 14th centuries).

The current chancel and parclose screens within were erected in 1911. However, in the north aisle are two fragments – a post and a door – from what was evidently a sturdy late medieval screen. The post, which may have been a standard, is a huge and unusual piece, with a crocketed and ogee-arched niche below and a shield above (painted with the symbol of the Trinity). The door is also a hefty piece. The lower panel is plain and the mouldings here are simply chamfered. The upper panel (originally divided by a mullion) is moulded with hollows and quarter-rounds and retains its head tracery. This consists of two trefoil heads with a flattened trefoil form above and between. Both fragments show faded paintwork, but this is likely to be later work and probably does not belong to the screen's original colour scheme.

High up on the north side of the chancel arch is the door that once opened onto the rood-loft. Below is the door that gave access to the rood-stairs. Halfway up is a small window designed to throw light onto the stairwell.

WITHINGTON, ST. PETER

Externally, Withington church offers very little to excite the onlooker, except perhaps for its attenuated spire, which perches on a diagonally buttressed tower of the late 13th century. The building consists of a nave, chancel and south porch, and has been much restored (especially the chancel).

At first, the interior also appears to offer very little. However, the rood-screen here turns out to be one of the most interesting in Herefordshire. It consists of four bays to either side of a wide central doorway, and is framed up on a chamfered sill that stands on a chamfered dwarf wall of ashlar blocks. Perhaps the most striking feature of the screen is the highly distinctive treatment of its standards. These are identically moulded to the west and east, and feature tall, thin, blind Perpendicular tracery lights. The door standards each have two lights: one above and one below; the wall standards three lights: two above and one below. Moulded uprights of this design can be found at only three other locations in Herefordshire: at Eaton Bishop (in the muntins), at Hereford

Withington: Detail of tracery heads with an arch brace that once supported the bressumer in front

Cathedral (in the portable pulpit made up of old screenwork that now stands in the south chancel aisle) and at Yatton (carved on one side only). The standards are moulded with a half-round, which is returned across the heads via a series of unusual, squared junctions. The mullions are also unusually moulded (upon both sides) with hollows and a squared face with a half-round.

The tracery heads are carved upon both sides and feature a design that consists of an ogee arch, cusped below and with the spandrels above containing flowers held by cusps (or, looked at differently, irregular trefoil forms). The door-head has spandrels similar in design to those found at Yatton and Aylton. The head-beam is currently obscured by two other beams (placed one upon another, *cf.* Elton) set up slightly to the west of the head-

beam. The upper beam has a curved face between half rounds; the lower beam a slightly curved face carrying mouldings below. A continuous slot runs along the underside of this beam for a lost drop-cresting that once extended around the spandrels. New woodwork added to the backs of these beams makes it difficult to identify their original roles. However, it seems likely that the lower beam was a bressumer (supported on posts with carved spandrels) and that the upper one, which has a new top-cresting, may have been the top-beam of the rood-loft. The disposition of the current screen is almost certainly the result of work carried out at the same time as the renewal of the chancel. At this point the loft may have been dismantled, the screen rebuilt above middle rail height upon a new sill and dwarf wall, and the beams that originally belonged to the loft front integrated to form a cornice.

YATTON, ALL SAINTS

All Saints stands alone on the brow of a hill. Architecturally, it offers very little, either inside or out. It was built in 1841, extended in 1901–3, and consists of a nave with transepts, a west bellcote and chancel. The church has no porch, but is entered instead through a door at the west end. The interior is whitewashed and austere and the church makes a striking contrast to Yatton Old Chapel, half a mile to the west.

The screenwork within, although fragmentary, is of considerable interest. The church was entirely new in 1841, so the pieces did not originate here. However, they look too big to have been employed at Yatton Old Chapel (and besides, this screen originally carried a rood-loft). As it now stands, it consists of three bays formed by two wall and two door standards. Each standard

Yatton: Detail of junction of standards and head-beam, with curved braces or spandrels similar to those found at Aylton, Fawley and Withington

has, upon its west face only, two tall, thin, blind Perpendicular tracery lights. These are very similar to those found at Eaton Bishop, Hereford Cathedral and Withington (though are slightly different in cross-section). The middle rail and everything below this height is new work. At the junction of the standards and the head-beam are six big spandrels of two different designs, carved upon both faces. Those in the outer bays have circles sliced up into five wedges, each containing a rounded dagger-type form. The two door-head spandrels, with their four swirling dagger or mouchette forms are similar to those at Aylton. These spandrels, in their scale and design, are also similar to those found at Fawley and Withington. The head-beam was originally a bressumer. It has seven mortise holes for the joists of the loft floor and a curved face above a big half-round, possibly for a carved trail.

WORCESTERSHIRE

ALFRICK, ST. MARY MAGDALENE

The church stands in an elevated churchyard, and is given a slightly odd appearance by its north transept and vestry, both of which were added in the late-19th century. The earlier fabric comprises a nave, chancel, south porch and timber bell-turret. The windows are perhaps the most interesting feature of the church for they belong to a number of periods and styles, from the Norman through to the Perpendicular, and contain several panels of Netherlandish painted glass of the 16th and 17th centuries.

Alfrick: Wainscot showing distinctive carved spandrels

In the north aisle is a small and unusual Norman font, together with a stone carved figure in the west wall.

The rood-screen offers little of value above middle rail height (this portion being a somewhat mechanical Victorian addition). However, the wainscot is predominantly old work and is of considerable interest. Below the middle rail, the screen is divided into three wide bays by chamfered muntins with ogees. These mouldings are returned over each head of the wainscot. The upper corners of all three panels to the south, and two of the three to the north, contain carved spandrels. These employ a number of leaf and flower motifs: crinkly leaves (sometimes diamond-shaped or overlapping), water-flowers, double flowers and even little ball-flowers. They are very similar to those found at Bishop's Frome, Stoke Lacy and Dilwyn in Herefordshire. The middle rail, which has a rounded top and is ogee-moulded below, is also old work. In its upper face on the south side it has a slot and mortise holes; to the north, just the mortise holes. The boarding of the wainscot has been renewed and the screen stands on a chamfered sill.

Above middle rail height, the screen consists of six bays to either side of the central doorway. The standards and mullions are new, but may follow the precedent set by the original uprights. Each bay is topped by dense Perpendicular grid tracery over cinquefoiled heads. Above this is a crenellated head-beam.

LITTLE MALVERN, ST. GILES

This mutilated Benedictine Priory church occupies a beautiful setting on sloping land below the wooded Wynd's Point in the Malvern Hills. The loss of its nave, transepts and chapels has played havoc with its proportions (just as similar losses have with the proportions at Abbey Dore and Pershore) and the structure appears altogether too lofty for its greatly reduced footprint. A small monastic community (with never more than a dozen monks) was formed here as early as 1125, and was well established by 1171. As it stands, the church has only a chancel and nave

Little Malvern: Screen (looking west) dividing the monastic choir into a parochial chancel and nave

(formed by dividing the original monks' choir) together with a west tower (originally the crossing tower). The side chapels (squints through from which still survive) and the transepts were walled off in *c*.1600. By this date, the nave and cloister had also disappeared. As befitting so incomplete a building, the interior contains fragments of stained glass, medieval floor tiles and decorative stonework (again, just as at Abbey Dore). Even the choir stalls were mutilated (although the decoration on the arms was left intact, the misericords were hacked off).

The screen that now divides the original monastic choir into a parochial chancel and nave was evidently erected here sometime after the loss of the monastic nave. Although it contains old work, it seems likely that its original form was altered when it was re-erected in this position. The screen now consists of two double bays to either side of a central doorway, which takes the space of two bays. The standards, mullions and middle rail are all chamfered. The sill (now hidden) is new, and the head-beam is simply moulded and has mortise holes and a rebate along its top. The English construction technique, of intermediate standards extending from the sill up to the head-beam with lengths of middle rail dowelled between, has enabled the builder to give the screen the highly unusual feature of a 'stepped' middle rail. This may have been done to give those in the choir stalls slightly more privacy, or simply to marry up the design of the screen with that of the stalls beyond. The wainscot below is plain boarded and has no muntins. The ogee-arched tracery is cusped above and below to give trefoil heads and trefoil forms to each spandrel. The door-head has a rounded arch (cusped below to give a big trefoil head) and plain spandrels.

Little Malvern: Detail of tracery heads and plain head-beam; above is the rood-beam

In spite of the mortise holes and rebate, there is no evidence that the screen in this position ever carried a loft overhead. However, it may have done so at an earlier date, perhaps when (and if) it was employed at the east end of the monastic nave. Dating the screen is difficult, though it seems likely that it is earlier than the rood-beam above (which certainly belongs to the late 15th century). The guidebook suggests an origin sometime in the 14th century for the screen. Given the plainness of the framing members and the relative purity of the tracery heads, such a date is just possible.

The beam overhead is, for once, a genuine rood-beam (as opposed to a bressumer). At one time it formed an isolated feature roughly halfway between the screen and the roof above. In 1888 it was still possible to see marks where the beam had been inserted high up into the north and south walls of the nave (or choir as was). The beam carries two carved trails: the upper (and narrower) one is a water-plant; the lower one a vine. Still inserted into the underside of the beam is a very fine drop-cresting. The upper face has three rectangular mortise holes and a series of smaller, round mortise holes either side. The central mortise hole for the Rood itself is the largest and has been cut slightly to the west of the flanking holes for the figures of Mary and John. The round holes north and south of these were for candles or tapers. The vine trail of the rood-beam, together with some of the timbers belonging to the screen below, has evidently been renewed.

It is just possible that the blind traceried fronts to the stalls once belonged to a late medieval screen. They feature tracery of a later date than that of the adjacent screen, which consists of a cusped ogee arch beneath a pointed arch, the intervening space divided by uprights. Two of the compartments have cusps holding little flowers, and flowers also terminate four of the cusps of the ogee arch below. The tracery is framed up between ogee-moulded muntins, the mouldings being returned over each head.

SHELSLEY WALSH, ST. ANDREW

Shelsley Walsh is tucked away in the Teme valley, close to the Herefordshire border. It is a small church, consisting of a nave and chancel in one, with a north porch and bell-turret. Its fabric dates from the 12th century, but has seen intermittent restoration, the most drastic programme of which took place midway through the 19th century. Aside from the screenwork, the church features an attractive chancel ceiling (painted pale blue and decorated with black stars), a sandstone font of the early 12th century, and some medieval tiles in the chantry chapel.

The screenwork within comes as a happy surprise, for not only is it substantially original and unaltered, it is also unusually complete. It consists of a rood-screen, a 'rood-beam' overhead, and a parclose screen to the west. The rood-screen consists of four bays to either side of a central doorway, which takes the space of two bays. The southern portion of the rood-screen doubles as the eastern 'wall' of the parclose chapel.

Perhaps the most striking feature of the rood-screen is the way in which the intermediate standards and the middle rail marry up. The standards are pierced to encase the middle rail, lengths of

Shelsley Walsh: Screenwork, including rood-screen, bressumer and parclose screens

which are butted together within each standard (thus hiding the joint and making the middle rail appear to run unbroken between the door and wall standards). This method of screen framing is exceptional. In other respects the standards (and mullions) are of a familiar design. They have ogee mouldings to the west, and the standards have boutell shafts upon little bases (but without caps: the shafts simply run straight into the head-beam). These uprights are chamfered to the east.

The middle rail itself is chamfered above and below, and (just as at Ludlow) has a deep hollow moulding cut in its western face. The top face of the middle rail contains little holes that probably once held thin metal bars. To the north, the wainscot has bold linenfold panels framed up between muntins that are bigger than the mullions above. The tracery heads that top each bay above middle rail height are uniform and of a simple yet effective design: a rounded arch above and a flattened ogee arch below enclose two cusped compartments that each contain an encircled Catherine wheel form. The spandrels are also cusped. The door-head tracery corresponds with that of the bays, and has a lovely curved fringe of 15 little flower cusps. The head-beam carries a vine trail and a rather big top-cresting (possibly added in the 19th century) which has been fixed against flimsy planking. This defeats the object of a cresting (namely that it should form a decorative silhouette) but was presumably done in order to support or protect the cresting.

The lovely beam above has two finely carved vine trails between half-rounds upon its western face, and a slot below that once housed a drop-cresting. Although it appears to be a rood-beam, it has five large mortise holes in its eastern face and a series of smaller mortise holes and a rebate in its upper face, all of which

Shelsley Walsh: Detail of tracery heads,
including the pretty door-head fringe

confirms that it was in fact the bressumer belonging to the rood-loft. Above the bressumer is a massive, simply chamfered tie-beam. This has two big mortise holes, into which may have been inserted the uprights of a tympanum. This spans the church next to another huge beam, also chamfered. Given that it is certain that a rood-loft once surmounted the rood-screen here, we are left with a problem: if the parclose screen is coeval with the rood-screen, no loft could have surmounted the rood-screen without overlying the parclose chapel in an awkward and unsatisfactory fashion. However, there is – or rather *was* – a precedent for such an arrangement. Although fragmentary when it was photographed in 1886 (and almost completely lost by 1926) the remnants of the loft coving and the adjacent parclose chapel (occupying the same position as that found at Shelsley Walsh) can clearly be seen at Downton on the Rock in Herefordshire.

One other faint possibility is that the parclose screen once occupied another part of the church (though precisely which part is not clear). Evidence to support this includes the crude way in which the southernmost bay of the western parclose screen has been cut short above middle rail height. Also, in the two southernmost bays of this screen, there are pairs of elevation squints. Why have they been cut through here? Surely not so that people kneeling behind this screen could see the elevation of the Host in the parclose chapel: if these squints looked onto the high altar it would make more sense. The wainscot on the south side of the rood-screen has also been meddled with.

In both construction and design terms the parclose screen corresponds closely with the rood-screen. Running west it has four bays, a door and a further bay, before turning and meeting the south wall after describing a further four bays. The bays are narrower than those of the chancel screen and the design of the tracery heads has been adjusted to fit. The parclose screen stands (just as the rood-screen does) upon a renewed and chamfered sill. Both the parclose and rood-screen feature the same big ogee-moulded muntins and linenfold below middle rail height. The middle rail itself has the same little holes in its upper face for bars, and the head-beam continues the vine trail of the chancel screen. There are boutell shafts to either side of the door and at the east and west ends of the screen.

Downton on the Rock: How Shelsley Walsh might have looked

GLOUCESTERSHIRE

AWRE, ST. ANDREW

The isolated village of Awre lies at the end of a narrow lane that winds through reed-beds, past signs that warn of tidal flooding. Given the small size and disparate nature of the settlement the church is surprisingly large. It consists of a nave with north aisle, a chancel, south porch and west tower. The body of the church dates from the mid-13th century, the tower and south porch from the 14th century. Inside is an interesting font decorated with trefoils and quatrefoils (probably of *c*.1400) and a massive dug-out chest of the late 13th or early 14th century, known locally as

'the Mortuary' because bodies recovered from the Severn were placed in it prior to burial.

The rood-screen has been much renewed, particularly below middle rail height. It consists of four bays to either side of a central doorway, which occupies the space of three bays. The lower half of the screen is mostly new. A plain-boarded wainscot (with no muntins) is framed up between the sill and middle rail, both of which are chamfered. The upper face of the middle rail on the north side shows two blocked, round mortise holes per bay, perhaps for later wooden (or metal) bars. The standards and mullions are simply moulded with flat faces and ogees to either side.

Awre: Detail of door-head, the larger cusps of the arch with leaf carvings like those found throughout Herefordshire

Awre: Detail of tracery heads and head-beam above (with vine trail, rather than pomegranate)

The uniform tracery heads are finely carved upon both faces and are original. The design consists of a trefoil beneath a pointed arch, enriched with cusps and sub-cusps. The door-head has a two-centred arch, again cusped and sub-cusped below, with crinkly leaves in the cusps. The spandrels each contain a big quatrefoil and dagger form. The head-beam has a carved trail above a half-round upon its western face, but this is not continuous. To either side of the central doorway there are lengths of a fairly good vine trail. Over the door, there is a less well carved length of what may be a pomegranate. To the east, the head-beam has a curved face above a half-round.

Awre: Rood-screen

In the north wall, adjacent to the screen, is the chamfered doorway to the rood-stairs, and above is the matching doorway that once gave access onto the rood-loft. From within the chancel the form of the stairwell (together with a tiny window) can be seen. The stairwell was excavated in 1970 and the doorways unblocked. The former was found to contain a chimney flue (of the 18th century) and had been filled with rubble.

ENGLISH BICKNOR, ST. MARY

The village is situated on high ground on the fringes of the Forest of Dean. Its church is unremarkable from the outside (having been largely rebuilt in the 19th century) so the retention within of so much fine late Norman work comes as a great surprise. The work includes the five bays of the nave arcade (complete with their carved capitals). Of these, the eastern arch of the north arcade, with its chevrons and beakheads, is especially significant, for it once formed the outer doorway of the Norman church. The church now consists of a clerestoried nave with side aisles, a chancel, south porch and west tower.

Inside, the church possesses not only a rood-screen, but also a set of parclose screens to the south. The rood-screen is mostly new and consists of three bays to either side of a central doorway, which takes the space of three further bays. The lower half of the screen is now boxed in with later boarding. The standards and mullions all have simple hollow chamfers along their edges. The tracery heads, with Perpendicular style loop lights and Tudor roses terminating the cusps, are also new. The head-beam has a curved face between rounds to both east and west, and is crenellated above.

The parclose screen to the south is a far more interesting piece than the rood-screen, and retains much old and valuable work. It has three bays to the north of a doorway (which takes the space of two bays) and four bays to the south. The treatment of the screen below middle rail height is identical to that of the rood-screen, only here it is possible to see that the middle rail has been removed and the mullions re-dowelled into the boarded-in wainscot below. The standards and mullions have corresponding

English Bicknor: Parclose screen tracery head: an ungainly design, but engaging and certainly unique

ogee mouldings and flat faces. These mouldings are returned over the heads of each bay. The tracery heads are rustic and engaging; the design evidently one of this carpenter's own invention. It appears nowhere else and consists of a many-cusped arch with a trefoil at its apex, and spandrels each containing a simple Perpendicular light and two other shapes. The door-head tracery also features an unusual detail: the outer parts of each spandrel have a Perpendicular light over a pair of half-circles. The head-beam is very similar to that of the rood-screen and also has a crenellated top.

The parclose screen dividing the chancel from the aisle has four wide bays and a door at its eastern end. Like the other two screens its lower half is boxed in with plain boarding. The tracery heads here are of a more familiar type, and consist of a flat, cusped arch, with cusped spandrels and little flowers terminating several of the cusps.

Mitcheldean, St. Michael

Mitcheldean grew wealthy on the backs of the local cloth and iron industries; a factor that partly accounts for the size and splendour of its church. The structure belongs mainly to the 14th and 15th centuries and consists of a clerestoried nave with one south and two north aisles, a chancel, south porch, north vestry and a south-west tower with spire. The interior is very wide, and contains some striking (though hardly lovely) fittings of the late 19th and the early 20th century. The current chancel screen was erected in 1892–3 and is a thorny, self-confident piece. The reredos beyond is an extraordinary creation, with life-size figures carved in white marble.

With its great width and want of a chancel arch, St. Michaels bears comparison with the churches of the South-west. Its original rood-screen, which spanned the entire width of the church and ran between the first and second bays of the nave arcade, also clearly echoed those of the South-west. The rood-stairs, which continue down into an ossuary below, can be seen projecting south of the south aisle. None of the original screenwork now survives. However, the late medieval boarded tympanum overhead does. This would be a rare enough survival in any state, but here it retains its original Doom painting and is thus especially noteworthy.

The work depicts (amongst other things) the Betrayal, Passion and Ascension of Christ on the lower panels, the Last Judgement with the Heavenly City to the north, and the jaws of

Hell to the south on the panels above. All of this has been painted (predominantly in greens and reds) on oak boards, and the whole is now supported upon a decorative archway with a crenellated top. This was added at the same time as the new screen below.

There is no painting of Christ upon the Cross: the carved and painted Rood, once fixed to the top of the rood-loft, would have fulfilled this role.

MONMOUTHSHIRE

BETTWS NEWYDD

Bettws Newydd contains the most complete set of rood fittings to survive in any church in Wales or England. This exceptional arrangement consists of a rood-screen, rood-loft, tympanum, stairs and doorway. There is no outward sign of these riches save for a tiny rood-window in the south wall; all else is unremarkable. The church is a small, mainly Perpendicular structure of single chamber form, with a bell gable and porch at its west end, and a vestry and organ chamber of the late 19th century to the north.

The screen of Bettws Newydd has five bays to either side of a central doorway, which takes the space of three bays. Following the familiar Welsh pattern the mullions and muntins are dowelled into a sturdy middle rail, which runs through between the stout door standards and the walls of the nave (there being no wall standards). The wainscot has been renewed: it once consisted of four rough-hewn panels to either side of the central doorway. The middle rail to the south is a replacement, but that to the north is original and matches up with the mullions above. The mullions are moulded with ogees and hollows to either side of a flat face. The tracery heads to each bay have been roughly worked from thick timber and show carving upon both faces. The repeated design is of three straight-shafted lights over a trefoil cusped arch. Eight of these tracery heads are original (those occupying the two bays adjacent to the door standard on the south side are replacements).

Bettws Newydd: Detail of loft front

Bettws Newydd: Detail of bressumer
showing the oak trail (above) and vine trail (below)

Bettws Newydd: Rood-screen, loft and tympanum

The door-head's Tudor arch and tracery have been cut from even thicker timber than that of the tracery heads to either side, and may be a later addition (perhaps inserted after the removal of the screen doors). The eastern face of each door standard features a boutell topped by a pinnacle.

The rood-loft overhead remains substantially unaltered. However, the plastering of its soffit is not original; the partially hidden head-beam shows the stops for the ribs that once ornamented its underside. These ribs did not correspond with the bays below, and originally formed eight compartments. The head-beam, whose underside is slightly convex and whose western side has a cavetto moulding followed by rounds and hollows, never held a carved trail. This is in contrast to the similarly moulded bressumer (now supported upon later posts) which has two. The upper one is an unusual oak trail (in that its leaves are more akin to a vine trail); the lower one is similar, but in place of the acorns are grapes. Like the carved trails at Mamhilad these are thinly rendered, and suffer from a lack of the modelling and cutting through which gives to the best work of this type its happy play of surface and shadow.

Above the bressumer rises the parapet of the rood-loft. This has 14 openwork panels divided by flat muntins. Nail holes on the muntins indicate the loss of enrichments which may have taken the form of pinnacled buttresses. A crocketed ogee arch has been superimposed before each panel. The treatment of each foliage crocket varies from arch to arch. Each of the arches frames the lower half of the panel behind, and specifically an openwork quatrefoil shape flanked below by two cusped trefoils. Deep cresting may once have hidden the series of plain, flattened triangles remaining at the base of each panel. The top beam above has a carved trail, possibly representing the water-leaf. This too suffers from a lack of three-dimensionality.

Filling the void over the screen and loft is the original late medieval rood-tympanum. Its posts correspond with the lateral ribs of the barrel-vaulted ceiling above. To the west, the central post forms the upright of a cross. This is unlikely to be a structural coincidence, and the Cross itself (rather than the figure of Christ alone) may have been attached to it, or at least before it. To each side of this is a three-light window, which would have allowed those in the rood-loft to look down into the chancel below.

CWMCARVAN, ST. CATWG

The church occupies an elevated site, and consists of a nave (with north and south porches) and a chancel of Old Red Sandstone; the stark west tower is of grey ashlar. The fabric dates from the 13th or 14th century, but may have earlier origins. Inside, beneath the tower arch is a screen which has been cobbled together using Jacobean panels that may or may not have come originally from a pulpit. The doorway and the framing are modern, but the head-beam, together with the arcaded panels to either side of the doorway and the three smaller panels above, all belong to the 17th century.

GWERNESNEY, ST. MICHAEL

St. Michaels is another of Monmouthshire's little churches. It stands amid a handful of houses and farm buildings, and consists of a nave and chancel, bell gable and south porch, all constructed out of the local sandstone. The church belongs mainly to the

Gwernesney: The spiky carved trail (possibly denoting hawthorn) over damaged tracery heads

13th or 14th century and was partially restored in 1853–4 by J.P. Seddon, who also worked at nearby Llangwm Uchaf.

Unusually for a Welsh church St. Michaels is architecturally divided and thus possesses a chancel arch. The space below the arch is filled with a tiny screen. This stands upon a low stone step and comprises two bays to either side of a central doorway, which takes the space of four bays. The wall and door standards extend from the sill up to the head-beam, and the middle rail is dowelled between. Below the middle rail the wainscot has plain boards (without muntins) faced with later panels bearing faded gold paintwork (traces of this decoration can be found elsewhere on the screen). Above, there are mullions whose double ogee mouldings correspond with both the middle rail into which they are dowelled, and the narrow standards to either side. Each tracery head has a

steeply-pitched ogee arch with cusps terminating in flowers, and spandrels each containing an encircled quatrefoil holding a four-petal rose. The pairs of tracery heads have been carved from a single board which has then been slotted through each mullion. The tracery is carved upon its western face only and the door-head tracery has all but disappeared.

To either side of the chamfered chancel arch is a stone corbel supporting the head-beam of the screen. This beam extends from the wall at its northern end to just over the corbel at its southern end. Judging from the way the mouldings die out the beam has not been substantially shortened. The mouldings consist of hollows and rounds, and retain some fragmentary lengths of a carved enrichment similar to that found at Langattock Lingoed. This ingenious, spiky design

Gwernesney: Detail of screen

employs opposed and interlocking arcades of half circles which have been cusped, giving the appearance of entwined briars. The top of the head-beam has mortises and a groove for the tympanum, and slots to the west for the joists of the missing loft floor. As late as 1954 Crossley and Ridgway reported finding the sawn-off remains of a second, unmoulded beam embedded in the wall of the nave higher up.[1] These once belonged to the rood-beam.

At the west end of the church is a pair of screens that now serve to enclose the font. These appear to be coeval with the rood-screen, but almost certainly began life as parclose screens[2] enclosing a chantry chapel at the north side of the rood-screen (they may have been removed to their present location when the pulpit was built). The screen adjacent to the entrance has two bays of three lights each, divided by a standard that extends from the sill to the head-beam. The longer screen is identical but for the door between its two bays. The wainscot is plain, with the muntins planted on (and thus not constructional). The mullions have a square cross-section where they spring from the unmoulded, square-cut middle rail, but quickly (and uncomfortably) evolve ogee mouldings further up, which match those found on the standards. None of the tracery heads survive, but the slots into which they were housed can clearly be seen. The head-beam also has grooves for the tracery heads and two rounds for carved trails (now lost).

Gwernesney: Parclose screen now enclosing the font, missing its carved trail and tracery heads

*Kemeys Commander:
Rood-window*

KEMEYS COMMANDER, ALL SAINTS

Tiny All Saints stands protected from the indignities of the adjacent farmyard by a wall that neatly echoes the rectangular floor plan of the church. It consists of a nave and chancel in one, and has a timber-framed porch and bell gable at its west end. It is memorable for having no windows in its north wall (*cf.* Llangeview).

Kemeys Commander: Detail of the little and much renewed
rood-screen

The old screenwork within is much mutilated, but enough of it survives to securely bracket it with that of Bettws Newydd, Mamhilad and Trostre in the same county. The screen has four bays to either side of a central doorway, which takes the space of three bays. Unlike at Bettws Newydd the wall standards are present here. The screen is framed up in the familiar Welsh fashion with the middle rail running through. While the mullions above have been retained, the muntins and wainscot panels below have not. The double ogee mouldings that link the middle rail, mullions and door standards are returned over the head of each bay via corresponding mouldings carved into the head-beam. The door standards have been cut away on their eastern side, possibly

for a later door. They each feature a squared then rounded boutell topped with a pinnacle. Unlike at Bettws Newydd, however, these adorn the west face of each door standard, rather than the east. The current tracery heads are replacements and were inserted in the first half of the 20th century. The head-beam has a large cavetto moulding to the east which probably once housed a carved trail. To the west are eight mortise holes for the ribs of the floor of the rood-loft. The top of the head-beam shows the mortise holes and groove for the framework and planking of the tympanum (which may have resembled the one that survives at Bettws Newydd).

LLANFAIR KILGEDDIN, ST. MARY THE VIRGIN

The church has a slightly mournful, left-behind look to it and could easily have been demolished but for the welcome intervention of the Victorian Society. It stands well away from the loose-knit village it once served, amid gravestones that lurch and topple through tangled bracken. For once, a Victorian rebuild has resulted in the addition of a feature of real value. Inside, lining the nave and chancel, is a complete scheme of Arts and Crafts sgraffito[3] wall decoration, completed in 1890 by the artist Heywood Sumner. The treatment of the subject matter (the Benedicite) shows a directness that prefigures the graphic poster art of the early 20th century.

The rood-screen at the head of the nave has been heavily restored and is something of a curio. Indeed, it may well be an impostor, for it bares little relation to anything else in the county. It stands beneath the chamfered chancel arch and consists of five and a half bays to either side of a central doorway, which takes the space of three bays. The half bays at either end have replaced

Llanfair Kilgeddin: Detail of screen

the missing wall standards. The middle rail runs through and is identically moulded to east and west with pairs of ogees, between which run deep grooves. The plain wainscot panels below are divided by flat muntins which do not correspond in their setting out with the ogee-moulded mullions above. The screen's new woodwork was added during the restoration of 1873–6. It includes the two screen doors (the bays of which are narrower than those of the screen to either side, and of a simpler design), all of the tracery, some of the mullions, the half bays at each end of the screen, and parts of the head-beam (including the cresting). The head-beam retains the mortise holes for a now-lost tympanum.

Local tradition once held that the screen originally came from a church in Somerset, or perhaps Ireland. Neither is very likely (and besides, as Crossley and Ridgway point out, it is improbable that 'such scanty and unimpressive remains should have been salvaged from so far').[4] A Welsh origin, given for example the continuous middle rail and the square heads, seems more likely, but to this little else can be added with conviction.

LLANGATTOCK LINGOED, ST. CADOC

The church stands high up, overlooking fields that slope steeply away to the south. It consists of a nave, chancel, south porch and embattled west tower. Although in essence a Perpendicular structure, its interior is characterised by Jacobean and Victorian fittings. The exterior of the church was recently cream-washed.

Of the original screenwork, only the damaged, sandy-brown bressumer of the rood-loft now survives[5] (*cf.* Pipe and Lyde in Herefordshire). This huge beam (18 by 11 inches in cross-section) is moulded to take four carved trails divided by half-rounds.

*Llangattock Lingoed: Detail of the superb bressumer;
the uppermost trail like that at Gwernesney*

be inhabiting the beam in 1947. Much of the original fleur-de-lys drop-cresting survives below. The top of the beam has mortise holes for the muntins of the rood-loft parapet, which indicate by their number that the loft front once consisted of 13 panels.

When Crossley and Ridgway visited in 1947 a great deal of the original pigment was still clinging to the woodwork. This included red and gold in a barber's pole design along the half-rounds that separate the trails of enrichment; blue on one of the trails, and scattered remnants of gilding. The exceptional quality of what little carving survives upon just one of the principal beams, together with the traces of paintwork and gilding, point to a late medieval rood-screen and loft of rare and glittering artistry.

Outside, the housing of the rood stairs can be seen projecting from the north wall in line with the chancel arch. A tiny window lit the stairwell; a two-light window further west lit the screen. The church has a number of blocked doorways associated with the rood-loft, and an arched recess and piscina in the south wall that once served a rood altar. A defaced but evidently fine set of royal arms can be seen over the chancel arch. Below the chamfered arch at the west end is a tower screen made up of modest Jacobean panels (*cf.* Cwmcarvan) carrying two dates: 1593 and 1617.[6]

LLANGEVIEW, ST. DAVID

Little St. Davids stands quite alone, but is denied the peace this spot deserves by the dual carriageway that roars past close by. As if forewarned of this the builders gave the church no windows in its north wall (*cf.* Kemeys Commander). The structure itself is Perpendicular in date and consists of a nave, chancel, west porch and bellcote. Besides its fragmentary screenwork it retains its box

Of the trails only two remain substantially complete. Both are representations of the vine with two leaves per compartment; the upper differing from the lower in having three bunches of grapes rather than one to each (slightly smaller) compartment. These are ingenious and lovely designs executed with flair; their pronounced convex profiles adding great life to the carving. Fragments of a narrower trail survive above (again finely carved, but this time featuring a series of mouchettes). In 1947 Crossley and Ridgway reported finding a portion of the fourth trail still *in situ*: 'Only 1ft. of this remains; a series of conjoined quatrefoils within squares set on edge, the spandrels cusped to form trefoils. This enrichment has been gilded'. This fourth trail has since been lost, perhaps a victim of the death-watch beetle that was found to

Llangeview: The skeletal rood-loft shorn of its wealth of carved decoration

pews, pulpit and reading desk, all of which date from the 18th century. Unusually, the structure was not greatly altered by the Victorians.

Although fragmentary, the screenwork within is of considerable interest and must have formed an arresting fitting in so small a church. Indeed, at one time it may have been the equal of that surviving at Partrishow or Llanfilo. The mutilated rood-screen occupies the chancel arch, and has two bays to either side of a central doorway, which takes the space of three bays. Of the framing, the wall standard to the north has gone and that to the south has been sawn off just above the middle rail. The sill into which the standards were mortised has also disappeared. The mullions are lost and, as at Gwernesney, there were never any

muntins (the wainscot being of plain boards only). The bay and door-head tracery is lost, but was originally slotted into both the uprights and the head-beam. The standards, middle rail and head-beam all carry double ogee mouldings.

The rood-loft beams (and the head-beam of the screen) span the full width of the nave and are embedded securely into the north and south walls west of the chancel arch. The convex surface running along the western face of the head-beam once housed a carved trail. Punctuating this beam higher up are a series of moulded stops with mortises for the nine ribs of the loft soffit (which was not flat but slightly curved). Over the stops are mortise holes for the floor joists of the loft, which spanned the gap between the head-beam and the bressumer to the west.

The massive bressumer (which in its mouldings is similar to that of Llangattock Lingoed) affords further evidence of the original richness of these fittings. Its western face has a series of curved surfaces that once housed further trails of running ornament, together with a slot along its underside for drop-cresting. The eastern face has the double ogee moulding seen elsewhere. Above the bressumer is the rood-beam, and between run the chamfered muntins of the loft parapet (four of which are missing). These formed bays containing plain panels that were slotted into the beams above and below and the muntins to either side. Peg-holes in the muntins and the bressumer to the centre of each panel hint at further ornamentation; possibly including the crocketed pinnacles and carved figures seen elsewhere. The rood-beam also has a curved surface that once housed a carved trail. The chamfered tie-beam above the head-beam may have formed a part of the loft and supported the tympanum.

Llangwm: Detail of rood-loft, whose near total absence of plain surfaces recalls the screenwork of Devon

The original means of accessing the rood-loft remain a mystery. The undisturbed state of wall fabric that we know to be largely un-restored suggests that the loft was reached via an open timber staircase or a ladder. However, there is no material evidence to support such a theory.

LLANGWM UCHAF, ST. JEROME

The church seems a little too large for its narrow valley setting. It consists of a nave and chancel, with a south porch attached to the nave and a north tower set against the chancel. The structure was rebuilt in the 19th century. According to one contemporary source, 'it had gone so far to decay that Divine Service could no longer be held within its walls and it became a receptacle for rubbish'.[7] The spectacular rood-screen and loft inside form the most dramatic legacy of this rebuild. Nothing else seems to matter.

The screen and loft at Llangwm Uchaf owe their current appearance to the work of the architect J.P. Seddon (who also worked at nearby Gwernesney) and thus belong in date as much to the 19th century as they do to *c.*1500. Seddon took great pains to incorporate as much of the original woodwork as possible and to find precedents in similar screenwork for his own additions. However, in its composition and detailing there is much for which an early precedent cannot in truth be claimed. Seddon also published a description of the rood-screen and loft, and of the works he carried out thereto.

The screenwork of Llangwm impresses in two principal ways: firstly, screen and loft together form an edifice of unusual height for a Welsh church (a factor accentuated by the large jump in floor levels at the head of the nave) and secondly the fittings are

Llangwm: Rood-screen and loft

281

superabundantly encrusted with carved decoration. Indeed, the nine carved trails and six crestings comfortably rival Devon screen levels of richness. The rood-screen does not fill the chancel arch (as it once did) but instead stands before it. It consists of seven bays (of which the three outer bays are blind) to either side of a pair of doors, each taking the space of of two bays. In a clear sign that the screen has been heavily restored there are no longer any wall or door standards. The sill and middle rail are both replacements. The middle rail, which is divided diagonally to give two rows and two half rows of blind decoration (with each cusped compartment holding a little flower) is one of Seddon's flights of fancy, for no precedent for such a design exists in Wales.

Llangwm: The sill, wainscot and middle rail,
all with elaborate 'planted on' decoration by Seddon

The wainscot bays are each carved with linenfold and intricate blind tracery. Much of this is new work, but the linenfold on the doors may be original. Some of the blind tracery heads of the wainscot replicate the tracery heads above, others do not. Of the 12 fine grid tracery heads at least seven are original. All of the mullions are new, for the underside of the head-beam has blocked mortise holes for the tenons of the original mullions. (If their profile, with its ogees and rounds, is accurate, then this may give a clue to the original profile of the middle rail.) The square-cut head-beam features a narrow carved trail of stems and flowers (much renewed) issuing from the jaws of two tiny dragons, and is fringed above and below by blind-cresting. The eastern face of the screen is entirely plain.

The bressumer beam above and to the west actually consists of two beams, one upon the other (the division comes below the carved trail that runs under the top-cresting). This arrangement occurs only very rarely and may represent an expedient of Seddon's, intended to yield a greater surface area upon which to place both original trails and new work.[8] The carved trails of the bressumer have been variously renewed. They are (beginning with the lowermost): an oak trail with acorns, a narrower band of intricate but regular overlapping tracery, a wide and especially good vine trail, another narrow band of finely wrought tracery (this one featuring little quatrefoil forms) and finally a narrow water-plant trail. All are separated from one another by half-rounds. The fanciful top-cresting may also be Seddon's (for, once again, there exists no obvious precedent for its design). The bressumer is supported at each end upon wall-posts and wall-brackets with pierced spandrels. The drop-cresting beneath the bressumer is carried around the quarter-circles of each brace, ensuring that these become components integral to the loft front.

The loft coving is entirely new, and the result of misguided supposition on the part of Seddon. He had no knowledge of the original appearance or setting out of the horizontal ribs, or of the bosses that mark their intersections with the vertical ribs. Quite reasonably, the vertical ribs have been fitted to correspond with the mullions (and muntins) of the screen below. Also reasonably, the horizontal ribs are placed to divide each strip formed by the vertical ribs into squares.[9] The carved fringes (like cresting) around the edges of each panel are also of Seddon's doing. The soffit, although coved, is pitched at 45 degrees between the head-beam and the bressumer. Welsh coving tends to be shallower than this (although Beguildy, albeit possibly an English import, affords an example of coving of a similar pitch).

The mullions of the rood-loft parapet correspond with the muntins and mullions of the screen, and the ribs of the loft coving. They are (except for those at each end and that in the centre) moulded with rounds and angle flats, and some retain pieces of their original, delicate carved framing. The panelling of the loft front was once housed in the narrow groove running along the underside of the top beam. Seddon has ignored this and instead set the panels against the muntins of the loft front. The highly wrought openwork panels of the loft parapet are replacements and bear little relation to anything surviving in Wales (though they sit happily enough in this context). The crocketed arches of various designs attached before the panels are mainly original, and probably once formed canopies for niches that once contained figures. Nail-holes suggest that buttresses also once framed each panel.

The top beam is set marginally west of the bressumer, and gives to the rood-loft a barely perceptible forward tilt. The lowermost enrichment of the top beam is a vine trail, different to and less successful than that belonging to the bressumer. Above this is a band of intricate tracery, similar to the upper of the two on the bressumer, though a little wider. The uppermost enrichment is a very fine and fluidly rendered water-plant trail (*cf.* Llananno). Again, all the trails are separated by half-rounds, and are fringed above and below by top- and drop-cresting respectively. The loft floor is original and is supported on joists that link the back beam (which has a slot possibly designed to take a drop-cresting) to the bressumer. Behind the loft, the chancel arch is filled with boarding from the original tympanum. This has squints allowing the occupants of the loft to see into the chancel. Access to the rood-loft was originally via a stair tower on the north side of the chancel.

Colour can still be seen on various parts of the screen; most notably along the middle rail (greens, reds and blues) and on the coving of the rood-loft. This belongs to the 19th century, but was added with uncharacteristic sensitivity (for the era) following identification of traces of the late medieval paint scheme by Seddon (plates 13–16). In 1877, on the wall above the chancel arch, a painted figure of Christ could still be seen. This probably belonged to a medieval doom painting, and would have formed a fitting backdrop to the other medieval feature now conspicuous by its absence; namely the Rood itself.

Aside from the details noted above for which no historical precedent can be claimed, there are fundamental problems with the composition of the screenwork as a whole as devised by Seddon. It appears that a certain architectural rigour has informed the deployment of horizontal and vertical elements, as well as decoration, across both screen and loft. In the case of the typical rood-screen and loft of the late 15th century it is virtually unknown for all of the vertical elements – screen muntins, mullions, soffit ribs, and parapet muntins – to all line up: they do not at Partrishow, Llanwnnog, Llananno, Llanfilo, Beguildy, or at St. Margarets over the border. In reality the various 'faces' were often considered independently, and thereupon the proportions also. Seddon's desire to have continuous verticals has constrained parts of the composition. Whilst it has worked with the screen and loft parapet, it has failed with the loft soffit, where the square panels appear too small and tightly packed (one need only compare the coving here with that at St. Margarets).

As regards to decoration, Welsh rood-lofts of *c.*1500 were generally enriched at the expense of the rood-screen below. At Llangwm, Seddon has attempted, through the addition of various new elements (such as his sill and middle rail etc.) to give to the screen a richness it would not normally have possessed by this date (at least in Wales). Consequently, the loft, although dazzling, does not enjoy the unequivocal visual superiority over the screen below that is the hallmark of Welsh screenwork of this date. In feel the decoration lavished across both rood-screen and loft, although effective, is more akin to that found in the South-west.

LLANSANTFFRAED, ST. BRIDGET

This very small church stands on open ground close to Llansantffraed Court Hotel. It has a nave and chancel, and a stone vaulted porch and bell gable at its west end. The reredos built into the east wall within boasts two fine alabaster panels of the 15th century, which depict the Burial and the Entombment.

The screen now dividing chancel from nave was erected in 1931, but incorporates (rather painstakingly) various fragments of old woodwork, some originally from a late medieval screen, some assuredly not. Prior to the new screen's construction, an oak coffer made up from pieces of an old screen was dismantled so that the parts could be worked into the new screen. The re-used pieces of old work include five of the tracery heads (three of the narrow heads and two of the double heads), two sections of double-ogee moulded mullion and some of the cresting on the head-beam. The tracery heads are of scissor (or double-scissor) form, with their spandrels cusped to form trefoils. The corner tracery in the door-head is also original, though mutilated. The five squared (and damaged) pinnacles crowning the head-beam are certainly early (see photograph p.95), but never belonged to a screen or loft and look discordant here.[10] The rest belongs to the 1931 rebuild, which was carried out by a workshop in Winchester.

MAMHILAD, ST. ILLTYD

This cream-washed church (*cf.* Langattock Lingoed) stands amid yew trees on the crest of a hill opposite a pub. It belongs mainly to the Perpendicular era and has a nave stepping down into a slightly lower chancel, along with two porches (one to the south and one to the west). It also features the double bell gable characteristic of so many Monmouthshire churches.

Of the screenwork within the interest emphatically lies with the old rood-loft which now forms a west gallery at the back of the church. The chancel screen is modern and nothing like as compelling. The old screenwork is closely related to that of Bettws Newydd, Kemeys Commander and Trostre in the same county. However, in the latter cases the rood-screen forms the only division in a single chamber church, whereas at Mamhilad it stood before a chancel arch. The surviving components here include the bressumer together with almost all of the loft front and the top-beam. The bressumer is moulded with rounds between which are two flats for carved trails. The lower of these is missing but the upper one, a tightly-carved oak trail with few acorns, survives. The brattishing and the corbels supporting the beam are new.

The 15 muntins of the loft parapet are mortised into the bressumer to give 14 bays, each of which contains an openwork panel with a tracery head. Some of the muntins have buttresses (those adjoining the walls have blind loop enrichments divided by quatrefoils) and most have hollow edges, possibly for buttressed pinnacles. The more elaborate muntins divide the series of panels into two groups of four at either end of the parapet, and two groups of three in between. The notches in the muntins once held ogee canopies of a water-plant design, pieces of which have been fixed to the top-beam.

The tall and thick tracery heads are very similar to those at Bettws Newydd, but here they consist of four grid lights (rather than three) over a cinquefoiled ogee arch, with roses terminating each cusp.[11] Although its upper face is mutilated, the top beam retains a trail of water-plant. Like the oak leaf trail below, this is a tightly-packed design well befitting the solid, uncomplicated feel of the rood-loft. In common with the screenwork of Bettws Newydd, Kemeys Commander and Trostre sturdiness rather than

Mamhilad: Detail of loft front

finesse characterises both the construction and the decoration of the rood-loft at Mamhilad. The survival of this loft almost certainly has less to do with historical preservation than the appropriation of an existing fabric for purely utilitarian ends.

RAGLAN, ST. CADOC

In the minds of most Raglan church will always come a distant second to the castle. However, the church is not without interest and possesses one of the finest towers in Wales. This has four stages and diagonal buttresses, and is crowned by pinnacled battlements. Like the castle, it dates from the 15th century.[12] The rest of the church consists of a nave, chancel and south porch (all of which is essentially Perpendicular in date, but was restored in 1867–8).

Raglan: Screen fragment

Inside, in the south wall of the nave, the door and stairs that once gave access to the rood-loft have been opened out and reworked to give access to the pulpit instead. This approach is still lit by the original two-light window in the nave wall. The pulpit incorporates five tracery panels of three different designs. These have dense grid tracery, Perpendicular in design and possibly dating from the early 16th century. The panels could have formed the enrichments on either a loft parapet or a screen wainscot (of the two, the latter seems more likely).

REDWICK, ST. THOMAS

Redwick church stands on the Levels: the peculiar no man's land bordered by the M4 to the north and the mouth of the Severn to the south. As befitting such a location it is an unusual (if fine) church, striking for its central tower and its chancel east window, whose fantastical ogee tracery marks an unequivocal antithesis to the rectangularity of the Perpendicular style of later centuries.

The screenwork within is also of singular appearance. It consists of a rood-loft supported at considerable height upon two substantial, diagonally set standards. These have recessed and deeply carved panelled faces in two stages, and are surmounted by crocketed trefoils and pinnacles. In 1948, war damage necessitated repairs to the church and the old bressumer was taken down to be replaced by the current one, which is actually a reinforced steel girder clad in wood to resemble the original. The old bressumer was a massive beam (more than 20 feet long and a foot square in cross-section). It was finely and unusually moulded with hollows and rounds, and had two narrow channels for carved trails. It also retained some of its original, mainly red and blue pigmentation. The beam also had three sets of mortise holes: one along the back top edge for the joists of the loft floor, one below for the ribs of the cove or soffit, and one on the top of the beam for the muntins of the parapet. The beam rested on the trefoil cusped braces visible today (though these, together with the tops of the standards, were somewhat mutilated when the alterations were made).

The current loft front stood on the old bressumer prior to 1948, but is of no great age. It has cusped, pointed arches with trefoils above on turned mullions. This unusual treatment echoes work typical of the 13th century (*cf.* Stanton Harcourt, Oxfordshire). At the time of the repairs a modern chancel screen was also taken down. This featured a length of vine trail from the old screen. This fragment now occupies a window recess in the north wall of the nave. The rood-loft is accessed via a door in the south aisle, a mural staircase, and a second door high up on the south side of the chancel arch.

ROCKFIELD, ST. CENEDLON

The church is approached from the east and is attractively sited on rising ground bounded by trees. The tower is medieval, but all else belongs to the Victorian rebuild carried out by Prichard and

Seddon in 1859–60. The church consists of a chancel with a north vestry, and a nave with a north aisle and south porch.

Inside, the chancel is divided from the nave by a little Victorian screen of iron. However, in the vestry a number of finely carved pieces from a late medieval timber screen survive, variously incorporated into two cupboards. The cornice of that nearest to the door has been ornamented with lengths of vine trail, each compartment of which contains two leaves and grape bunches.

Rockfield: Finely carved screen fragments, including vine trail and tracery heads, incorporated into two cupboards in the vestry

The doors below re-use six panels of grid tracery of two different designs, possibly from a loft parapet. On the back wall is a second cupboard, incorporating a wider vine trail of a different design. This features spiralling tendrils and is altogether finer and more varied than the narrower trail on the first cupboard. Below are two further tracery panels. Some cresting from the old screen has also been retained. It is not known for sure whether these fragments belonged to a rood-screen that once stood in Rockfield old church, or whether they were brought in from elsewhere. Overall, the quality of the carving is of a high order.

St. Pierre, St. Peter

Few churches could be as unhappy in their current setting as St. Peters. It lies almost lost amid the paraphernalia of a sprawling golf club, hotel and hospitality complex. Close by stand rank upon rank of green golf buggies, wired up and waiting. To be fair the church never did enjoy glorious isolation, but has been accompanied by a manor house for centuries. St. Peters is of single chamber form and belongs mainly to the Perpendicular era (although parts of the structure belong to the 12th century or earlier: it has some herringbone masonry in its north wall). It was restored mid-way through the 19th century.

The little screen within was also restored in the 19th century, yet retains a significant amount of old woodwork. It is of six narrow bays (actually three double bays) to either side of a central doorway. The wall and door standards extend from the sill up to the head-beam and are substantially original. The head-beam, with its embattled top, is also original. However, the middle rail, the wainscot panelling and the mullions above are all replacements.

St. Pierre: The small rood-screen that divides chancel from nave

The Perpendicular tracery heads to each narrow bay are carved upon both sides. The door-head features a two-centred arch with blind-traceried spandrels (again carved on both sides). This door-head is 'supported' on attached shafts with caps.

SKENFRITH, ST. BRIDGET

Skenfrith church enjoys a memorable setting on a bank of the river Monnow next to the impressive remains of Skenfrith Castle. Like the castle, it belongs mainly to the 13th century. It has a nave with side aisles, a south porch and west tower, and a chancel and vestry. In the 14th century the aisles were widened and the chancel rebuilt. The distinctive tower, with its timber belfry and pyramidal roof, would have been higher, but problems with its foundations

restricted its growth. Inside, at the eastern end of the north aisle is an exceptional survival: a beautiful and complete *opus anglicanum* (literally 'English Work') cope of the early 15th century.[13]

The church has a rounded chancel arch supported upon moulded capitals that match those of the nave arcade, but retains only a tiny fragment of the screenwork that once stood beneath and within this arch (as is confirmed by the mortises cut into the face of the arch piers). On the south side of the chancel is a reading desk in which pieces of the old screen have been re-used. Framed above by a length of the original middle rail and below by a new base are four plain wainscot panels, each pierced with crudely cut elevation squints.[14] The uprights are original and are chamfered to match the underside of the middle rail. Projecting from each arcade wall to the west of the chancel arch is a stone corbel; the one to the north higher than that to the south. At one time these must have carried the rood and head-beams of the loft. The arch to the south aisle also incorporates part of the stairs that once gave access to the rood-loft.

TROSTRE, ST. DAVID

The tiny church of St. Davids stands high up and all alone, looking out over a great, shallow bowl of farmland. Like the nearby churches of Kemeys Commander and Bettws Newydd, St. Davids consists of a nave and chancel in one, and has a porch and double bell gable at its western end. Its fabric displays the familiar mix of the Perpendicular and the Victorian.

The screen that divides chancel from nave, although comprehensively restored, also has much in common with those at nearby Kemeys Commander and Bettws Newydd (see photograph

Trostre: the tiny rood-window set high up in the nave wall

on p.119). It consists of six bays to either side of a central doorway, which takes the space of three bays. The middle rail is dowelled in between the wall and door standards. Each door standard has a squared boutell attached to both its eastern and western face: at Bettws these appear only to the east, while at Kemeys they appear only to the west. The wainscot is plain panelled but for two tracery fragments. The panel-tracery to the head of each bay has been renewed but closely follows that found at Kemeys and Bettws. The head-beam is moulded with a series of hollows, half-rounds and quarter-rounds to both the east and the west. Its eastern side also has a slightly convex face framed above and below by rounds, which may once have held a carved trail. The top of the head-beam also has seven joist holes cut into it for the floor of the rood-loft. Slots in the wall-plates that support the roof also attest to the existence at one time of a rood-loft in the church.

USK, St. Mary

St. Marys originated as the church of a Benedictine priory in the second half of the 12th century. In the 13th century, however, a north aisle was added for the use of the townsfolk, and following the Dissolution in the 16th century the priory church became the parish church as the nave too was appropriated. The crossing tower was vaulted to form a sanctuary below in 1844, the chancel and transepts of the priory church having been swept away at the Dissolution.

The screenwork within presents a striking edifice, for whilst the portion at the head of the north aisle shows only dark wood and no colour at all, that occupying the nave is brightly painted in red, green and gold (see plate 12). Aside from the obvious colour alterations the screen as a whole has endured numerous material alterations, and there is compelling evidence to suggest that it may no longer occupy its original position. It currently stands one bay to the west of the east wall of the nave; a position it has occupied since at least the first half of the 19th century.[15] However, the doorway high up in the east wall of the side aisle and the one at floor level (now blocked up) suggest that the screen once stood against the east wall; as does the fact that the vaulting only springs to the west. However, if this is the case then how did one get from the aisle portion of the loft across onto the nave portion? (given that there is no obvious blocked doorway through the wall above the arcade). This factor at least leaves open the possibility that the screen does indeed stand in something like its original position.

The screen as a whole now stands raised up upon a stone base (or dwarf wall) which has been encased in wood. When this was

*Usk: Detail of the loft vaulting and tracery heads
of aisle portion of screen*

done the middle rail and wainscot were removed to allow an unimpeded view of the high altar beyond (the sill was also lost at this time). The points at which the middle rail once met with the standards betray the original form and height of the middle rail. Its top was ogee moulded and its east and west faces were plain. The wainscot boards were slotted into the standards and almost certainly the underside of the middle rail, and were ornamented with blind tracery. At one time, when the screen was lower than it is now, the bressumer extended unbroken from the south wall of the nave across to the north wall of the side aisle. However, now that the screen is higher the nave arcade interrupts the progress of the bressumer across the church. The loss of the original middle

rail and wainscot, and the addition of the new rail and tracery, has significantly and adversely altered the proportions of the screen. The original loft floor survives above the vaulting.

The nave portion of the screen has four wide bays to either side of a central doorway, which takes the space of two bays. It contains very little original woodwork (a fact well masked by its *c.*1900 paintwork, added by G.E. Halliday). The intermediate standards extend from the sill up to the head-beam (following the familiar English pattern) and were evidently interchanged when the screen was altered. Each has ogee mouldings to the north and south, and a little battlemented capital crowning a boutell which in turn surmounts the offset of a buttress upon its western face. The ribs of the vault spring from each of the capitals. A new rail has been dowelled between each of the standards and the new 'heads' formed by this rail have been given trefoiled and cusped arches with roses to match those above[16] (though the arches are slightly less flattened). The main head of each bay contains deep panel tracery, carved on its west face only and subdivided by internal, pointed arches. The door-head tracery has also been substantially renewed; as has the top- and drop-cresting that frames the bressumer above and below.

Although the aisle screen is apparently identical to the nave screen (but for the obvious lack of colour) it deviates from its neighbour in a number of significant ways. It does not have a central doorway (but rather three bays to the north of its doorway and four to the south) and is marginally shorter than the nave screen. Significantly, it retains far more of its original woodwork than the nave screen and far fewer later additions.[17] Where the tierceron vaulting to the south is almost completely new, the vaulting ribs

Usk: Parker's drawing

291

Usk: Door-head tracery of the much-renewed nave portion of the screen

Usk: Detail of the east side of the aisle portion of the screen, showing carved spandrels reminiscent of those at Bronllys

to the north are all original (though the canvas infilling between them is not). The vaulting of the entire screen springs only to the west, thus leaving spandrels to the east behind the vaulting. In the aisle screen these spandrels contain carvings, echoing the treatment employed at Old Radnor. The well-moulded bressumer is original across both portions of the screen, but has been less adulterated in the aisle screen. However, the head-beam, unlike that to the south, is new.

Usk, like Old Radnor to the north, affords the rare instance of an English screen in a Welsh church. However, where the screen at Old Radnor has a clear prototype in the form of the parclose screen at Cirencester, that found at Usk can make no such claim. Its origin is entirely unknown (although a Gloucestershire or Somerset workshop has been suggested as a possible source).[18]

Glossary

Ambone A large, marble pulpit found in continental churches.

Ambulatory A semicircular or polygonal aisle, often running behind the apse.

Apse The semicircular or rectangular east end of the chancel.

Arabesque Elaborate and fanciful ornament usually based on geometrical designs and using combinations of flowing lines, tendrils etc.

Arcade A series of arches supported by piers or columns (can apply to a screen).

Arch(ed) brace A curved timber strut found at the junction of a post and beam.

Architrave The lowest of the three main parts of the entablature (sometimes used to describe the suspended horizontal element in early basilican screens).

Aumbry A small cupboard or recess for sacred vessels, usually located close to the altar.

Baluster A short post or pillar in a series, usually supporting a rail (thus 'balustrade').

Basilica A single-chamber church of oblong plan form, with a longitudinal axis terminating in an apse, and no dividing wall between the nave and the sanctuary.

Bay The space between the columns in an arcade (can apply to a screen).

Bema Another name for the sanctuary in an early Christian church.

Billet Romanesque ornamental motif consisting of raised rectangles or cylinders with spaces in between.

Blind arcade An arcade of piers or columns attached to a wall.

Blind tracery Unpierced, applied tracery (e.g. that 'planted on' to a solid wainscot).

Bouttel An attached shaft, usually round in cross section, forming a moulding on the standard of a rood-screen.

Bouttel cap The decorative top to a bouttel shaft, from which the ribs of the loft vault spring.

Brattishing An ornamental cresting, often in the form of miniature battlements.

Bressumer The lowermost of the western beams of the rood-loft, often richly carved.

Buttress A masonry form projecting from, or built against, a wall to give it extra strength or to shift the weight-bearing burden away from the wall itself (e.g. to allow for more expansive windows).

Cancelli An early, low type of continental screen (from which the word 'chancel' derives).

Carved trail The undulating, naturalistic ornamentation of a beam.

Capital The element that caps a pier or column.

Cavetto Type of hollow moulding, a quarter circle in cross-section.

Celure An extra decorated area of roof forming a canopy of honour over the rood-figures.

Chamfer A flat bevel or slope made by paring away the edge of a right-angle.

Chancel The east end of the church (where the main altar is located).

Chancel arch The archway between the nave and the chancel.

Chantry chapel A chapel endowed for the saying of Masses for the soul(s) of the founder(s) after death.

Chevron Norman zigzag moulding found around arches and windows.

Choir screen (Or Quire) Screen dividing the choir and chancel from the nave.

Cinquefoil An ornament divided by cusps into five lobes.

Clas church A type of Celtic mother church (akin to an English Minster church).

Cornice Strictly, the top section of an entablature; however, sometimes refers to the heavily decorated bressumer of a rood-loft.

Coving The concave underside of e.g. a rood-loft.

Crocket	A stylised leaf-shaped ornament, often projecting from the angles of spires, pinnacles, canopies, gables etc.
Crossing	In a cruciform church, the space at the intersection of nave, chancel and transepts.
Curvilinear	Tracery consisting of curves and ogees.
Cusp/ sub-cusp	The projecting point between the foils in e.g. a Gothic arch.
Dagger	A tracery motif common to the Decorated era, of lancet shape, pointed at the foot, rounded or pointed at the head, and cusped within.
Decalogue	The Ten Commandments.
Decorated	Division of Gothic architecture, covering the period *c*.1300–*c*.1350.
Doom	Name given to depictions of the Last Judgement (often in combination with the Resurrection).
Door standard	The door post of a rood- or chancel screen.
Door-head	The top of the doorway of a rood- or chancel screen, often containing tracery.
Drop-cresting	A carved decorative fringe along the bottom edge of bressumer, head-beam etc.
Drop-finial	A hanging finial (i.e. of pendant form).
Early English	Division of Gothic architecture, covering the period *c*.1200–*c*.1300.
Entablature	The horizontal members above a column (architrave, frieze and cornice). Sometimes used to describe the suspended horizontal element in early screens.
Enterclose	A fenced-in recess for an altar, formed e.g. between the wainscots of a double screen.
Fillet	A moulding in the form of a narrow, flat, raised band.
Finial	A formal ornament (i.e. ball) topping a canopy, gable or pinnacle.
Fluting	Mouldings in the form of shallow, parallel concave grooves.
Foliated	Decorated with leaf ornament.
Four-centred arch	A type of late medieval flattened arch consisting of four arcs.
Fretwork	*See Openwork.*
Frieze	Strictly, the middle division of an entablature; however, can refer to a decorated band (e.g. along the head-beam of a screen).
Gable	The triangular upper portion of a wall at the end of a pitched roof (sometimes found as a non-functional form on post-reformation screens).
Gothic	Style of architecture characterised by pointed arches and rib vaults, sub-divided into the Early English, Decorated and Perpendicular.
Gothic light	*See Loop Light.*
Great Rood	The principal depiction of Christ Crucified, located over the entrance to the chancel.
Green man	A human mask with foliage issuing from the mouth.
Hagioscope	An opening cut through e.g. a screen wainscot or tympanum to allow a view of the main altar. Also known as a Squint.
Half-round	*See Round.*
Head-beam	The top beam of a rood- or chancel screen.
Hollow	A concave moulding.
Hollow chamfer	The concave paring away of a right angle.
Iconostasis	Formerly a screen in Byzantine churches dividing sanctuary from nave; in the Middle Ages, a parapet covered with icons surmounting a series of columns.
Jacobean	The era of James I (1603–1625) characterised by e.g. distinctive carved decoration.
Jubé	A continuous gallery forming a continental precedent for the monastic pulpitum.
Lenten veil	A ceremonial cloth covering the Great Rood from the first Sunday in Lent until Palm Sunday (also known as the 'Rood-veil').
Light	A vertical division of a window or of a bay in a rood- or chancel screen.
Linenfold	Panelling on which the vertical carving resembles parallel folds of linen (popular in the 16th century).
Loop light	A tracery form common to the Perpendicular era,

	consisting of a thin, vertical light, cusped at the top to give a motif akin to a burning candle.
Middle rail	The horizontal beam that tops the wainscot of a screen.
Mortise and tenon	A joint formed by a projecting piece (or tenon) fitting into a socket (or mortise).
Mouchette	A tracery element of curved dagger form belonging to the Decorated era.
Moulding	The contours given to the face of a beam or post (e.g. ogee).
Mullion	A vertical post dividing a screen or window into two or more lights.
Muntin	A vertical post dividing a wainscot (etc.) into separate panels.
Naos	The 'choir-nave' in an early Christian church.
Narthex	The outer nave in an early Christian church.
Nave	The western body of the church, for the parishioners.
Niche	A vertical recess in a wall or pier, often arched and intended for e.g. a statuette.
Norman	Relating to the period 1066–1200 and to a distinctive massive, Romanesque architectural style.
Offset	The part of a post exposed horizontally when the portion above is reduced in thickness (often sloping).
Ogee	A double-curved line comprising concave and convex elements (an 'S' or inverted 'S' shape).
Openwork	Carved work that is cut through, and thus transparent (e.g. fretwork).
Ovolo	Type of convex moulding, the same as a quarter-round.
Parapet	The gallery front or back of a rood-loft.
Parclose screen	A screen separating a chapel from the body of the church (the chapel is sometimes called 'a parclose').
Perpendicular	The third division of English Gothic architecture (*c*.1350–*c*.1550).
Perpendicular light	*See Loop Light.*
Pinnacle	A small pyramidal or conical shaped crowning element, often ornamented with crockets.
Piscina	A basin with a drain for washing vessels used in Masses (usually located in the wall adjacent to the main altar).

Presbytery	That part of a monastic church east of the choir.
Pulpitum	A stone screen in a major church designed to shut off the choir from the nave.
Putti	Small boy or cherub figures (singular: Putto).
Quarter-round	*See Round.*
Quatrefoil	An ornament divided by cusps into four lobes.
Rebate	A groove or channel, generally rectangular, cut along the face of a piece of wood to receive the tongue or edge of another piece.
Rectilinear	Tracery consisting of straight lines intersecting at right angles.
Reeding	Parallel convex mouldings cut along a beam or post.
Rendering	The plaster facing of an outer or inner wall.
Reredos	The ornamental screen found above the altar on the east wall of the chancel.
Respond	A half-pier carrying one end of an arch and bonded into a wall.
Rib	A projecting band on a ceiling or vault (can be structural or purely decorative).
Riddel Post	Type of post from which curtains can be hung.
Romanesque	The architectural style supplanted by the Gothic, characterised by round arches and massive forms.
Rood	The figure of Christ upon the Cross.
Rood-beam	A free spanning beam to support the rood-figures above the rood-screen; or the top beam (either western or eastern) of the rood-loft.
Rood-figure	Christ or the attendant figures of Mary or John.
Rood-group	Christ accompanied by Mary and John.
Rood-loft	The galleried platform that surmounts the rood-screen.
Rood-screen	The name given to a pre-Reformation chancel screen (deriving from its location beneath the Great Rood).
Rood-stairs	The access stairs to the rood-loft, often cut into the nave wall at the east end of the nave.
Rood-tympanum	The hoarding – of either planking or plaster over wattle and lath – used to block up the chancel archway above the height of the rood-screen and rood-loft.

Rood-veil	*See Lenten Veil.*
Round	A moulding which is semi-circular (more than 180° of a circle) in cross section; a half-round is exactly 180° of a circle in cross section, and a quarter-round is 90° of a circle in cross-section.
Royal Arms	The coat of arms of a king or queen (frequently taking the place of the Rood after the Reformation).
Sanctuary	The space occupied by the high altar.
Sentence	A short religious text painted upon the wall of a church.
Sill	The lowermost beam of a rood- or chancel screen (found at floor level).
Soffit	The ornamental underside of a rood-loft, arch, canopy, etc.
Sounding-board	A canopy or tester over a pulpit.
Spandrel	The triangular space between the side of an arch, the horizontal drawn from the level of its apex, and the vertical of its springing.
Squint	*See Hagioscope.*
Strapwork	Ornament consisting of interlacing bands with the appearance of cut leather.
String course	A projecting moulding running horizontally round the walls of a church or tower.
Tabernacle work	Ornamentation in the form of applied canopies and elements leading to the creation of small niches (i.e. on the parapet of a rood-loft).
Tester	A suspended canopy (i.e. over a pulpit etc.)
Top-beam	The uppermost beam – either eastern or western – of a rood-loft.
Top-cresting	A carved decorative fringe crowning the top edge of bressumer, head-beam, top-beam or rood-beam.

Tracery	The openwork decoration found in the lights of a screen or rood-loft; or in a window.
Transept	The transverse portion of a cruciform church.
Trefoil	An ornament divided by cusps into three lobes.
Tudor arch	A type of late medieval flattened, pointed arch (similar to a four-centred arch) whose shanks start with a curve near to a quarter circle.
Tudor Rose	A distinctive, stylised five-petalled rose form.
Vault	Arched roof or ceiling (applicable to rood-lofts as well as churches).
Barrel:	(Or Tunnel) The simplest type of vault, semi-circular in cross-section.
Fan:	Vault sub-divided by ribs that spread evenly from a common source.
Groin:	Vault created by the intersection at right angles of two barrel vaults.
Lierne:	Rib vault with (purely decorative) tertiary ribs that do not spring either from one of the main springers or the central boss.
Tierceron:	Rib vault with secondary ribs that spring either from one of the main springers or the central boss, and which meet with the rib-ridge.
Wainscot	The solid, panelled lower portion of a screen.
Wall standard	The wall-post of a rood- or chancel screen.
West gallery	A raised timber singing gallery at the west end of the nave.
Wyvern	A dragon with the legs and wings of a bird and with a serpent for a tail.

Bibliography

Abulafia, D. (ed.) *et al. The New Cambridge Medieval History, Vol. 5, c.1198–c.1300*, C.U.P., 1999.

Addison, W. *Local Styles of the English Parish Church*, Batsford, 1982.

Allmand, C. (ed.) *et al. The New Cambridge Medieval History, Vol. 7, c.1415–c.1500*, C.U.P., 1998.

Batsford, H. & Fry, C. *The Cathedrals of England*, Batsford, 1934.

Batsford, H. & Fry, C. *The Greater English Church in the Middle Ages*, Batsford, 1943-4.

Betjemen, J. (ed.) *Collins Guide to English Parish Churches*, Collins, 1958.

Binney, M. & Burman, P. *Change and Decay – The Future of Our Churches*, Studio Vista, 1977.

Black, J. *A New History of Wales*, Sutton, 2000.

Bond, F. *Screens and Galleries in English Churches*, Henry Frowde/ O.U.P., 1908.

Bond, F.B. & Camm, The Rev. Dom Bede. *Roodscreens and Roodlofts, Vol. I*, Sir Isaac Pitman, 1909.

Bond, F.B. & Camm, The Rev. Dom Bede. *Roodscreens and Roodlofts, Vol. II*, Sir Isaac Pitman, 1909.

Braun, H. *An Introduction to English Medieval Architecture*, Faber and Faber, 1951.

Brown, R.J. *The English Village Church*, Robert Hale, 1998.

Bury, T.T. *Remains of Ecclesiastical Woodwork*, John Weale, 1847.

Cambrensis, G. (transl. Lewis Thorpe). *The Journey Through Wales* and *The Description of Wales (1188)*, Penguin, 1978.

Camm, Dom Bede. *Some Devonshire Screens and the Saints Represented on their Panels*, Ampleforth Abbey, 1906.

Clapham, A.W. *English Romanesque Architecture before the Conquest*, O.U.P., 1930.

Clapham, A.W. *English Romanesque Architecture after the Conquest*, O.U.P., 1934.

Clifton-Taylor, A. *English Parish Churches as Works of Art*, O.U.P., 1989.

Clifton-Taylor, A. *The Cathedrals of England*, Thames and Hudson, 2000.

Cox, J.C. & Harvey, A. *English Church Furniture*, Methuen, 1907.

Cox, J.C. *English Church Furniture and Accessories*, Batsford, 1923.

Cox, J.C. *The Parish Churches of England*, Batsford, 1937.

Crossley, F.H. 'An Introduction to the study of Screens and Lofts in Wales and Monmouthshire with especial reference to their Design, Provenance and Influence', in *Archaeologia Cambrensis, VOL. XCVII*, 1943.

Crossley, F.H. & Ridgway, M.H. 'Screens, Lofts and Stalls situated in Wales and Monmouthshire, PART 5, SECTION VII: Montgomeryshire', in *Archaeologia Cambrensis, VOL. XCIX*, 1947.

Crossley, F.H. & Ridgway, M.H. 'Screens, Lofts and Stalls situated in Wales and Monmouthshire, PART 6, SECTION IX: Radnorshire', in *Archaeologia Cambrensis, VOL. C*, 1949.

Crossley, F.H. & Ridgway, M.H. 'Screens, Lofts and Stalls situated in Wales and Monmouthshire, PART 7, SECTION X: Brecknockshire', in *Archaeologia Cambrensis, VOL. CII*, 1953.

Crossley, F.H. & Ridgway, M.H. 'Screens, Lofts and Stalls situated in Wales and Monmouthshire, PART 10, SECTION XIII: Monmouthshire', in *Archaeologia Cambrensis, VOL. CVIII*, 1959.

Crossley, F.H. & Ridgway, M.H. 'Screens, Lofts and Stalls situated in Wales and Monmouthshire, PART 11, SECTION XIV: Border Influences', in *Archaeologia Cambrensis, VOL. CXI*, 1962.

Crossley, F.H. *The Church Screens of Cheshire*, R & R Clark, 1918.

Crossley, F.H. *English Church Craftsmanship*, Batsford, 1941.

Crossley, F.H. *The English Abbey – Its Life and Work in the Middle Ages*, Batsford, 1942-3.

Crossley, F.H. *English Church Design, 1040-1540 A.D.*, Batsford, 1945.

Davies, J. *A History of Wales*, Allen Lane, 1993.

Davies, J. *The Making of Wales*, CADW (Sutton), 1996.

Dirsztay, P. *Church Furnishings*, Routledge & Kegan Paul, 1978.

Dodd, A.H. *A Short History of Wales*, John Jones, 1998.

Duffy, E. *The Stripping of the Altars*, Yale, 1992.

Fenton, R. *Tours in Wales (1804–1813) Edited from His Journals in the Cardiff Free Library by John Fisher*, Bedford Press, 1917.

Friar, S. *A Companion to the English Parish Church*, Sutton, 1996.

Hall, J. *Hall's Illustrated Dictionary of Symbols in Eastern and Western Art*, John Murray, 1994.

Haslam, R. *The Buildings of Wales, Powys*, Penguin, 1979.

Heath, S. *Our Homeland Churches*, The Homeland Association, 1907.

Howard, F.E. *Screens and Rood-Lofts in the Parish Churches of Oxfordshire*, Hunt, Barnard, 1910.

Howard, F.E. *Mediaeval Styles of the English Parish Church*, Batsford, 1936.

Howard, F.E. & Crossley, F.H. *English Church Woodwork*, Batsford, 1927.

Hubbard, E. *The Buildings of Wales, Clwyd (Denbighshire and Flintshire)*, Penguin and University of Wales Press, 1994.

Huchard, V. *et al. The Musée National du Moyen Age – Thermes de Cluny*, Réunion des Musées Nationaux, (n.d.).

Hunt, T. *The English Civil War at First Hand*, Phoenix, 2002.

Hutton, G. & Smith E. *English Parish Churches*, Thames and Hudson, 1957.

Jones, L.E. *The Beauty of English Churches*, Constable, 1978.

Jones, M. (ed.) *et al. The New Cambridge Medieval History, Vol. 6*, c.*1300–*c.*1415*, C.U.P., 2000.

Laing, L. & J. *Art of the Celts*, Thames and Hudson, 2000.

Leonard, J. *Churches of Herefordshire and their Treasures*, Logaston Press, 2000.

Little, C.T. & Husband, T.B. *The Metropolitan Museum of Art – Europe in the Middle Ages*, M.O.M.A., 1987.

Lloyd, D. *The Parish Church of Saint Laurence*, Studio Press, 1980.

Lloyd, T *et al. The Buildings of Wales, Pembrokeshire*, Yale, 2004.

MacCulloch, D. *Reformation – Europe's House Divided 1490–1700*, Penguin, 2003.

Murray, P. & L. *The Oxford Companion to Christian Art and Architecture*, O.U.P., 1998.

Newman, J. *et al. The Buildings of Wales, Gwent/ Monmouthshire*, Penguin and The University of Wales Press, 2000.

Parker, J.H. *ABC of Gothic Architecture*, Parker, 1888.

Peate, I. *The Welsh House*, The Honourable Society of Cymmrodorion, 1940.

Pevsner, N. & Wedgwood, A. *The Buildings of England, Warwickshire*, Penguin, 1966.

Pevsner, N. *The Buildings of England, Shropshire*, Penguin, 1958.

Pevsner, N. *The Buildings of England, Herefordshire*, Penguin, 1963.

Pevsner, N. *The Buildings of England, Worcestershire*, Penguin, 1968.

Pevsner, N. *The Buildings of England, Northamptonshire*, 2nd edn., revised by Cherry, B., Yale, 1973.

Pugin, A.W. *A Treatise on Chancel Screens*, Charles Dolman, 1851.

Robinson, J.M. *Treasures of the English Churches*, Sinclair-Stevenson, 1995.

Royal Commission on Historical Monuments, England (RCHM). Herefordshire *Vol. I South-west*, 1931; Herefordshire *Vol. II East*, 1932; Herefordshire *Vol. III North-west*, 1934. H.M.S.O.

Scarisbrick, J.J. *The Reformation and the English People*, Blackwells, 1984.

Short, E.H. *A History of Religious Architecture*, Philip Allan, 1936.

Thomson, J.A.F. *The Transformation of Medieval England 1370–1529*, Longman, 1983.

Thoresby Jones, P. *Welsh Border Country*, Batsford, 1946.

Thurlby, M. *The Herefordshire School of Romanesque Sculpture*, Logaston Press, 1999.

Vallance, A. *English Church Screens – Being Great Roods, Screenwork & Rood-Lofts of the Parish Churches of England & Wales*, Batsford, 1936.

Vallance, A. *Greater English Church Screens – Being Great Roods, Screenwork & Rood-Lofts in Cathedral, Monastic and Collegiate Churches in England and Wales*, Batsford, 1947.

Vallance, A. 'Rood-Screens and Rood-lofts in Kent' in Ditchfield, C. *Memorials of Old Kent*, Bemrose, 1907.

Verey, D. & Brooks, A. *The Buildings of England, Gloucestershire 2 – The Vale and the Forest of Dean*, Yale, 2002.

Verey, D. *The Buildings of England, Gloucestershire 1 – The Cotswolds*, Penguin, 1970.

Walker, D. *Medieval Wales*, C.U.P., 1990.

Walker, D. *Rood Screens and Timber Work in Powys Land*, Powys Land Club, (n.d.).

Williams, G. *Recovery, Reorientation and Reformation in Wales – c. 1415-1642 (History of Wales Vol. III)*, Clarendon Press, 1987.

Williamson, P. (ed.) *The Medieval Treasury*, V&A Publications, 2002.

Zarnecki, G. *et al. English Romanesque Art 1066-1200*, Arts Council of Great Britain, Weidenfeld and Nicolson, 1984.

References

Introduction
1. In this way it formed a legal, as well as a physical, demarcation.
2. The screens at Rodmersham in Kent and Chivelstone in Devon are apparently of Spanish chestnut.
3. In *English Church Woodwork*, B.T. Batsford Ltd., London, 1917.
4. More than 5,000 detailed descriptions of English and Welsh churches by Glynne survive in manuscript form.
5. Fenton's *Tours in Wales* was eventually published in 1917.
6. Walker in the *Montgomery Collections*, and Thomas in *Archaeologia Cambrensis*.
7. In *Archaeologia Cambrensis*; Section VII, Montgomeryshire.
8. *Ibid.*
9. In *English Church Screens, being Great Roods & Rood-lofts of Parish Churches of England and Wales*, B.T. Batsford Ltd., London, 1936.
10. *Ibid.*
11. Camm had already written, *Some Devonshire Screens and the Saints Represented on their Panels*, which was published in 1906.
12. F.E. Howard also wrote, *Screens and Rood-lofts in the Parish Churches of Oxford-shire*, which was published in 1910.
13. F.H. Crossley also wrote, *The Church Screens of Cheshire*, which was privately printed in 1918.
14. In *The Buildings of England: Herefordshire*, Penguin Books, London, 1963.
15. *English Church Furniture*, EP Publishing, Wakefield, 1973.

The Origins of Ecclesiastical Screenwork
1. The Jews it was who originally conveyed the Gospel across the Roman Empire and out into the pagan world beyond, and it is natural, therefore, that the organisation of their places of worship should inform that of the earliest Christian churches, and specifically their modes of partition.
2. St. Matthew, xxvii: 50 – 51.
3. In *The History of Arians*; cited by Frederick Bligh Bond and the Rev. Dom Bede Camm in *Roodscreens and Roodlofts*, Pitman & Sons Ltd., London, 1909.
4. In his *Epistle 67*; also cited by Bond and Camm, *Ibid.*
5. Metal screenwork is a notable feature of Spanish and Low Country churches in particular.
6. The term 'basilica' refers to the function of this building, but when used to describe a basilican church refers instead to its form.
7. Constantine attributed his victory over Maxentius at the Milvian Bridge a year earlier to the Divine intervention of the Christian God.

8. These are St. Pancras, Canterbury; St. Andrew, Rochester; St. Mary, Lyminge; St. Peter, Bradwell, and St. Mary, Reculver.
9. In *English Romanesque Architecture before the Conquest*, Clarendon Press, Oxford, 1930.
10. Fawley chapel in Herefordshire has a triple arcade separating nave from chancel, but this is a Victorian addition.
11. In *English Romanesque Architecture before the Conquest*, Clarendon Press, Oxford, 1930.

The Great Rood
1. *Archaeologia Cambrensis*, 6th series, vol. iii.
2. In 'The Medieval Wooden Crucifix Figure from Kemeys Inferior, and its Church', *The Monmouthshire Antiquary*, ed. David H. Williams, Vol. XVI, 2000.
3. The Great Rood was occasionally referred to as the *Good* or *High Rood*; the *High, Great* or *Greatest Cross*; the *High* or *Great Crucifix*; and the *Patible* (from the Latin *patibulum*, meaning gibbet).
4. The doctrine of the essential duality of Christ – that he embodies both the divine and the human – was further strengthened in 451 at the Council of Chalcedon.
5. And, interestingly, in the large number of surviving metal Romanesque Crucifix figures.
6. This is a small altar-cross of copper-alloy, engraved and gilded. This, together with the mid-11th-century Lundo Crucifix, is the only complete altar-cross of the Romanesque period to survive.
7. A small hollow-cast copper-alloy figure belonging to the University Museum of Archaeology and Anthropology in Cambridge, z. 11501.
8. The Great Rood also occasionally appeared in painted form on the wall over the chancel arch.
9. The fragmentary Saxon Rood at Bitton in Gloucestershire is an exception. It is located over the chancel arch in this important Saxon Minster church.
10. *English Romanesque Art 1066-1200*, Weidenfeld and Nicolson, London, 1984. The fragments can be seen in the British Museum.
11. J. Charles Cox and Alfred Harvey in *English Church Furniture*, Methuen & Co., London, 1907.
12. In *English Church Woodwork*, B.T. Batsford, London, 1917.
13. In 'The Medieval Wooden Crucifix Figure from Kemeys Inferior, and its Church', *The Monmouthshire Antiquary*, Volume XVI, 2000.
14. Another very fine – albeit later – rood-beam existed at Salisbury Cathedral until its removal by James Wyatt in the 18th century (who also worked on Hereford Cathedral).

15. List courtesy of Aymer Vallance in *English Church Screens*, B.T. Batsford Ltd., London, 1936.
16. In *The Buildings of England; Herefordshire*, Penguin Books, London, 1963.
17. By Pevsner and Wedgwood in *The Buildings of England; Warwickshire*, Penguin Books, London, 2000.
18. Other fine painted 'Doom' tympana survive at Mitcheldean in Gloucestershire, Dauntsey in Wiltshire, Ludham in Norfolk and Winsham in Somerset.
19. A late canvas Decalogue still survives in the rood-loft at St. Margarets.
20. Others include those at Woolpit in Suffolk (vaulted), Mobberley in Cheshire, Hennock in Devon, Dummer in Hampshire and Ivinghoe in Buckinghamshire.

The Development of the Rood-screen in England and Wales

1. In some larger churches, such as Bosham in Sussex, the chancel archway is much larger, as befitting a Minster church served by a body of clergy.
2. They did not all share the same internal layout. St. Brigit's church at Kildare in Ireland, erected in the 5th century (and known from a manuscript source), appears to have had a double nave, one side of which was reserved for men and the other for women, with separate doorways at its west end communicating with the sanctuary beyond.
3. Frederick Bligh Bond and the Rev. Dom Bede Camm, *Roodscreens and Roodlofts*, Vol. 1, Pitman & Sons Ltd., London, 1909.
4. Walsoken in Norfolk provides an example of a late Norman church with aisles; while Ledbury in Herefordshire and St. Peters in Northampton are particularly unusual for having aisles that continue eastwards to flank the choir.
5. F.E. Howard and F.H. Crossley in *English Church Woodwork*, B.T. Batsford Ltd., London, 1927.
6. Interestingly, just like the screen at Thurcaston, this also has polygonal as opposed to turned mullions.
7. It retains its original doors, together with their original hinges, sliding bolt and hasp.
8. The apparently decorative piercings in the wainscot at Stanton Harcourt are in all probability Elevation squints, and were certainly added at a later date.
9. This screen corresponds in its composition with the screen in the church of St. Nicholas, King's Lynn.
10. The churchwardens' accounts for Thame in Oxfordshire, for example, contain a list of subscribers responsible for building the church there.
11. It was first seen more than a century before in the 1380s, at North Walsham in Norfolk.
12. The parish was originally in the diocese of Hereford.
13. Quoted by M.H. Ridgway and F.H. Crossley in 'Screens, Lofts and Stalls in Wales and Monmouthshire', *Archaeologia Cambrensis*; part 6, section xi.
14. A considerable amount of research has been carried out on the figure paintings of rood-screens: for example by Dom Bede Camm, who wrote, *Some Devonshire Screens and the Saints Represented on their Panels;* published in 1906.
15. The restoration of the screen and loft at Llangwm in Monmouthshire, by J.P. Seddon in 1876–8, shows a light touch. Seddon found traces of red and blue pigment, and reapplied some of this scheme as part of his restoration. G.E. Halliday's re-colouring of the screen at Usk on the other hand shows a heavier touch.
16. Alec Clifton-Taylor in *English Parish Churches as Works of Art*, B.T. Batsford Ltd., London, 1974.
17. In *Roodscreens and Roodlofts*, Sir Isaac Pitman & Sons Ltd., London, 1909.
18. According to Howard and Crossley in *English Church Woodwork*, B.T. Batsford Ltd., London, 1917.
19. These include Prophets, Apostles, Latin Doctors of the Church, Sibyls, the Annunciation, the Visitation, the Expulsion from Eden, & etc.
20. The term is Francis Bond's, used in *Screens and Galleries in English Churches*, OUP, London, 1908.
21. Ashby St. Ledgers – also in Northamptonshire – is a rare example.
22. Here they include John the Baptist, the Blessed Virgin Mary and St. John the Evangelist.

Minor Screens

1. 'Parclose' sometimes appears in early documents as *enterclose*, *perclose*, *pertclose*, *parclos*, or *perclos*. The word derives from the old French verb *parclore* – to enclose – and was in use from at least the 14th century.
2. There is a stone parclose screen at Easton-on-the-Hill in Northamptonshire.
3. And at Astbury in Cheshire, which almost certainly originated from the same workshop source as Aymestrey.
4. However, it should be remembered that the parclose screen in this context still performed a utilitarian role – namely that of asserting the legal rights of the Guild to the fabric of the chapel.
5. In *Screens and Galleries in English Churches*, Henry Frowde, London, 1908.

The Rood-loft

1. This was also occasionally referred to as the *soler*, *soller* or *pulpite*.
2. Although Bond and Camm assert that early lofts were often at least 12 feet deep.
3. The loft at Llanfilo in Breconshire is an exception to the rule. Although located in an architecturally divided church its coving springs to both west and east of the dividing wall.
4. The rood-loft parapets at Besford and Leigh in Worcestershire are exceptions, being divided into three wide bays in each case.

5. Atherington's rood-loft is unusual for employing horizontal boarding.
6. Hereford Cathedral housed a stone pulpitum, until its demolition in 1841. St. Davids Cathedral in Pembrokeshire retains an extremely fine stone pulpitum.
7. Indeed, Aymer Vallance suggests a date of *c*.1200 for Colsterworth, citing the nail-head ornament as evidence for this early date (whilst conceding that the doorway may have been later adapted to its usage as an access to the rood-loft). *English Church Screens*, B.T. Batsford Ltd., London, 1936.
8. Quoted by Vallance; *ibid*.
9. Cox and Harvey report that 'traces of the rood-altar slab' survive at Daglingworth in Gloucestershire, but no such fragments exist there now; *English Church Furniture*, Methuen & Co., London, 1907.
10. In *English Church Screens*, B.T. Batsford Ltd., London, 1936.
11. In *Screens and Galleries in English Churches*, Henry Frowde, London, 1908.
12. At this church's restoration, the stairs were discovered built into the wall.
13. Only rarely were such doors enriched, as at South Cove (painted), and Lavenham (carved with linenfold); both in Suffolk.
14. *Screens and Galleries in English Churches*, Henry Frowde, London, 1908.
15. In *Roodscreens and Roodlofts*, Sir Isaac Pitman & Sons Ltd., London, 1909.
16. *Ibid*.
17. At Montgomery, the space below the loft was appropriated in the 17th century for a pew. At Madley in Herefordshire a curtained, private chapel, re-using late medieval elements, was erected in the north aisle in the 17th century.
18. In fact this did occur from time to time, as with the screenwork of Chirbury Priory, now gracing the church at Montgomery.
19. W.R. Hughes, *Llanegryn Church*.
20. *Ibid*.
21. In *English Church Furniture,* Methuen and Co., London, 1907.
22. That the coving does survive in so many instances is at least consistent with the Elizabethan Order of 1561 which states that the loft be taken down 'unto the up-per parts of the vaults and beams running in length over the said vaults'. At Great Rollright in Oxfordshire, the coving has been retained, but re-set as a celure high overhead.

The Reformation
1. The 'Annates' are the first year's revenue of a see or benefice, paid to the Pope.
2. In 1538, the burning of lights before images was forbidden; while in 1547, all lights were banned, save for two on the altar.
3. By Eamon Duffy in *The Stripping of the Altars*, Yale University Press, London, 1992.
4. In *The Reformation and the English People,* Blackwells, Oxford, 1984.
5. By Scarisbrick *ibid*., and others.

6. BM MS. C. 25, g. 18. Quoted by Aymer Vallance in *English Church Screens*, B.T. Batsford, London, 1936.
7. Today, many rood-screens retain the vaulting or coving only of the previous rood-loft; such as those at Old Radnor and Beguildy in Radnorshire.
8. It has been suggested (by Vallance in *English Church Screens*) that the retention of a disproportionate number of rood-lofts in Wales was because the Welsh were ever a nation of singers, and clung with great tenacity to such traditions, and consequently to the fittings which served these traditions.

The Post-Reformation History of Church Screens
1. Proceedings of the Society of Antiquities, vol. iv, 1859; cited by Vallance in *English Church Screens*, B.T. Batsford Ltd., London, 1936.
2. According to Rev. C.R. Norcliffe in a paper for the Yorkshire Architectural Society of 1862.
3. In *Archaeologia Cambrensis*, part six, section ix: Radnorshire, 1949.
4. In *Archaeologia Cambrensis*, part five, section vii: Montgomeryshire, 1947.
5. In *Welsh Churches*.
6. From ms. notes, in *Archaeolgia Cambrensis*, vol. XCVII, part II, 1943.
7. A faculty (or licence from a diocesan consistory court) must be sought before any alterations, additions, removals or repairs can be carried out to the fabric, ornaments or furniture of a church.

The Welsh March
1. 'March' derives from the Anglo-Saxon word *mearc*, meaning boundary.
2. Doubtless, much to the relief of the English king, who was then preoccupied with the re-conquest of Normandy.
3. Just as Offa's had been in the 8th century: his dyke was essentially an admission by the King of Mercia that the English were unlikely to gain any meaningful control in Wales.
4. This demarcation oversimplifies the reality of the March, for within *Marchia Wallie* there were a number of pure Welsh districts, outliers of *Pura Wallia*, known as the 'Welshries'. These districts were every bit as Welsh in culture and social structure as any to be found in the Welsh heartlands.
5. In *Welsh Border Country*, B.T. Batsford, London, 1946.
6. In *A History of Wales*, Allen Lane, The Penguin Press, London, 1993.
7. *Ibid*.
8. The lowland winter quarters were known as the *hendre*, the upland summer pastures as the *hafod*, and this seasonal farming system as *transhumance*.
9. In *The New Cambridge Medieval History, vol. VII*, CUP, Cambridge, 1999.
10. The most conspicuous legacy of this turbulent past is the 600 or so castles traceable

in Wales. These occupy an area of just 8,000 square miles, making Wales the most densely fortified country in Europe.

11. By professor Gwyn Jones in his introduction to *The Mabinogion*, J.M. Dent, London, 1998.
12. This was carried out by William Salesbury; an exceptional humanist scholar from Denbighshire.
13. By William Morgan; the vicar of Llanrhaeadr-ym-Mochnant.
14. Glanmor Williams, *Wales* c.*1415-1642*, Clarendon Press, Oxford, 1987.
15. Influential Pope (1088–99), who took the Christian reform message across Europe to great effect.
16. Glanmor Williams, *Wales* c.*1415-1642*, Clarendon Press, Oxford, 1987.
17. John. A.F. Thomson, *The Transformation of Medieval England 1370-1529*, Longman, London, 1983.
18. *Ibid.*
19. The *Valor's Ecclesiasticus* of 1535 records that a quarter of all parochial livings in Wales were, at the time, worth less than £5 per year. This, according to Glanmor Williams made them 'wretchedly poor' (*Wales* c.*1415-1642*, Clarendon Press, Oxford, 1987).
20. In *Mediaeval Styles in the English Parish Church*, B.T. Batsford Ltd., London, 1936.
21. The organising of groups of commoners into guilds was less common in Wales, although guilds of craftsmen maintained chapels at Brecon, and fraternities existed at Presteigne.
22. By Iorwerth Peate in *The Welsh House*, the Honourable Society of Cymmrodorion, London, 1940.
23. F.H. Crossley, *Archaeologia Cambrensis*, Vol. XCVII, Part II, 1943.
24. F.H. Crossley and M.H. Ridgway, *Archaeologia Cambrensis*, Section V, 1947.

The Screenwork of the Southern Marches

1. The rood-screen at Old Radnor in Radnorshire extends to flank the side aisles also, and has two further doors giving access to the chapels. Here, the sill is continuous and is flush with the floor.
2. In Midlands screenwork, the chamfered middle rail remained commonplace up until the Reformation.
3. Bond and Camm did something similar for Devon, identifying 12 distinctive types of screenwork in the county; in *Roodscreens and Roodlofts*, Vol II, Sir Isaac Pitman & Sons, London, 1909.
4. At this time Ludlow was a town of considerable import, not only in the border context but also the national one. The first son of Henry VII, Arthur, on marrying Katherine of Aragon, was made Lord of the Marches and given Ludlow Castle. Arthur's friend, Sir Richard Pole, commissioned a screen for Aberconwy to commemorate the marriage. For these and other reasons, the case for the presence of a workshop centre in or near to Ludlow is compelling.
5. In *Archaeologia Cambrensis*, Part eleven, Section XIV, Border Influences, 1962.
6. It must be acknowledged, of course, that all of this screenwork has been greatly meddled with, and that the work in Stoke Lacy (and possibly Lea) was imported from elsewhere.
7. In *Archaeologia Cambrensis*, Part six, Section IX: Radnorshire, 1949.
8. In *English Church Woodwork*, B.T. Batsford, London, 1917.
9. It should be remembered that there never has been (nor is there now) a Celtic race or nation, and that 'Celt' refers merely to a speaker of a group of Indo-European languages. The term 'Celtic art' is too broad and vague to be of real value: it covers a period stretching from 700 BC to 1200 AD; it was produced by the peoples of any number of European countries, and it variously appropriated elements from Oriental, classical Greek, Roman and Viking art.
10. In *The Art of the Celts*, Thames and Hudson, London, 1992.
11. Found at Elmswell in Yorkshire and now in the British Museum.
12. The exquisite screen at Colebrooke is closely related in its openwork carving to the rood-screen and loft at St. Fiacre-le-Faouet, and was in all probability made by Breton craftsmen.
13. The exquisite cresting at Newtown, seemingly depicting seaweed, may be an exception.
14. In *Heraldry*, Guillim, III. xxvi., 1610.
15. In *Roodscreens and Roodlofts*, Vol II, Sir Isaac Pitman & Sons, London, 1909.
16. Cited by A. Vallance in *English Church Screens*, B.T. Batsford, London, 1936.

Montgomeryshire

1. One imagines that Parker would not have approved of the new screen. For him 'the effect of dazzling richness is injured by extreme precision'. Manuscript notes, 1829.
2. *Ibid.*
3. In *Welsh Churches*: 'there are stone steps leading to the rood-loft'.
4. Hamer, 'The Parish of Llangurig', *Montgomeryshire Collections*, Vol. II, 1869.
5. In *The Buildings of Wales; Powys*, Penguin Books, London, 1992.
6. M.H. Ridgway and F.H. Crossley, *Archaeologia Cambrensis* 1947; Montgomeryshire.
7. Dodson also claims to have found, carved into one of the bands of enrichment, 'geese, and a dog': sadly, there is no sign of these creatures now.
8. The usually reliable Rev. Parker, for example, incorrectly states that the late medieval screenwork of Newtown originally came from Cwmhir Abbey.
9. In *Archaeologia Cambrensis*, April, 1903.
10. In his *Tours in Wales*, 1810. This closely echoes his comments on Partrishow in

Breconshire.

11. Manuscript notes, 1829. Parker made extensive notes and drawings of the Newtown screen and loft; most of them excellent and of inestimable value now.
12. Manuscript notes, 1829.
13. *Ibid.*

Radnorshire

1. In 1917, R. Tudor (architect) and J.H. Lloyd reported finding the 'oak screen is painted'. The colour perhaps belonged to the Victorian restoration of the building of 1878.
2. These are similar to those found on the celure at Talyllyn in Merionethshire.
3. According to Crossley and Ridgway in *Archaeologia Cambrensis* 1949; Radnorshire.
4. Parker found much original colour on the screen itself (mainly green and red on the mouldings and tracery).
5. In 1945, the upper part of the tympanum could still be seen in the gable of the roof (according to Crossley and Ridgway in *Archaeologia Cambrensis* 1949; Radnorshire).
6. In *The Buildings of Wales: Powys*, Penguin Books, London, 1979.
7. *Archaeologia Cambrensis* 1949; Radnorshire.
8. *Ibid.* It should be acknowledged that the pair describe a water-plant trail at Newtown as 'the finest example of this type we possess'.
9. They are fewer in number because each is very slightly wider than its counterpart to the east.
10. This now unusual feature can also be seen at Bleddfa church, near Knighton.
11. According to S.W. Williams in *Archaeologia Cambrensis*, 1873.
12. The cusped timber chancel arch with its arcade of cusped openings also belongs to the restoration.
13. A motif also found on the bressumer beam at Bronllys.
14. RCAMW, *Radnor*, No. 546, 1911.
15. *Archaeologia Cambrensis* 1949; Radnorshire.
16. The organ fills the other bay.
17. A double middle rail can also be found at Llanegryn in Merionethshire, but the feature is extremely rare in Wales. At Old Radnor, the top rail has ten quatrefoils per bay, the middle rail four per bay, and the lower one seven per bay.
18. In the north aisle, for example, is a design composed of three cusped half-circles with rose cusps.
19. Jonathan Williams MS., 1818 (*Archaeologia Cambrensis* 1949; Radnorshire).
20. We know this from drawings by the Rev. John Parker.

Breconshire

1. Both Glynne in *Welsh Churches* (1840), and H.S. Davies in *Arch. Journal*, VII, (1850), refer to this decoration.
2. In *A History of the County of Brecknock*, 1809, vol. 2.
3. In *Churches of Brecknockshire*.
4. The north aisle was removed during the 1907 rebuild. The church was also comprehensively reconstructed in 1831–3.
5. 'The part of the rood-loft next the chancel remains. It was some years ago converted into a gallery with seats in it, but the church was thereby so much darkened that it became necessary to take it down'. From the notes of Theophilus Jones, 1809, II.
6. F.H. Crossley and M.H. Ridgway, *Archaeologia Cambrensis* 1953; Brecknockshire.
7. In *Welsh Churches*.
8. According to Richard Haslam, *The Buildings of Wales: Powys*, Penguin Books, 1992.
9. According to Crossley and Ridgway: *Archaeologia Cambrensis* 1953; Brecknockshire.
10. In *Church Builder*, July, 1913.
11. Plate XXX in *Roodscreens and Roodlofts*; Frederick Bligh Bond and the Rev. Dom Bede Camm.
12. In 1840, prior to the restoration, only the rood-stairs remained *in situ*.
13. By Crossley and Ridgway: *Archaeologia Cambrensis* 1953; Brecknockshire.
14. According to Glynne in *Welsh Churches*.
15. In *Archaeologia Cambrensis* 1953; Brecknockshire.
16. In *Welsh Churches*, 1864.
17. This unusual feature has its own entrance, hagioscope, and an altar over the grave of the saint.
18. *Tours of Wales*, 1804–5.
19. *Ibid.*
20. In *Welsh Churches*, 1864.
21. *Ibid.*

Herefordshire

1. Roland Paul made these discoveries during his excavations of the site in 1895. He was able to identify, for example, the foundations of the altars belonging to the pulpitum and screen.
2. The west gallery against the back wall is coeval with the screen, and probably by the same hand.
3. Nikolaus Pevsner, *The Buildings of England: Herefordshire*, Penguin Books, London, 1963.
4. Royal Commission for Historical Monuments, *Herefordshire*, Vol. 1, 1931.
5. *Ibid.*

6. This is evidenced by plans in Browne Willis's *Survey* of 1727, James Storer's *Cathedrals* of 1815 (etc.); and by a painting of 1830.
7. In a *Brief Enquiry into the Ancient and Present State of Hereford Cathedral*, 1827; quoted by Aymer Vallance in *Greater English Church Screens*, B.T. Batsford Ltd., London, 1947.
8. Bishop Audley was successively Bishop of Rochester, Hereford and Salisbury.
9. Skidmore also produced screens for the cathedrals at Lichfield and Chester.
10. The work took 38 conservators more than a year to complete, and cost £800,000.
11. By Nikolaus Pevsner in *The Buildings of England: Herefordshire*, Penguin Books, London, 1963.
12. Bond and Camm, *Roodscreens and Roodlofts*, Issac Pitman & Sons Ltd., London, 1909.
13. Nikolaus Pevsner in *The Buildings of England. Herefordshire*, Penguin Books, London, 1963.
14. Consisting of three wide boards divided by possibly chamfered muntins to each side of the door.
15. M.H. Ridgway and F.H. Crossley, *Archaeologia Cambrensis*; Section XIV: Border Influences, 1962. During the *c*.1900 restoration much of the loft was painted white, yellow-ochre and light red.
16. According to Nikolaus Pevsner, *The Buildings of England: Herefordshire*, Penguin Books, London, 1963.
17. Roman physicians who, during the 4th century, practiced Christianity in defiance of imperial authority.

Monmouthshire

1. *Archaeologia Cambrensis* 1959; Monmouthshire.
2. The medieval use of screenwork to box in a font is unknown.
3. This involves the application of coloured plasters, which are then cut back to reveal the desired colour for the particular scene being depicted.
4. *Archaeologia Cambrensis* 1959; Monmouthshire.
5. The rood-screen once stood within (rather than before) the chancel arch.
6. These are roughly coeval with the two sets of pews in the chancel (the set to the south is dated 1634).
7. *The Usk Gleaner and Monmouthshire Record*, published by J.C. Clarke at the *County Observer* office. Usk. Vol. 1. August, 1875.
8. Crossley and Ridgway speculate that the second beam may have come from nearby Llangwm Isaf, which was shorn of its fine screenwork in the 19th century. Paired beams are occasionally a feature of mutilated post-Reformation screens, where the rood-beam or bressumer of a dismantled loft has been placed over a screen's head-beam. This feature is found at both Elton and Withington in Herefordshire.
9. In cross-section the vertical ribs are moulded with a round and hollow (for which there exists ample historical precedent).
10. In 1947, Crossley and Ridgway reported finding six pinnacles present and make no mention of any damage. *Archaeologia Cambrensis* 1959; Monmouthshire.
11. One of the tracery heads shows a slight variation, with narrower loop lights yielding a wider space between the pairs of lights.
12. The cusped panels that decorate the upper third of the tower are similar to the decorated jambs of the rear windows of the gatehouse of the castle.
13. A cope is a semi-circular cape worn during ceremonies or processions. Such was the finesse of their needlework many were cut up and used as altar frontals (for example).
14. These are similar to those found in the tympanum at Llanelieu in Breconshire and in the wainscot at Stanton Harcourt in Oxfordshire.
15. There was also a parclose screen between the first two piers of the arcade, dividing the aisle from the nave, at this time.
16. Only one of these is old. It is carved upon one face only (where the new ones are carved upon both).
17. The bressumer for example has not had its missing carved trail replaced, nor inappropriate top- and drop-cresting added. Furthermore, a new middle rail has not been inserted.
18. *Archaeologia Cambrensis* 1959; Monmouthshire.

Index

Most entries concerning construction, style, decoration etc, have been grouped under Rood, Rood-loft and Rood-screen. Page numbers in italics refer to illustrations, in bold to the main entry for that screen (which often also includes illustrations).

Also from Logaston Press

Romanesque Architecture and Sculpture in Wales
by Malcolm Thurlby

This is the first comprehensive study of Romanesque Architecture and Sculpture in Wales. As the project has progressed, so ever more Romanesque work was found to remain. Unsurprisingly some of the most lavish survivals are found in southern Wales (and to a lesser extent in central eastern Wales), where the Normans penetrated early on and where relative security allowed work to proceed. St Davids was rebuilt in 1182 in a very late Romanesque style after an earthquake largely destroyed the previous building erected some 65 years earlier.

Yet much survives in North Wales too, largely thanks to the patronage of Gruffudd ap Cynan and his aspirations on the European stage. In decyphering the work of Gruffudd ap Cynan, for example, there are few people better placed than Malcolm Thurlby, for he can bring his huge knowledge of the Romanesque to draw out the wider story—making comparisons with work across Europe in terms of overall design, and more locally and in the detail of the work to ascertain from where the masons and sculptors were drawn. Thus the book is not just about the individual examples of the style, but about why certain work has adopted the particular design and ornamentation that it has, with the ability to now read 'backwards' from what we can still see to the mind of the patron who was commissioning the work those centuries ago.

The book takes the building of Llandaff cathedral in 1120 as a juncture in the development of the Romanesque in Wales, its appearance being then on a massive and lavish scale for the country. Thus chapters deal with Romanesque work prior to 1120, the creation of Llandaff cathedral and its effect, notably in southern Wales, the work of Welsh patrons and then a chapter devoted to the unravelling of Romanesque St Davids, rebuilt when Gothic was well established in France and had been successfully introduced into England and Wales.

Malcolm Thurlby was born in England but is now the Professor of Visual Art at York University in Toronto and the author of countless articles in a variety of journals.

ISBN 1 904396 50 X
400 pages, over 500 black and white photographs and 16 colour plates
Price £17.50

The Churches of Worcestershire
by Tim Bridges

Introductory chapters tell of the spread of Christianity across Worcestershire and the majoe events that affected church building in the county over the centuries. The core of the book is a gazetteer to the 270 Anglican churches in the county, detailing their building history, furnishings and tombs.

Tim Bridges lectures widely on church architecture and history and works as Collections manager for Worcester City Museums.

ISBN 1 904396 39 9   288 pages, over 200 illustrations   Price £14.95

The Churches of Shropshire & their Treasures
by John Leonard

This book explores 320 parish churches of Shropshire, half of them medieval. Chapters guide the reader through changing architectural styles, from Anglo-Saxon origins to the 21st century and then detail the treasures of the churches, including towers and spires, porches roofs, sculpture, fonts, memorials and monuments, stained glass, rood-screens, pulpits, pews and chancel furnishings. The county is then divided into geographical areas, with descriptions of all the individual churches in each area.

John Leonard is a retired consultant physician who lives in Shropshire and has written numerous books on churches.

ISBN 1 904396 19 4   336 pages, over 530 illustrations   Price £12.95

The Churches of Herefordshire & their Treasures
by John Leonard

This book adopts a similar approach to that for Shropshire noted above, but covering Herefordshire.

ISBN 1 873827 91 1   240 pages, 290 illustrations   Price £12.95